THE BEST OF
ED ZERN

Books by Ed Zern

To Hell with Fishing
To Hell with Hunting
How to Tell Fish from Fishermen
How to Catch Fishermen
Are Fishermen People?
A Fine Kettle of Fish Stories
Hunting and Fishing from A to Zern

THE BEST OF
ED ZERN

Fifty Years of Fishing and Hunting

from One of America's

Best-Loved Outdoor Humorists

THE LYONS PRESS

Guilford, Connecticut
An imprint of The Globe Pequot Press

The Lyons Press is an imprint of the Globe Pequot Press.

Originally published by The Lyons Press as *Hunting and Fishing From "A" to Zern*

Printed in the United States of America
10 9 8 7 6 5 4 3 2 1

Library of Congress Cataloging-in-Publication Data is available on file.

ISBN 1-58574-342-9

CONTENTS

Preface

Don't look at me. This book was Nick Lyons' idea. It grew from one of mine, which was simply to put a collection of "Exit Laughing" columns from *Field & Stream* between covers, in hopes that at least those readers who had written complaining that there wasn't such a collection available would buy it in sufficient numbers to enable me to continue to avoid honest work.

Nick felt it should have some fishing articles and other stuff not screamingly funny, and so there are some of those. There are even some odd-ball advertisements for products no longer on the market, which may simply be a coincidence.

Many of the real people mentioned in the book have died since the pieces appeared, and I haven't altered the references. If you knew them you know they're gone, and if you didn't it doesn't matter.

On that topic, I'm reminded of the Alabama sharecropper walking through a rural cemetery and seeing a headstone on which was carved "Not Dead But Sleeping." The farmer shook his head sadly and said, "Mister, you ain't foolin' nobody but yourself." The only immortality I'm sure is available to fishermen is achieved by people like Izaak Walton and Theodore Gordon and Lee Wulff and Roderick Haig-Brown and a few other writers and innovators among whom I'm not numbered. And as I grow older and more skeptical of the parson's promises it seems to me this is the kind of deathlessness I'd settle for. It may not last long after the last pint of fresh water is polluted, which may not be awfully long, but when the fishing goes I'm willing to go with it.

ED ZERN

PART

I

THE
BOOKS

Forty years ago I sold two short stories to *Collier's*, then the chief competition for *The Saturday Evening Post*. One was about a guy who got drunk in church, and the other was about a funeral. I had written them to prove that the so-called taboos of the popular magazines against references to religion or dying weren't applicable if the subjects were treated humorously. My editor at *Collier's* was Denver Lindley, who left there to join Appleton-Century Publishers as a book editor. When he asked if I'd write a novel of the same genre as the stories, I said no. When he asked if I'd write a novel about fishing, I said, "Oh, the hell with fishing."

"That's a great title," Denver said, and I said I'd write a book to go with it. When I fell behind schedule, I called H. T. Webster, the cartoonist who invented "The Timid Soul" and "Life's Darkest Moment" and who occasionally drew cartoons about trout and salmon fishing, and asked him if I could use some of his cartoons to help complete the book. He said go ahead. The book came out in 1945 and over the next ten or fifteen years sold several hundred thousand copies. I don't think many fishermen bought it; people bought it to give to fishermen.

After that came *To Hell with Hunting* (1946), *How to Tell Fish From Fishermen* (1947), *How to Catch Fishermen* (1951), *Are Fishermen People?* (1951), and *A Fine Kettle of Fish Stories* (1964). All of them are out of print today, and available only through dealers specializing in sporting books, and garage sales.

TO
HELL
WITH FISHING

(1945)

HOW TO DISPOSE OF DEAD FISH

A recent survey showed that roughly two-thirds of all fishermen never eat fish. This should surprise nobody. Fish is brain food. People who eat fish have large, well-developed brains. People with large, well-developed brains don't fish. It's that simple.

The question a fisherman faces, then, is how to get rid of the fish he has caught. There are several schools of thought on this problem.

The Pilgrim Fathers buried a dead fish in each hill of corn to make it grow. Unfortunately, few fisherman have access to cornfields. Most farmers would sooner have a cyclone.

Some fishermen try to palm off their catch on kindhearted friends and neighbors. Naturally, it doesn't take *those* folks long to learn that when a trout has been lugged around all day in a hot creel, it is poor competition for a pork chop.

Other methods of fish disposal are (1) stuffing them in a corner mailbox when nobody is looking, (2) hiding them under potted palms, (3) checking them at the Union Depot and throwing away the check, (4) hurling them from fast-moving cars on lonely roads late at night, (5) mailing them to the Curator of the Museum of Natural History, requesting an identification of the species and giving a phoney name and return address, and (6) baiting walrus-traps with them.

None of these methods is satisfactory. (1) is probably illegal, (2), (3), (4), and (5) are in lousy taste, and (6) brings up the problem of walrus-disposal. Walrus-disposal makes fish-disposal seem like child's play.

My friend Walt Dette puts back all the trout he catches in the Beaverkill, and keeps

3

only chubs to feed to his seven Siamese cats. This is dandy for people who have (a) sense enough to put back trout for future sport and (b) seven Siamese cats. Few fishermen have both.

Both, hell. *Either*.

AIN'T IT THE TRUTH? NO

Fishermen are born honest, but they get over it.

When a fisherman is going to tell you about the big musky he caught, he knows you will subtract ten pounds to allow for his untruthfulness.

So he adds ten pounds to allow for your subtraction.

The other ten pounds he adds on account of being such a liar.

Then he adds five pounds for good measure because what is five pounds more or less on such a big fish?

As a matter of fact, he didn't even catch that musky. He found it floating belly-up.

It died laughing at a Hokum's DeLuxe Weedless Streamlined Hollow-ground Galvanized Non-skid Semi-automatic Husky-Musky Lure with Centerboard Optional, $1.50 at all sporting-goods stores.

Lizzie Greig, the Gal Fly-tier of the Angler's Roost, was born in Scotland on the River Tweed. It was too late at night to borrow the greengrocer's scales, so they used the one her father used for salmon.

She weighed 17 pounds, 5 ounces.

HOW TO CATCH FISH WITH FLIES

Some wiseguy once defined a fishing line as a piece of string with a worm on one end and a damn fool on the other.

This is a silly definition, of course—for many fishermen use flies instead of worms. They think it is more hoity-toity. If worms cost two bits apiece, and you could dig Royal Coachmen and Parmacheene Belles out of the manure pile, they would think differently. This is called human nature.

Fly fishermen spend hours tying little clumps of fur and feathers on hooks, trying to make a trout fly that looks like a real fly. But nobody has ever seen a natural insect trying to mate with a Fanwing Ginger Quill.

Of course, every once in a while a fly fisherman catches a trout on a trout fly, and he thinks this proves something. It doesn't. Trout eat mayflies, burnt matches, small pieces of inner tube, each other, caddis worms, Dewey buttons, crickets, lima beans, Colorado spinners, and almost anything else they can get in their fool mouths. It is probable they think the trout fly is some feathers tied to a hook. Hell, they're not blind. They just want to see how it tastes.

Trout flies are either wet flies or dry flies, depending on whether they are supposed to sink or float. If you ask a wet-fly fisherman why a natural insect would be swimming around like crazy under water, he gets huffy and walks away.

Many fishermen think trout are color-blind, but that is nothing to what trout think of fishermen.

HOW TO WADE A TROUT STREAM

Nothing is so disturbing to the joys of trout-fishing as to step on a slippery rock while wading a stream and go hip boots over tincups. There are several ways of avoiding this. Some people wear nonskid chain devices attached to their boots. Some people wear stocking-foot waders and hobnailed or felt-soled shoes. Some people with more gray matter just stay the hell out of trout streams.

Statistics show that one-legged fishermen seldom fall down while wading. I only know one one-legged angler personally. He lost the other one while poking good-natured fun at a buzz saw, and had it replaced with an aluminum job, made by the Dodd Artificial Limb Company. He is very proud of it. When somebody suggested that he turn it in during an aluminum scrap drive, he indignantly refused.

"I don't give a good Dodd gam!" he said.

AIN'T NATURE NATURAL?

When fishermen come home from a day's fishing empty-creeled, and you say well, where are the fish, ha, ha, they say look, bub, can't you get it through your thick skull there is more to fishing than catching fish.

But when you say what, for instance, they are stumped.

Sometimes they mumble around about getting next to nature. But the fact is, fishing has no more relation to nature than Spit-in-the-ocean with deuces, treys, and one-eyed face-cards wild.

Take trout fishing.

Trout are raised in hatcheries and fed on ground-up horses. They are not even allowed to have normal sex relations. When a boy trout starts sidling up to a girl trout, a couple of nature-lovers grab them and squeeze their milt and roe into a pan.

The little trout are kept in tanks until they're several inches long. Then they're loaded into nice natural tank-trucks and hauled out to a stream or pond and dumped in.

When they find there is no horse meat in the water, they go around gnawing at beer bottles, mattress springs, tin cans, old galoshes, worn-out girdles, Silver Doctors, and the other natural articles found in trout streams.

As a matter of fact, the most popular trout in America—the brown trout—isn't even natural to this continent. It was imported from Europe in 1884. If it knew how to get back there, it would probably go.

The only reason there is any trout fishing in most states is that Conservation Departments have learned to kick Mother Nature in the teeth every time she comes messing around.

When you hear a fisherman talking about the beauties of nature, you can rest assured he would not know the old lady if she knocked him down and sat on him.

And if you got a better idea, let's have it.

ALL ABOUT BIG-GAME FISHING

People who are just taking up big-game fishing are called learners. People who know more about big-game fishing than anybody else put together are called Lerners.* This is so confusing that many people just throw up their hands and change the subject.

The only difference between big-game fishing and collecting old millstones is that millstones aren't slimy.**

In between fishing expeditions, big-game fishermen go around lifting Percheron horses off the ground and pulling loaded freight cars with their teeth. In the evening, they gather in small groups and feel each other's muscle.

Big-game anglers and fresh-water anglers sneer at each other.

And why not?

Life's Darkest Moment

* This is a pun, and refers to Mr. and Mrs. Michael Lerner, who invented horse-mackerel fishing.
** Contrary to popular misconception, whales are not fish. Otherwise, there is little to be said in their favor.

How to Torture Your Husband

Please note that the obnoxiously successful angler in the upper left corner is not wearing waders—probably because she once wore a pair in front of a full-length mirror. If I ever got the job of eliminating sex as a factor in American life, my first step would be to compel all women under fifty to wear stocking-foot waders with felt-soled shoes. If this failed, I'd know I was licked, and hand in my resignation.

The Thrill that Comes Once in a Lifetime

Probably, deep in his heart, the kid feels a certain contempt for the fancy-pants fisherman with the elegant equipment.

Driving along beside a beautiful stretch of a closely posted stream one afternoon, Jack Rowles and I beheld a gentleman in a cashmere sport coat and neatly pressed doeskin slacks, seated languidly on a shooting stick on the bank and casting a fly, while his gentleman's gentleman stood by—presumably to disengage fish from the hook when necessary, change flies, announce callers, serve tea, etc.

This sight so unnerved us that we considered stopping the car and chucking some large, plebeian stones at the toff, but the evening rise was due to start shortly, and we had several miles to drive to public water.

The Timid Soul

Every man has at least one chink in the armor of his honesty. I once knew an Episcopal bishop who stole bird dogs. And it's a rare stretch of water that doesn't look more inviting for a couple of "No trespassing" signs.

A well-known professional flytier once told me that her father, who lives beside a famous Scottish salmon river, had poached the preserved water all his life, and was the terror of every bailiff for miles around. On the old man's seventieth birthday, the owners sent word that henceforth he had their permission to fish their water, and would no longer be bothered by the wardens.

This action so demoralized the gaffer that he went into a profound funk and refused to go near the river for several months. When he appeared to be wasting away, his wife persuaded the owners to withdraw their devastating offer of immunity, and the old man took up his poaching where he had left off. The last I heard, he was well in his eighties, and still good for a brace of salmon every evening during the runs.

Life's Darkest Moment

Fishing the Willowemoc last year, I rose a trout to my next-to-last-remaining Blue Spider, but left the fly in his jaw when I struck too hard.

I hated to lose that fly—good naturally-blue hackle is hard to come by—and so I rashly announced to my companions that I'd get it back the next morning. I also described the fish as at least a sixteen-incher. I could tell by the feel when he took the fly.

Jack Rowles, Founder and President of the Beaverkill Chub Club, denied hotly that (a) I could raise a trout that had a fresh hook in its jaw and (b) that I could judge the size of a trout by breaking off a fly in it, and we argued these points until the bartender started putting out the lights.

The next morning Jack went with me to the pool, and on the first cast of my only other Blue Spider a trout took the fly and was netted. The fish (a) had my original Blue Spider stuck in the corner of his jaw, and (b) was nine inches long.

We called it a draw.

How to Torture Your Wife

I think this is a very funny cartoon, because I suggested the idea to Mr. Webster. I expected it would be signed: "WEBSTER—IN COLLABORATION WITH ED ZERN, THAT DELIGHTFULLY CLEVER PRINCE OF GOOD FELLOWS." Instead, all I got out of it was a rather cavalier "plus Z," and in the wave of speculation as to the identity of "Z" that swept the United States and possessions, I came off a poor second to Joe Zilch.

The Thrill that Comes Once in a Lifetime

This shows how well-meaning people go around messing up other people's lives. Up to the moment illustrated, the luckless laddie was perfectly content with his pole, string, and bent pin. From now on, he'll eat his heart out until he can own a $60 rod, a $20 reel, a $15 tapered line, and the expensive trimmings that go with them. But in order to get those items, he'll have to turn down his parents' pleas to stay on the farm, and go to make his fortune in the city. Since he has no special talents or abilities, and is not very bright, he'll spend forty years working his way up to be assistant manager of the shipping department. When his kids have grown up and married, he'll be able to afford a fairly good fishing outfit, but he'll be too decrepit to use it.

When I meet a country boy on the stream, and he starts eyeing my rod, I threaten to wallop his bottom with it. Some people don't know when they're well off.

Life's Darkest Moment

Probably the well-intentioned host is in the advertising business. There is an unwritten but quite rigid rule around advertising agencies that, wherever a fishing scene is illustrated, the tackle should be as ill-assorted as possible.

If you will find me an advertising illustration of a fishing scene in which the artist has not put a bait-casting reel on a flyrod, or vice versa, or in which a character is not flyfishing with a plug rod, or some similar incongruity, I will send you a brand-new, soft-iron hobnail free of charge.

THE HONEYMOON

Life's Darkest Moment

Personally, I don't get the point of this cartoon. As far as I can see, it's an ideal honeymoon, and I don't know what Mr. Webster could be driving at. I spent my honeymoon fishing for small-mouth bass. I had to. The trout season had ended.

The Thrill that Comes Once in a Lifetime

Here Mr. Webster shows how a seemingly kind act can wreck several lives:

The kid retrieves the leader and fly, only to discover that in order to handle nine feet of leader and a dry fly, he needs at least a $20 rod. In order to get the twenty, he holds up a filling station and inadvertently assassinates the proprietor, who leaves a wife and eleven children in utter, abject poverty. The kid is sent to a reformatory, where he contracts whooping cough and dies. His parents commit suicide from grief and shame. Meanwhile, the guy who was too lazy to hunt for his leader and fly in the brush pile is going around telling all and sundry what a helluva generous fellow he is.

16

TO
HELL
WITH HUNTING

(1946)

HOW TO HUNT LIONS IN DESERT REGIONS

In southern Libya and northern portions of the British Sudan, the so-called desert lion occurs, and occasional specimens are bagged by sportsmen.

Most hunters, however, complain of the difficulty of finding lion under desert conditions—and admittedly, they are not as plentiful as in Kenya, Nyasaland and other sections of Africa. I am indebted to Mr. Leonard Lionni of Philadelphia for a simple but effective method of locating lions in the Libyan Desert or other sandy regions.* In applying this method, the hunter equips himself with a fine-mesh sieve, and—having arrived at the edge of the desert—proceeds to sift the desert sand through the sieve. Since the lions are too large to pass through the mesh of the sieve, this method cannot fail to produce satisfactory results.

* Mr. Lionni is also the author of the Lionni Simplified Plan for National Defense. Reduced to its essence, this plan calls for complete abolition of the Army and Navy. In the event of an attack on this country, the enemy would be permitted to land his forces unmolested on our shores. When all enemy troops had landed, a delegation of inspectors from the U. S. Immigration Bureau would approach them and demand to see their passports and visas. When the invaders failed to produce passports in proper order, they would be sent to Ellis Island, and deported as undesirable aliens.

THE DIETARY HABITS OF LIONS

Many authorities claim that only crippled or senile lions will attack humans unless provoked, and that a healthy lion, able to obtain his natural forage, is as harmless to humans as a kitten.

One of the most eminent of these experts on lion behavior recently took a set of Dr. Eliot's Five-Foot Shelf of the World's Best Literature and went out in the middle of the South African veldt, hellbent on getting culture.

He had read about six inches when he looked up and observed a young, healthy lion on his right. Unperturbed, he returned to his reading, and when he had read about a yard, he looked up and noticed another young, healthy lion on his left. The lion authority merely sniffed contemptuously and went on reading.

When the expert had scarcely three-quarters of an inch remaining between himself and cultural fulfillment, the lions moseyed over and bit him into small, easily digestible pieces.

This shows what happens to people who read too much between the lions.

POSITIVELY THE LAST CHAPTER
ABOUT LIONS IN THIS BOOK

The history of lion-hunting abounds in curious and unusual departures from the normal sporting procedure.

During the early days of World War II, two young cadets in training at a Royal Air Force base in Rhodesia fell to boasting of their respective prowess as hunters. Since several lions had been reported in the vicinity, they agreed to a friendly contest, and each put up a pint of Guinness's—the first one to kill a lion to get both bottles.

While one of the cadets armed himself with a borrowed Mannlicher rifle and set out to kill his lion in the conventional way, the other, being somewhat more enterprising by nature, secured permission from the commandant to borrow one of the combat airplanes used in training at the base.

Loading the wing guns with live ammunition he took off hastily, and after reconnoitering for a few minutes, spotted a splendid specimen trotting across the plain. In almost less time than it takes to tell it, he dove at the unfortunate beast, riddled its tawny carcass with machine-gun bullets, and returned to the base, where he quickly polished off both bottles.*

* As far as the writer can discover there is no particular moral to this story, except possibly that a strafed lion is the shortest distance between two pints.

ALL ABOUT GUIDES

Hunters like to talk about the shrewdness and sagacity of back-country guides, and their picturesque qualities. City-bred hunters think anybody who knows a rabbit from a razor-back hog is shrewd and sagacious, and anybody who wears a shirt two days in a row is picturesque.

The truth is, most guides are not smart enough to hold down a steady job at the local sawmill, and are obliged to choose between guiding and burglary.

And although burglars meet a better class of people, the hours are not attractive.

Sometimes guides have other businesses on the side.

I know a guide in East Glandular, Oregon, who runs a small crossroads general store when he is not poking around the hills with a party of hunters, hoping to stumble on some game.

I stopped in to see him last summer, at his store. Every shelf was stacked high with boxes of black pepper. There was more pepper piled on the counter.

There was also pepper under the counter, on top of the stove, and on the floor.

"Quite a stock of pepper you've got in," I observed.

"Hell," said the guide, "that ain't nothing. You'd ought to see down in the cellar."

"You must sell an awful lot of it," I said.

"Nope," said the guide. "I don't sell hardly none to speak of."

"But there was a salesman in here last month," he said wistfully. "Now, *there*'s a feller sells a lot of *pepper!*"

THE KING OF SULLIVAN COUNTY

Frank King lives near Monticello, New York, in the midst of the countryside that has been his stomping grounds for sixty years. For a number of years he has run hunting camps in various parts of Sullivan County, and guided hunters and fishermen. Before that, as a boy and young man, he was an "outlaw"—a professional market hunter—and the terror and despair of every game warden and keeper in the district. Back in the days when conservation was just a four-syllable word, Frank shipped four barrels of ruffed grouse to New York City every Monday morning from early fall to late spring, and enough venison to feed a heavily-populated township.

I'm not sure when Frank quit outlawing, but I've heard it was immediately after the one and only time the forces of law and order came close to catching up with him. "I guess I ain't so goddam spry as I used to be," Frank is alleged to have said, and thenceforth walked the straight and narrow.

I don't know how spry Frank used to be, but judging from the way he goes through the woods and over mountains today, he must have been a very elusive gent in his heyday.

Here are a few Frank King stories.

FISH STORY

Guin Polevoy and I drove up to Frank King's place one June day to fish the Neversink. As we pulled up in front of the house, Frank came charging down to meet us, his blue eyes blazing and his voice throaty with righteous indignation.

"Why the almighty hell wasn't you birds here last night?" he howled, hopping up and down with excitement. "Lemme tell you! I went down to the hardware store yesterday evening and bought four of them goddam newfangled leaders that's made out of some goddam chemicals or something. Forty-five cents apiece they was. 2X. Then I took the truck and drove her back through that wagon-road to the Slide Pool. Got there about eight o'clock, and there wasn't a goddam fish showing nowheres in the pool. So I put on one of them big spider-flies with the guinea hen hackle that you gimme on opening day, and I hadn't no sooner throwed it up by the head of the pool than a twenty-inch brown come up and ate it. Made one jump and that leader busted at the knot, and the fish went jumping all over the goddam pool trying to shake that fly off his snoot. So I put another one of them same flies on, and son of a bitch if the same damn thing don't happen!"

Frank paused to catch his breath and shift his chaw and let his indignation get untangled from his tonsils, and went on:

"Well sir, I stood in that goddam pool until all four of them leaders was wore pretty near down to the butts, what with big trout busting off a inch or two with every fly, and all them trout was hopping two feet out of water trying to shake the flies loose, and by the time it was too dark to fish any more I had three-four of them in the air all around me all the time. Boys, I been fishing that river fifty years, and if I had of had just one goddam decent leader I'd be showing you the finest mess of big brown trout you ever seen, right now! Go to hell if I wouldn't like to find the man that invented them leaders and shove a barrel of chemicals clean up his goddam chimney!"

I have seen a lot of big fish lost, and heard a lot of heart-rending fishing stories, but never have I seen anybody as visibly outraged by the double-dealing of Destiny as Frank King when he stomped back to the house, still sputtering and pop-eyed, to get ready to go with us, and my heart bled buckets for a brother sportsman.

I was still clucking my tongue sympathetically when Mrs. King came around the corner of the house with a basket of wet clothes. "Did Frank tell you about the fishing last night, Ma?" Guin asked.

"Yes, indeed," Frank's handsome white-haired wife replied.

"Do you believe those fish were as big as he said?" Guin asked.

"I guess I would," Ma King said patiently, hanging a shirt on the line, "if I didn't know for a fact Frank was down at the fire-house playing cards from noon to midnight."

THE BEST WINGSHOT IN THE UNITED STATES

Back in Frank King's market-hunting days, he was somehow appointed one of the assessors for the township—probably because he knew every inch of it thoroughly, and if his respect for property lines was not highly developed, his knowledge of them was unsurpassed.

It happened that a portion of an immense private shooting preserve, owned by a wealthy New York sportsman named Milford, lay within the township boundaries, and also that a great many of the deer and grouse Frank shipped to market came from within its closely patrolled confines.

In pursuance of his official duties, Frank learned that Milford was present at the main lodge one day, and so he put on his best bib and tucker, carefully picking off any stray partridge feathers that adhered thereto, and drove over to discuss the property's assessment with the owner.

The owner explained to Frank that he kept the place merely as a shooting preserve, primarily for the large numbers of grouse it harbored, and politely inquired whether Frank ever did any bird-shooting. Frank looked at the city man suspiciously, but when it seemed clear that the question was asked out of prime innocence, Frank allowed that he sometimes fooled around with a scattergun, and knew a grouse from a groundhog.

The owner then went on to remark that he considered himself the best wingshot in the United States. Frank pricked up his ears, and allowed that the United States was a pretty big country. "I know it's a big country," said the owner. "But I've shot birds from one end of it to the other, and always with the best wingshots in the area, and I've yet to meet a man I couldn't outshoot. And the same holds true for England and Scotland.

"Of course," he explained, "I *ought* to be the best wingshot in the country. I've never done much of anything else since I was a youngster, except fish for salmon. Got my first English shotgun as a gift on my twelfth birthday, and been shooting upland and lowland ever since."

"Well now," said Frank, "mebbe you *are* the best wingshot in the United States. Like you say, you *ought* to be. But if you're the best, I figure I'm a real close *second-best!*"

"Really?" said the owner. "Well, Mr. King, I'll tell you what. I'll wager one hundred dollars that we can shoot grouse over the same dog for one day, and I'll grass two birds to your one. How does that strike you?"

"It strikes me fine," Frank said. "When would you like to settle this here wager?"

"How does Saturday suit you?" Milford said. "I've a fine grouse dog up with me that needs a work-out, and we'll make a day of it."

Thus the next Saturday morning found Frank and Milford setting out from the lodge with a good English setter, and it was a matter of minutes before the dog came to point on birds.

"How do you want to work this, Mr. Milford?" Frank asked. "If we're shooting alternate points, you take the first one."

"None of that, Mr. King!" chuckled the owner. "I'm not going to do you any favors, and I don't want you to do any for me. When those birds flush, you shoot as many as you can, and I'll do the same. This is every man for himself!"

"Suits me," Frank said. (Afterwards Frank said, "That's where that feller made his mistake. For ten years back I hadn't never let a ruff fly more than eight-ten feet, and mostly I hit em less than five.")

When three grouse flushed, Frank doubled on the two that came up on Milford's side while Milford was still bringing his gun up—and by eleven o'clock, Frank had killed twenty-seven birds to Milford's three.

"It looks like you've won yourself a hundred dollars, Mr. King," Milford said. "Let's go back and have lunch. And may I say that this has been one of the most disconcerting days of my life, and that you, sir, are beyond the slightest shadow of doubt the greatest wingshot in the world!"

"You'd better not tell that to nobody around these parts," said Frank. "Some of these Sullivan County boys can *really* shoot."

After lunch, Frank took the hundred dollars, thanked his host for a pleasant morning's shoot, and drove home. That afternoon the head gamekeeper of the preserve appeared at the lodge in a black fury, and announced his resignation.

"What's the matter?" Milford asked his usually mild-mannered minion.

"Matter!" screamed the enraged bailiff. "Yesterday I hired two extra watchmen to keep Frank King off this place—and today you *invite* him in!"

Once a year thereafter until his death, Milford (which isn't his name, of course) invited Frank to the lodge for a day of companionable (and non-competitive) shooting. "It's the only way I can give the watchman a day off," he explained one time to Frank, and they both chuckled.

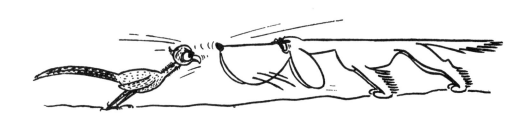

HOW
TO TELL FISH
FROM FISHERMEN

(1947)

JOKE

Runt Wood told me the story about the hotel chambermaid who entered a room to perform her chores and found the guest in the bathroom. He was attired in waders, felt-soled shoes, hat-with-flies, wading jacket, creel and net, and was engaged in casting a dry fly into the bathtub, which was full of water. He was annoyed when the chambermaid intruded, but after whispering "Shhh!" went right on casting.

The chambermaid shrugged her shoulders and went down to the manager's office. "There's a loony in 719," she said, "and you'd better get him out of there if you want me to tidy the room."

The manager went up to the room, opened the bathroom door and saw the guest still casting into the tub. Thinking it best to humor the guest, he inquired cheerfully, "Catching any fish?"

The guest looked at him in amazement. "*What*?" he demanded incredulously. "In a *bathtub*?"

THE FISH ON 42ND STREET

If you happened to be walking down 42nd Street near Times Square one Monday afternoon several years ago and noticed several large brown trout in reasonably fresh condition lying around on the pavement, you may have wondered how they got there. I'll tell you:

One Sunday in early May, Jim Deren,* Larry Madison† and Ernie St. Clair†† drove up from New York City for a day's fishing on the Neversink. They left before daybreak, in Deren's station wagon, and were on the stream by nine o'clock. After an hour or so of fruitless fishing, during which they met another metropolitan angler, whose car they had seen parked near theirs, Deren suggested calling it quits and trying another stretch of water about ten miles distant. When Larry and Ernie balked, Jim said he'd take the station wagon and go by himself, and would pick them up at the bridge along about nightfall, and they agreed.

Late in the afternoon things picked up a bit, and after the other chap had left in disgust, both Larry and Ernie stuffed several sizable trout into their creels before they began working their way back down to the bridge. When they got there it was dark and cold, and knowing that Jim might have marked down a lunker and be spending an hour of darkness trying for it, they weren't concerned when ten o'clock came around and no Deren. But they were godawfully cold, and their waders had leaked enough to soak their underclothing, and so they decided to do a little night-fishing under the bridge, hoping the exercise would keep their blood circulating until Deren arrived with their dry clothes.

Along about midnight, though, the cold became unbearable, and so they came out of the water and built a fire and huddled around it, all the while making interesting if somewhat implausible conjectures as to Deren's ancestry and sex life. By two o'clock there was a heavy frost on the ground, and they had burned all the combustible material within toting distance. At three o'clock they decided that Deren had almost certainly fallen into a deep pool and been drowned, and they had better starting shifting for themselves.

The nearest village was eight miles away on the other side of the mountain, and they reached it about five o'clock—foot-sore, famished and with a total of fifteen cents between them, since their wallets were in Jim's car. They stood around the sleeping town for a while listening to each other's teeth chatter, and when a New York-bound bus came along they flagged it, and by threats and cajolery persuaded the startled driver to take them aboard. It was high noon when they arrived at the Times Square bus terminal—clad in

---

* Proprietor of the Angler's Roost, which has since moved to the Chrysler Building and become disgustingly respectable. Cf. *To Hell With Fishing*, p. 86.

† A documentary movie-maker and excellent angler and fly-tyer.

†† Onetime manufacturer of the famous St. Clair nymphs—the most incredibly lifelike and deadly lures you ever laid eyes on. I lost my last two in monstrous Beaverkill trout, and since Ernie disappeared several years ago, the few remaining St. Clair nymphs are now collector's items.

multi-patched waders, vintage fishing jackets and fly-bedizened hats—clutching rods and reels and draped in strong-smelling creels complete with defunct fish.

They tried to slip unobstrusively through the lunchtime throngs on 42nd Street, but their hobnails made an embarrassing clatter on the pavement and their landing nets kept catching on people's buttons, and as a sort of extra-special attraction the bottom fell out of Larry's creel and spilled sixteen-inch brown trout up and down the sidewalk. Even though he let them lie, it was some time before they could find a taxi and direct the driver to the Angler's Roost, where they could borrow money to pay the cabbie and also learn if Deren's remains had been found.

When they stumbled into the Roost, Deren was behind the counter, going about his business as usual, and when he saw them come through the door he lay down on the

floor among the stray feathers and clutched his sides and howled with laughter, in which neither Madison nor St. Clair was disposed to join. However, they were too enfeebled by hunger and exposure to do more than glower at him, and when he was able to control his merriment, he explained that he had had a flat tire on the way back to the bridge, and had arrived late, and had been unable to find them. After honking his horn and hollering for almost an hour (he alleged), he had decided that they must have gone back to the city with the chap they had met on the river, and he had driven home alone.

He said the roar of the fast water under the bridge must have drowned out the sound of his horn, and further that it was not his fault that a couple of birds walking around New York City in full trout-fishing regalia were a mirth-provoking spectacle. He went around the corner to the garage and got their clothes, and when they had changed they staggered out of the Roost as haughtily as anyone who has not slept or eaten for thirty-odd hours, and who has spent a long cold night huddled under a Catskill Mountain bridge, and who has walked eight miles over a mountain in hobnailed shoes and wet waders after a full day's fishing could be expected to stagger, and it was several weeks before either of them could discuss the matter with any degree of dispassion.

Larry is now inclined to be philosophic about it, and even says it had certain advantages. He says he can now dream he is standing around the Waldorf-Astoria lobby in his underwear, and it doesn't faze him a bit.

BOOM GOES THE WEASEL

One time I went over to Bucks County, Pennsylvania, to spend the night with Lyman and Mary Clark at their home. After dinner Lyman showed me the Old English gamecocks that he breeds selectively for color and quality of feather, and never have I seen such splendid hackle, on or off the hoof. When it got too dark to admire the birds we went inside, and after we had hashed over a lot of past fishing trips and plotted some future ones, I went to bed in the guest room and slept like a log until 5 A.M. Probably I would have slept even longer if a shotgun hadn't been fired in Lyman and Mary's room, which adjoined mine.

I am a notoriously sound sleeper but the first blast—accompanied by a shattering crash of glass—brought me sitting upright, and was followed by a second shot which seemed even louder, if possible. Although not by nature a busybody, I was intrigued.

Lying back in bed, I soon had the solution. Obviously, either Lyman (Mary) had shot Mary (Lyman) and thrown her (him) out the window; or he (she) had missed and she (he) had jumped out the window to escape. This latter theory seemed most plausible, as it accounted for the second blast, fired at her (his) retreating figure. I also recalled that Lyman and Mary had had a trifling disagreement as to the precise shade of blue that is desirable in a Gordon Quill hackle, and after considering how one thing often leads to another, I rolled over and went back to sleep.

When I came down to breakfast I was astonished to note that both Lyman and Mary seemed in excellent health, and after bracing my courage with a stiff slug of orange juice I ventured to inquire whether by any chance they had flushed a covey of quail in their bedroom just about daybreak.

Lyman then explained that he had heard some of the gamebirds squawking, and on looking out of the window had seen a weasel chasing one of his prize hens up and down the lawn. In a half-waked condition he had grabbed a twelve-gauge shotgun from the closet, loaded both barrels and blazed away at the weasel through the lower section of the window. Unfortunately the window was open at the top instead of the bottom, and the load had gone through a double thickness of glass, producing the subsidiary sound effects and making it necessary to despatch the weasel with the second barrel. The de-weaseled hen then went about its business, and Lyman went back to bed.

While I found this account somewhat lacking in dramatic and human-interest values, I was relieved, and ate an extra helping of scrambled eggs in celebration.

JE M'EN FISH

As far as I know, I am the only living human being who has ever caught a fish in the Seine River within the city limits of Paris. At least, I spent a number of weeks hanging around the less fashionable quais watching the fishermen, and never saw anyone catch a fish, or even heard of one being caught. One day I was sitting on an embankment below the Pont Neuf and an elderly gentleman came over and handed me his fishpole, explaining that he had to see a *homme* about a *chien*, and would I take charge of his tackle until he returned. His hook was baited with sliver of raw turnip, and after I had dangled it in the river for a minute or two I felt a nibble, and hauled in a fish that was four inches long if it was an inch. Five or six other fishermen immediately came over to learn what bait I had used, but it had come off the hook during the fierce struggle to land the fish, and I didn't know the French word for turnip.* When the proprietor of the tackle reappeared I handed him the rod and the fish and went about my business. For a long time I hoped that the editors of *Field & Stream* would hear about it and give me a special award in their fishing contest, but they never did.

* I *think* it was a piece of turnip, although it might have been rutabaga or horse-radish. It didn't much matter, because I didn't know the words for rutabaga or horse-radish either.

STYLISH
FISHERMAN

AFFABLE
FISHERMAN

SEA-SICK
FISHERMAN

LOCAL
EXPERT

HONEST
FISHERMAN

OUTDOOR
TYPE

PURIST

INTELLECTUAL
FISHERMAN

YOUNG, INNOCENT
FISHERMAN

TAKE IT OR LEAVE IT

When I first began trout fishing I carried a pocket fly-tying kit in my jacket. Liz Greig had taught me to tie "in the hand," and when a fly came on the water that I couldn't match from my flybox, I would whip out the kit with a fine dramatic flourish and cook up an imitation.

This monkey business impressed some of my more insouciant companions, but the trout regarded it as sheer dam-foolishness, and gave most of my ad-libbed creations the go-by.

Now, in my dotage, I carry a reasonable assortment of sizes and patterns in my flybox, and I figure any trout that doesn't like my selection can go patronize some other angler.

PARABLE FOR POACHERS

Every time I drive along a stretch of posted water (which, because I suffer from chronic human nature, always looks fishier than unposted water), I think of a story my father used to tell, about a man who went walking through a forest, and was suddenly accosted by the owner of the property.

"This is my land," said the owner, scowling ferociously, "and you'll have to get off!"

"Your land?" said the startled stroller.

"Of course it's my land!" said the owner indignantly.

"Tell me, sir," said the trespasser, "how did you acquire it?"

"I inherited it from my father!" said the owner.

"Really?" said the stroller politely. "And how did your father acquire it?"

"He inherited it from *his* father!" snapped the owner impatiently.

"And how did *his* father acquire it?" asked the inquisitive trespasser.

"Why, damn your impudent eyes!" roared the owner. "He *fought* for it!"

"Good," said the stroller, removing his jacket. "I'll fight you for it."

I have always been tempted to try this routine on some owner of choice and posted lake or stream, but unfortunately the ones I've encountered have invariably been large, burly individuals with bulging biceps and great clumps of hair growing out of their ears, against whom I could not last two rounds; and so I keep my trap shut and drive on down to the open water.

Still and all, it's a nice story.

THE PERILS OF FLY-TYING

Lyman Clark sent me a packet of rusty dun hackle that he'd plucked from one of his gamecocks, and I sat right down at my fly-tying table and compounded a dozen of the juiciest dry flies that a trout ever turned up his nose at.

When I'd whip-finished the final fly, the desk and floor were a litter of fur and feathers, and because my daughter was then crawling around the house eating all the matches and razor blades she could lay her prehensile little hands on, I went and got the vacuum cleaner and ran it over the floor and tabletop.

While doing this, I happened to think of an elderly brown trout I knew who lived under a boulder in the Schoharie, and was wondering how he would regard this particular shade of rusty dun, when I came to in time to see the last of the dozen flies disappear down the nozzle of the vacuum cleaner.

By the time I had retrieved the flies from the dustbag (which had not been emptied for some years, by the looks of it), and spent a good hour trying to restore them to their original succulence, I understood better than any deep-domed professor of physics why Nature abhors a vacuum, and damned if I blame the old jade.

When I got up to the Schoharie the next week I learned that someone had horsed my speckled friend out from under his rock with a length of clothesline and a six-inch chub for bait, but I caught a few of his great grandchildren on the vacuumized duns, and had a pretty good time.

ALL ABOUT WESTERN TROUT FISHING

I'd be the last guy in the world to go around stirring up sectional animosities—but the fact is, several of my acquaintances have told me that the average Eastern trout fisherman, accustomed to hard-fished streams, low clear water and circumspect fish, makes the average Western trout fisherman look like a bum. I wouldn't know, and if I did I would be too politic to take a partisan position—but a friend of mine nearly got his face kicked in on the Deschutes River one time. He's a veteran Catskills angler, and an accomplished nymph fisherman, and one time he took his tackle along on a business trip to Portland, Oregon.

After his chores were attended to, he rented a car and drove to a recommended stretch of the Deschutes. The next morning he studied the stream for a while, and the only fly he could see was a tiny midge that was hatching sporadically. When he saw several trout bulging, he put a Number 20 nymph on his 4X leader and proceeded to have himself a field day. He lost quite a few large fish in the fast water, but at the end of the day he had five brown trout in his creel, from sixteen to eighteen inches, and had released a number of smaller ones.

Walking back to his car he met a party of three local fishermen, all over eight feet tall (he claimed), who asked him what luck. He showed them the five keepers, and they asked what kind of bait he had taken them on. When he showed them the tiny fly they became moody, and one of them picked him up by the scruff of the neck and threatened him with multiple contusions. "In these parts, stranger," the petulant Westerner said, "when a man asks us what we caught our fish on, we don't try to kid him. Now git!"

My friend got, but before he could reach the car he ran into another party, who looked equally large and choleric. They asked to see his basket, and after admiring the trout, asked what he had caught them on.

"A great big gob of salmon eggs," said my friend, and while the tall-timber boys were digging their salmon-egg jars out of their packs, he snuck off to his car and drove back to the city like a bat out of hell.

OPTIMISTIC FISH

ROCOCO FISH

RECALCITRANT FISH

RISIBLE FISH

NERVOUS FISH

UNEASY FISH

DISILLLUSIONED FISH

FLABBERGASTED FISH

LUNATIC FRINGE

THE GREATEST FISHING STORY IN THE WORLD

I suppose that if *Moby Dick* were a fishing story, it would be the greatest fishing story in the world. But it is disqualified on the technical grounds that whales are not fish, and so Melville's ghost will have to console himself through eternity with the thought that it is merely one of the great novels of the English language.

For my money, gents, the greatest fishing story ever written is Ernest Hemingway's "Big Two-Hearted River." I don't mean the most amusing story, or the cleverest story, or the most exciting, but simply the one that comes closest to putting all the feeling of fishing into words. It happens to be a trout-fishing story, and even a special kind of trout-fishing story, and not the best of Hemingway's short stories, but there is in it the universalness of a man going fishing, not for food or money or even for sport, but because it is the only way he can break a pattern of experience and emotion and ideas and people and work and fear and all the little things and big things that press on him. It is a matter-of-fact story, told matter-of-factly, but there is mystery in it. And it is mystery that makes fishing special, in a way that skiing or gunning or golf or riding to hounds can never be special.

I read "Big Two-Hearted River" for the first time in 1932. I was in Paris, and broke, and in September it started to rain and kept on raining, and my friends left, and I bought a copy of *In Our Time*, a collection of Hemingway short stories in a cheap paper-bound edition, and went back to the creep-joint I lived in and read it. When I finished "Big Two-Hearted River" I went to sleep with a bad case of homesickness, and the day after that I was headed for home.

There was no fishing when I got back here, and if I hadn't read the story I might have hung around over there and become a reporter on the Paris *Herald* or the leading figure in a white slave ring, and really amounted to something. On the other hand, it may have been the rain that was really to blame. The point is, "Big Two-Hearted River" is a great fishing story, and if you haven't read it, it's high time you did.

HOW
TO CATCH
FISHERMEN

(1951)

CRIME DOESN'T PAY WHOM?

Several years ago a friend of mine grew weary of elbowing his way through hordes of fishermen along the banks of every trout stream within driving distance of New York City, where he then lived, and having no particular ties with the metropolis he pulled up stakes and headed west. When he found a western city with a nice climate and an even nicer trout stream flowing nearby, he bought a house on the outskirts of town and settled down as a permanent resident. Shortly thereafter he sent me a long letter with a rapt description of the nearby fishing, with special emphasis on the fact that anyone who fishes the several local streams may not only latch onto large numbers of sizable brown and rainbow trout but may also have a mile or more of water all to himself, even on weekends. It sounded sensational.

Last year, though, the same friend sent me a batch of newspaper clippings describing his off-season activities. It seems he had organized 3,000 (or maybe it was 3,000,000) youngsters of the city into a gigantic Junior Sportsman's Club and was teaching them the basic elements of fly fishing—with classes in casting, fly tying and all essential phases of the sport. He was manifestly pleased with himself, and in an accompanying note he explained that the club would undoubtedly help to reduce juvenile delinquency and make fine, cleancut, wholesome citizens out of boys who would otherwise end their days in the hoosegow, if not actually in the hot seat.

Personally I feel that this guy is a menace to his fellow fishermen. If his program is successful he will have that mob of moppets sloshing around in trout streams, instead of loitering around pool rooms and gin mills, where they belong. And in a short while the

35

streams in his neighborhood will be as crowded with anglers as the Esopus or the Housatonic or any other eastern river. It simply doesn't make sense. Instead of letting those kids go happily about their business of rolling drunks, holding up filling stations, smoking reefers, and other normal pastimes my friend is trying to herd them into streams and lakes, where they will be a real nuisance.

And regardless of what you may think of our penal system, the fact is that every man in jail is one less potential fisherman to clutter up your favorite pool or pond. Frankly, if there were more people in penitentiaries and reform schools and fewer on rivers and lakes it would suit me fine. They could all be paroled on the last day of the fishing season, with orders to report back to the warden and be locked up again on the following opening day; the money saved on prison food bills through this arrangement could be used for general stream improvement work.

In fact I am about to start, in my own neighborhood, a campaign to interest all youngsters in joining a Junior Crime Club, with courses in petty thievery, hijacking, pocket-picking, marijuana culture, breaking and entering, arson, counterfeiting, safe-blowing, disposal of stolen goods, felonious assault and other larcenous arts, criminal crafts and sinful sciences. Any member of the Club who is caught within five hundred feet of a lake, stream or pond containing any species of game fish will be stood in a tub of concrete until it hardens, and then sunk in the deepest part of the water that led to his downfall. And the only "tight lines" that Club members will ever know are the ones by which they swing from a gallows.

Here—have an application blank.

OYEZ, OYEZ

Fishing the Gunnison River in Colorado one day, Larry Madison met a justice of the Supreme Court of a certain western state. The trout weren't moving, so they sat beside the stream a while and Larry asked the legalist how a man gets appointed to a state Supreme Court bench.

The judge said there were a number of factors governing such appointments, but offered one concrete suggestion to aspiring jurists. He said that while on a lower bench he had devised a compact little fly-tying kit, with a small vise which could be clamped onto the rostrum in such a position that it couldn't be seen by anyone else in the court. By hunching over and appearing to concentrate fiercely on the fine points of the case under argument, the judge had been able to turn out five or six carefully tied optic bucktails in the course of a day's session and still maintain a fairly good grasp of the proceedings.

Only on a few occasions, the judge said, did he become so absorbed in cocking the fan-wings on a dry fly at the proper angle that he completely lost the thread of the arguments advanced by the opposing lawyers; in these cases, the judge said, his verdicts were considered such models of objectivity, lucidity and jurisprudential wisdom that they came to the attention of the governor, who promptly appointed him to a vacancy in the highest court of the state.

PLUG STORY

When I first began putting this book together, it seemed to me to be weighted on the fly-fishing side—possibly because fly fishing is, if possible, somewhat more ludicrous than plug casting. When I met a non-fishing British friend on Lexington Avenue and mentioned this dilemma he seemed puzzled, but then brightened up and said he knew a pretty good plug story.

During the buzz-bombing of London, he said, a whole block of flats was demolished by an almost direct hit. An hour later a rescue squad, digging through the debris, came upon an old man sitting naked in a bathtub. He was stunned and dazed but otherwise uninjured, and in his hand was the tub's rubber stopper.

"I can't understand it," the old man said, shaking his head in disbelief. "I just pulled out the plug, and the house blew up."

I explained to my friend that it wasn't the kind of plug story I could use, but to show him there were no hard feelings I took him to the Men's Pub at the Waldorf-Astoria and stood him a pint of bitters.

HOE HUM

My friends Marvin and Grace Marie Chase recently bought a farm near the Esopus Creek, and last summer I dropped in to find them busy with the thousand-and-one chores that people who buy farms find themselves busy with. But Marvin knocked off whitewashing the manure pile, or whatever it was he was doing, and conducted me around the place, showing me the various points of interest. These included an acre of eating corn which he was endeavoring to keep free of weeds—and he showed me the hoe with which he chopped the offensive flora. It looked more like a child's toy than a regular hoe, and woefully inadequate to cope with a field of weed-infested corn.

"That's an awfully small hoe, isn't it?" I said. "Why don't you get a full-sized one?"

Marvin eyed me indignantly. "Of course it's a small hoe!" he said. "Any nincompoop can chop weeds with a full-sized hoe. But with this hoe, it takes skill, strategy and weedcraft—and the weeds have a fighting chance! Furthermore, just feel this—" and he

handed me the skimpy instrument. "Feel that balance! Not too much whip, either—plenty of backbone in that handle, and the action's sort of semiparabolic. It's exactly the kind of hoe that Payne or Jim Lindsay or Garrison would make if they made hoes!"

And so, when I had admitted that it was indeed a beautifully balanced stick, light in the hand and ideally suited to precision hoeing—in short, calculated to make weed control a thoroughly sporting proposition—we continued our tour of the Chase acres.

Having worked on a farm in my youth, I spied several other items that aroused my curiosity. But I kept my big mouth shut.

INCREDIBLE OCCURRENCE ON THE LITTLE LEHIGH CREEK, FAMOUS PENNSYLVANIA TROUT STREAM. OR ANYWAY, FAIRLY INCREDIBLE

On June 17, 1943, a newly wed fisherman from Hazleton, Pa., having solemnly promised his bride that he'd bring back at least one good trout for her breakfast, fished four miles of the Little Lehigh without so much as pricking a fish. Walking up from the stream just at dark, troutless and dejected, he was suddenly seized by one of those unaccountable whims to which fishermen are frequently subject, and decided to walk back to the water and make just one more cast. After scrambling down the bank he carefully cast a large night crawler so that it drifted appetizingly past a large submerged boulder.

When nothing happened, he decided to try just ten more casts and call it quits. After making ten more casts he got in his car and drove back to Hazleton

ZERN SPURNS URN

If, some day in the future—the reasonably distant future, I hope—you should see my wife standing on the bank of the Beaverkill, or the Brodheads, or the Ausable, or some other good reliable trout stream with a jar in her hand, don't bother to ask her what's in it. I can tell you right now.

It'll be me.

I've asked her, as a personal favor, to splash my ashes into the upper stretch of one of my favorite trout streams when, as it sometime must, the problem of their disposal comes up. I've explained that there would be no particular hurry, but that when she got the opportunity and it wasn't inconvenient and the weather was nice and she was getting tired of seeing the urn standing around in the spare closet among the busted table lamps and the Christmas-tree stand, she should run this errand for me, and she has agreed.

I had several reasons for this request. One was simply that it's a less expensive way to dispose of ashes than to hole them up in a cemetery with a lot of deceased golfers, bridge players and other riffraff who probably wouldn't be very good company anyway. Another reason was purely sentimental: I like trout streams and, dead or alive, I like to horse around in them. But another reason has a good, practical conservation angle: fish food.

And that, gents, is the theme of this essay. Because actually, I'm not at all sure that my cinders, even when soaked in clear, cool mountain water, would be the sort of thing a finicky brown trout would choose to chew on. Certainly not if he had much choice. In fact, I am advised by a leading stream biologist that while a few fishermen disposed of in this manner would serve to enrich the mineral content of the stream and promote the growth of plankton and some of the smaller crustaceans, the practice could—if carried to extremes—completely upset the chemistry of the water, with dire consequences to the fish life in the stream.

However, he had an alternate suggestion. He pointed out that many men of high intellectual attainment bequeath their brains to various institutions, to advance research and perforce shed light on the nature of greatness; he proposed that since most of the fishermen he knew were not particularly distinguished by an abundance of gray matter, but instead ran more toward a general meatiness—and since the cost of liver, horseflesh and the other staples of a hatchery trout's diet had increased tremendously in recent years, creating a serious budgetary problem—it might be that a popular movement could be fostered among fishermen to leave their bodies (including any brains that might be present) to the nearest state or federal fish hatchery.

It was this man's opinion (and he has had a great deal of experience in hatchery

POEM FOR A JULY WEEKEND

Ah, happy barefoot youth with bent-pin hook,
  As innocent as saints long dead or latter-day,
Seeking the wily trout in fern-rimmed brook,
  You got Monday, Tuesday, Wednesday, Thursday and
  Friday to splash around this water, you little hick; why
  can't you let me fish it in peace on Saturday?

management) that the average fisherman, when run through a grinder, would compare favorably with the lower-priced cuts of a milk-wagon horse, and would be an advantageous supplement to the more traditional foods on which hatchery trout are fed; also that, if a trend should set in, a substantial saving could be effected in the cost of nourishing hatchery trout to releasable size. It was likewise his feeling that there would be a certain poetic justice in the establishment of this cyclical relationship between trout and angler—a relationship which is at present, he feels, too one-sided from a dietary point of view.

I was sufficiently impressed by the basic wisdom of the biologist's suggestion to speak to my wife about it, but she had other ideas—based on practical as well as sentimental considerations—and insisted on sticking to the original agreement. And it's true, as she pointed out, that an empty urn can be used as a cookie jar.

TAG, YOU'RE IT

At the covered bridge on the upper Beaverkill one cold and cheerless Opening Day I met Warden Roy Steenrod, creator of the Hendrickson dry fly and former fishing companion of the now legendary Theodore Gordon. Roy was supposed to be creel-checking tagged trout, but at noon, with nine cars parked by the bridge, nobody had caught a fish.

"When they start tagging fishermen," Roy said darkly, "we will be getting somewheres." At the time I thought he was kidding, but the more I think about his proposal the more sense it makes. What happens, for example, to all the vast schools of fishermen after the close of the season? The fact is that little or nothing is known about the whole subject of fishermen during the off-season, and perhaps it's time we did something about it. I know a man who has devoted ten years to the study of plant lice, and I'm sure that the average fisherman is just as interesting as a plant louse.

Or almost as interesting.

WILL WONDERS NEVER CEASE? NOT IF *I* CAN HELP IT

Fishing is a strange and unpredictable business.

For example, I one time sat beside a pool on the Brodheads Creek and watched a veteran fly-fisherman, famous all over the Atlantic seaboard for his skill and streamcraft and armed with the most expensive equipment, fish the stretch carefully without raising a single trout.

Five minutes later, a man from Philadelphia who had never fished for trout before and whose rod would have been spurned by any self-respecting junk dealer, awkwardly cast a night crawler into the same pool.

You may imagine my astonishment when he, too, failed to catch a fish.

TRUEBLOOD IS THICKER THAN BUTTER

About fifteen years ago I started to gather up a few books on angling, and by the time I had several hundred volumes collected I commenced to feel pretty cocky about it, and occasionally I referred in a studiously casual way to my "library" of fishing books. Then one evening at a dinner party I met a man who, when I brought up the subject, admitted that he too had a modest angling library. "You don't say?" I said politely. "How many volumes?"

"I'm not sure," he said, "but it's somewhere between five and six thousand."

Up to that moment I hadn't known there *were* six thousand books on fishing, and I slunk off into a corner and hid behind a potted palm for the rest of the evening. But although I gave up collecting at that time, I've added a volume, now and then, to my shelves—and last March a professional book reviewer offered me a pile of current fishing books which publishers had sent him for reviewing. He explained that he would as soon review a brochure on tea-leaf reading as sully his syndicated column with mention of a fishing book, but he thought I might find something of interest in the stack, and I graciously agreed to take them off his hands.

One of the books was *The Angler's Handbook* by Ted Trueblood, which I found to be highly readable, and remarkably free from the delusions of omniscience which assail most fishing experts when they get within ten feet of a typewriter. In fact, I found a lot of good, practical information in the volume, and one paragraph (on Page 30) made an especially strong impression. It reads:

> If your rod weighs six ounces, your reel nine, and your line another ounce or two, it means that you are holding a pound of weight in your casting hand—much of the time at arm's length—all the time you fish. Try carrying a pound of butter around that way for four or five hours.

The following Saturday, at noon sharp, I purchased a pound of butter at the A & P store and started holding it at arm's length. (My wife insisted that oleomargarine would do just as well, but I pointed out that if Trueblood had meant oleomargarine he would have *said* oleomargarine; whereas, in point of fact, he specifically said butter. "He probably owns a cow," my wife said, "and is prejudiced. For carrying purposes, I'm sure oleomargarine would do just as well. You could color it, and nobody would ever know the difference.'' And then people wonder why women seldom make good fisher-men.)

The first fifteen minutes went well enough, except that when I got back to the house and tried to take off my topcoat I found that the pound of butter wouldn't go through the sleeve, so I kept the coat on. After a while I began to feel awfully warm, so I went outside again, and met one of my neighbors. "How's tricks, Ed?" he said.

"Not too bad, George," I said.

"Good," he said. "What's that in your hand?"

"A pound of butter," I said.

"What are you doing with it?" he said.

"Carrying it," I said.

"Why?" he said.

"On account of Trueblood," I said. "He said I should try carrying a pound of butter for four or five hours. I've only got three and a half hours to go."

When George tiptoed away and whispered something to another neighbor and they both kept staring at me and shaking their heads, I decided to go back in the house where I wouldn't have to answer a lot of damfool questions. It was still very warm in the house, and after the butter got soft I figured I could get it through the sleeve of my topcoat, so I made another try. It worked fine, except that when I was squeezing the cartoon to get it started through the sleeve about a quarter pound of melted butter squirted out onto the living-room rug. This disturbed me at first, until I recalled that actually I seldom use a rod heavier than four ounces or a reel heavier than six, so that the three or four ounces of butter on the rug really didn't matter. In fact, I figured that even the butter that dripped onto the topcoat and my suit didn't make too much difference, because most of my fishing is done with a three-ounce rod and a correspondingly light reel. My wife, however, thought differently, especially after she stepped on the butter on the rug and sat down in it rather suddenly, and while she was making some remarks I put the topcoat back on

over the butter, went outside and dropped what was left of the carton into the garbage can. It's amazing how excitable women are.

Come to think of it, though, I'll bet Trueblood *does* own a cow.

BEST BY TEST

Sitting around in the Antrim Lodge bar one evening, Jack Rowles and I were appalled at the number of strange fishermen milling about, and we decided to draw up a written examination for Beaverkill anglers. Our idea was that after grading the papers it would then be possible to sort out the really serious fishermen from the canasta players and the guys who were simply on the lam from their wives and were going around disguised in waders. By the time Frank started closing up for the night we had several dozen pertinent questions, of which I recall only a relatively uncomplicated one. It was a field problem, and it went like this:

> You are standing, rod in hand, at the head of Cairn's Pool on the Route 17 side, when simultaneously (A) a case of bonded bourbon whisky bounces off a passing truck and lands undamaged in the middle of the highway, where the next passing motorist is sure to see it and pick it up, (B) at the lower end of the pool a beautiful and shapely blonde who has been swimming starts shrieking that she has lost her bathing suit and urges you to hurry down and restore her circulation by any means you choose, as she is getting chilly, (C) across the river a barefoot boy gets his foot caught in a switch of the Delaware, New York and Ontario Western tracks and hollers for you to cross over and pry him loose before the Binghamton Express, which is due in three minutes, comes around the bend and (D) a brown trout of at least four pounds begins to feed greedily on large mayflies within easy casting distance, and is obviously a cinch for a #10 Light Cahill. In one sentence, state what you would do.

I don't intend to tip our mitt on this because some day we might want to use it in another examination. But it might help to bear in mind that four-pound trout in the Beaverkill are a lot harder to come by than bourbon, blondes or barefoot boys.

THEORY SCHMEORY

While loitering around fishing camps and tackle shops all up and down the eastern seaboard and bickering with the fishermen who hang out there, I have discovered that two basic theories are held by almost all trout fishermen. And that both these theories are not only wrong, but specifically contrary to fact.

The first theory, as propounded by millions of fly fishermen, holds that a dumb trout is easier to catch than a smart trout, and that fish which survive the opening-day assault are of a higher order of intelligence (or at least of a lower order of stupidity) than those which succumb to the first artificial fly to come within eating distance.

This, of course, is nonsense, as anybody who has ever compared an artificial trout fly with its natural counterpart can testify. The fact is that only a highly intelligent fish would have sufficient imagination to realize that the most cunningly-fashioned Hendrickson ever tied was intended to simulate a living specimen of Ephemeroptera. A dull-witted trout would simply and unimaginatively assume that it was a clump of fur and feathers tied to a hook, obviously deficient in vitamins and other nutritive values; it would never occur to him that anybody expected him to start gnawing on it.

I am obliged to concede that the imaginative trout's imagination is of a rather childish sort, closely related to that which enables a group of small boys to play at war when armed only with sticks, or permits a little girl to pull the stuffing out of a doll and dreamily make believe she is disemboweling her mother. But childish or not, the trout that takes an artificial fly is displaying imagination, and imagination is most certainly a sub-function of intelligence.

The second theory is equally preposterous, if not more so, and could be summated in the simple proposition that smart fishermen catch more trout than dumb fishermen. I don't know how this theory ever came into being, much less gained widespread acceptance, but its absurdity should be apparent to any thinking person.

In the first place, to be a successful fly fisherman requires absolute concentration on the fly. The angler must be alert and ready to tighten instantly at the rise to a floating lure, before the trout has a split second to discover his error and spew out the bogus bug. With the wet fly or nymph he must be even more steadfast in his concentration, sometimes sensing rather than actually feeling the arrested motion of the sunken fly, and failure to respond instantly usually means a missed fish.

Accordingly, if a trout-fishing contest should ever be held between a team of notably brilliant scientists and a team of demonstrably feeble-minded inmates from a county sanatorium, my money would be on the feebs every time. For while the brain-boys fished, their minds would be wandering off in all directions—thinking up new and better ways for blowing the human race higher than a kite or perfecting an improved formula for a salve to smear on the survivors—and any trout that came to their lures would have ample time to detect the fraud and spit out the hook before the professors came out of their trigonometric trances and tried—too late—to set the hook.

Whereas their opponents, being off their rockers and therefore unaware that mass extermination is socially desirable, would have their minds free to concentrate on their fishing. In no time at all they would have their limits, and after collecting my bets I would head for the fleshpots.

Easy come, easy go.

PHILADELPHIA STORY

Mr. Wesley Gilman, a Maine man who neglected his fishing to such a disgraceful extent that he became president of a good-sized advertising agency, once met me on Chestnut Street in Philadelphia and told me he was moving from a large downtown apartment house to a suburban home.

He said that on the grounds of the apartment house, between the twenty-story building and the street, there was an ornamental garden pool about twenty feet in diameter and three feet deep. He said that four years before, he had got hold of a dozen fingerling brown trout and dumped them into the pool, because, he explained, it had seemed like a good idea at the time. He said he had intended to try catching them but had never quite got around to it, and that as far as he knew they were still there. He asked if I'd like to have a try at them, and when I said I would he said he'd clear it with the building superintendent.

I drove around to the apartment house shortly after dawn the next morning, and having found the pool right where Wes had said it would be, I set up a 3-ounce flyrod and began fishing a #12 dry Light Cahill, with no results whatsoever. In fact, I didn't really expect any results, because the water was murky, stagnant and patently as barren of brown trout as a YMCA swimming pool.

While I was changing to a large variant fly, more to humor Wes than in hopes of raising a fish, people began coming out of the apartment house. I hadn't realized that anybody in Philadelphia got up so early, and I was distressed when the people gathered in a little cluster, standing off at a safe distance and watching me cast. When about ten of them had accumulated they apparently felt there was strength in numbers and moved in closer. Finally one of them got up courage to ask what I was doing, and when I said I was fishing for trout, all the spectators exchanged meaningful glances and several of them pointed their fingers at their temples and twirled them clockwise.

While I was changing to an even larger fly I observed that a policeman had joined the growing gallery, and that he seemed to be making up his mind whether to send for a rope and lasso me or to attempt persuasion. I had a sort of trapped feeling, but couldn't think of any better course than to cast the fresh fly and try to appear nonchalant, so I did.

When the fly settled on the water there was a splashy strike, and in no time at all I hauled a fourteen-inch brown trout out of the pool. It was a singularly unlovely fish, lean of frame and large of head, but unmistakably a trout. I rapped it on the head and stuffed it into the canvas creel I had thoughtfully brought along. Then, after disassembling my rod, I walked with magnificent dignity to my car, got in and drove off, while the gallery stood and gaped.

Back at my own apartment I cleaned the trout and found it full of small snails and Japanese beetles; the flesh had a much stronger smell than seemed necessary, but the janitor's cat appeared happy to have it. As far as I know the eleven other trout are still in the pool; if so, you ought to be able to pick up a brace of three-pounders there in an evening, if you hit it right.

Tight lines!

CHESTNUT

My friend Noel Dickson claims he was sitting in his car beside the West Branch of the Ausable one day, with his pretty wife; they were hoping to spot a good fish working, when they noticed an elderly man, obviously a native, walking slowly toward them on the road. He had a flour sack full of some sort of dust, and was sprinkling it about him as he shuffled along. When he came abreast of the car, Noel asked him what he was doing.

"Just sprinkling this panther powder, bub," he said.

"Beg pardon?" said Noel.

"Panther powder," said the old man. "Keeps panthers away."

"But there *aren't* any more panthers in the Adirondacks," Mrs. Dickson protested.

"That's right, ma'am," he said. "Good thing, too. This here powder ain't worth a damn."

HOW TO RUN A TACKLE SHOP

If I had to name my favorite sporting goods store, it would probably be the Angler's Roost, even since it moved into the Chrysler Building and became mildly respectable. Because so far as I know it's the only shop in which the customers either wait on themselves or are waited on by other customers.

This state of affairs, which makes for a certain comradely chaos, exists because any

Unbalanced
Fisherman

Hung-over
Fisherman

Night
Fisherman

Domesticated
Fisherman

Armchair
Fisherman

Early-Rising
Fisherman

Late-Rising
Fisherman

Furtive
Fisherman

Ice
Fisherman

salespeople present are invariably deep in violent discussion with one or more habitués of the place concerning the relative merits of dyed versus naturally blue hackle on a Quill Gordon or some equally controversial and friendship-shattering topic, and they can't be bothered with dropping it just because someone wants to buy a rod or a rifle. However, the chances are that one of the lay brothers will fall out of the discussion for a few minutes to let his larynx cool off, and if he notices someone standing around muttering about the lack of service he will slide behind the counter and wait on him.

I dropped in one time to pick up an HEH line and met Dorian St. George, who needed a new pair of felt-soled shoes. After Dorian got behind the counter and sold me the line, we switched places and I sold him the shoes, and after putting the money in the cash register we fought our way out through a group that was arguing whether or not the so-called coffin fly is actually the spinner of the green drake, and went about our business. I was surprised that Dorian could pass up the coffin-fly argument, and told him so, but he said hell, he had started it the day before and was bored with it.

HOW TO WRITE FUNNY STUFF ABOUT FISHING

Three years ago a large weekly picture magazine suggested that I cover the opening day of trout season for them, and write a funny piece about it. I said I would, for a consideration, and when we had agreed on that, and that I should confine my coverage to the Beaverkill, I asked what they had in mind, exactly.

"Make it very funny," the editor in charge of stories about the opening day of trout season said. "I'm not a fisherman myself, but I know that fishing has some very humorous aspects. For example, the fisherman who gets his fly caught in a tree, and has to climb up and fetch it down."

"That's it exactly," the assistant editor in charge of stories about the opening day of trout season said.

"Well, frankly," I said, "that business of the fly in the tree has been done before. In fact, it seems to me to be rather on the trite side—like the fisherman falling into the stream."

"Wonderful!" said the editor. "By all means, have a fisherman falling into the stream—a great idea! Of course, we want a *factual* report—this is, after all, a news magazine—but with all those fishermen milling around, there's sure to be somebody falling into the river, isn't there?"

"Oh, sure," I said. "But I still think the fly in the tree and the fisherman falling in are too obvious—and not very funny, either. Have *you* ever fallen into an ice-cold river?"

"You must understand," said the editor, "that we have ten million readers, and that what is obvious to you, with your specialized interest in fishing, is not at all obvious to them."

"Of course not," the assistant editor said.

"Therefore," said the editor, "by all means include the fly in the tree and the fisherman getting good and wet."

"Well, it's your magazine," I said, and when opening day came I went up to the Beaverkill, and was on the river at 5 A.M., notebook in hand and pencil poised.

Several hours later I was still waiting for somebody to get his fly and leader caught in a tree; I concentrated on sections of the stream where trees overhung the bank, and finally I went over to Willowemoc, where there are more trees, but with no success. In fact, I even went so far as to pay a fisherman from Poughkeepsie a dollar to flip his backcast into a tree and tangle his fly and leader in the branches; I knew that this was unethical, but time was going fast and I was desperate. He made about twenty-five backcasts into a large, bushy tree overhanging the water, but it was no use; the leader wouldn't tangle and the fly wouldn't catch.

After having failed to convince the fisherman that he ought, in all fairness, to give me back the dollar, I realized that the sun was getting low in the sky, and that I had better give up on this and devote the rest of the day to finding somebody who had fallen into the water. I drove frantically up and down the lower river, from the Junction Pool to Peekville, but every fisherman I saw was dry as a bone. I saw one man standing beside the river below Painter's Bend, and got out of the car and snuck up behind him and attempted to shove him in, but he sidestepped me and chased me back to the car and around it ten or twelve turns and would have caught me if I hadn't ducked in and locked the door when he cut a corner too close and tripped over the front bumper, and while he was prying a large rock out of the ground I drove off.

As a last resort I thought of wading out into the river and falling in myself, but I felt that this wasn't what the editors wanted, and furthermore the water temperature was barely over forty degrees, so when it got dark I conceded defeat and drove back to the hotel and got drunk.

I wrote the article the next day and took it into the editors, but they said what they wanted was flies caught in trees and fishermen falling into the river and funny stuff like that, and although they paid me for the piece, they never ran it.

I went fishing on the Beaverkill the next weekend the river was lined on both banks with fishermen climbing trees trying to retrieve flies and thousands of trout were maimed and crippled by fishermen falling on them, and if the editors had the right slant on humor it was a sidesplitting scene. Personally, I didn't crack a smile.

JERSEY JUSTICE

It is generally considered bad form for a man who writes about fishing to get pinched for violating fish and game laws. The closest I ever came to being incarcerated on this particular count was in New Jersey. Having just moved to Philadelphia, I bought a nonresident Jersey license and began fishing some of the bass lakes across the Delaware.

One fall evening I was on Lake Atco and had excellent fishing with a popper plug. When I rowed back to the dock, arriving after dark so that I had to use a flashlight to find a mooring place for the boat, I had three largemouth bass between four and five pounds on my stringer, and had released several nearly as large.

There were four or five other fishermen standing around on the dock, and while they were inspecting my catch a scowling, six-foot-tall kid in his early twenties advanced upon me and snarled, "All right, you! You're under arrest!"

"Who, *me*?" I said in astonishment. "What for?"

"For plenty!" the youngster declared. "You was fishing with a light! And I seen you with my own eyes, so don't pull no fast talk—I got you dead to rights! It's high time some of you city fellers was—"

"Just a minute, now," I said. (I can stand being called almost anything except a city feller.) "Who are you, anyway?"

"I'm a deputy warden, that's who!" said the kid, glaring ferociously around the circle of fishermen.

"May I see your badge?" I said. He fished it out of his shirt pocket and flashed it at me.

"When did you get it?" I asked.

"Yesterday," he said. "And futhermore—"

"Now you listen to me, kid," I said. "If you want to keep that nice shiny badge, you'd better run along home and study up some more on the fishing laws. They don't say you can't use a flashlight to find the dock. You'd better just forget it, and wait until you get used to all that authority."

"He's right, sonny," one of the other fishermen said. "You'd better beat it before he sues you for false arrest."

The deputy sputtered and fumed, but when each of the other spectators assured him that he was wrong, he stomped sullenly off into the darkness. I then delivered myself of a few well-chosen remarks to the effect that law-abiding citizens should not be subjected to such inconsiderate treatment.

"That's a fact," one of the fishermen said.

"Anybody who actually violates the law should be punished, naturally," I declared.

"Naturally," said another fisherman.

"It is the bounden duty of every sportsman to learn the law, and abide by it!" I said, my voice quivering with moral indignation. "Any fisherman who's too dim-witted to learn a simple set of regulations *deserves* to get into trouble!"

"Yes sir," said another bystander.

"If I broke a conservation law, I would *want* to be punished!" I said in my best Spartacus-to-the-gladiators style.

"In that case," said one of the fishermen, "you better hurry and catch that deputy before he gets away. You caught them bass on an illegal plug."

"That's right, mister," another fisherman said. "We got a three-hook law in this state, and them two gang hooks on that plug counts as six. It's a twenty-five-dollar fine, and if the judge don't like your looks it's the same for each illegal plug in your tackle box. You got fifteen or twenty in there."

"I think that deputy went up that way," said another bystander. "I could run up and fetch him, if you'd like."

After reflecting that nobody had ever really liked my looks except my mother, and that even she had never been genuinely enthusiastic about them, and that twenty-five times fifteen or twenty is an appalling sum, I declined the fisherman's offer to fetch the deputy and withdrew in confusion. Since then the statute of limitations has set in, I have gone straight, and New Jersey has amended the three-hook ruling in regard to plugs. And I wouldn't be surprised if, after the shine wore off his badge, the kid made a pretty good deputy.

ARE FISHERMEN PEOPLE?

(1951)

HOW TO STUFF A FISH

Recently I dropped into the Trail & Stream shop in New York in search of some correctly tied Light Edson Tiger bucktails. (Most tyers use pure-white bucktail dyed yellow for the wing, when the proper hair isn't white but only white-flecked, which becomes yellow-flecked after it's dyed—a distinction much too subtle for a trout to grasp, I'm sure, but one about which I am obnoxiously adamant.) They didn't have any Light Edson Tigers, correctly or incorrectly tied, and while Vic Soskice, the proprietor, was offering to have a batch whipped up for me by one of his stable of skilled tyers, I glanced up at the wall and saw a stuffed fish.

"My God!" I said. "What's that?"

"It's a stuffed fish," Vic said.

"I know," I said, "but what's it doing up there?"

"Hanging," Vic said, and went on to explain that it was the world-record broadbill swordfish recently caught by Lou Marron at Iquigue, Peru. It had weighed 1,182 pounds, with a length of fourteen feet, eleven inches, and had been landed in an hour and fifty-five minutes on thirty-nine-thread line. Vic told me that they had had to remove the large plate-glass window in front to get the fish into the store, which I believed, and that an old gentleman with a goatee had paused to watch the fish being unloaded from the moving van and had said, "That is a confounded lie!" which I did not believe. Also, the longer I looked at the fish the more I felt there was something amiss, and finally I asked Vic if this was the actual fish or a phony.

"The sword and the tail and fins are the actual fish," Vic said, "but the body's plaster.

54

It just wouldn't be possible to skin a fish that large and keep the skin intact. So they make a number of measurements and give the dimensions to a taxidermist, along with the sword and fins. He reconstructs the fish according to the measurements, and —*voila*!''

"*Voila* yourself!" I said. "This damn fish is an impostor! In fact, it's not even a fish! It's a fraud! A hunk of plaster painted up to look like a fish, with a couple of fins stuck to it! You could just as well call a ten-dollar fiddle a Stradivarius because one of the strings came off a genuine Strad!"

While I was developing this thesis a man came in, looked at the monster on the wall and said, "What was it caught on?"

"A Light Edson Tiger bucktail," said Vic courteously, "tied with pure-white bucktail dyed yellow."

"Thank you," the man said. I walked out with him and headed for the Angler's Roost. They had no Tigers either.

MATUTINAL

Last year I was driving down Route 17, along the Beaverkill, and picked up an old man walking hatless in the cold May drizzle. He was grateful for the lift, but said he didn't mind the walking *or* the rain; he was only going down the road about two miles to see his sister, and he figured the exercise was good for him. When I asked him, he said he was eighty-three years old, and had lived along the river all his life, and had worked in the acid factory below Roscoe from the time he was fifteen until his eightieth birthday. I asked if he ever fished the river, and he said no, not any more. Said it hadn't been very good fishing since the dry spell in 1897.

I asked him if he'd traveled much, and he said, "Some. Never been to New York, but I been to Binghamton five times, and twice to Elmira, and once I went clean to Syracuse. Last year, that was. Visited my son and my daughter-in-law, but I didn't get along with them very good, so I come on back here."

"What was the trouble?" I asked.

"It was just a lot of little things," he said. "You know how them little things get under your skin. But mostly, I guess, it was the way they'd lie a-bed until seven, seven-thirty in the morning."

I agreed it must be a sad thing to raise a slothful son, and left him off at his sister's farm.

WESTWARD HOKUM

The other day I was talking to a man from Ohio or Oregon or one of these far-western states and he complained that too many books about fishing were written from such a blatantly eastern point of view that western anglers could hardly stand to read them, and that somebody ought to do something about it.

I can't think of anything to do about it personally, except to tell about the first time I met a western fisherman. He had never previously been east of the Rockies, and he was an ardent trout fisherman. As I recall he was roughly eight feet tall, and he made no effort to conceal his scorn for the East, which he allowed was effete beyond the endurance of a man from the wide open spaces.

However, he had heard and read about the Beaverkill as being the best trout stream in the East (as it may well have been at that time), and he had flown to New York City for the express purpose of wetting his waders in that famous river. He had arranged with Jim Deren, from whom he had been buying fly-tying materials by mail, to meet him at

the airport late on a Friday night and drive him up to the stream, and Jim had rounded up several Beaverkill fishermen, including me, to make it a party.

We picked him up in Jim's station wagon at the airport about three o'clock Saturday morning—the flight had been delayed by weather—and in order to get better acquainted before setting out for the Catskills we repaired to a nearby all-night gin mill. There, after tossing off several hookers of straight rye whiskey, the stranger advised us that he was accustomed to fishing big, wide, western-type rivers and that he fully expected to be disappointed in the Beaverkill.

We were obliged to admit that the river was awfully tame except when in flood, and for the next couple of hours we sat in the tavern while the westerner regaled us with hair-raising stories of the rough, tough rivers in his native region. When we got out of the tavern and into the station wagon, it was nearly daylight, and as we headed for the northbound parkways all of us were feeling terribly effete; all, that is, except the westerner, who was tired and sleepy after the long plane trip and the all-night bull session, and who curled up in a corner of the station wagon and fell sound asleep.

By the time we got onto the Sawmill River Parkway, about twenty miles outside of the city, it was broad daylight, and Harry Braun kept staring moodily at the Sawmill

River, a weary trickle of muddy water that runs alongside several miles of the six-lane concrete highway, and can be easily jumped across at almost any point.

"Stop the car," Harry finally said. Jim pulled off the concrete onto the carefully mowed grass that separates the brook from the road and stopped the car. When Harry explained, we all piled out of the station wagon and began unloading our duffel and tackle, while Harry shook the sleeping guest.

"Wake up, pardner," Harry shouted, to make himself heard above the traffic. "We're here!" The visitor sat up, rubbed his eyes, saw his hosts busily setting up rods and scrambling into waders, and then looked at the skimpy brook.

"Ye gods!" he yelled. "That's the Beaverkill?"

"Yup," said Harry, cheerfully. "In perfect shape, too. Water height's just about right. Let's get going."

The westerner slowly climbed out of the station wagon and walked to the stream, which was a good ten feet wide at that point and all of eighteen inches deep. He stared at the murky water. He looked back at us, who were already in our waders and had most of our tackle set up. He looked back at the water again.

Then he sat down on the grass and began to sob—loud, anguished, western-type sobs.

I forget who it was who got up nerve to tell him it wasn't the Beaverkill, but somebody did, and we went on up to the Catskills. He turned out to be a nice guy and a good fisherman and we had a fine week end, with excellent hatches and the larger trout moving.

HOW TO TELL YALE MEN

In a book called *How to Catch Fishermen* which I wrote several years ago I included the following anecdote:

One fine October day Marvin and Grace Marie Chase were chugging along the Jersey beach in their beach buggy, looking for signs of feeding stripers, and passed another fisherman standing in the surf. I don't know what the guy was wearing, but as they went by, Marvin (Tufts, '29) remarked to his wife, "Nobody but a Yale man would wear that kind of clothes for fishing."

"That's a silly thing to say," said Grace Marie, and when Marvin maintained that it was *not* a silly thing to say, they spent the next ten minutes arguing whether it is or is not possible to tell a Yale man by the clothes he selects to go surf fishing in. Finally, Marvin swung the beach buggy around and drove back to the bar where they'd seen the controversial character. He was still there, and Marvin pulled up beside him.

"What college did you attend?" Marvin demanded.

"Yale," the man said.

"Thank you," Marvin said, and drove back down the beach.

Grace Marie had told me the story. I thought it was a fine commentary on matrimony, male fashions and that marvelous intuition with which people who fish a lot are sometimes gifted.

Shortly after the book came out, I bumped into Marvin at the Angler's Roost, and asked if he'd seen the story. He said he had.

"Was it true?" I asked.

"Sure," said Marvin.

"Tell me," I said, "what was there about that guy's dress that made you think he was a Yale man?"

"He was wearing a white sweater," Marvin said, "with a big blue Y on it."

THE GREAT INDOORS

By now all but the most hopeless optimists must be convinced that fishing for trout in public waters in these United States is, except for a handful of inaccessible waterways, a snare and a delusion, with the hordes of fishermen increasing almost but not quite as fast as the numbers of fish decrease. (I know a stream in Pennsylvania where, by wonderful good fortune, two fishermen in one season were bit by timber rattlesnakes; and since most fishermen fear rattlesnakes, you could have a longish stretch of that mountain river all to yourself for several seasons thereafter. I tried to start a movement among some select angling friends to breed rattlesnakes and stock all streamside areas heavily with the creatures; Gottlieb Kuhn, the Lackawaxen snake-catcher, agreed to furnish the breeding stock in exchange for a dozen hellgrammite hooks on nylon snells; and we had even agreed, among the score of us involved, to draw straws to see who deliberately got bit, in case no outsider unwittingly obliged, so that we could be assured of an authentic newspaper story that might scare off faint-hearted fishermen. Unfortunately Gottlieb got a job on the D. L. & W. along about then, so we had no breeding stock, and the chap who'd been going to raise the rattlers in his garage said his wife had got wind of the scheme and was being unpleasant about it. Now, of course, it's too late, because no sane rattlesnake would linger in the neighborhood of an eastern trout stream waiting to be trampled to death unless he was tethered.)

And so I have a scheme. Not only will it solve a lot of the problems facing the trout man today, it will also make me moderately rich—or, at least, that's my hope. I propose to construct, somewhere in the vicinity of Grand Central Station in New York City, *The World's First Indoor Trout Stream*.

This stream will be approximately one block long as the crow flies, but thanks to a cunningly contrived system of meanders and switchbacks it will offer a fishable length of more than a quarter mile, in the course of which the angler will discover all types of water, a meadow section with slow, still pools, a white-water stretch of typical rainbow water, shallow riffles, pocket water, etc. The normal flow will be approximately that of the West Branch of the Ausable above the Ski Jump about the second week in June, with a maximum width of twenty feet, but by a twist of a valve the operator in charge can produce drought conditions for the man who wants to practice low-water techniques, or bring on a spring freshet for the guy who likes to fish a weighted bucktail.

Another valve will regulate water temperature, and a control panel will govern lighting, so that you may, as you prefer, have either early-morning or late-evening fishing at any hour of the day or night. (When the lighting dial is set to "Early Morning" a fog-producing machine will automatically go into action, laying an appropriate early-morning mist on the water.)

The maximum number of fishermen permitted on the stream at any one time will be five (giving each angler more than eighty yards of water to himself—or roughly eight times as much as he'd get on the Beaverkill or Esopus any week-end day of the season). The fee will be $5 per hour per angler—or, if someone wants the entire stretch of river to himself, he can have it for $20 per hour or fraction thereof. There will be additional fees, of course, for additional services: the management will provide a rising barometer (by means of a pressurizing system) for an extra $3.50 per hour; for an additional $2.75 hourly the operator will make the water slightly murky so that heavier leaders may be used without fear of spooking gut-shy fish.

Persons wishing to try a bit of night fishing for big brown trout may do so by arrangement; the stream can be blacked out, even at midday with the sun shining brightly outside, and the desired degree of moonlight will be provided by the operator.

For those who wish it, the management will provide a cold, raw drizzle, or a falling barometer, or muddy water, or black flies, mosquitoes and no-see-ums. There will be a fee for those extras, of course, but only enough to cover the cost; the management will recognize that a number of trout fishermen are constitutionally unable to enjoy themselves unless they're thoroughly miserable. These persons will also be able to rent torn or porous waders, exquisitely mismatched rod-and-line combination, dry-fly leaders guaranteed unsinkable, dry flies guaranteed unfloatable, sopping-wet cigarettes and many other items designed to make them happy as larks.

Space prevents me from filling in all the details of this project, but I take this opportunity to appeal to all trout-fishing readers to forward any suggestions that might be incorporated in the final plans now being drawn up. All ideas will be gratefully received, and the best ones adopted. For example, my friend Larry Koller suggested, "Why not stock different species of trout in the different stretches of the stream?"

Who said anything about stocking *any* species of trout in the stream?

HOW TO CATCH BIG TROUT ON DRY FLIES

Last year I ran into a friend who showed me a snapshot of a 25½-inch brown trout which he said he had taken on a Number 14 Quill Gordon dry fly.

"How was that again?" I said.

"Well," he said, "I was fishing at a very fancy club upstate, with a strict rule about fly-fishing only, and I hooked this five-inch chub on the Quill Gordon floater. Well, sir, that chub put up such a battle that it took me down through four of the best pools on the club water, and on the fourth pool this large brown trout came out from under a boulder and ate the chub. Naturally, I was terribly upset by this, and managed to play the brown into my net in short order, so it wouldn't go around molesting other people's chubs. But it just goes to show that the Quill Gordon is a grossly underrated dry fly.

"If I get invited back again," said the friend, "I'm going to try a different fly. Who knows what a Number *Twelve* Quill Gordon might produce?"

"Who knows?" I said, and hurried home to patch my minnow bucket.

HOW TO DRINK WHISKEY

When I dropped by the Trail & Stream shop to pick up some of Alex Rogan's elegant salmon flies last September I found Alex there, and we got into a discussion about the ideal fly box. Alex told me that he often fished with a friend who was hard of hearing; the friend used one of those circular plastic fly boxes that clip to a button of the angler's vest and have a number of compartments. They were fishing a salmon river one time, Alex said, and an elderly native came by and got to talking with them. When Alex explained that his friend was hard of hearing the old man said, "Ah, yes, so he is!" and after that when he wanted to say something to the friend he would bend down, grab the circular fly box that hung on the man's vest and shout into it at the top of his lungs. "He hasn't used anything but an ordinary fly box since then," said Alex.

It was while fishing a Maine lake in a canoe with this same companion, Alex went on to say, that they paddled in to shore and broke out a bottle of rye whiskey. "It was a few months after I'd come to this country," said Alex. "I had never drunk anything but Scotch whiskey, and back home I'd heard terrible things about American whiskey. But when my friend handed me the bottle I closed my eyes and took a stiff drink, and when I opened my eyes I saw a strange beastie stickin' its head out of the water and glarin' at me something savage! 'It's a hulloocination,' I thought to myself, 'indooced by a single wee nip of American firewater!' and in order to make it go away I picked up my fly rod and flicked a streamer fly at the creature, the meanwhile resolvin' never to touch a drop of anything but Scotch whiskey the rest of my life.

"Unfortunately," said Alex, "the fly caught in the poor creature's hide, and it scrambled ashore and galloped into the woods. 'Ye've hooked a beaver!' my friend hollered. So I jumped out of the canoe and run through the woods after it, yellin' at my friend to bring the gaff, but although I played it skillfully it took out all my backin' and broke off.

"It just goes to show," said Alex, "that you shouldn't close your eyes when you drink whiskey."

ESTIMATE

I met Brian MacKenzie at a party last Christmas and asked him what he'd been up to in the year since I'd seen him. Traveling, he said, and went on to tell me about being in Dublin on business, and arranging to squeeze in a day of trout fishing. He went to a little village, whose name I've forgotten, and engaged a local guide. The guide was diligent enough, but the weather was unsettled and the fish weren't rising, and at the end of the day all he had was a single brown trout of a scant three ounces.

Walking back to the inn the guide said, "Well now, it's only one fish, but it's a nice one. About three to the pound, I'd say."

"Three to the pound?" Brian said. "You're daffy!"

"Ah, but sure," said the guide, "and the other two might be bigger."

BOOK REPORT

While leafing through a British book on pike fishing, published in 1843, I came across this sentence:

> For we may observe that the fisherman is a kindly man, not given to lustful excess or vile thought, but marked by gentility of word and deed; the very mist that rises from loch and river is like a cleansing vapour, banishing worldly care and sordid passion alike; indeed, do you meet a person of mean and greedy nature, or vain disposition, be assured, gentle sir, he is no angler.

Evidently the mist that rises from the Beaverkill, the Miramichi and other streams and lakes I frequent doesn't have the antiseptic qualities of the British product, because not too long ago I met an angler, and an exceptionally skilled one—he can lay out sixty feet of double-tapered line and twelve feet of light leader with a four-ounce rod and drop a #16 Goldribbed Hare's Ear on a rising trout's nose as nicely as you please—who has a police record as long as your arm, and as a matter of fact if he hadn't been given to lustful excesses and vile thought, not to mention worldly care and sordid passion, he wouldn't have become the anonymous proprietor of a chain of disorderly houses, and couldn't have afforded to travel all over North America on fishing trips while the poor slobs who were marked by gentility of word and deed stayed home with their noses to the grindstone and tried—not very successfully—to make an honest dollar.

ARS LONGA

Mr. Ed Dodd of Atlanta, Georgia, draws a widely syndicated cartoon strip called ''Mark Trail,'' relating the adventures of a fish-and-wildlife biologist with a talent for getting himself into fairly dire predicaments—which Marse Dodd, who is aware which side his bread is buttered on, promptly gets him out of.

Recently I was telling Ed a story about Al Harris' Aunt Cora, who once wrote a fine Georgia book called *The Circuit Rider's Wife*. The story had to do with a covered bridge, and Ed said it reminded *him* of a story. He said that several years ago he was traveling through that same mountainous section of the South and while driving down a lonely back road he came to an old covered bridge. It impressed him so much that he took an easel and sketch pad out of the car and began making a large drawing of the bridge, and while he was working at it a gaunt and ancient mountaineer came trudging down the road with a dozen baskets in his hand, and stopped to watch Ed drawing.

When Ed questioned him, the mountain man said he'd lived all his life within a few miles of the bridge; that, in fact, he had been baptized in the swimming hole underneath the bridge, and had proposed to his wife while riding in a mule-drawn shay through the same venerable structure. Now, he said, it was one of the few things in the mountains that hadn't changed much since his boyhood; he walked past it each day on his way to the crossroads store where he sold his home-made baskets; and just last week he had learned that a new road was going through soon, and the covered bridge would be torn down to make way for it.

"That's a pity," Ed said. "I suppose you'll miss it pretty badly." And when the mountaineer reckoned he would, Ed asked him if he'd like to have the drawing that was nearly completed on the easel. The native said yes, indeed, he would surely admire to have the drawing.

"In that case," said Ed, who knew the backwoodsman's traditional reluctance to accept an outright gift, "I'll make you a proposition. You give me one of those baskets, and I'll give you the picture."

"Ha!" snorted the old man. "I reckon you would! *I get two bits apiece for them baskets!*" And he stalked off down the road, muttering in his beard about city slickers.

YOU, TOO, CAN BE OBSOLETE

Well, there was this farmer in Nebraska named Herb Toelke, and he liked horses and he liked hunting and he liked mountains. He liked Nebraska, too, but there weren't enough horses or game or mountains in Nebraska, so he up and went to Montana and settled in Ronan, a small town near the Idaho border.

There were plenty of horses there, and deer and elk and bear and even a few goats to hunt, and there were mountains—the Mission Range and the Swan River Range and other saw-toothed tributaries of the Continental Divide.

To get in to where the hunting was best, a man had to make a pack trip, and one time some of Herb's neighbors invited him to come along with them, back into the Bob Marshall Wilderness Area where the grizzlies are supposed to be thicker than anywhere in the United States. "It was quite a trip," Herb says. "We had twenty-four boxes of corn flakes and one can of milk. Somebody forgot to bring sugar and salt, but we had nearly two pounds of pepper. It wasn't well organized."

So Herb Toelke decided to go into the pack-trip business, and he did. He got hold of some good pack mules and a string of horses, and learned to snake the train along a six-inch-wide track notched into the steep side of a mountain, and learned what to do when a new mule shied and the whole string threatened to slide half a mile down a talus slope. His wife was already a good cook, and she learned how to get the same bill of fare out of a cook tent at the base camp that she got out of the kitchen back in Ronan. His boy,

Bob, was a natural-born horse wrangler and a natural-born nice guy, who could do tricks with a lasso to amuse the small fry, and what with one thing and another there isn't a finer pack-trip outfit in the Northwest today than Herb Toelke's.

One recent summer my then-eleven-year-old son Brook and I met Herb and Bob Toelke at Holland Lake, where the trail starts up over the 9,000-foot Swan River Range and then skids down the other side to the upper reaches of the south fork of the Flathead. Mike and Frances Hudoba were there, too, and Joe and Mary Brooks, and Martin Bovey. I didn't know about them, but I knew I hadn't been in a saddle for twenty years, and that Brook had never been within fifty feet of a horse, to my knowledge, and that we were scheduled to ride thirty-one miles along mountain trails that day.

There were nine of us on horseback, and eleven mules loaded with food and gear for the eight-day trip, and early in the morning we all started up the steep west side of the mountain.

An hour later we had gained several thousand feet in altitude, and when Herb started threading the pack train across what seemed to be a purely perpendicular cliffside, and when my horse stumbled and slithered in the loose shale that littered the wisp of a trail,

and when I looked down and saw that if the horse lost his footing we'd have a hundred-foot drop before we hit the tops of the scrub pines that clung to the cliff, I was scared stiff. That poor kid, I thought. I bring him along on this trip and tell him it's going to be lots of fun, and then I lead him right smack into the jaws of death. It was all I could do to screw up courage to turn around in the saddle, but I wanted to tell Brook, who was right behind me, to be brave.

When I finally looked back, I saw that Brook was still there. He sat sideways with one leg hooked over the horn of the saddle, with all the glacier-streaked glory of the Rocky Mountains rising around him, and if his face was somber with awe or pale with terror it was impossible to tell, because it was buried deep in a Gory Story comic book.

When we rested an hour later, I snuck the literature out of his saddle bag and hid it. And so if you ever ride in with Herb Toelke to the Bob Marshall Wilderness country, to fish the Flathead and the White River for cutthroat trout or to let the stuffing out of a big trophy elk, and get bored with the sight of bear grass and cinquefoil and Indian paintbrush and Ponderosa pine and Douglas fir and two-mile-high peaks with the snow still under the ridges in early August, you can dismount at the first campsite, about ten miles in, and under a large rock at the foot of a big tamarack you'll find a Gory Story comic book in practically mint condition. Help yourself.

(As long as I've dragged my son's name into this, I might also mention that methods of evaluating one's chums have changed since I was a dozen years old. When I asked Brook recently about a friend of his, he said, "Oh, he's a nice enough kid, but he's obsolete."

"He's what?" I said.

"Obsolete," Brook said. "I mean he's interested in P-40's and those old-fashioned propellor jobs, and most of us kids only care about supersonic jets."

"Watch your language," I warned him, and went to look at my bald spot in the mirror. It was still there.)

THE CASE OF THE FLYING TROUT

I wrote a story once and titled it "How My Old Man Come to Resign from the Shohola Corners Zion Reformed Evangelical Gospel Association." It was about a man who accidentally got drunk, but when a weekly magazine bought and published it, they changed the title, and called it "High and Dry."

I threatened to sue, but they said titles always had to be short and snappy, and since I was new in the business, I bowed to their judgment.

But recently I came across a book, published in 1694, with a title nearly as long as that short story. The book was authored by Captain Richard Franck, and was called "Northern Memories Calculated from the Meridian of Scotland, Wherein Most or All of the Cities, Citadels, Seaports, Castles, Forts, Fortresses, Rivers and Rivulets, Are Compendiously Described, Together with Choice Collections of Various Discoveries, Remarkable Observations, Theological Notions, Political Axioms, National Intrigues, Polemick Inferences, Contemplations, Speculations, and Several Curious and Industrious Inspections, Lineally Drawn from Antiquaries, and Other Noted and Intelligible Persons of Honour and Eminency. To Which Is Added the Contemplative and Practical Angler by Way of Diversion. With a Narrative of That Dextrous and Mysterious Art, Experimented in England and Perfected in Remote and Solitary Parts of Scotland. By Way of Dialogue. Writ in the Year 1658 but not till Now Made Publick, by Richard Franck, Philanthropus—Plures Necat Guala Gladius.''

The title is followed by eleven fairly windy Dedications, four Addresses, including one to ''Gentlemen Piscatorians Inhabiting in, or near, the Sweet Situations of Nottingham, North of Trent,'' and seven prefatory poems.

By the time I'd got through the poems I was too bushed to read the book, but it did start me to mulling over that Dextrous and Mysterious Art, and I recalled the time I

nearly caught a big trout. It was nearly twenty years ago on the Brodheads Creek in Pennsylvania. I was fishing the lower river where the railroad runs close by the stream, and noticed a butterfly flutter down the embankment, obviously injured. I watched it, because I thought that at any moment it would fall into the river and I might mark down a good fish rising to eat it.

It didn't fall, though. Instead, a brown trout that must have been thirty inches long stuck his head out of the water, slow and easy, and inhaled the butterfly as it fluttered a good ten inches above the surface. I waded ashore as fast as I could. There I changed my 4X leader to a brand-new salmon leader that a healthy calf couldn't have busted on a straight pull. Then I pawed through my fly boxes for something resembling a butterfly, and came up with a brown-and-yellow bivisible roughly the size of a hen's egg. It would take something that big and juicy, I figured, to elevate that big brown again.

I tied it on and carefully waded into position to cast to the fish. There was only one spot from which I could present the fly without the heavy leader showing too much, and I knew that if the first cast didn't raise the brute it wouldn't do any good to keep on casting. After ten minutes of working into position in the deep water I found a good-sized rock that made a perfect casting platform, but I chose to wait a bit in case my wading had alarmed the big fish. So I stood there for what seemed an hour, and then began false casting to get out line.

When I had the range, I prayed a little prayer and dropped the big floater onto the water. It landed perfectly, right where I'd intended, and began riding the current toward the trout's hideout behind a large boulder. I tensed myself, waiting for a possible strike with every muscle a-quiver—and when it came, I reared back on the rod so violently that the small trout that had taken my fly went shooting back over my head like a speckled comet; at the end of the line it ripped off the hook and kept right on going, and I saw it sail over the railroad tracks and then on out toward the highway that runs a hundred feet or so beyond.

I was too disgusted to go look for the fish, and after taking my rod down I walked back to Charley's hotel.

"Where's Mac?" I asked. Mac had been three days without a fish, and I thought my story might cheer him.

"He left for home half an hour ago," Charley said. "Said he knew when he was licked."

Back in town the next week I ran into Mac.

He said, "You won't believe this. Nobody does. I don't really believe it myself. But it's true! I fished that damn river three solid days and never saw hide nor hair of a trout. Then I start to drive home, and I'll be go to hell if a ten-inch trout doesn't jump a hundred feet from the river right through the car window into my lap!"

"A likely story!" I said, and went on my way.

THE HAPPY FISHERMAN

One of the more fraudulent myths that make up the folklore of fishing is the one that depicts fishermen as carefree people. The fact is, if you show me a man who enjoys himself while fishing, I'll show you a man who's a second-rater, if not actually a bum, on a trout stream, bass pond or salmon river. In order to be a good fisherman, you've got to acquire knowledge, which is an excruciatingly painful process; having acquired it you've got to apply it; this involves making a number of decisions (what stream shall I go to this weekend? Shall I fish wet fly, dry fly, nymph, bucktail, streamer, spinner or worm? Shall I try for that rising fish from below or above him? Should I stop fooling around with this Yellow-bellied McQueen and try a Rat-faced MacDougal? Shall I keep on using this 3X gut and have a big, gut-shy brown refuse the fly, or tie on a 6X tippet and have the fish break off? etc., etc.), and there is not one man in ten thousand who can make decisions without suffering acutely in the process.

During this past season I met hundreds of trout fishermen on a dozen streams, and only one of them was actually having a good time. I discovered this bird on the Ten Mile River, a mediocre New York trout stream, when I came wading down through a fast run that flattened out into a wide, shallow pool. It was mid-afternoon of a bright, hot day, and such trout as were moving about were in the riffles. On the bank sat a middle-aged pleasant-faced man with a spinning rod in one hand and a bottle of beer in the other. When I went over and sat down beside him, to rest my bones and ask how he was doing, I saw that the line led out from the rod tip to a copper wobbler lying on the sandy bottom in a foot of slack water.

Also, when he offered me a bottle of beer, I saw that he had five empties beside him and another four bottles cooling in the water; I declined, and asked if he'd had any luck.

"Nope," he said cheerfully. "Been here since nine o'clock this morning, and haven't had a nibble."

"Where were you fishing?" I asked.

"Right here," he said. "Salesman at the tackle store said trout would bite on that thing, but I guess they're not very hungry. You sure you won't have a beer?"

"Thanks, no," I said. "You mean you've had that wobbler lying there for six hours, waiting for a fish to eat it?"

"Yep," he said. "Fact is, this is the first time in my life I've ever been fishing. Darned if I'm not enjoying it, too! Always wondered what people saw in it. Thought they were crazy. Well, you live and learn."

"That's right," I said. "But you can't catch trout with that lure lying motionless on the bottom. You've got to cast it across the stream and reel it back in. Then it flashes like a shiner, and a trout might try to eat it. Also, there's nothing in this pool right now but some chubs and a few small bass. I'll show you where to fish, and how to cast with that outfit, if you'd like."

"Well, that's mighty kind of you," said the man, "but I'll tell you what. Suppose you fish your way, and I fish my way, and we let it go at that? And while you're up,

would you mind handing me one of those bottles—they ought to be nice and cool by now. Thanks. Sure you won't join me?''

I thanked him and went on my way. Thinking about it later, I realized that this was the first happy fisherman I'd met in years—but I'm confident that before the season ended he had learned enough to enable him to be moderately miserable.

Actually, of course, it takes several years of serious fishing before a man learns enough to go through a whole season with an unblemished record of physical and spiritual anguish. But after a man really gets the hang of it, he can be put down on any water, under any conditions of wind and weather, and can immediately give you half a dozen excellent reasons for being despondent. The stream, for instance, is either too high, too low, too cold, too warm, too roily, too clear, too shallow, too deep, too swift, or too slow. If there are other fishermen on the stream he complains it's too crowded, and if there's no one else in sight, he's unhappy because he knows a really good piece of water always has several fishermen loitering about. If the sun's shining, his leader will cast a shadow, and if the sky's overcast, it means the barometer's probably falling.

Maybe this doesn't make sense, but it's really simple. As I said before, the only really good trout fisherman is the one who *works* at it—studies the fish, studies the rivers they live in, studies the insect life they feed on, learns to tie good imitations of the natural flies and nymphs, learns to cast well under the worst conditions, learns to wade fast, rough water, and in general takes fishing as seriously as a bricklayer takes laying bricks, or a banker takes banking, or a burglar takes burglary. He doesn't have much fun, of course, but he isn't interested in having fun. He's interested in being a good fisherman. When he's fishing, he's unhappy, frustrated and embittered, and that's the way he wants it.

In fact, it's possible for a good fisherman to be unhappy even while he isn't actually fishing. For instance, last month I met a fishing friend in Grand Central Station, and inquired why he was scowling so fiercely.

"Ha!" he yelled. "Do you know what a freshwater fishing license costs in New Zealand?"

"No," I said. "How much?"

"Thirty-five dollars!" he bellowed. "It's an outrage. A man goes ten thousand miles to fish, and they nick him thirty-five bucks just for a license!"

"I didn't know you were going to New Zealand," I said. "When do you leave?"

"I'm *not* going to New Zealand," he snarled. "I can't even afford to go to Kensico Reservoir. *But suppose I did?* Thirty-five dollars for a license—do they think I'm *made* of money?"

"Gosh, I don't know," I said, and watched him hurry off to catch his train, muttering to himself about highway robbers.

Now *there*, by God, is a fisherman.

A LA CARTE

About ten years ago I spent four months on the west coast of Florida with my family. I was supposed to be writing a book, but the salt air corroded the works of my portable typewriter, and so I was obliged to spend my time fishing for snook, redfish, sea trout, tarpon, jack crevalle and occasionally for freshwater black bass and bream. Once in a while I would mate on a local charter boat, when the regular mate was off on a toot and the skipper, Mac, had a party. I did it for kicks and because after the day's fishing Mac would break out a bottle and lean back and tell some of the most godawful and entertaining lies that mortal tongue ever uttered. Mac had been a commercial fisherman for thirty years or so, and it is my observation that commercial fishermen are generally even bigger liars than amateur fishermen, as indeed they ought to be, being professionals.

And when I recently had lunch with Dave Newell, of Homosassa Springs, and inquired if he'd ever run across Mac, he told me six or eight Mac stories I'd never heard before. One of them was about the time Dave was tarpon fishing in the Shark River area with an elderly cracker for a guide, and when they passed a deserted settlement the guide got to reminiscing.

"Thirty years ago," he said, "there were people living in them shacks. I put in here one day in my mullet boat, and seen this good-looking girl on the dock—oh, a real stunner, she was, about eighteen years old and wild as a colt—and durned if I didn't talk her into coming aboard and sort of keeping house for me, you might say.

"Didn't have nothing to feed her but fish, but she seemed mighty contented, and it seemed like I was going to enjoy the trip more'n I'd figured.

"Then, by God, who comes piling in here one morning but Mac, with a galley full of fresh supplies, and ties up alongside me, and before sundown he had ham-and-egged her away from me!''

HOW TO SAVE FISH HOOKS

Last year I was fishing the long pool below Cook's Falls on the Beaverkill, using my own version of the Dickey Fly tied on a No. 6 3X-long Allcock's Model Perfect hook. This is a freak hook, and even when Allcock's hooks were plentiful it was hard to find. If I hadn't cadged a few from Walt Dette, the Roscoe fly-tyer, I'd have been out of them long ago.

I hooked a twelve-inch brown at the head of the pool, and since I didn't want the fish I brought him in close and reached down to twitch the fly out of his jaw. Somehow I got my hand messed up in the slack leader, and the fish broke off and swam away with the Dickey Fly hanging on his jaw.

I tied on a new fly and was just about to start fishing again when I noticed something flash in the water nearby, and saw it was the same fish, lying on his side in a foot-deep riffle and rubbing his jaw against a rock to dislodge the hook.

Because I wanted the hook back, I unslung my landing net, tiptoed slowly and carefully up behind the fish and slammed the net down on the water. It made a fine, big splash, but when I looked there was no fish in the net. In a minute I saw the fish about twenty feet away, still trying to rub off the fly.

Again I snuck up behind him, as cautiously as I could, and slapped the net down on him, and again he ducked away. When the fish and I had repeated this routine three more times I heard voices, looked up and saw that six carloads of fishermen had stopped and were watching me.

"It was bad enough when they brought in their spinning rods," one of them was saying. "This goofy bastard don't even use a rod!"

I thought of wading across the river and explaining the whole thing, but it seemed simpler just to throw rocks at the cars until they went away, so I did.

A
FINE KETTLE
OF FISH STORIES

(1964)

THE TRUTH ABOUT IZAAK WALTON

On a number of occasions I have tried, out of a sense of duty aggravated by a suspicion that my literary taste buds might have been defective on previous attempts, to read Izaak Walton's *The Compleat Angler* beyond, oh, say page 25 or 30. It was no use. By the time I had endured the compulsively dreary discourse of Piscator, Venator, and Auceps through a dozen pages I was bored so stiff that my wife had to call the children to help get me out of the chair and up to bed. As a result I suffered from an habitual feeling of moral, intellectual, and spiritual inferiority, and would slink abjectly from the room whenever my fellow anglers commenced to boast of the number of times they had read this hallowed tome or the number of editions of it they had accumulated in their sporting libraries.

Recently, however, it occurred to me that although most of these friends referred to Izaak Walton on terms of easy familiarity, it was possible that none of them had any actual knowledge of the man. I thereupon took it upon myself to investigate the background of the author and his work, with results that astonished me and will, I have no doubt, astonish you. Here, then, are the true facts about this much-discussed but little-known book and its author (to be read at your own risk, if you cherish illusion).

First, the man who called himself Izaak Walton was in reality an adherent of Charles II named Matthew Hornaday, who, so far as is known, never fished a day in his life or cared to. He was, in fact, scornful of all outdoor sports or games, although there are records indicating that he occasionally bowled at St. James Green in London until caught cheating in a minor tournament and expelled from the club.

Second, the book *The Compleat Angler* has nothing whatsoever to do with fish or fishing. It is, in every detail, a turbidly tedious political allegory intended not for the amusement or instruction of anglers but simply for the advancement of the Caroline cause and the confusion of the forces of Cromwell. The gist of Hornaday's thesis is the fundamental illegality of the Cromwellian regime, in the furtherance of which viewpoint he assumed the pseudonym of "Walton," which is, quite obviously, a backwards spelling of "Not law"! Similarly the name of Charles Cotton, purportedly the collaborator who apprehended the book's later sections on fly fishing, is a heavy-handedly humorous reminder that he is "pulling the *wool* over the eyes" of the disestablishmentarian authorities.

Hornaday was an admirer of the English theological writer Richard Hooker (1553-1600), whose two-volume *Laws of Ecclesiastical Polity* dealt lengthily with the controversial problem of the role of the established church and its relation to the civil government and to royalty; Hornaday chose the angling allegory as an obfuscatory reference to the theologian, since a fisherman is, of course, a hooker of fishes.

Quite naturally the book abounds in veiled or disguised references to ecclesiastical and political figures of seventeenth-century Britain; the famous admonition on the handling of the frog as bait, for example ("use him as though you loved him . . . that he may live the longer"), often cited as an instance of the author's compassion, is in fact a clumsily obscured incitement to anti-Cromwellian insurrection, in which the word "live" is, of course, "evil" spelled backwards, and which—if we attach to its front and back the two inner letters of "frog" and again spell it backwards—becomes "Oliver."

After I had made this discovery it further occurred to me that some of the current literature ostensibly devoted to shooting and fishing might in fact be this same insidious sort of political propaganda. It did not, therefore, greatly surprise me to find in an article on fishing in Europe a reference to having watched a blue bird flit along the bank while fishing a German river ("Elbe jay" = LBJ!) or to notice that the current Abercrombie & Fitch catalogue of used guns lists several elephant rifles.

HOW TO PROVOKE A WOLF

Once upon a time there was a girl named Little Red Ridinghood. One fine day her mother gave her a bottle of Italian vermouth to take to her grandmother, who lived in a cottage deep in the forest. "Be careful while going through the forest," said Little Red Riding-hood's mother, "as there are reports of a wolf in the area. However, your grandmother is very anxious to get this vermouth, as it is one ingredient in a magic potion she makes every evening before dinner—oh yes, and take along this jar of olives."

"Yes, Mama dear," said Little Red Ridinghood, "but I have no fear of the wolf, for there are no authenticated instances of an unprovoked attack by a wolf or wolves on a human being. Also, in *The Wolves of Mount McKinley* by Adolf Murie, published in 1944 as No. 5 in the National Park Service's Fauna Series, it clearly says——"

"Buzz off," said Little Red Ridinghood's mother, "or I'll give you a fat ear."

"Yes, Mama," said Red Ridinghood, and skipped merrily down the path that led to the forest. No sooner had she got into the woods, where the shadows concealed Heaven knows what nameless dangers, than who should step out from behind a tree but a wolf. "Hiya, cutie," said the wolf. "Whatcha got in the basket?"

"Among other things," said Red Ridinghood, "I got a bottle of Italian vermouth and a jar of olives, for my grandmother who lives in a cottage about a mile down this path. And please, sir, let's not have any unprovoked attacks—I'm in a hurry."

"Certainly not, sis," said the wolf, and ran off into the forest. As soon as he was out of sight he lit out for the cottage of Red Ridinghood's grandmother. On arriving there he entered and said, "Greetings, Granny! How's about a generous slug of that magical potion, for a desiccated denizen of the forest?"

"Beat it, buster," said Red Ridinghood's grandmother. "If there's one thing I can't stand, it's a looped *lupus*."

"Wow!" said the wolf. "Hoo boy! If that don't constitute provocation, I never encountered none!" After eating Red Ridinghood's grandmother, he put on her cap and got into her bed. Soon Red Ridinghood came skipping into the room, with her basket.

"Hiya, girlie," said the wolf, assuming a grandmotherly expression. "Whatcha got in that basket for your poor old granny?"

"I'm glad you asked that question," said Red Ridinghood, "because among other interesting items in this basket I got this Ruger .44 Magnum revolver, fully loaded and guaranteed to let the sawdust out of transvestite wolves at ranges up to 300 yards." So saying, Red Ridinghood raised the Ruger and drew a bead on the beast—when who should jump out from behind the door but a Federal agent.

"Hold it, Red!" said the agent. "According to the provisions in this here newly enacted Federal anti-gun legislation, I'm obliged to heist that heater. See you in court, kiddo."

"Thank goodness," said the wolf, and as soon as the agent had confiscated the gun and left, he gobbled up Red Ridinghood and headed back for Mount McKinley.

UNCLE ELWOOD AND THE STRANGER

My Uncle Elwood had a fine collection of fly rods, and when I learned of his death a couple of years ago, of a coronary thrombosis, I wondered what would become of them. So I wrote to my Aunt Amy, after a decent interval, saying I'd like to buy the Paynes and Thomases, suggesting a fair price.

I didn't get any of the rods, it turned out, because in his home town of Connell's Forks in Pennsylvania Uncle Elwood was a well-known sportsman with a lot of close friends among fishermen there, but Aunt Amy did send me a Vom Hofe salmon reel I had asked about and two clip-boxes of standard-pattern salmon flies. She also sent me Elwood's fishing diary, saying he had been making an entry in it when he died and that although she had found it dull reading and had given up after a few pages she thought it might interest me, as I was a writer. It turned out to be a large, battered notebook with entries dating back to 1934. I browsed through it a few pages at a time all through this past summer and found most of the entries too cryptic to be of much interest—"Tried Slocum Branch with Tom G., no luck," "Took limit of natives before noon above CCC camp," "Showers all day, four small browns on #16 Bread Crust, one 15-incher on white maribou streamer"—that sort of thing.

Between the entries of May 1965, and the final one there were six or seven references to a huge brown trout supposed to live in the lower end of the Wagon Pool in Fishing Creek; it had been christened "Gangbuster" by Uncle Elwood or one of his cronies. Since Fishing Creek usually produces at least half-a-dozen browns of five pounds or better, any fish that rated a nickname must have been quite a trout. The last entry in the journal was the only lengthy one in the entire diary, and I quote it verbatim:

Saturday, May 23, 1967. Returned Charley Haskauer's power saw and drove on over to Musser's Bridge, left station wagon back of dry wall and started fishing at first bend.

Had usual Leadwing Coachman for dropper and picked up five small trout on it before I got to Tent Rock, but except one chub nothing touched the tail fly, #10 Hare's Ear, same on which took three-pound rainbow opening day. Met Dave Sneeder at Tommer's Brook Pool, he had no trout but said some were raising at lower end of fast run below RR bridge. Ate lunch on bench at Boy Scout camp and watched water but saw only chub rises. Walked across meadow to avoid bog and took path to Hankin's Run Pool where I lost good rainbow last week, fished both sides but took only two small browns and released.

About 3 PM walked down along creek to Wagon Pool, sat beside upper end and watched small natives splashing at natural March Browns. Joined by city fellow in new waders and fancy tackle but pleasant, eager to learn. Had small beard but respectable looking, maybe college professor or doctor. Said he owed great debt to fishing, didn't say why, probably health. Had three dandy browns in creel, biggest about 19″, said had taken all on dry fly he ties himself, calls it Fallen Angel. Something like Hendrickson but body more sulphur-colored. Gave me one. Inquired about any big trout. Told him about "Gangbuster" and how George Harvey, best fisherman this area, had hooked him three times and lost him. Said I'd seen him chasing minnows twice, would sell my soul just to latch onto him for five minutes.

After city fellow went upstream, saw fair trout rise nicely to natural Red Quill so tied on stranger's fly, dressed line, and started fishing dry but no luck. At bottom of pool ten-inch chub took fly just above boulder at head of fast water and ran down into riffle. Then something took chub. Felt enormous weight and power when tried to bring chub in, then line stripped off reel in screaming run across riffle and up into main pool again. Knew it was Gangbuster when he ran upstream. Held rod high and walked upstream above boulder, waded into channel far as possible to head him off from coming back downstream into fast water again.

Kept pressure on much as possible with two-pound tippet but he was sulky, finally when arm almost dropping off from holding rod high, tapped butt to stir him up. Monster

took off, came down around boulder and into fast run, never even slowed up when came to end of backing. Pop! Reeled in feeling sick, decided to call it quits, maybe give up fishing for good. On way back to car met city fellow on path, told him I'd hooked Gangbuster. More than five minutes, wasn't it, he said. It surely was, I said. Fine, he said, laughing, I'll be around at midnight to collect. Collect what, I said. You, he said, that was the deal, wasn't it. I'm in no mood for jokes, I said, and he said sorry, no offense but a deal's a deal, midnight sharp. I went on up to car, drove home.

Thinking of it just now, got to wondering about city fellow. Where from? Strange accent. Can't understand how anyone could see how upset I was by loss of big trout and make feeble jokes. But it is now five minutes after midnight so my slight nervousness about stranger was unwarranted.

Just remembered I set watch ahead five minutes this morning so must be exactly midni

*   *   *

Aunt Amy found Uncle Elwood the next morning, with his fountain pen still in his hand. I'm glad he hooked Gangbuster before he died, but I wish I'd got one of those rods.

SNAKE STORY

I don't know Andy Markham very well, but well enough to know that he always had a nice head of wavy brown hair, and had lost little of it despite his forty-odd years, and naturally I was surprised to bump into him in Grand Central Station the other day and see that his hair was almost pure white. "For Pete's sake, Andy," I said, "what happened to your plumage?"

"I've just missed the 5:17," Andy said, "so let's have a quick one at the Biltmore bar and I'll tell you all about it.

"You remember that stretch of Big Piney Creek that runs under the bridge at Route 128 and disappears down the mountain?" Andy said, when we had found an open space at the bar. "We studied it on the map one time at Gene Hill's house and figured there must be some great pools in that wilderness stretch before it gets down to the Delaware River—and you said nobody ever fishes more than a couple of hundred yards, or maybe half a mile, beyond the bridge. Remember you said there must be some brown trout in there as long as your leg?

"Well, sir, I was up in Ontario for some small-mouth fishing in June, for nearly a month, and somehow while driving back I got to thinking about that stretch. And the more I thought about it the itchier I got, so I figured I'd take one more day and have a whack at it. I reckoned if I got an early start I could cover at least three miles of it and be back at the car by dark.

"I stayed overnight at a motel near Milford, and was parked by the bridge and had my rod set up by 6 A.M. I worked my way downstream fishing a Leadwing Coachman in the riffles and pocket water and not getting much action—a few ten-inchers—and along about noon I came to a stretch that was real nasty. Lots of blowdown timber, probably from the '56 hurricane, and it jutted way out into the river from both banks. I'd kept three small browns, so I built a little cooking fire beside the stream and broiled them on a stick for my lunch, and drank a bottle of ale I'd brought along in my creel, and felt pretty good despite the disappointing fishing.

"Then I shoved on downstream, looking for that dream pool that had to be in there somewhere, and darned if I didn't find it! First, though, I found a falls. About a quarter-mile below where I ate lunch the creek narrowed up and took a 40-foot dive off a ledge, and at the foot it had dug a terrific pool. I had a devil of a time getting down to the foot of the drop without breaking my rod or my neck, but after I'd fished that big black pool a few minutes I raised an enormous trout to a dry White Wulff.

"I kept pounding away at the eddy where the fish had showed, and pretty soon he came back and took a Fanwing Royal Coachman solidly, and for the next hour I had my hands full. Finally I had him so pooped I could slide him halfway out on the bank and

kick him out the rest of the way. He was 23 inches long and just shy of eight pounds, and beautifully shaped—just right for hanging over the mantel in my study. It wasn't until after I'd caught my breath and admired the fish for a while that I noticed it was starting to get dark, and I had a long upstream hike ahead of me. So I stuck the big brown into the bellows pocket of my jacket, took my rod down and started upriver. When I was about fifty yards above the falls, edging my way along the bank, I almost stumbled over a bear cub. It let out a woof, and before I could back off, mama came charging through the brush with blood in her eye. I jumped into the river, and before I knew it the current had bowled me over and was sweeping me toward the falls and the rocks below them.

"I figured I was a gone goose, but one of those old blowdown trees was sticking way out above the river about ten feet away from the brink of the falls, and I grabbed a branch and swung myself up on the dead tree. When I'd inched my way toward shore a yard or so I heard a buzzing sound, and knew what it was. That rattlesnake was a good five feet long, coiled on the tree trunk between me and dry land.

"Pretty soon it was pitch dark, but as far as I could tell the snake hadn't budged. There wasn't anything I could do except sit there all night, not daring to move a muscle and wondering how long that rotten tree trunk would bear my weight. Brother, that was a long night.

"Finally it got light enough so I could see the rattler had vamoosed, so I worked my way along the trunk to the bank and collapsed in the brush. After a while I recovered enough to walk back to the car, and when I looked in the mirror I looked sort of funny. It took me a minute or two to realize that my hair had turned completely white, literally overnight."

"At least you'll have a nice trophy to hang over the mantel," I said.

"Ha!" said Andy, gulping his drink and looking at his watch. "While I was teetering on that rotten log, I figured the more I could lighten ship the better my chances were. So I dropped all eight pounds of that trout in the river. And believe me, Ed, I'm not going back there to get its brother."

At the dinner table that evening my wife asked me why I looked so pensive and I said I had heard a harrowing story on the way home. "You always hear harrowing stories," she said, "and all I hear are silly ones. Why, just today I met that nice Mrs. Markham we met at the Hills' last Christmas, and she told me the silliest story I've heard in ages. She said her husband started dying his hair about ten years ago when it started to go gray, and last May his company got an important new client who hates men who dye their hair, and her husband was going to have to handle the account. So he went up to this camp in Canada and shaved all his hair off and let it come in white, and now he's going around telling people some awful cock-and-bull story about bears and rattlesnakes and all sorts of scary things, and pretending his hair turned white from fright. Isn't that just the silliest thing you've ever heard?"

"It sure is," I said. "What's on TV?"

THE STRANGE CASE OF HERMAN THE GERMAN

I went over to Pennsylvania one day last May and fished the Brodheads, and didn't raise a trout or see a trout move all day long. There was a time when this was a great fishing river, perhaps the best in the East, with some awfully big fish up and down the length of it, and I'll tell you a story about one of them.

You've probably heard of Charley Rethoret, the cantankerous Alsatian and master chef who owned and operated the Hotel Rapids at Analomink. When I first started fishing that part of the river, and staying at Charley's hotel, there were all sorts of jokes about the big brown trout—maybe six or eight or ten pounds—that lived in the Railroad Pool upstream from the hotel a quarter mile and was nicknamed Herman the German. But jokes or no jokes, if you walked up after dark and sat beside that pool you could hear trout as long as your arm sloshing around in the shallows after minnows, and every so often there'd be a splash that sounded like someone had thrown a calf into the pool, or at the very least a six-weeks shoat, and you'd wonder how anyone would have the nerve to wade that pool even in broad daylight when one of those monsters might come by and bite your leg off. And of course, once in a while somebody'd hook a real big fish in or near the pool and it would smash his tippet or bust his rod, and since it was usually somebody who had handled his share of eighteen- and twenty-inchers, you'd know it was no ordinary trout.

I guess it was about the third year I fished there that this young fellow from New York City showed up on opening-day weekend, having heard about Charley's from Bache Brown or Gene Connett or Jack Knight or somebody, and along about dark that evening, when most of us had finished dinner, he walked in the door white as a sheet and began

stammering about having hooked the grandfather of all brown trout at the tail of the Railroad Pool. Or rather, he said he'd hooked a seven- or eight-inch trout and was bringing it in when this enormous something-or-other had riz up and inhaled the small trout and then had gone back into the deep water. Harold—that was his name—said he'd kept a tight line on the monster for nearly half an hour, but that finally it had got annoyed and had moved upstream slowly but surely until his backing was all out and the leader snapped.

When Charley laughed and said that was Herman he'd hooked, Harold bristled up and said it wasn't a laughing matter, and that he'd by God catch that trout if it took all season. And he meant it. From then on he was there every Friday night, and sometimes Thursday night, fishing through until late Sunday night, and never anywhere but in the Railroad Pool. Sometimes he'd fish all night, with bass bugs and big wets and salmon flies and bucktails, and I suspect sometimes with minnows. I forget how many trout he took out of that pool that were over eighteen inches, but it was more than a dozen, and three or four were well into the twenties. Charley used to tell him to stop being foolish about Herman, and some of us were annoyed because he was always in the Railroad Pool, and seemed to regard it as his private water. As the season began to peter out he told Charley he was coming up for the entire last week, and when Charley told me about it I could see he was troubled. A few days later I got a card from Charley inviting me to be his guest at a special dinner at the hotel the following Friday, and since I'd planned to spend the weekend there anyway, I left Philadelphia early and got to the hotel about six. There were, oh, maybe a dozen others there, all the ones who rarely missed a weekend, and young Harold was there to.

It was a good dinner, of course, and while we were eating our apple pie Charley came out of the kitchen and joined us. "I'm glad you all could come," he said, "because this is probably the first testimonial dinner you've ever been to that was given in honor of a trout." And then one by one he called on each of us to stand up and make a little speech about Herman. I said I'd heard him at night once or twice, but Joe Lord said he'd hooked him on a Fanwing Royal Coachman, and several others claimed they'd had him on for a minute or two. After we'd each had a turn, Charley stood up and said sadly, "My friends, this is a confession. You remember about five years ago when that new hotel opened up near the Paradise Forks? And some of my best customers began staying up there, because they thought the water was better? Well, to take your minds off that place, I decided to invent a giant brown trout. You all knew there were some real lunkers in the Railroad Pool. So I started talking about this godawful big fish, and even telling what you might call lies about having him on one night and seeing him rise and gobble a swimming chipmunk and that sort of stuff, and I nicknamed him Herman the German. I figured there'd be no harm done—and there wouldn't have been, if Harold here hadn't made an idiot of himself, and put me in the position of taking money under false pretenses. Well, I'm going to refund Harold's money for the entire season—and that's *my* story about Herman, friends. *There's no such trout in the Railroad Pool!*"

"Not any more there isn't, buster," said a girlish voice, and in through the side door came a girl. She was blonde and pretty and petite, and she was dragging a brown trout that looked as big as she was, or bigger.

"Herman!" yelled Joe Lord and Lyman Clark and three or four others.

"Lucille!" yelled Harold.

"For the love of Pete," said Charley, "what's going on here?"

"I'll tell you what's going on," said the girl, glaring at Harold. "A year ago I got engaged to that two-timing so-and-so there, and we spent every weekend planning our marriage. Then last April he said he wanted to spend one weekend alone, trout fishing, and I said go ahead. Well, since then I've seen him once or twice on weekdays, but mostly he's too busy resting up for the coming weekend, or tying new flies, or patching his waders or putting fresh hobnails in his boots. So after I'd sat at home and cried for a few weeks, hoping he'd get over this silly Herman business, I suddenly thought of the answer. The reason he couldn't catch Herman is because Herman's a girl! Harold doesn't know beans about girls."

"Please, Lucille!" said Harold.

"Thirty-three inches, eleven pounds ten ounces!" said Jim Deren, who had brought out a tape measure and Charley's kitchen scales.

"So I tied a girl-type fly," said Lucille. "I used mutation mink for the body, and some feathers from a Schiaparelli hat for the wings, and gold thread to tie it with. This is it." She held up a horrible-looking mess of wet fur and feathers lashed onto a hook that would have held a mako shark.

"Great day in the morning!" said Deren.

"It even *smells* funny," said Joe Lord.

"That's Toujours L'Amour," said Lucille. "Fifty dollars an ounce. I sprinkled some on it to make it more alluring. Because, gentlemen, in our family the women don't sit around and twiddle their thumbs while some hussy alienates their fiance's affections— they fight! To the death—as you can plainly see!"

"Lucille!" said Harold, his voice brimming with adoration. "You're even more wonderful than I'd thought! Imagine catching a trout like that on a fly you tied yourself!"

"If that thing is a fly," said Lyman Clark, "I'm Little Lord Fauntleroy. I think Herman bit it just to put it out of its misery."

"See here, sir," said Harold, "be careful how you talk about Lucille's flies. Some day she's going to be my wife, and——"

"Some day my foot," said Lucille. "Right now. There's a justice of the peace in East Stroudsburg—let's go." And she took Harold firmly by the arm and headed for the door.

"Just a minute," said Charley. "What are you planning to do with this trout? It won't fit into the freezer."

"I'm planning to have it stuffed," said Lucille, "and hung over the door to our bedroom, as a warning to designing females who get ideas about Harold. Bring it along, Harold—that justice of the peace is a taxidermist, too." And off they went into the evening, looking happier than human beings have a right to be.

"Well," said Charley, "at least I won't have to refund his money, like I was going to."

"And I'll be able to fish the Railroad Pool again," said Joe.

All in all, everyone agreed, it was a satisfactory evening, and after a round of nightcaps at the bar we all turned in to be ready for the early-morning fishing, which turned out to be fairly good. In fact, it had been a good season altogether, and when it ended a few days later I stopped at the private hatchery at Paradise Valley to say hello to my friend Mike, who ran it. "By the way, Mike," I said, "whatever became of that tremendous big old breeder trout you had here last year?"

"By golly," said Mike, "that's a funny thing. About closing time last Friday a good-looking blonde marches in here waving a fistful of—"

"Never mind," I said. "I'd rather not know about it."

THE DEATH, IN A MANNER OF SPEAKING, AND TRANSFIGURATION OF CHARLEY GUNN

On my way one time to fish the great big eddy where the Lackawaxen River joins the Delaware (and where Zane Grey lived until he invented the West), I stopped in my favorite general store in a town not far from there to buy a couple of dozen bandanna handkerchiefs and say hello to my friend Ike Tussle who runs the store and with whom I fish for trout occasionally, in a secret stream known only to Ike and me and perhaps fifteen hundred other anglers. It was a nice July day, and Ike said, "By golly, Ed, I'm coming with you! Haven't fished that eddy for ten maybe twelve years, and been meaning to for the last eight or nine. Hold on whilst I get my stuff."

An hour later Ike was rowing one of Gollop Kuhn's rental rowboats slow and easy around the big pool while I trolled a June-bug spinner with a lamprey eel hung on the hook behind it, but we weren't having much action. (Ike had a line out, too, and held the rod under one knee while he rowed.) Finally Ike said, "Ed, what do you do with all them bandanna hankies you keep buying from me? I must of sold you a gross in the last five years. Do you eat them?"

"No sir," I said, "I do not. What I do is blow my nose on them, or soak them in fly dope and tie them around my neck in black-fly time, or wipe my windshield with them, or clean my shoes, or tie them on my antenna so I can find my car in a parking lot—hell, there are hundreds of uses for a good bandanna handkerchief. But mostly I blow my nose on them. There's nothing like an old-fashioned bandanna handkerchief for a really satisfactory nose-blow—a man can put his heart into it, and not worry about the consequences. Does that answer your question?"

"Yup," Ike said, but I could see he was thinking about something, and when I asked him what was on his mind—I thought perhaps he hadn't approved of my using his good bandannas to clean shoes, or something—he said, "All that talk about blowing your nose reminded me of Charley Gunn. Did I ever tell you about Charley?" When I said he hadn't, he let the boat drift a minute while he cut himself a fresh chew of plug tobacco, and when he got it properly clamped in his jaw he told me about Charley.

This here Charley Gunn, he said, he was a real nice old galoot that lived so far back in the woods the bull moose used to bust into his pasture and make eyes at his mooley cow. Seems like Charley only come to town about twict a year, to buy salt and flour and the like, and he always done all his trading at my store. Maybe it was because living so far out in the woods like that, Charley had got to be kind of feeble in the head, and folks would play jokes on him and devil him, but I never let nobody pester Charley around the store, and he appreciated it.

One of the ways Charley was a mite queer, he could never stand to hear nobody blowing their nose. Seems like one time Charley got hisself treed by a bear, and for dum' near a week that critter went snorting and snuffling around the tree waiting for Charley to come down and be et, and every time Charley hears a nose blowed, it puts him in mind of that varmint, and he just naturally takes to his heels.

So, whenever Charley used to be in town, the boys would gather round him and start talking about something and then one of them would whip out his hanky quick and blow his nose something fierce, and Charley would skedaddle away from there like he just saw seventeen devils! Matter of fact, it got so Charley would start running as soon as anybody made a motion to reach in their pants pocket.

Some of the boys tried blowing their noses at Charley in the store sometimes, and I throwed them out, and after that Charley knowed he was safe there, and done all his shopping with me.

This particular time, Charley come into the store to do his fall shopping before he got snowed in, and I could see he had something on his mind. So after he'd bought a big mess of ordinary provisions, he hemmed and hawed a while and then he asked me if I got any coffins.

Running a general store you get some queer requests, but it ain't so often you get an order for a coffin. Especially when there's an undertaker two doors down the street.

But Charley told me he figured he ought to have a coffin, on account of not feeling so good lately and living so far out in the woods. He said if anything happened to him in the wintertime, old Hiram Simpson that lived up the road a piece would stop by to find out why Charley's chimbly wasn't smoking, but it might be weeks before Hiram could get into town for a coffin, and Charley wasn't sure he would keep that long. Charley said if there was a coffin there, why he had already dug a hole up the hill a way while the ground was still soft and Hiram wouldn't have no trouble burying him.

Looking at it that way, it seemed like a sensible thing to have a coffin handy, so I told Charley to wait while I went and seen Luke Holmes that was the town undertaker about getting one for him. And when I told Luke about it, he said he had a pretty fair coffin in stock that Charley could have real reasonable, so I paid him for it, and him and me carried it out and put it in Charley's buckboard, in front of the store.

There wasn't nothing fancy about that coffin, but I knowed Charley was a man of simple tastes, and when he come out and looked at it he said it suited him good.

I guess everything would of been fine, only just while we was getting Charley set to head back to the woods, along come Tom Sprangley. Tom is a fellow that always likes a practical joke, but he knowed I didn't like folks to torment Charley around my place like blowing their noses at him and such, and besides, when he seen the coffin he serioused up and said what's going on? So I told him how Charley wanted to have a coffin handy, him not feeling so chipper, and Tom agreed it was a real sensible idea.

"It don't seem right, though," Tom says, "for Charley not to have no funeral. I would surely hate to think that a man that loves his neighbors and lives honest and upright as long as Charley should not get the benefit of a proper Christian burial. I surely would."

"You know durn' well Charley don't have no neighbors," I says. "Not to speak of."

"That ain't Charley's fault," Tom says. "If he had 'em, he'd love 'em."

So I said it didn't make a lot of difference, because after the spring thaw run off, one of the town preachers could take a day off and drive out to Charley's place and conduct a funeral service, and everything would be hunky-dory.

"That's all well and good," Tom says. "*Perviding!*"

"Perviding what?" Charley says.

"Perviding it don't come the Day of Judgment before that preacher can get there!" Tom says. "The way I hear it from Reverend Moley over at the Methodists, a feller that ain't been buried proper won't even hear that horn blow, let alone rise up!"

"What horn?" says Charley. I could see he was commencing to get worried.

"Gabriel's, you durn' fool!" says Tom.

"Now looky here, Tom," I says. "That horn hasn't never blowed yet, and I reckon Charley can take a chance it won't blow before a preacher can get through that road."

"Suits me," Tom says, shrugging his shoulders. "If a man wants to gamble on eternal perdition, it's his own business."

"Now, Tom," I says, "all you're doing is getting Charley upset. The chances are he's going to live to be a hundred, and, if he don't, the chances are the Day of Judgment is a long ways off, and, besides, there ain't nothing Charley can do about it."

"Yes, there is!" says Tom. "He can get hisself buried right now!"

"But, Tom, Charley ain't even dead yet," I says. Charley didn't say nothing at all, but only sat there and looked kind of scared.

"Of course he ain't dead," says Tom. "But it seems to me if a man can buy hisself a coffin whilst he's in good health, there ain't no reason he can't get hisself buried in advance and get it over with. Especially living way to hell and gone out in the woods like Charley, and the Judgment Day getting closer every day!"

I seen Charley look around like he figured the Angel Gabriel might come walking around the corner any minute, and I says, "You mean honest-to-God burying? Like in a hole?"

"Certainly not!" snorts Tom. "What I mean is to kind of prefuneralize him. Then he can pass away anytime he's a mind to, and, thaw or no thaw, he won't get caught short, so to speak, when that old horn starts a-blowin'!"

"How come you're getting so religious-minded lately, Tom?" I says. "All this here stuff about horns and all. You sure got that Gabriel business on your mind."

"You bet I got it on my mind," Tom says. "I ain't like some folks I could mention that would play fast and loose with a friend's eternal soul, and maybe leave him holding the bag while everybody else is resurrecting like hot cakes. Sell him a coffin and then hustle him out of town."

"Now, wait a minute, Tom," I says. "You know doggone well I didn't make a nickel on that coffin. And if you're so all-fired set on funeralizing Charley, why, I'm willing if Charley is. How about it, Charley?''

Charley was looking mighty unhappy, but he always figured I knowed best, so he nodded his head yes-wise.

"That's better!" says Tom, looking pleased. "Now all we got to do is find a preacher and a place to hold the services.''

"How about right inside the store?" I says. "Otherwise I'll have to get somebody to mind it for me.''

"I shouldn't think Charley would care much for being buried out of a store," Tom says. "After all, the deceased had ought to have something to say about his own funeral.''

"Stop calling Charley deceased," I says. "Charley ain't no more deceased than you or me.''

"He claims he don't feel good, don't he?" Tom says.

"You won't feel so good, neither, the day of your funeral," I says. "How about it, Charley? Is the store okay?''

Charley, he just gulped and nodded.

"Trouble with some folks," Tom says, "they don't have no standards. Now me, I wouldn't want to be buried out of even the Bon Ton Dry Goods Emporium, much less—''

"You run your funeral," I says, "and let Charley run his. Tom, how about you trot over and see if Reverend Moley can come right down, and we'll get this over with. Charley's got a long ways to go home tonight.''

So Tom lit out for Moley's house, and Charley and I went and set in the store, only pretty soon Tom come back and said how Moley said nothing doing. He said Moley claimed it was against the principles of the Methodist religion to have a funeral for anybody that wasn't properly deceased.

"Did you tell him about Charley living so far back in the woods and all?" I says.

"I didn't get a chanct to," Tom says. "He got kind of huffy soon as I mentioned the corpse was in a hurry to get back home, and—''

"There you go again!" I says. "Charley ain't no corpse! He ain't even going to be funeralized. You know so durn' much about Gabriel's horn and all, and you don't even know it's against religion to bury a man alive! Getting everybody all upset and then—''

"That's the *Methodist* religion!" Tom says. "Hell, we ain't even tried the Baptists or the Lutherans or the Episcopals yet.''

"You know good and well anything the Methodists won't do, the Episcopals won't do neither," I says. "No, sir, I figure we just better let Charley take his coffin and go home.''

"Wait a minute!" Tom says. "I just got it! All our troubles is due to Charley ain't dead yet. Ain't that so? So all we got to do is—''

I seen Charley start to edge toward the door, so I quick busted in, "Doggone you, Tom, that's the last straw! First you call Charley deceased that ain't even hardly sick, and now you're aiming to—''

"No, I ain't!" Tom says. "All I'm saying is there don't nobody need to *know* he's alive! Now, lookit here—you and Charley bring that coffin in and set it up there on the counter. Charley can lay down inside, and you cover him up good with a sheet. Meantime, I'll go fetch a reverend." And Tom hightailed it out the door and down the street before I could grab him.

Well, sir, I sure was in a fix. I sure didn't like the idea of palming off Charley as his own mortal remains, because there can't no good come of pulling the wool over people's eyes. But then I knowed Tom would be back pretty quick with a preacher, and I'd have a hard time explaining it was all a mistake, and he might figure I was playing a joke on him, and the first thing you know there wouldn't be none of that congregation trading at my store.

So me and Charley h'isted the coffin up on the cheese counter, and Charley laid down and I covered him up with a bran'-new sheet from off the dry-goods shelf. I hadn't much more than got him laid out proper and told him to lay good and still until I give him the word, when Tom come back with a reverend.

I never seen such a reverend in all my born days. He was pretty near seven foot tall and, even so, his nose was a couple of sizes too big for his face. He was wearing a swallowtailed coat that must of been in the family for generations and pants that the cuffs was six inches shy of his shoe tops.

"Ike," says Tom. "Shake hands with Reverend Gabe Appletree, that's going to give poor Charley a decent Christian funeral. The reverend just come over this morning from Traverse City—he's fixing to run off a three-day revival over to the Hosanna Reformed Tabernacle next week. Seen him coming out of Miz Slocum's boardinghouse and recognized him right off for a shepherd of the Lord. Hell, there wouldn't nobody else dare to wear a coat like that except maybe—"

"Glad to know you, Reverend," I says, keeping one eye on the coffin. But Charley was laying low like I told him, and Tom went right on talking.

"The Reverend says I got the right idea about Judgment Day," Tom says. "He agrees most folks don't take it serious enough, and he aims to say a few words on the subject at the funeral. Don't you, Reverend?"

"You're durn' tootin," says Appletree. "This here world is plumb full of sinners that's going to find theirselves up Satan's crick without no oars when Gabriel blows his trumpet! I presume that there is the deceased," he says, looking at the coffin.

"That's Charley, all right," I says. "But you better not go poking around the remains, Reverend, because he might have some kind of mysterious dis—" Just then the door opened and in come Miz Slocum and a dozen or so other ladies. All of them was looking very solemn, and some of them was even sniffling and dabbing at their eyes.

"Howdy, Miz Slocum," says Tom. "You ladies just be seated on them benches and we'll get right on with the funeral. The Reverend Gabe Appletree is going to officialize."

"Now, wait a minute!" I says. "What's going on here, Tom?"

"Charley's funeral, you durn fool!" says Tom. "The reverend happened to mention he don't preach his best without he has a congregation, so I ast Miz Slocum to drum up some mourners. Are you going to begrudge poor Charley a few measly mourners? What kind of a—"

Just then Miz Slocum come over to where we was talking. This Miz Slocum, she doesn't never miss a funeral, and I guess she was grateful to Tom for tipping her off like he done, but she was trying awful hard to look sad. "Poor Mr. Gunn," she says, "what did he die of?"

"I don't rightly know, ma'am," Tom says. "The way I figure, he must of had a relapse or something. It come on real sudden."

"For the land sakes!" Miz Slocum says, and she went back and whispered to the others, and they all started to sniff and sob louder than ever.

But they quieted down some as soon as Appletree stood up behind the cracker barrel that Tom had fixed to use for a pulpit and went harrumf, harrumf, a couple of times to clear his throat. And then he commenced to preach.

Well, sir, I got to hand it to that feller, he could preach like nobody's business. He started out nice and slow, taking it easy, and getting warmed up like. He said how all of us was awful sinners what with card-playing and cussing and carrying on, and he even got in a couple of good licks at elderberry wine.

And by the time he worked up to how the Judgment Day is coming, he was starting to hit his stride. His eyes was popping halfway out of his head, and he was hopping up and down like a churn-plunger, whooping and howling and waving his arms like a crazy feller. He was a caution, all right! When he hollered about sinners sizzling in the fiery pit, I would of swore I could feel them flames! And, by golly, so could the reverend! When he talked about sulphur and brimstone you could see his nose twitch on account of the smell, and when he talked about Old Nick lighting into a sinner with a pitchfork you could see him jump like a yellow-jacket hornet had stang him! I seen some powerful tall preaching in my day, but I never seen the like of this fellow! He had them poor old ladies fit to be tied, and even me and Tom got all choked up when he commenced to talk about the sinners and the heathen that was going to miss the glory boat come Judgment Day.

The way he told it, you could just hear them unbelievers and blasphemers and heretics and backsliders howling bloody murder while Lucifer's gang sorted them out and plunked them into the fiery pit. It was plumb pitiful, he said, what was going to happen to them folks that hadn't never repented, and even though they was sinful and wicked and had it coming to them good and proper, he couldn't help feeling terrible sorry for them.

And I guess he really meant it, because even when he was preaching the tears rolled down his face, though it wasn't nothing to the way Miz Slocum and them ladies was blubbering and bawling, and even Tom Sprangley was crying like a baby.

And the reverend choked up so he couldn't hardly talk when he said how that terrible day was coming when Gabriel would stand up there on the hilltop and blow a mighty blast on his trumpet and all the departed would rise up to be judged and I seen Tom reach for his pocket just in time to grab his arm but it wasn't no use.

Because just when I was grabbing Tom's arm, the Reverend Appletree up and pulled out *his* hanky. And maybe this here Appletree had a sure-enough gift for preaching, but, believe me, it wasn't *nothing* compared to his gift for noseblowing! Like I said, he had the biggest nose I ever seen or likewise heard tell of, and he knowed how to make every inch of it count.

And I guess if I hadn't of been holding Tom's arm, Tom would of been able to step aside and let Charley go by, although he still would of had to do some tall stepping.

Because Appletree's nose wasn't no more than halfway blowed when Charley rose up out of the coffin, sheet and all, and lit out for the door like a scared bunny rabbit. And when he went by Tom, that there sheet whipped around Tom's ankles somehow, and Charley drug him clean out the door and two blocks down Main Street before the sheet come untangled from his legs.

Like I told Tom a couple of days later when he could sit up and see visitors, I figure he was just as lucky not to of stayed around with all them ladies screeching and fainting all over the store, and I figured his doctor bills wasn't no more than I paid to have the stove fixed that Appletree knocked over going out the back door.

And you might think how a lady as homely as Miz Slocum, that's a widow to boot, would be real grateful to the parties which fixed for her to meet her second husband. Because Appletree dislocated hisself in several places from not quite clearing the back fence, and by the time he was up and around, Miz Slocum had him hooked good and proper.

And, believe it or not, me and Tom didn't even get an invite to the wedding. Hey, by golly, I think you got a walleye bumping that bait!

I didn't, though. It was just bottom.

ODDS and ENDS— MOSTLY ODDS

When I got out of college in 1932, I went to Paris and stayed there, pretending to write a novel, until I had spent the $400 I had been paid by the campus newspaper for writing a weekly column. It lasted four months, and I arrived back in New York without enough left for a bus ticket to my home near Pittsburgh. The only way I could afford to travel, then, was as a paid instead of paying passenger, and I spent eighteen months as a merchant seaman, jumping ship in Baltimore after a dentist at the Naval Hospital pulled a perfectly good tooth rather than bother to fill a small cavity but having developed a strong taste for new sights and new sounds.

That's why most of the pieces in this section involve travel as well as fishing and/or shooting; they appeared in *Field & Stream, Sports Illustrated,* The Sunday *New York Times* Travel Section, *True,* various publications of Steve Ferber's Aqua-Field Publishing, Inc., and Jim Rikhoff's National Sporting Fraternity/Amwell Press library.

Something
Was Fishy About
Stonehenge

While in England a few years ago I spent some time in a small village in Hampshire, home county of such sacrosanct trout waters as the Test, the Itchen and the Tichborne. Not long after settling myself at the inn I began to hear stories of the local fishing wizard, a Mr. Smythe-Preston, whose incredible success in extracting limit bags of large trout from hard-fished chalk streams at times when other anglers were going fishless was the talk of the sporting community. Naturally my curiosity was aroused, and I determined to seek Mr. Smythe-Preston out and, if possible, learn his secret.

"It's no use," said the innkeeper, himself a veteran angler and skilled flytier. "He won't say a word. All we know is that he prefers fishing alone, observes all the local regulations as to hours and tackle and, although generally friendly, is somewhat peculiar in his habits. The fact is, there are those who say he's a practicing Druid, and there is talk of witchcraft and ancient rites. Some even say he has a pact with the devil. But, of course, that's all nonsense, and for myself I think he's a topflight trout man who's also exceptionally lucky."

Later, at a dinner party, I met the local curate, another dedicated trout fisherman, and asked him about the fabulous Mr. Smythe-Preston. "I know him only slightly," said the reverend angler, "and he seems a nice enough chap. As for his remarkable success at fishing, I simply don't know how to account for it. Twice I've met him along the stream and observed him carefully, and although he handles a rod and presents a fly as well as most of us, the truth is, he's not really a brilliant—ah—technician. Some of the villagers claim they've followed him on several mysterious predawn expeditions, and declare that he drives to Stonehenge—it's not far from here, you know, less than an hour—where, they say, he goes through some sort of ritualistic rigmarole just as the sun rises over Salisbury Plain. Frankly, I suspect those self-appointed gumshoes of having had one too many at the Crown and Creel—at any rate, he doesn't seem the sort of chap to belong to a pagan sect, and I can't take it seriously.''

Ironically, it was at the Crown and Creel, the village's one and only pub, that I finally met the mysterious man in person, and was surprised to find him the most unmysterious-appearing of mortals, about as sinister in aspect as an Iowa Sunday-school superintendent. The grayness of his face and mustache was alleviated only by the mild twinkle of his eyes, and not at all by the drab and rumpled tweeds that failed to disguise a middle-aged paunch. When I asked if I might stand him a pint he accepted politely if not cordially, but when I said I had heard of his phenomenal ability to produce limits of large trout each time he went fishing and asked straight out if he would tell me his secret, he modestly laughed and said the talk was exaggerated. ''Although I must admit,'' he added, ''that I *am* fairly lucky occasionally. And I try not to fish on an east wind—the usual sort of stuff every fisherman knows. But tell me about American trout fishing—your Large Hole River that I've read so much about, and all that.''

I told him about the Big Hole and the Madison, and was starting on the Letort when I overheard one of a group of villagers at the next table laughingly offer to take a lie-detector test over some boast he had just made. It was then that I recalled the tiny envelope in my wallet, and realized that it might be the answer to my problem.

The packet had been given to me by a young friend who, while interning at a New York hospital, had been involved in some research experiments with sodium pentothal, the so-called ''truth serum.'' In this case, however, it had been produced in the form of pills that could be administered orally and, when dissolved in liquid, affected neither color nor taste. ''Frankly,'' my friend had said, ''I don't know how effective this stuff will turn out to be, but I thought you might use it to help in locating some of your friends' woodcock covers. Slip a couple of these into their martinis—it can't do them any harm, and it might start them chattering like magpies!'' He had meant it for a joke, but I had put the packet into my wallet and forgotten it, until that instant.

At the same moment, by one of those fortuitous coincidences that occur more often in real life than in fiction, Mr. Smythe-Preston was called to the telephone; on a reckless impulse I took the pills from my wallet and popped two of them into the half pint of beer in his mug; then, seeing that there was only one pill left, I popped that one in, too. On returning, Smythe-Preston drained his tankard and said he'd have to be getting back to his cottage. When I said I needed some exercise and asked if I might walk with him, he agreed without much enthusiasm and we set out.

I had no idea how soon the pills would take effect, or indeed if they would take effect at all. For the first half mile I was sure they wouldn't—it would not have been beyond my medical friend to have given me some kind of sugar-pill placebo together with a cock-and-bull story—and then, as we started across the village common, I thought I detected a change in the tone of Smythe-Preston's voice. He had been mumbling non-committal answers to my questions about local history, but when I asked about the remnants of what seemed to be a Roman wall he began talking at considerable length, in a slightly higher-pitched voice and quite rapidly. When my next remark brought an even more effusive response and a reference to some personal matter that an Englishman would ordinarily not mention to a stranger, I pretended to stumble and twist my ankle.

He could hardly refuse when I asked if he'd mind sitting on the wall with me for a minute, until I could determine if the ankle was sprained.

Naturally, as soon as we were seated I asked him point-blank to tell me the secret of his fishing prowess. Not to my surprise, he commenced talking at once, in the manner of a man who is slightly tipsy and feeling well pleased with the world and himself. "Oh, that?" he babbled happily. "Damndest thing, old chap. I've always been a bit of an archaeologist, y'know—fascinating hobby, and something to do between fishing seasons. And, of course, with that Stonehenge thing so close at hand I did a lot of rummaging around there, taking measurements and calculating meridians and sidereal angles and generally trying to outguess all the others who were trying to unriddle that ring of great boulders. I say, am I boring you, old chap?"

"Not at all," I assured him.

"Well, then," he said, "it could hardly have been that I was the first really keen fisherman to poke about there, and I may not have been the first to discover it. Possibly others unearthed it too, and kept their faces shut, as I did."

"Discovered what?" I asked eagerly, and Smythe-Preston laughed.

"Discovered what all those monstrous stones were put there for," he said. "It was all so absurdly simple, once I'd broken the code. And to think that it took me nearly five years to see what should have been obvious right from the start."

"For heaven's sake, man," I said, "*what* should have been obvious?"

Smythe-Preston looked at me in disbelief. "Look, old boy, since you seem a bit dense I shall spell it out for you. These chalk streams you've been fishing all week—they were here before man, of course. God knows who kept the weed cut then, but the trout were here, too, and when the ancient Britons came tromping onto the scene they found old *Salmo fario* ahead of them, and well established. And so they did what any self-respecting Briton would have done—they started fishing for trout! Of course, it wasn't easy. The poor brutes weren't much on finesse—just barely down out of the trees, you might say—and the arts of angling weren't highly developed. But, of course, the trout weren't so awfully sophisticated either, and that helped. At any rate, they fished—for food at first, and then, of course, for sport as well, since they were British.

"And being fishermen," Smythe-Preston went on, a mile a minute, "they soon developed most of the appurtenances of anglers everywhere—crude rods and lines, no doubt some type of artificial fly, since the principal food of the fish was, even then, natural insects. Do you follow me?"

"Yes, indeed," I said.

"Good," said Smythe-Preston, "because, frankly, you don't strike me as frightfully bright. Well, then. Along with the rods and such, these primitive trout fishers invented other necessities—the alibi, for example. The trout that keeps growing after being caught, more rapidly than it ever did in the water. The pre-Potter one-upmanship of the flyfisher over the worm-soaker. And—as you've undoubtedly seen by now—the fisherman's calendar."

"Undoubtedly seen what by now?" I asked, bewildered.

"Sir," said Smythe-Preston, "if you will forgive my saying so and, indeed, even if you will not, you are most incredibly obtuse. Frankly, I wonder I waste my time with you. But you have asked me a question, and for some peculiar reason I feel impelled to answer it—truthfully!''

"For God's sake, *do*!" I urged.

"Can't you get it through your thick colonial skull," he said, "that Stonehenge, that so-called riddle of antiquity, is nothing more nor less than a fishing calendar—a monstrous, megalithic solunar table, so to speak, constructed by a prehistoric race of trout fishermen! Once I got to wondering why it had been built in the heart of the chalk-stream country, everything fell into place. And so, you see, I go there every morning I'm able, during the season, and by observing exactly where the sun's rays strike at sunup—which means crawling about on my hands and knees sometimes in the outer ring—I know precisely, virtually to the split second, when the trout will be voraciously, passionately, uncontrollably on the feed, and will take almost any fly that's presented to them. As I've long ago learned where most of the larger fish lie, it's a simple matter to be there at precisely the right time. And while that overpowering compulsion to feed is affecting the trout, sometimes for as long as three or four minutes, I can take every fish within reach of my cast. The problem is that, having hooked a three- or four-pounder, I may need the entire feeding period to land him. However, there are usually several such periods during the day, sometimes of as short a duration as 15 seconds, and by the time the sun has been up a few minutes I can have determined exactly when they will occur and arrange my itinerary accordingly.''

"Fantastic!" I said, and meant it. "But tell me, how do you determine the exact times of day?"

"Look here, old man," said Smythe-Preston, peering at his watch. "I can't stay here any longer. My wife is frightfully jealous and has the silly notion that I dally sometimes with a widow on the other side of the common, no matter how convincingly I deny it. And, of course, it might be that she has reason—bound to be a bit of fire where there's that much smoke, eh? But since I've told you this much of my secret, I suppose I might as well fill in the details. If you'll meet me here tomorrow morning at five o'clock, I'll take you over to Stonehenge and show you."

"You will?" I said incredulously, thinking even as I spoke of the story I'd be able to tell my friend at the research center. "You're not just putting me on?"

"On my word of honor," said Smythe-Preston sadly, "although, for the life of me, I can't imagine why. Good night, sir." And he hurried off down the lane.

That night I lay awake calculating the possibilities of a genuinely accurate system of forecasting fishing; it was certain that the secret of Stonehenge, once known, could be adjusted for latitudinal, longitudinal and altitudinal variations to apply to any part of the world on which the sun shines, and that the pattern of recurring feeding periods could be projected far in advance.

When five o'clock came I was at the appointed spot, but waited in vain. At seven, having formed some uncharitable opinions as to the value of an English angler's word of honor, I walked back to the inn, where I was informed by my host that Mrs. Smythe-Preston had just been arrested for the murder of her husband, into whose gizzard, in the course of a family discussion, she had plunged a carving knife.

I suppose I shouldn't have used that third pill.

—*Sports Illustrated*, 1956

How to Put the "Ask" in Alaska—an Interview

I kept waiting around, hoping someone would interview me about a recent trip, so I could use the transcript in *Field & Stream* this month and avoid the bother of writing an article. But nobody did, and then it occurred to me that I could interview myself. Why not? These days anglers not only tie their own flies and mold their own jigs and whittle their own plugs; they also make their own glass and graphite rods from blanks and, in a few extreme cases such as Stan Bogdan's, make their own reels; it's just a matter of time until somebody starts extruding his own monofilament or braiding his own backing.

To minimize the confusion I've dubbed the auto-interviewer Walter Wego (as in "Over the river and through the woods to Grandmother's house wego") or W.W., a set of initials once employed by another journalist-interviewer. The interview went something like this:

WW: Hi there, Ed. Been anywhere interesting lately?

EZ: Howdy, Walt. Yes indeed, I sure have been anywhere interesting lately.

WW: Do tell. Like where, exactly?

EZ: I've been to Alaska lately. Or anyway, last September.

WW: My, my! Do you go to Alaska often?

EZ: I certainly hope so, from now on. But this was my first trip.

WW: Why did you go?

EZ: I went to catch a big rainbow trout.

WW: Did you catch it?

EZ: No.

WW: Did you catch a small rainbow trout?

EZ: Yes.

WW: How small was it?

EZ: The smallest was about three pounds, but most of the small ones were between four and eight pounds.

WW: Come off it, buster. I've seen you darn near swoon over a two-pound rainbow, and not all that long ago. Anything over five pounds would have sent you screaming for a taxidermist.

EZ: True, true. But try to get it through your skull, Wego, that "big," rainbow-trout-wise, is a relative adjective. There are lots of rivers where a two-pounder's a swoonable fish. But not where rainbow trout grow to fifteen or twenty pounds, and maybe twenty-five.

WW: Those are steelhead, aren't they?

EZ: No, those are strictly fresh-water, non-seagoing rainbows. Unless you consider Lake Iliamna a sea, which it isn't, in my book.

WW: What makes you so sure there were fifteen- or twenty-pound trout in that water, if you only caught some piddling three-pounders—see, now you've got *me* doing it.

EZ: I'm sure fifteen-pounders were in there because my friend Ed Rice, who master-minded the expedition, caught one that weighed 15¼ pounds on a moderately reliable scales. It was caught on a weighted wet fly and sink-tip line. I took several rolls of film of it with my new automatic-focus camera. Also, I got busted off twice by really big rainbows, which I estimated to weigh sixteen pounds four ounces and seventeen pounds six ounces respectfully.

WW: You mean respectively.

EZ: I mean respectfully.

WW: Oh. How did you feel about Mr. Rice's big fish?

EZ: I felt he was being ostentatious.

WW: Might I see the photographs you took of it?

EZ: No, you might not. The thing about an automatic-focus camera is that you don't have to focus it. You just have to point it. Thus you aren't likely to notice the big smear of reel grease or crankcase oil or walrus blubber or whatever it was on the lens. I would prefer not to discuss it.

WW: Fair enough. Now then, exactly where were you, and how did you get there?

EZ: I was staying at the Kulik Lodge, which is about 200 miles southwest of Anchorage and about 40 miles south of Lake Iliamna, which is about 60 miles long. Those rainbows get big and fat in the various lakes, then come into the rivers in August and September to get bigger and fatter on salmon eggs.

WW: I thought salmon buried their eggs in the gravel, so other fish couldn't get at them.

EZ: Indeed they do. But in that part of the world, there are always a lot more salmon than the redds, or gravel beds, can accommodate, so that incoming schools of salmon dig up last week's deposit of eggs to make room for their own, and the result is a river full of free lunch, not to mention breakfast and dinner and in-between snacks, for the rainbows that move up out of the lake to get in on the goodies. This goes on for a month or so. As for how I got there, I met Ed Rice, Ernie Schwiebert, Mel Krieger, Jack Hemingway, Charley Meyers, Leo Eichhorn, and John Fabian in Seattle, flew to Anchorage, stayed overnight at the Captain Cook Hotel, flew next morning to a town called King Salmon, and transferred to a float plane, which flew us to Kulik Lodge in two trips. No sweat.

WW: So the big trout aren't there all the time?

EZ: There are almost always good rainbows in the rivers, but sometimes they're badly outnumbered by salmon moving in to spawn, and at that time the salmon are still strong, willing to take a fly or spinning lure and able to put up a fierce battle. Also, anglers staying at the Kulik Lodge can fish several other excellent rivers: the American, where I had fast and furious fly fishing for rainbows to seven pounds; the Brooks, where we saw some nifty bears but didn't try to establish any real relationship; the Battle, which has some big grayling along with the rainbows; and two branches of the Talarik.

WW: Interesting. Do you always talk with a lot of semicolons?

EZ: No, but there's a Semisopochnoi Island in the Aleutians, if you go about 1,500 miles further west than I went.

WW: You don't say. What does Semisopochnoi mean?

EZ: I presume it means half a sopochnoi. Let's get on with the fish stuff, shall we?

WW: Anything you say. How would you rate this Kulik River scene, compared to trout waters in Argentina and New Zealand? And how much fishing pressure can it take before it starts going to hell?

EZ: I'd rate it as good or better than anything I've experienced anywhere, ever. As for pressure, the Kulik River—which is only 2 miles long, connecting two lakes—has a two-fish limit and allows fly-fishing only, but I'd guess our party of eight caught upward of 500 trout during our five days there, and so far as I know only six trout were killed, and those by request of the Lodge kitchen. And with the vast amount of available water, and the small number of fishermen—limited by a scarcity of accommodations and the expense involved—I'd guess there'll be mind-boggling fishing there for a lot of decades to come.

WW: You mentioned expense. How expensive is it?

EZ: Very—but as a once-in-a-lifetime experience, it ought to be considered by every right-minded, God-fearing fisherman. There are other camps and lodges in that area offering splendid sport without some of the la-de-da stuff like cabins with showers and gourmet cooking and good-looking waitresses. Why don't you ask me what flies they were taking?

WW: Oh. Sure. Tell me, Ed, what flies were they taking?

EZ: I'm glad you asked. Actually, it didn't matter which fly one was using—

WW: Which fly one *what* was using?

EZ: Actually, it didn't matter which fly you used, so long as it was fished near the bottom, which is where the trout were slurping salmon eggs drifting out of the gravel. So a sinking or sink-tip line was in order, and in the deeper, faster runs a bit of lead wire on the fly, or some split-shot ahead of it, made a big difference.

WW: Look, I know you're the Fishing Editor and all, but I wonder if a feeding trout would really make a *slurping* sound under water?

EZ: Feel free. Most flies we used had a touch of orange or red in the dressing, on the theory that the trout were conditioned to eating stuff that had a salmon-egg color, such as salmon eggs, and in fact those flies worked every bit as well as flies without a touch of red or orange. Also, flies tied to imitate a single salmon egg—just a small gob of orange chenille on a bare hook—produced some pretty big trout in the fast, shallow riffles, even when those flies were held stationary. Rainbow trout aren't noted for deep thinking, and apparently it didn't occur to most of them to say, "Hey, why is that salmon egg swimming upstream against the current, and why does it have that hook coming out of its whatchamacallit? I think I'll give that one a pass."

WW: How bad were the mosquitoes?

EZ: Not bad at all. I took a head net but never bothered to wear it. I wouldn't advise anyone to walk around stark naked after sundown, and calm days are worse than breezy days, but all in all it wasn't nearly as buggy as some states I've been in.

WW: Good. What about bears?

EZ: What about them?

WW: Well, *you* know. Did anyone get eaten?

EZ: Shucks, nobody even got gnawed on. There were a few bears munching on dead and dying salmon, but if a bear can hear you coming, it'll almost always move out of your way. Fishing the Babine in British Columbia, I remember, everybody was given a lard bucket full of rocks and told to rattle it when walking along the river, so the bears would hear us coming and clear out. The din was deafening—it was like fishing in a boiler factory.

WW: You're kidding.

EZ: Incidentally, the Kulik Lodge camp has been there for thirty-five years and hasn't lost a guest or guide to bears yet.

WW: Did you see much other wildlife?

EZ: Flying into camp we saw a few moose, one a bull with a rack well over 70 inches, and along the rivers there were a number of bald eagles. I had brought along a duck gun, thinking there might be some waterfowl or ptarmigan shooting, but never took it out of the case. No caribou in that area—the game trails, and you see a lot of them when you're flying into the various rivers, are mostly made by bears.

WW: Have you anything further to say before we sign off?

EZ: Yes indeed. I'd like to propose a rousing vote of thanks to Old Man Seward.

—Field & Stream, 1981

The Hooker Hooked

I caught my first trout at the age of five, from a mountain brook that flowed into the Cheat River in West Virginia not far from our summer cottage, using a piece of white wrapping-string tied to a stick and a small safety pin on which I had impaled a cricket. It was a splendid brook trout, at least five inches long and beautifully formed and colored, and it fought fiercely, or would have if it hadn't been derricked onto the pine-needled bank the instant it bit the cricket, but on the way home I stopped to watch a man shoot a rattlesnake that had crawled under the porch of his cabin, and lost the fish in my excitement.

That ended my trout-fishing for a long time, as my family moved to a suburb of Pittsburgh, and the creeks that ran near my home flowed yellow and malodorous with coal-mine drainage. Summers I went to camps and caught smallmouth bass in Ontario, a brace of rather puny muskellunge in Conneaut Lake and one no larger in Lake Chatauqua, and various pickerel, perch, bullheads, walleyes, rock bass and sunnies in assorted waters. But no trout. I went to college surrounded by some of the best limestone creeks in Pennsylvania, when a limit of browns over two pounds with a five-pounder among them was no unusual feat, but it was in the midst of a depression—*the* depression—and a fishable split-cane fly-rod complete with reel and fly line cost upwards of ten dollars, which was more than I allowed myself for spending money for a month. (The three Leonard rods and Meek reels my father had left had been burned along with our house and most of its contents a few years previously.)

After college I shipped as a seaman on freighters for a year, then lucked my way into a writing job in a Philadelphia advertising agency. They paid me fifteen incredible dollars a week for a mere 44 hours (the shipping line had paid me the going rate of $26.50 a month for a 56-hour work-week, plus, of course, a bunk and food of sorts) and I saved enough during the first year to buy an extremely used Ford coupe for $35. One June day

I was in the office of a senior vice-president of the company, and while waiting for him to finish a telephone call I studied a photograph on his wall, of him in a canoe netting a big squaretail.

"Like fishing?" he asked.

"I do indeed," I said, "but it's a long time since I've done any."

"Ever fish for trout?" he asked.

"Only deep-water lakers," I said, "and it was too much like laying the Atlantic cable."

"Got a car?" he asked, and when I said I did he changed the subject to business. The next Friday morning he called me up to his office and handed me an aluminum rod case in which was a three-piece 8-foot 4-ounce Thomas rod, a reel with a silk double-tapered fly line on it, an envelope of leaders, a cardboard box with a dozen wet and dry flies in it and a pair of hip boots two sizes too large for me.

"Duck out at noon," he said, "and drive up 611 to East Stroudsburg. Take 209 there until you see a big frame hotel on the left, right beside the road, with a sign that says 'Charley's Hotel Rapids.' Go in and tell Charley I said for him to see that you catch some trout. Good luck."

I couldn't leave at noon because I had a lot of work to do, and in those days you didn't take chances with a job that payed that well, but at five o'clock I rushed out, packed my sea-going dungarees and sweatshirt which was the closest I could come to a sporting ensemble, and drove as fast as I could up 611. I found the hotel, a barn-like white-painted frame building so close to the D.L. & W. railroad tracks that the building shuddered and shook when trains roared by, and went in and introduced myself to Charley Rethoret, a stumpy, volatile, fierce-looking Alsatian with a ragged mustache. When I gave him the message from Wes Gilman he assigned me to a room upstairs and told me to change clothes and come back down. It was nearly dark, but I got into my dungarees and boots and went back down. Charley seemed startled at my outfit, and asked if I had ever fished for trout. I said no, and he thought for a minute, then said okay, he thought he could help me catch a trout.

On the porch outside the bar I set the rod up while Charley pawed through the flies Wes had lent me and picked out a fairly large White Miller, probably a #6. I had tied a heavy leader to the line because that was the only kind Wes had lent me, but Charley said no, that's not the right leader, and went back of the bar into a cigar box and dug up a much lighter one, probably 3X or 4X. When he had tied the fly to it he handed me the outfit and a flashlight—it was now quite dark—and led me across the tracks to the top of a high bank beside the creek. "Take that path down to the water," Charley said, "and right at the bottom there's a boulder with an iron spike in it. It's all that's left of an old foot-bridge. Cast your fly straight out from there about two rod lengths, no more, and let it swing in the current until it's straight downstream. Don't use the light unless you have to. Don't use more than ten feet of line or you'll get hung up behind you. Keep doing that until something happens."

"What if nothing happens?" I said.

Charley shrugged. "Then come back and have a drink and dinner," he said, and walked back across the tracks to the hotel, where several other cars had pulled up since

I arrived. I slid cautiously down the steep path to the water, not using the light at all, and by the time I had felt my way to the creek my pupils had dilated and I could dimly see a boulder at the water's edge, with an iron spike stuck in it.

I peeled about six feet of line off the reel and flipped the fly awkwardly into the water. When it had swung downstream I peeled off a few more feet and flipped it out again. The third time I flipped the fly onto the dark, rushing water I saw something swirl violently in the current, making a wave almost a foot high, and at the same instant there came a yank on the line that nearly tore the rod from my hand, and no doubt would have if the leader hadn't popped like a rotten thread.

I was too dumbfounded to do anything but sit down on the boulder and light a cigarette with trembling fingers, and when the cigarette was finished I walked back up the bank to the hotel, changed clothes and sat down to one of those "Analomink Charley" meals that drew non-fishermen from a hundred miles around and helped to make up for the abominable beds and the noise and the cinders of the railroad. By the time Charley came by the whole episode seemed somehow unreal, but when I told him what happened he didn't seem at all surprised. "Better luck next time," he said cheerfully, and hurried off to greet Gene Connet or George LaBranche or Jack Knight or Preston Jennings or Jim Leisenring or some other now-legendary figure of the trout-fishing world, none of whom I had then ever heard of but some of whom it would be my great privilege to know and to fish with in coming seasons on the Brodheads.

For although I didn't know it at the time I had been hooked as surely and solidly as that big brown trout, and although he probably rubbed the hook out of his jaw that same night I've never recovered from the one he stuck into me.

It wasn't until I had fished that splendid little river for several seasons and had come to know Charley Rethoret well that I realized why he had me use a light leader that night: he believed that a few really big trout give a stream character and fishermen something to talk about, and saw no reason to risk having a novice angler horse one of his biggest trout out of the home pool. (When I wanted to try for the Leviathan another night, Charley asked me not to, giving some totally implausible reason, and I never did.)

Charley's gone now, and the hotel's gone, and the skinny kid in dungarees with the borrowed tackle has been transformed into something grosser and grayer and grumpier although better equipped. But the river's still there, having survived even the Army Corps of Engineers after one big flood, and it may be that that big trout's great-great-great-great-great-great-grandson is finning himself in the current behind that same midstream boulder.

I hope so.

—Random Casts, 1978

A Day's Fishing, 1948

I had been three July days on the West Branch of the Ausable in the Adirondacks and had seen few trout moving and brought fewer to the fly; in the evening there would be fifteen minutes of lackadaisical rising to a small sulfury mayfly, perhaps a *dorothea*, and while that was going on a trout or two might suck in a sparsely tied Light Cahill, but the bigger fish weren't having any, thank you. In the daytime the river was dead, and there are few things deader than a dead brown trout stream. Then I recalled that Wendle Collins had told me of a bigger river ninety miles to the north, and had praised it, and I thought it might not be as slow as the West Branch. The next morning I got up early and drove to the town Wendle had mentioned, and looked up the doctor who had been his companion when he fished there. "Ah, yes," said the doctor, "but the river's in terrible shape. Low and warm. There's another, though, that you might try since you've come so far. Small, but at least it has water. Here it is on the map—a rainbow river, with a few natives in the slow runs, and once in a while a two-pounder. The best stretch runs through the place of a man named Thompson—drive down this dirt road and his is the first farmhouse after you pass a white church.

"This Thompson," said the doctor, "is a queer bird. A widower, in his seventies. If he likes your looks he may let you go through his place to get to the river, and if he doesn't he won't, and that's that. You can say I sent you—I've treated his arthritis for a long time—but if he doesn't like the way your chin dimples it won't do any good at all. He owns three miles of the river—in fact, he owns a good chunk of that township— and he turns away a lot of people for no reason, since he doesn't fish and has no stock on the place nor land in cultivation. If there's ever an unpopularity contest in this county he'll win it hands down."

I drove out the highway to the dirt turn-off, and after passing a white church came to a large frame farmhouse beside the road; the mailbox was marked "Thompson." I parked the car in the driveway to the barn, across the road from the house, and walked across the road and up onto the front porch. When nobody answered my knock on the door I walked around to the back, where I found the door open to the kitchen but could see no one. I tried several outbuildings behind the house, then went back to the front porch and knocked again, louder. When it occurred to me that I'd forgot about the barn I turned and saw a man leaning back against it, blending his weatheredness into the barn's and watching me without much interest. He was six feet and a few inches tall, in soiled, faded overalls and shirt and badly needing a shave and haircut. He's the hired man, I thought, but as I walked closer and saw him more clearly I changed my mind. "I'm looking for Mr. Thompson," I said. He looked at me for four or five seconds, still without interest, and then said, "You've found him." "I'm a friend of Dr. Summers," I said. "He told me if you liked my looks you'd let me go through your place to the river, and if you didn't you wouldn't."

He looked at me some more while he mulled this over, then unfolded his arms and shifted onto his own frame the weight the building had supported. "I'll show you the way to the river," he said. I got into my waders, took my rod in sections and followed him across the road and over several fallow fields. Walking beside him I said, "Do you eat trout? I don't keep them, usually, but I'll bring some back if you'd like."

A hundred paces later, when I was sure he hadn't heard me, he said, "I guess I could use some. If they're cleaned." We had come to the edge of a field and the remnants of a stone fence, and down the slope from it through a sprawl of alders I could see the sparkle of water. "There it is," he said, and turned and walked back across the field. I went down through the blackberry tangle on the slope and through the alders to the stream; it was a fast, pretty river, only slightly swamp-stained and with good pocket-water where trout can lie and rest while the current brings manna, and where a nymph or wetfly on a long, light leader will linger a second or two—long enough for a fish to seize it before the rush of water whirls it on downstream.

It was noon then, and I fished half a mile down the river and took two ten-inch rainbows before eating the sandwich I'd packed in my vest the night before. Both trout had taken a small wet leadwing coachman, but when I came to a beautiful deep pool with a foot-high falls at the head I changed to a tiny red-and-white maribou streamer and struck a fourteen-inch rainbow under the falls and a thirteen-inch brook trout in the tail of the pool. Then I changed reels to have a floating line and fished a dry fly back to where I'd entered the river, picking up three more nine- and ten-inch fish and losing a sixteen- or seventeen-inch rainbow that caught me with my rod-tip down and broke the 4X gut on his first wild jump.

It was almost seven o'clock when I got back to the farmhouse, and as I came up to the kitchen door I could see that Thompson had just finished putting away his supper dishes. The white-enameled sink was just inside the door, and so I stepped inside and slid the seven cleaned and still beautiful trout out of my grass-mat creel onto the sink top. "I'll trade you these for a glass of cold water," I said. The old man came across the kitchen and peered down at the fish. Then he picked up a pail that was three-quarters full, poured it into the sink and started out the door; "I'll get some fresh," he said.

I followed him outside and around the back of the house to an uncovered dug well with a wooden windlass; he hooked the bucket onto the rope and let it drop into the water, then reeled it back up. It was the first time I'd seen a wooden windlass since my boyhood in West Virginia, and I said, remembering that the doctor had said he was well-to-do, "Why don't you get a pump for this?" He finished winding in the bucket; when it rested on the edge of the well-wall he said, "Had a pump once. It froze. This don't freeze." We went back to the kitchen, and he got a glass from the shelf, filled it from the bucket and handed it to me. While I was drinking it he wrapped the trout in waxed paper and put them in the ice-box. Then he took a chocolate layer cake from a cupboard and set it on the kitchen table. "There's cake," he said, in the way he might have said it was raining. I waited to see if he meant to pursue the subject, and then asked if I could have a piece of it. He seemed relieved, and took a knife from the table drawer. While he was cutting a slab from the cake I said it looked home-made, and he said it was.

"A neighbor?" I said. He looked at me in genuine surprise, and when he saw I was serious he said, "I do my own cooking." It was good cake. I stepped outside and sat on the bench beside the kitchen door while I ate it, so as not to get crumbs on the floor, and when he'd put the cake back in the cupboard he came out and sat down on the other end of the bench. Through a mouthful of cake I asked him if he fished the river much.

"Don't fish it a-tall," he said. "Don't see the sense on it." "Trout are pretty good eating," I said. "Not that good," he said. "Not good enough to go traipsing up and down a river all day getting bit by black flies."

I finished the cake, and asked if I could come back sometime and fish the upstream water, and he said, "I guess so. But don't bring nobody with you. I don't want all creation tramping across them fields." I said I'd come alone, and asked if he had any help around the place. "Don't need none," he said. "Used to have a man for the milking, but I don't have cows now. You ever milk a cow?" I said I had, but that I wasn't very good at it, and he said he had known. "I can tell a man that's milked cows," he said. "Never missed a one." I asked him how he could tell, and he thought for a minute and said, "I couldn't rightly say. But I can tell, all right."

I said it was nearly nine o'clock and I had to drive ninety miles back to the motel, and had better be going, and the old man was silent while I gathered up my creel and rod and vest. I thanked him for the fishing and the cake, and he said, "This is the first time I been up after eight o'clock in a long time. Maybe ten years." He followed me across the road and watched while I stowed the rod and gear in the station wagon. I got in and started the motor and said so-long and was turning out of the driveway onto the road when I heard him call. I stopped, thinking I'd left some gear on the ground, and he walked across the barnyard and stooped to put his head in the opposite window.

"You can bring somebody, if you want," he said. I said thanks, I'd be back the first chance I got, and would only bring someone who had milked a cow. I meant to go back, of course, but I never did.

—*The Gordon Garland*, 1965

Trout in the Morning—
Death in the Afternoon

"It was a long walk and the country was very fine, but we were tired when we came down the steep road that led out of the wooded hills into the valley of the Rio de la Fabrica."
—THE SUN ALSO RISES

In 1932 I was in Paris pretending to write a novel and actually being homesick for Pennsylvania pinewoods and mountain brooks, and when I reread *The Sun Also Rises*, then six years old and already a classic, the part about trout fishing in Spain shook me up. A kindly old Parisian sold me a bicycle for 100 francs and I headed south, figuring I could borrow or steal some tackle when I got across the Spanish border. By the time I got to Rambouillet, twenty-eight miles below Paris, I knew why the kindly old Parisian had sold the bike for $4, and after giving it to an astonished ten-year-old I hitchhiked back to Rue Monsieur-le-Prince.

In 1966 I was in Seville for Holy Week and the Fair, and when it occurred to me that I was missing the opening of the trout season in New York I thought I might see if I could have more success in reaching Hemingway's rivers by approaching them from the south. I telephoned Max Borrell, the indestructible fishing pundit of the Ministry of Tourism in Madrid. He assured me that the Rio Irati, which Hemingway wrote about in the novel, was still there and still a good trout river, but he admitted to ignorance of the Rio de la Fabrica. However, he told me where to get a ten-day provincial license in Pamplona (at the Regional Forestry Office, for $1.65) and wished me tight lines. I flew from Seville to Madrid and on to San Sebastian, where I rented a Seat, the Spanish version of the Fiat, and drove sixty-five kilometers to Burguete, which had been Hemingway's headquarters, over a mountainous but well-paved road.

Burguete, as Hemingway noted, is one street wide with whitewashed houses banked solidly on either side, and after pulling off onto the mini-plaza beside the schoolhouse to let a funeral procession go by, with six men carrying a plain black coffin behind a cross-bearing priest and surpliced altar boys, I found the Hotel Burguete a few steps ahead. The proprietor sized me up instantly as a rich American and said I could have a large room without bath and three meals for 185 pesetas, or $3.10, a day. As it turned out, the meals were highly edible in a hearty farm-kitchen way, and the tab included a bottle of more-than-adequate Rioja with lunch and dinner.

In the morning I backtracked forty kilometers into Pamplona where I got a license and saw posters announcing a corrida the coming Sunday with Curro Giron—one of four Venezuelan Indian brothers, three of whom were fairly classy matadors—getting top billing. When I got back to Burguete it was too cold and raining too hard for comfortable fishing, so I cornered Julio Urdiroz, the proprietor, and asked him if he remembered Hemingway. He said yes, he remembered him well, the American who had stayed there and had had a remarkable intelligence and had walked across the mountain to fish. Urdiroz brought out a ragged topographical map and showed me the river—not the Irati, but a tributary called Rio Legarza—to which Hemingway had walked, and which must have been the stream that Jake Barnes walked to in the novel. I asked Urdiroz about the Rio de la Fabrica and he said he knew of no such river.

In the morning there was fresh snow on the hilltops, but the sun shone and the air was springlike. I drove over the mountain to the crossroads village of Arive and the Irati River, which was running slightly high and murky with snow water, and turned upstream on the road that runs alongside the river. The macadam ended after three miles at a cluster of houses called Orbaiceta, but I followed a dirt road a few kilometers until I saw a Frenchman worm-fishing with a twelve-foot rod and thread-line reel. He told me that the water he was fishing was private, but that for 100 pesetas a day I could get a permit from the forester at Orbaiceta that would entitle me to fish private as well as public water on the Irati. This arrangement with the landowners and syndicates that control much of the choice fishing waters applies only to weekdays.

The Frenchman, a wholesale meat dealer from Bayonne, was very friendly. He told me he had thirty-five brown and rainbow trout, counting the ones he had stashed in the luggage compartment of his Citroen, and that as the limit was fifteen he would explain to the forester-warden, if one came by, that half the trout were mine. I don't know how he planned to account for the other five trout, but in any case, I assured him that the honor was more than I could bear and that if questioned I would deny any knowledge of the fish. He was saddened by my lack of the NATO spirit but shrugged and went back to his fishing. Later I learned that the forester had caught him with trout over the limit and had forbidden him to fish the Irati again that season.

I drove on a few hundred yards to public water and fished a dry fly upstream through some riffles and several deep, slow runs, getting a few splashy rises from small trout. Coming back down with a brace of wet flies, I caught three browns from eight to ten inches and released them. The river is stocked, but there were enough fingerlings to indicate good natural reproduction, and many of the trout I took during five days of fishing looked and behaved like wild fish. None was more than ten inches, but with the evident abundance of aquatic insects and the river's limestone purity, there were indications of bigger fish for anyone with the time and inclination to work the heavier water, especially late in the evenings. I did try it one evening but chickened out when, with the sun gone, the temperature dropped rapidly into the 40s and my fingers got too numb to tie on a fly.

The Irati is heavily spin-fished and worm-fished by local and visiting Spaniards and a number of Frenchmen who come across the border just fifteen miles from Burguete. Of twenty-odd Spanish anglers I met on the Irati and the Urrobi only one was fly-fishing, using a twelve-foot rod and a cast of three wet flies. Most of the water is easily reached from the road, and, although a guide might be helpful in pointing out the best pools, none is necessary. I had asked about guides at the inn and was told there were none available in Burguete. Anyone familiar with trout water should be able to spot the better stretches. After three days at Burguete I had a note from Señor Borrel suggesting that I fish various other rivers of the region, some of which he felt might produce more and larger trout, but I had only two more days of fishing before meeting my family in Paris and was anxious to find what Hemingway had meant by the Rio de la Fabrica; in this mountainous, wooded, agricultural region a factory seemed unlikely. The next morning, when a boy came down the river road driving a herd of goats and stopped to watch me release a trout, it occurred to me to call him and ask, ''Where's the factory?'' Instead of saying ''What factory?'', he told me to drive upriver on the dirt road and take the first branch road to the left. I took it, and after the road had straggled up the side of the hill for two country miles, it petered out in a muddy square surrounded on two sides by whitewashed houses, on another side by a large, unused church with the roof partially caved in, and on the other side by the ruins of what had once been, obviously, a group of large stone buildings, now with only a few walls and stone arches still standing and with goats grazing on the grass and shoots of trees growing among the fallen stones.

I parked the car in front of the church and when a man of about thirty came by carrying a post-hole digger I asked him if the ruins were the factory. Of course, he said. What had the factory manufactured? I asked, and he said armas. What kind of armas? I asked, and he said cannonballs. How long since the factory had stopped making cannonballs? I asked, and the young man thought a minute and said fifty years. Is that all? I said, only fifty years? and he thought about it some more and said seventy-five years. When a very old man came by and stopped to listen I asked him the same question, and he said, a long time ago. How long? I said, and he said maybe 100 years, maybe 200, who knows? Is that the Rio de la Fabrica, that small stream running behind the factory? I asked. He said, of course, but its true name is the Rio Legarza. Are there trout in it? I asked, and he said yes, many trout, but all small. It was starting to rain hard, and I said, thank you, and got back in the car and drove back to Burguete.

The next morning was Sunday, my last day, and I drove down the road toward Aoiz (pronounced *ahohweeth*) and fished the Urrobi, which runs more or less alongside it. When it began to rain again, a Spaniard who had been fishing below me put up his rod and invited me to join him in the shelter of an ancient abbey, which I did. He said the abbey was even older than the original Roncesvalles Abbey, which is up the road from Burguete toward France, but had been abandoned several centuries ago. He told me he was a lawyer from Aoiz and that although he spoke no English, he could read it fairly well, and asked if I knew the writings of an American whose name I could not understand, until I realized it was a Spanish phoneticization of John Alden Knight. I told him I had fished with Mr. Knight on several occasions and knew and admired his work, and, sad to say, had just had a letter telling me of his death a few weeks before. The lawyer took a flask of Spanish brandy from his creel and proposed that we drink to Señor Knight's memory. We did, and I was sorry I would not be able to tell Jack about it. In a few minutes the sky cleared and we went back to our fishing.

At 3 o'clock I drove down on the road past Aoiz and turned right on a road that took me into Pamplona, where I ate a long, vinous lunch and arrived at the bullring in time to buy a front row *sol y sombra* and sit through an exhibition of bullfighting so bad that it took five minutes, on two occasions, to clear the ring of flung cushions. (Curro Giron and one of the other matadors were awarded an ear each for their first bulls, apparently for not having tripped over their muletas.)

On the other hand, of course, it was a better bullfight than you can see on a Sunday afternoon in the Beaverkill country or within a short drive of the Deschutes, and I suppose I have a hell of a nerve to complain.

—Sports Illustrated, 1965

Are Fishermen Really Liars?

EXHIBIT A: I stole a trout one time—and I mean ripped it off, causing the rightful owner all sorts of anguish (but not as much anguish as if I had *not* stolen it). It was at the Antrim Lodge on the Beaverkill, still a favorite fishing inn for Catskill trout anglers, and I think the year was 1944. There was a kid there, home from basic training at an Army camp and using his few days of leave to do some serious trout fishing—probably the last he'd do for a long time, and possibly the last he'd ever do. He wasn't much of a trout fisherman, in years of experience or technique, but he made up for it in enthusiasm, and I offered to take him down the river one afternoon, as he had no wheels.

Driving down the old Route 17 beside the river I learned his largest trout ever was barely ten inches, and how much he'd like to get a really good brown this trip, to think about while he was overseas or wherever he'd be going. So when we stopped at the long pool below Cook's Falls, and he hooked and netted a nice fish after it had put up a respectable tussle, I made quite a fuss about it. "How big would you say it is?" he asked, eagerly, and I stretched things a bit and said, "That's a real nice fish—I'd say maybe fifteen, sixteen inches." "Wow!" the kid said. "Sixteen inches!" "Maybe more," I said, figuring it wouldn't do any harm.

At the bar that evening I told the group about the youngster's fish, and somebody asked him how big it was. "I didn't have a chance to measure it before I stuck it in the freezer," the boy said, "but I'd say, oh, sixteen-seventeen inches." "I watched you net it from the road," someone said, "and it looked bigger than that." "Might have been," the soldier said, looking pleased, and an hour and several bourbon-and-waters later I heard him describe it as "about eighteen inches." "Hey, that's the top fish of the day!" someone said. "I'd like to see that baby!" "Okay," the boy said, happily. "Soon as I finish this drink."

I ducked out the back door beside the bar, went into the freezer room and found the kid's trout in a paper bag with his name on it. It measured fourteen and one-half inches on the ruler hung by the door. I threw the bag into the trash can, stuffed the trout in a bag with my three keepers and rejoined the group at the table in the bar. When the boy and three or four others went up to look at his prize trout, and couldn't find it, the kid was furious. "What kind of lowdown, rotten so-and-so would steal another man's trout?" he demanded, but finally he simmered down and said, "Well, hell, if somebody needs a nineteen-inch trout that bad, he's welcome to it." And later he told me he'd always have the memory of it, which was true—and in this instance, a big improvement on the reality.

EXHIBIT B: Thirty-odd years ago I was fishing for smallmouth bass in the Thousand Islands section of the St. Lawrence River, staying at Cape Vincent with "Hike" Newell, a partner in the company I worked for, and some important clients. One morning I was baitfishing in a boat with Carl W., who was advertising manager of a large corporation, and a guide, and shortly after Carl had caught the first smallmouth of his life, a two-pounder or thereabouts, I lucked into one just under five pounds, and boated it. That evening Hike took me aside and told me that Carl wanted to have his catch mounted, but that being smallish it had already been filleted for breakfast; he asked if I'd mind if he had my bass mounted for Carl. "I don't mind a bit," I said, "but Carl's sure to know it's not his fish—it's more than twice as big as the one he caught." "Kiddo, you've got a lot to learn about fishermen," Hike said, and went to telephone the local taxidermist.

As a result, for several years after that I would walk into Carl's office in Chicago two or three times a year, to show him an advertising program or discuss budgets, and always I would admire the mounted bass on his wall, then listen while Carl explained, in excruciating detail, how he had let it toy with the shiner until the precisely right moment, and what a fierce battle it had put up after he had set the hook, while I nodded and assured him it was a splendid fish, which of course it damn well was.

I wouldn't say that either Carl or the soldier were liars, really, but I think that in their readiness, if not actually eagerness, to exaggerate the size of their catch they exemplified most of the anglers I know, including me. Most real fishermen are by nature dreamers, with few occasions on which we can let our imaginations off the leash, and the line between dreamers and liars is a thin one, which tends to dissolve in the running waters of a trout or salmon river, and even in the still water of a bass lake or bullhead pond.

Personally I make it a rule never to weigh or measure a fish I've caught, but simply to estimate its dimensions as accurately as possible, and then, when telling about it, to improve those figures by roughly a fifth, or twenty percent. I do this mainly because most people believe all fishermen exaggerate by at least twenty percent, and so I allow for the discounting my audience is almost certain to apply, so that the net figure in their minds will be about right. Thus, if I catch a four-pound brown on a #16 Adams in the Madison River I tell my friend Dave Dubious, "Dave, I took a five-pound brown on a #18 Adams just below the Varney Bridge last week." Dave thinks to himself, "In that fast, heavy water this klutz couldn't handle a five-pound brown on an #18 fly. It was probably a four-pounder, if that—and like as not it wasn't an #18 but a #16 or #14 fly." "Say, that's great!" Dave says. "Let me tell you about the twenty-one-inch rainbow I took out of the Big Hole three weeks ago, on a 6X leader." I instantly mark Dave's rainbow down to eighteen inches, beef up the leader to 4X, and say, "Wow! Tell me about it!" Thus we both come away with a fairly accurate understanding of who caught what, nobody has been injured, and life goes on.

There is, among hard-core fishermen, a conviction that truth, like pure water and the fish that live in it, is a precious commodity, not to be squandered or over-used. I respect that conviction, and those who hold it. And if the philosophers ask, "What is truth?", I answer, "I haven't the foggiest notion, gents. But one thing it *ain't* is those stories you hear at Bud Lilly's or Phil Wright's or Dan Bailey's or any other tackle shop or fishing camp."

As for me, I get all the truth I need in the newspaper every morning, and every chance I get I go fishing, or swap stories with fishermen, to get the taste of it out of my mouth.

—*Field & Stream*, 1977

The Ethics, Perhaps, of Fly-fishing

I agreed to write something about the ethics of fly-fishing because I hadn't thought much about it at the time, and it's always pleasant to be able to impose, or try to, your own ideas and ideals on other people, especially from a stance that makes back-talk difficult.

But now, faced with a blank sheet of paper and forced to think about it, it seems to me that all the problems of living and dying and of work and play are ethical problems, and to attempt to separate out the ethics of fly-fishing is akin to prescribing a special inflection of voice to be used when addressing bishops or billionaires or Internal Revenue agents. And perhaps it isn't really ethics that we have in mind, but rather attitudes, a code of behavior, a concern for tradition and a hope for conservation of both fish and values. Perhaps, too, in my own case I tend to confuse ethics with aesthetics (and perhaps ethics is the aesthetics of behavior).

Since such an approach is highly subjective I can hardly do better than to set down some of my own beliefs about fly-fishing; any ''ethical'' attitudes I have would grow out of these:

1. The essence of sport is skill, and the voluntary imposition or acceptance of arbitrary conditions demanding skills. There is nothing immoral about shooting sitting ducks, but the sportsman shoots them flying, and may decline shots that require little skill.

2. Fly-fishing generally requires more skills than fishing with lures or natural baits; fly-casting generally requires more skill than spin-casting or bait-casting; fly-fishing encourages development of collateral skills, in insect identification and imitation, in stream-craft and in fly-tying. It is therefore a more sporting way of taking those fish which sometimes feed on insects on or below the surface of the waters they inhabit or on small fish imitable by streamer flies. (The fact that skilled fly-fishers may be able under certain conditions to take more fish than the bait or lure fisherman is irrelevant; the honest man

is often able to accumulate more wealth than the thief, but this is a shoddy argument for honesty.)

3. Fly-fishing, or any other sport fishing, is an end in itself and not a game or competition among fishermen; the great figures in the historic tradition of angling are not those men who caught the greatest numbers of fish or the biggest fish but those who, like Ronalds and Francis and Halford and Skues and Gordon and Wulff and Schwiebert, made lasting contributions of thought and knowledge, of fly patterns and philosophy, of good writing and good sportsmanship. There have always been men who could accumulate a larger number of dead fish than other men, because it was important to them; but no one remembers who they were, or should.

4. One of the greatest privileges of the fly-fisher is to release his catch, not out of sentimental avoidance of the act of killing but out of awareness that in most waters of this continent, capable of sustaining a fish population from season to season, a game fish is far more valuable as sport or the promise of sport than as food for belly or vanity.

5. There can be no fly-fishing without pure waters in which game fish can live; there can be no such waters without proper management of watershed forests and farmlands, or without control of pollution through erosion or industrial or human waste. Therefore, the fly-fisherman should be deeply concerned with measures to conserve or restore pure waters, and will involve himself when possible in efforts to promote such measures, recognizing that they are inseparable from the conservation of all renewable natural resources. He will bear in mind the legend of the African chief who said, "This land belongs to my people. Some of them are living, some of them are dead, but most of them have not yet been born."

—Random Casts, 1966

"Sí, Señor–Mucho Ducks"

When Ed Zern got back from Yucatán last March, where he'd gone duck shooting, we asked him for a report. It read as follows:

Flew from New York to Havana, where camera was stolen. Flew from Havana to Mérida in Yucatán, where Mexican army confiscated my shotguns. Showed Mexican army officer my permit for shotguns issued by Mexican consul in New York. Officer studied permit carefully, locked shotguns in barred room and went away. While arranging with lawyer to get guns out of hock, learned that duck camp operator had broken up camp, dismissed Indian guides and sold decoys. After recovering guns, rode around northern Yucatán one full day with camp operator rounding up Indians and decoys. Went shooting next morning at 5:30 a.m., quit at 7:30 a.m. Too many ducks. Went to Uxmal and Kabah, ancient Mayan cities, and climbed around ruins. Went to a fiesta in Campeche, drank tequila to show Pan-American solidarity. Went to Champotón and up Champotón River in leaky launch. Drove fast back to Mérida to catch 4:35 airplane to Havana and New York. Arrived at airport at 3 p.m., found 4:35 airplane had left at 11 a.m. Was told not to worry, another left in two days. After speaking sharply to airline man, was told might get airplane next day to New Orleans. "This would entitle you to $16 refund," said airline man. "Good," I said. Before plane left next day airline man said he'd made a mistake—it was $1.60 not $16. "We'll send it to you," he said. Early in April got a letter from airline. "Enclosed find check for $1.60," it said. No check enclosed.

This seemed skimpy, and we asked him to elaborate a bit. For the edification of duck shooters, conservationists and other gringos we present this report on a paradise for wildfowl and wildfowlers.

—THE EDITORS
(Sports Illustrated)

Six hundred miles due south of Louisiana on the Mexican coast, the Yucatán peninsula stretches out into the Gulf of Mexico. It is a low, flat land, studded with the ruins of Mayan temple cities that were built a thousand years ago and abandoned to the jungle. Yucatán is inhabited now by descendants of the Indian temple builders and by white and mestizo Mexicans. Culturally it is almost an independent state, and even today there is no decent road and only one narrow-gauge railroad connecting Yucatán with the rest of Mexico.

The Mayan Indians, when found in their own villages, are poor, cheerful, intelligent, self-respecting and honest. The nourishment they scratch out of their state's thin limestone soil is so low in protein that a North American could scarcely survive on it.

Capping the northern tip of Yucatán is a 300-mile stretch of lagoons along the Río Lagartos (Alligator River). These mangrove-choked, brackish waters, from which almost all of the alligators have been killed off, are the winter home of millions of ducks that come down the flyways from the U.S., Canada and Alaska.

The rich forage plants in the shallows of the lagoons attract pintail, teal (mostly bluewing), widgeon, lesser scaup, gadwall, shoveler and an occasional redhead and mallard. The first ducks, generally teal, arrive at the end of August; by the first of April they have all gone back north. Between November 15 and March 15 the ducks are so abundant that the shooting is almost invariably excellent and sometimes fabulously so.

I had heard about Yucatán's wildfowling from an acquaintance, whose recommendation was almost hysterical; accordingly I jumped at a chance to try it last year. The Mexican consulate in New York City gave me a permit to take in two shotguns (a Browning 12-gauge over-and-under, choked full and modified, and a Winchester 21 bored fairly open for quail) and 500 rounds of ammunition (which is difficult and expensive to buy there, except for reloads of doubtful reliability). The consulate failed to tell me that a permit from the Mexican army might be required so the firearms could be taken directly through customs in Mérida. (The hunter who follows me should inquire about this military permit. It costs about $8 U.S.)

Thus when we arrived at Mérida Airport I discovered that 1) a Contax camera had been taken from a duffel bag somewhere between my hotel in Havana and the Mérida customs office, 2) the army refused despite the consular permit to let my shotguns go through, although they admitted the ammunition, and 3) my letter to the camp operator had gone astray and he had closed down for the season—dismissed the Indians who worked for him and even sold his decoys to a local sportsman. It took two days to get the shotguns released and then, while my wife went off to visit the ruins at Chichén Itzá, I went by hired car twenty-two miles due north to the state's leading seaport, Progreso, then a few miles east along the coast to the tiny but pleasant seaside resort, Bahia Bonita. There I was met by Shaun Viguerie of Metairie, Louisiana, a young but competent sportsman who had just finished his first season as a hunting camp operator. With his assistant, Ted Joanen, we piled into a truck and drove through the coastal jungle to an Indian village where we picked up three native hunters.

On the way, Shaun explained something about the hunting. The three Indians were market hunters; they kept a careful check on the movement of ducks along the lagoon, but when Viguerie engaged them they refrained from gunning in the area to be hunted so as not to drive the flocks away. Instead they helped plan the best location for the blinds; then, when the hunters were posted, two of the Indians and their canoes were trucked to points about a mile on either side of the blinds. At daybreak they would start slowly poling their canoes between the myriad islands of the lagoon toward the gunners, pushing the ducks ahead of them in short flights. Without this stirring-up there would be no shooting, since with the abundance of food and the mildness of weather there would be no reason for ducks to fly. The third Indian would act as a retriever.

The Indians, Jose, Vidal and Humberto, turned out to be enthusiastic hunters who spoke no more English than I spoke Spanish or their native language, Mayan. They obviously liked Viguerie, probably because he was a hunter like themselves and was trying to learn their difficult language, which is full of strange hissing, spitting sounds. (In the blinds they speak a sort of "duck English" consisting mainly of "*wee-jun!*" "*peentail!*" and "*er zey kom!*"

As any conservation-minded duck hunter would be, I was shocked to find market hunting widespread all along the Yucatán coast. Usually hunters work in teams, shoving a grass-camouflaged bateau up close to a feeding flock, then firing into it with old, overloaded guns. They reload their own brass cartridges. If a visiting sportsman gives them a few factory-loaded shells, they supplement the factory loads by pouring an extra ounce or two of shot down the barrel on top of the shell and wadding it with a banana leaf. In a good day two skilled hunters may kill several hundred ducks, for which they get from two cents to eight cents (U.S.) apiece, drawn and plucked. (On a bad day they may kill none, which gives the operation a sporting flavor.)

Considering the amazing concentration of ducks in the area and the poverty of the Indians, it would be quixotic to expect observance of arbitrary bag limits that don't make much sense to an Indian. To the Indians, who see vast flocks concentrated in the area, it's obvious that the few thousands they kill for market can't affect the population. It's useless to explain that those are the ducks of a whole continent and that when they leave they'll spread out over more than a million square miles; the Indians don't know much about continents and their arithmetic stops well short of a million. What they do know is that for eight months of the year they get almost no animal protein or fat in their diets; and that suddenly a benign if whimsical providence sends millions of pounds of fat meat to them, neatly packaged in feathers and needing only to be shot, drawn, plucked and popped into the pot.

One Yucatán hunter may tell you the hunting limit is 50 ducks a day, and the next one may say the limit is 100 a day. Actually Mexico has a republic-wide limit of 15 ducks a day from November 5 to March 15; but the game laws are little known. For lack of a warden in Yucatán, enforcement is up to the local police, so to all intents and purposes there *is* no limit, except that set by the conscience of the gunner. Since it's no trick for a fair wing shot to kill 150 ducks a day if he is so inclined, there's a lot of leeway for conscience. If the gunner considers that he is tying up two or more market hunters as guides, who otherwise might kill 50 to 100 each, he can shoot a hundred ducks and still tell himself he's conserving wildfowl.

At 4 o'clock the next morning Viguerie, Joanen and I had breakfast, then picked up our three Indians and drove back through Progreso and another five miles to westward of the port. By 5:30 I was sitting in an improvised blind that Shaun and Jose had hacked with machetes out of a mangrove island. In front of the blind rode a dozen nondescript decoys that Shaun had found discarded around the camp, including three or four made by rough-shaping a coconut husk with a machete and painting it black. By 7:30 I had killed my limit, shooting only pintail and widgeon.

Driving back to Bahia Bonita, Viguerie told me that early in the season pintail are the dominant species but that most of these handsome birds apparently keep on going to Central and South America; that mosquitoes are seldom a problem, even in the marshes, during the dry winter season; that along the northern shore there are no poisonous snakes; that when gun dogs of the region aren't suffering from heartworm they're likely to be crippled by cactus spines in their pads; and that he personally believes a trap load is the best choice for Yucatán duck shooting over decoys, since No. 6 shot cripples too many birds and magnum loads are unnecessary.

After lunch we walked through a banana plantation for an hour and put up four coveys of quail, at which I shot very badly; then I drove back to the Mérida Hotel and rejoined my wife.

We visited the magnificent ruins at Uxmal and Kabah before going by rented car to Campeche and Champotón. These, with the buildings at Chichén Itzá, are as archeologically impressive as the Egyptian pyramids. They should be seen. If the duck hunter's time is limited, he should send his wife, who will find the majesty and mystery of the ruins ample solace for duck widowhood.

At Champotón I tried the local tarpon fishing and hooked one, despite the services of the most incompetent guide I've encountered in a lifetime of fishing. A trip up the Champotón River produced no fish but a medley of noises, presumably made by birds and monkeys in the jungle that loomed above the river and sounding like a third-rate sound-effects record.

Yucatán, in short, is a land with a variety of promises, but not one altogether geared for the wildfowler—casual and aggravating when it comes to the fine details of bag limits and permits. However, the guides (when you find one) know their business, and the abundance of ducks makes Yucatán a tempting midwinter range for U.S. hunters. Shaun Viguerie, my guide, is active again this year, and can be reached in care of the Club Yucatán, 5243 Canal Boulevard, New Orleans—they'll forward mail or telegrams. Khaki trousers or shorts and shirts are all the clothes you'll need, but take along a light wool shirt and sneakers. Be sure to have someone get the proper army permit for gun entry; Viguerie will do this if you give him two weeks' notice (and can even lend you a serviceable gun, in a pinch). All licensing arrangements can be made on arrival. Flying time to Mérida is two hours from Havana, two hours and 40 minutes from New Orleans. Be sure your local airlines office or travel agent has up-to-date schedules of flights to Mérida. Mine didn't, and the resulting foul-up cost me a day.

And you might stop at the desk at the Mérida Airport and find out what happened to my $1.60.

—Sports Illustrated, 1958

Reflections of a
Lousy Wingshot

I hunted bobwhite quail in Arkansas one time with a former Yankee ballplayer and Hall-of-Famer, a superb athlete even after long retirement from professional sport. When he had fired fourteen shots on seven covey rises and collected fourteen birds (to my eight or nine), I asked him if he ever missed. He thought a minute and then said that honestly, he couldn't recall the last time he had missed a bobwhite quail, but then of course he only hunted one or two or, at most, three days a week. It was said in all modesty and I believed him.

I also recall thinking what a dull sport bird-shooting must seem to someone as proficient as that. It would be like watching a ball game knowing for sure who was going to win, or reading a murder mystery knowing from page one who done it. Whereas, gents, when I swing on a bobwhite or dove or woodcock, it is close to even money that the bird will continue in perfect health after I've pulled the trigger.

Oh, I have my days, of course, as we all do. I had my limit of ten Arizona whitewings with twelve cartridges one morning, and figured I had the whole thing licked, dove-wise, once and for all. And so informed anybody in our party who would listen, that evening, so that next morning I had a mildly interested gallery when I shot off a full box of 8's for barely enough doves to feed a small, not very hungry schoolgirl.

And the truth is, I like it that way. Not that I enjoy shooting poorly, because I don't. But if I were as good and consistent a wingshot as that old ball player, I'd give up bird-hunting and find something more unpredictable. A large part of the excitement of bird-shooting is simple suspense, and when I walk up on a covey of bobwhite and step in ahead of Old Joe the senile setter who's locked up tighter than the Bank of England at midnight, not only am I in suspense as to how many birds are going to get up and what direction they're going to fly—I'm also in suspense as to whether this is going to be one of those days when I couldn't hit the Empire State Building from across 34th Street (or if I did hit it, would only wing-tip it and have a runner on my hands).

But it's the bad days, I keep telling myself, that make the good days so satisfactory, and a diet of nothing but caviar must get awfully tedious. I remember one time when a men's magazine sent me to Czechoslovakia to report on the hunting there. Through the Ministry of Forests, which has charge of most hunting in the country, I was invited to join a party of paying gunners, mostly German and Austrian, at a famous shooting preserve not far from Prague, and was assured I'd enjoy the finest driven-pheasant shooting in that part of Europe.

But on arriving at the former Habsburg estate we found that the master of the shoot had been told only that a journalist would join the party, and had expected the guest to be armed only with a typewriter. He was upset when he learned from my interpreter that I was to shoot, and I didn't blame him, as the safety of the party was his responsibility and for all he knew I might never have seen a shotgun before. Reluctantly, he assigned me, on the first drive of the day, to a corner of the field where I couldn't have shot anyone else even if I had tried to, and also, I expected, where there wasn't likely to be much action.

I was shooting a favorite 16-gauge double, with a loden-coated *jaegermeister* assigned to be my loader and keep score on hits and misses; several of the party, I noticed, had matched pairs of guns so that their loaders could hand them a loaded gun the instant they fired the other, in case the birds came in droves. (If you'd like to, you may write to me in care of this publication and explain that pheasants don't come in droves, even when driven.) But soon after the drive started, signalled by the ritual tooting of a hunting horn, an even two dozen ringneck roosters, nicely spaced to allow ample time for reloading, came barreling over the trees and across my stand at various angles, and to everyone's astonishment, and especially mine, I killed the twenty-four of them with twenty-five shells.

By the end of the day I was high gun by a dozen or so birds, with seventy-odd pheasants killed, one pricked and lost, and two clean misses. It was as well as I have ever shot feathered game, and the fact that I went to another preserve near Bratislava the next week, this one specializing in waterfowl, and killed six ducks with twenty-six shells, or maybe it was twenty-seven, doesn't dim the recollection of that great day on pheasants. On the contrary: it's the prevalence of so-so days and occasional downright disastrous days that make the good ones so memorable.

I started a ruffed-grouse season one year, long ago, by lowering the first four birds my Labrador retrievers flushed, even though three of them were difficult snap-shots in heavy cover—a fact I became adept at introducing into conversations on any given topic during the next two weeks. When I got out again and missed the only four birds I put up, I figured I still had a .500 average, which is fancy shooting in any partridge gunner's book. And of course by the end of the season I was down to my usual average of one grouse for every four shots taken, give or take a few grouse (mostly give). But if I were some sort of supershooter who seldom misses a partridge, I wouldn't have enjoyed those wonderful two weeks of self-delusion when I thought I had finally gotten it all together, ruffed-grouse-in-heavy-cover-wise.

In Dublin one time I was invited to shoot driven pheasants as the guest of a syndicate that leased Lord Dunsany's estate 40 miles from the city. There were eight or ten stands each situated so as to provide sporty shooting as the birds came over high trees, with the guns moving from stand to stand always in the same order, so that all during the day I had one of the all-time great Irish trap and live-pigeon shooters on my right, usually 50 to 60 yards distant but sometimes closer. It was a splendid day, with lunch in the richly panelled gun room of the 900-year-old castle built with 20-foot-thick walls by the Danes (''to keep the heat in and the Irish out,'' as Lord Dunsany, son of the famous poet and himself a keen sportsman, explained). Incidentally, some great shooting sport can be arranged for visiting Americans in Ireland, during the season, through the Irish Tourist Bureau in Dublin—remind me sometime to tell you about woodcock shooting not far from Galway City, or the snipe bogs along the Shannon near Athlone.

At the end of that day I was high gun, with something over fifty pheasants credited to me, and I told no one that nearly half of them had been shot while approaching my stand by my sharp-shooting neighbor on the right. When the announcement came that I was high gun I looked his way, and he gave me a solemn, impish, Irish wink—and I don't know to this day if he was trying to make me look bad or make me look good with his poaching, or if he didn't really care either way. I do know that some of those birds were killed at unbelievable distances—but not by me.

(Incidentally, if you're unfamiliar with the economics of driven-bird shooting in Europe or Britain or Ireland, whether grouse or pheasant or snipe or partridge, and are wondering what the gunner does with sixty or seventy pheasants at the end of a good day's shoot, the answer is simple: he does nothing with them. Each gun is entitled to a brace—two birds—and the others are sent to market, to help pay the cost of maintaining the shoot. In some syndicates, guns may elect to take a cash payment instead of their birds. But as always with shooting in most parts of Europe, game is regarded as a cash crop, the same as sugarbeets or sheep; and there are no illusions that the game would survive if hunting were abolished).

And so I plan to go right on being a bum most days and a hero infrequently, remembering and savoring the good days and feeling sorry for those unfortunate super-shots who never, or seldom, fail to bag a bird per shell.

The poor guys don't know what they're missing.

—*Ithacagun Annual*, 1976

First Turkey

If you should ever, through some not likely but on the other hand not utterly inconceivable circumstance, find yourself entered in a flatulence tournament, and if you accept that tenet of the competitive creed that anything worth doing is worth doing well, then by all means arrange to gorge yourself beforehand on prime zebra meat, preferably the backstrap; you will be a shoo-in to win in a breeze, so to speak. The meat of this equine is so rich that in the process of digestion it produces a vast cubic footage of sundry mists and vapors, all of startling pungency and so mephitic as to be hazardous in the vicinity of open fires.

I learned this because it is my practice to shoot nothing of which I do not intend to eat at least a portion, so that when I killed the three Burchell's zebra on my license while hunting near Lake Magadi with Denis Zaphiro, then Senior Warden of the Southern district of Kenya, and Wendell Swank, who once headed Arizona's fish-and-game department and is presently conducting pilot programs in game-cropping for the United Nations in East Africa, and having previously announced my no-eatum-no-shootum policy in a voice vibrant with equal parts of Glenlivet and righteousness, I was forthwith obliged to gnaw on broiled zebra until my jaws ached and the eyes of those downwind of me watered.

This is the principal reason, then, that most of my shooting is at creatures on the wing, as not only are they, in general, a more sporting proposition for the shooter but with the exception of such eminently edible ungulates as eland and gerenuk, and of course the delectable Tommy, they are likely to be a more satisfying proposition for the eater. And if the odd mallard or pintail proves to have been queer for clams or a veritable ancient among Anatidae, at least there is not half a ton of it on hand as in the case of an elderly elk or Methuselish moose.

(Two trips to East Africa have convinced me that big-game hunting is to bird-shooting as a Wagner overture is to a Mozart quartet—or, in the case of solitary woodcocking, perhaps, to a Bach suite for unaccompanied cello—and that by taste and inclination I am, in all such matters, a chamber-music type. True, I'd like someday to take a good Cape buffalo, and perhaps even a really fine greater kudu—but I doubt that any shot at such game, however well placed, could provide greater satisfaction than I've had from a clean-killed downhill grouse on a steep Pennsylvania mountainside or my one honest right-and-left on woodcock in a west-of-Ireland thicket. And although as I write this I'm planning a trip to the Ungava region of northern Quebec for caribou, I have as much pleasure in anticipating the ptarmigan shooting of that splendid region as in the prospect of reducing a reindeer to possession.)

And so, when invited last December to join a party of turkey hunters on a Texas ranch some hundred-odd miles west of San Antonio in Real County, I accepted, and went, although warned (by a very pretty lady, who had shot one) that wild gobblers are, chewability-wise, in a class with underdone innertubes.

My previous experience with Texas had consisted chiefly of a few days at the port of Galveston in the early thirties, while working as a merchant seaman and of having lost an otherwise mint-condition tooth during a politico-philosophical discussion in an I.W.W. meeting hall, and so I was pleased to find, on arriving at the Rancho Real, that at least a portion of that sprawling state is rolling sand hills covered with pines and live oaks, well grassed and well watered, with deep ravines cut through the loose soil by clear-flowing creeks and rivers in whose bottomlands whitetail deer, wild turkey and a number of feral pigs find abundant cover.

In fact some of our party were more interested in deer than in turkeys, and I shall spare you and myself the embarrassment of describing my clean miss one afternoon, of a standing ten-point whitetail at an easy 200 yards, although I have alibis as brilliantly inventive as any you've ever heard. But what most of us wanted was a turkey, especially those (including me) who had never shot one—even though I had been warned that not only are most gobblers in that area (as in most others) killed on the ground, but are even, sometimes, hunted with rifles.

And so I found myself, before dawn the next morning, crouched with another gunner, a local man, in a blind made of slabs of sandstone open at one end and with crude log seats. By peering through the brush heaped high in front of the blind we could see, as dawn dispelled darkness, a baseball-diamond-sized clearing in the piney woods. It was, I'm sure, baited regularly (and quite legally), and before long my companion held finger to lips, and rolled his eyes toward the path behind us. Sure enough, I could hear a faint, almost mouselike scuffling in the pine needles, and when I turned my head very slowly I saw a flock of a dozen turkeys pussyfooting their way through the lingering mist, peering intently at every bush. Ten feet behind the blind the flock stopped, and one of the hens detached herself from the bunch, walked cautiously up to the open end of the blind, peered in at two motionless, breath-holding hunters (one of whom, at least, peered back) and slowly returned to the waiting flock.

When the old girl had whispered something to the others, they turned and scampered back into the brush: end of turkey hunting that morning. We sat awhile, until the sun rose bright and hot, then fell back a long mile to the ranch house and regrouped.

Three days later there had been two deer killed and several missed, but nobody had got a turkey (although a famous wildlife artist in the group had had a shot at one feeding at fifty feet and, although I had seen him go 24/25 on his first attempt at skeet, had missed it cleanly: "Turkey fever?" he had said, in wonderment). But the weather, the whiskey and the company had been first-rate, and the countryside had been beautiful in a soft, un-Texan way, and when I turned in that night I was happy, although the hunt was ended.

In the morning we breakfasted at four-thirty, but at five our host said the cars to pick us up would be an hour late and urged us to relax and have more coffee. When I asked if he'd mind if I wandered back to that first-morning turkey blind, he whistled up a ranch hand with a pick-up truck, and, off I went, wearing a business suit and clutching a Winchester Model 21 bored full and full and with a half a dozen high-brass 4s in my pocket. It was still dark, but the driver dropped me at a path and said it led directly to the blind. I walked in and found it, then walked across the clearing, pulled some sticks into a heap in front of a live oak and sat behind the sticks with my back against the tree and my gun in my lap. It was lighter now, and I recalled our host declaiming on the remarkable eyesight of wild turkeys and especially the Rio Grande subspecies of that area. "A Rio Grande turkey," he had assured us (pronouncing it, proudly, *rye-oh*), "can see through a thin rock."

The lighter it got the more foolish I felt sitting virtually in the open, and when I had about decided to quit making a spectacle of myself and go get in the blind, I saw a movement across the clearing. It was a flock of about a dozen turkeys, tiptoeing cautiously up the same path I had come by and peering right and left. Ten feet behind the blind they stopped, and one of the hens walked cautiously to the open end of the blind and peered in. Then she walked happily back to the flock, which trotted out into the clearing and began scratching and feeding in the grass.

I expected at any moment to be spotted, especially after my nose started itching, but after a few minutes one of the darker-hued, short-bearded spring gobblers (which unlike the old gobblers run with the hens) detached itself from the bunch, and I shot it. This seemed to surprise the other turkeys, which got the hell out of there. Unlike the turkey killed by that pretty lady this young bird was delicate in flavor and texture, and my wife and I ate it for our Christmas dinner. It was far, far tastier and tenderer than zebra, and made me glad I had heeded my host's warning and not hid behind a thin rock.

—The Wild Turkey Book, 1973

How to Put the Whamois on a Chamois

"For God's sake, hurry!" I wanted to holler. "Those people are dying!" That was years ago, as I watched a TV newsreel showing a rescue team of Swiss mountaineers setting out to save some people buried by an avalanche. The team, roped together, started up the slope in slow motion. Clump . . . clump . . . clump. One slow, plodding step at a time. I never did find out if they got there in time to save anyone.

I should have thought of that one November day, a few years ago.

With a rucksack on my back and a 30-06 Remington-*cum*-P.O. Ackley Springfield with a 4X Unertl scope in my mitted hand, I was halfway up a medium-sized snow-blanketed Austrian Alp. I had got that far in a Jeep that had started from the farmhouse where Helmut Dschulnigg had left his car, when even with chains on all four wheels it couldn't buck the drifts. But we still had two steeply uphill miles to go, on foot, through spruce forests and nearly two feet of fresh snow, to get to Helmut's hunting cabin.

And so when Dschulnigg, a man of much mountain experience (in Alaska and British Columbia as well as several European countries), started off with that same deliberate, shuffling, almost slow-motion stride, I skipped on ahead of him. What the hell. I could see the trail, and even though Helmut was nearly twenty years my junior I was in fairly good shape.

So off I went, plunging through the fluffy stuff and casting admiring sideways glances at the magnificent mountain scenery all around us and straight-ahead glances at the forested slope that led up the side of 8,000-foot Tennen Geb. Old stick-in-the-mud Dschulnigg slogged along far behind me, putting one foot in front of the other in slow, metronomic rhythm.

After plowing several hundred yards through the thigh-high drifts I heard a sort of thumping sound, like a distant tom-tom, and thought what an odd place to hear jungle drums. It took me a moment to realize it was my heart beating. Also, something had happened to my breathing, and my lungs were full of broken glass. By the time Helmut came plodding by, not even breathing hard, I had caught my breath and was able to fall in behind him (and behind Helmut's stumpy-legged dog Burgi, who obviously knew more about climbing Austrian mountains than I did and was happy to let her master break trail). Pretty soon both of them were so far ahead of me that the wind drifted snow into the trail, and it was all I could do to follow it.

After a while Helmut waited up for me and offered to carry my rifle; I thought well, he's twenty years younger than me, and I let him. If he had offered to carry *me*, I'd have jumped on his back. By this time I had remembered that TV news clip, and had figured out why those guys started off slow and easy.

About the time I was getting my second (or it might have been third) wind we rounded an enormous boulder and were in front of Helmut's hunting chalet—or rather, in front of one of his hunting chalets: Dschulnigg, proprietor of the ''Sport Und Waffen'' (sport and firearms) sporting-goods store in Salzburg and a leading Austrian sportsman and gunsmith, owns or leases seven chalets in the Salzburg area, so that under almost any conditions of season or weather there'll be good hunting from at least one of them. The one we had arrived at lies on the steep slope of Tennen Geb (Spruce Mountain) above the village of Abtenau, and we had come here to shoot a chamois. (Pronounced ''shammy'' if you're washing your car with a piece of very soft, absorbent leather; pronounced ''sham-wah'' if you want to be stuffy about it and give the correct French pronunciation to the runty ruminant the piece of leather is supposed to have come from but didn't.)

You wonder why I had just come 4,000-odd miles—via Rome, on one of Alitalia's splendid 747s—to shoot a 75-pound animal with horns so pint-sized a Florida Keys deer would sneer at them, that looks like a cross between a poorly designed billy goat and a hunchbacked antelope? And had agreed to pony up several hundred dollars if and when I shot one (or shot at one and missed)? And would wait half a year to get the horns and ''beard'' (more about that ''beard'' later) because it's the custom to keep all trophies until after a big exhibition each March, when the season has ended? Okay, I'll tell you.

I wanted to find out why this ungainly ungulate is one of the most prized trophies in the hunting world. I wanted to learn why some of Europe's greatest sportsmen count that year lost when they fail to add another set of chamois horns to the collection on their trophy-room walls. Also—a tourist at heart—I wanted to see what I had been assured was one of the most magnificently scenic hunting areas in the western world, the Austrian mountains.

There was no trophy room in Helmut's chalet. One of the two rooms was a combination kitchen-dining-living room, the other a sleeping room with four bunks. After a supper of hot soup and wiener schnitzel cooked up by Helmut and washed down with a very drinkable Austrian white wine, we turned in, and it seemed five minutes later that the alarm, set for 6 A.M., went off. During breakfast, Helmut gave me the bad news: it had snowed more during the night, and the radio was broadcasting avalanche warnings for the area.

''We'll hunt today,'' Helmut said, ''but if we don't find a chamois—and in this deep snow they're hard to find, because they take shelter under a thick stand of evergreens, or in caves—we may have to call it quits." He took me out on the porch of the chalet, overlooking the famous Dachstein ("Stone Roof") mountain, and pointed out the slope on which eight school children had been killed by an avalanche a few years before, and the bare sweeps made on the sides of several nearby mountains by avalanches that had swept away parts of the forest as they roared into the valley.

It *was* bad news, because I wouldn't be able to hang around until the snow set firmly enough to reduce the avalanche danger, which might be a week or three weeks. And so, right after a plate full of fried eggs and sausages (obviously cooked up for the American visitor, since this isn't a normal Austrian breakfast), we started out through the deeper-than-ever snow. I was wearing the same rubber-bottomed leather-topped boots I've worn in most of my hunting, to Helmut's undisguised disapproval. "Those are for wearing when you get up at night to go to the outhouse," he scoffed. "What you need here are heavy mountain-climbing shoes with cleated soles, and those snow-proof leggins I showed you at the store." He was right, of course—maybe before I'm too old to walk without a cane I'll learn to listen to guides and local experts. And Helmut was both.

I would have explained to him that par-mocs were good enough for my daddy and by God they were good enough for me, but my feet kept slipping out from under me on the steep slopes and I was too busy picking myself out of snowdrifts. One time, inching along the almost vertical pitch of a slope my feet shot out from under me and I slid fifty feet down the mountain in a cloud of powder snow, holding my rifle high so as not to clog the barrel. Helmut waited patiently while I angled my precarious way back up to the trail through the fresh snow, then gave me his alpenstock and showed me how to use it.

Halfway through the alpenstock lesson (you hold the six-foot, iron-spiked wooden pole in both hands and jab it into the uphill side of the mountain, leaning slightly against it and using it almost the way a canoeist uses a paddle), something caught the corner of Helmut's eye. "*Gams!*" he said, pointing straight up the mountainside. I recognized the German word for "chamois," and looked where Helmut pointed. High above, three tiny black spots were moving across the snow between two clumps of scrubby spruce trees. "Those are chamois," Dschulnigg said, "with just their heads showing above the snow. The first two are does, I think, and the third is probably a buck." I had unslung my rifle, but Helmut said, "Too far. That's at least 400 yards, maybe 450, and they'll take off now they've seen us." As he spoke, the chamois angled up the slope and disappeared behind a ridge of rock. I think Helmut might have tried a long, roundabout stalk if I hadn't been having so much trouble with my footing, but we went on along the side of the mountain, the alpenstock making the going easier.

Even with Helmut breaking trail through the deep snow, I had to stop occasionally to catch my breath. Each time, the scenery below us was spectacular: tiny farmhouses lay miles below us in the valley (through which flowed a trout stream in which, Helmut said, Peter Barrett had caught some fine rainbows two summers previously), and in the crisp, clean air the snow sparkled like a billion diamonds in the sunlight. Frequently, as we walked through clumps of scrub spruce, an upper bough would unload its burden of snow on us; the powdery stuff filled the air like fine-chopped feathers, and Helmut said one of the dangers in avalanche country is suffocation from inhaling powder snow stirred up by big snow slides. I started to say the scenery was almost worth suffocating for, but decided not to tempt fate.

"Speaking of avalanches," Helmut said, "we'll have to leave for Salzburg this evening—more snow tonight could make it dangerous even to get back to the farmhouse. That means we have only about two hours of hunting time left—and frankly, our chances aren't good. In snow this deep the chamois usually get in the thick stands of trees, where the snow doesn't penetrate, and stay there." We headed back toward the chalet along the remnants of an old logging road cut into the side of the mountain, stopping every fifty feet or so to scan the slopes ahead. Then Helmut saw it.

The chamois buck was holed up in a cave near the top of a bare rock slope, 200-odd yards ahead of us and perhaps a hundred yards above the road. Only his horns showed, and even after Helmut pointed them out I had trouble finding them against the bare rock background of the cave's interior, in my 7x35s. We backtracked cautiously, since the animal could have seen us if it had lifted its head a few inches. "We'll climb to his elevation through this stand of spruce," Helmut whispered, "and hope we can get a clear shot at him." It took fifteen minutes to clamber through the thick timber and work our way to the edge of it, moving slowly so as not to spook the quarry, if he was still there. He was—but lying behind a rim of rock that exposed only part of his head and neck.

"We'll wait 'til he stands up," Helmut said. I found a tree, and braced the rifle against it and waited. "You're sighted in for a hundred yards," Helmut said, "and he's about 175. Hold right on the heart." I knew where the heart was if he stood up broadside to us, because before starting out Helmut had taken me to his gun club's range, where I sighted in the 30-06 on a lifesize painting of a *gams* at a measured hundred yards. (Ostensibly this was purely a sighting-in operation, but I'm sure it was primarily to see how well and safely I handled firearms.) But now, watching the chamois through the 4-power glass, I felt sure Helmut had underestimated the range, and that it was at least 250 yards across the snowy expanse. Maybe 300. Even magnified four times the animal looked hardly bigger than a well-fed woodchuck, and I decided to hold an inch or two high when I shot.

Fifteen minutes later I was sorry I hadn't picked a more comfortable tree to brace the rifle against, but the chamois was looking in our direction and I feared to move even slightly. Suddenly the buck jumped to its feet, offering a perfect heart shot; I knew, even as I pulled the trigger, that I had held even higher than I meant to, and was disappointed to see a goatlike creature dashing up the mountainside from the cave. "I'm sorry I missed, Helmut," I said. "You didn't," Helmut said. "That one going up the mountain is a female—she must have been in the back of the cave. But I think you hit him high—he reared up and fell over backward behind the rocks."

"I knew I was too high," I said unhappily. "Let's go find him."

"Not in those boots," Helmut said. "Even with cleats you couldn't walk across that rock slope." He had taken a set of wrought-iron ice spikes out of his rucksack and was strapping them onto his boots. "Go back down to the road," he said, "and I'll cut across the slope. If the chamois's dead, I can bring it down to the road. If it isn't—." He shrugged and started cautiously across the icy slope, with Burgi floundering happily along behind him.

On the drive from Salzburg to Abtenau (past a signpost that pointed to Berchtesgaden 15 kilometers down a side-road), Helmut had explained that Burgi, a smallish, shaggy bitch about the size of an English springer spaniel, was trained to track wounded game, and that to hunt chamois or red deer without a dog to follow up a wounded animal is illegal in Austria. He told me, too, that resident Austrian hunting licenses are granted only after the applicant has passed oral and written examinations on gun safety, game identification and hunting laws and traditions; game limits are set area by area, and in a particular district the game managers will specify that a certain number of trophy specimens may be taken, but require also that small or deformed animals be shot, so that a healthy breeding stock is maintained in each forestry area.

Back down on the logging road I walked a straight line to a spot directly below the cave, then backtracked and paced off the distance: just over 200 yards. I had overestimated it, probably because I hadn't realized how small a chamois is; a full-grown specimen seldom weighs over 100 pounds, and may be closer to 60. (Back in Salzburg the next day I visited the *"Haus Der Natur,"* a natural-history museum just around the corner from Helmut's store, and saw a mounted *gamsbocke* that wasn't much larger than a Chesapeake Bay Retriever.)

But regardless of the reason, the fact was I had made a lousy shot and perhaps merely wounded an animal that might travel a considerable distance before it could be tracked down and put out of its misery, and I felt rotten about it. When Helmut appeared out of a stand of spruce and slid down the slope to the road, he had no chamois. "Probably it's dead," he said, "but we won't know until later. It fell about ten feet onto a ledge behind the overhang, and I can't get down there without a rope, or even see down there. But there's lots of blood, and I'm sure the buck's too badly wounded to move any distance. When the snow's firmer I'll come back with a forester and climbing equipment and bring him out. Right now, we've got to get back to the cabin and start down the mountain." He pointed to clouds that probably meant more snow, and we slogged our way back to the chalet.

A week later, back in New York, I had a letter from Helmut: he had gone back to the mountainside with climbing gear and had found the chamois dead where it had fallen onto the ledge. He had told me that each March an exhibition of trophies is held by the Regional Forestry Office, and until then he couldn't send the horns and the *Gamsbart* (literally, chamois' beard), a small bundle of light-tipped hairs from the animal's back, about six inches long and wrapped at the root end to form a brushlike ornament sometimes worn on Tyrolean hats. I never did find out why it's called a beard in German. The horns, he wrote, would score only about 85 points (to score 100, they'd have had to be ten inches around the curve and thick at the base; mine were nine inches and only medium-thick). In late March they arrived, mounted with part of the skull on a wooden shield, and if they aren't as impressive as a Cape buffalo's boss or a Kenai Peninsula moose's headgear at least they're easy to hang, and wouldn't hog a lot of wall-space in my trophy room if I had a trophy room. And if I ever get a Tyrolean hat I'll wear the *Gamsbart* on it.

Travel's educational, even when you're traveling with a gun, and during this trip I acquired the following educational goodies:

1. Austria is a country of splendid cities and magnificent scenery, with a long tradition of field sports and a ready welcome for the visiting sportsman.
2. Chamois are neither goat nor antelope, but a little of each (although they smell more like the former). They're related to the Rocky Mountain Goat and the Asiatic takin, and are found in the Appenines, the Pyrenees, the Balkans, the Carpathians and the Caucasus Mountains, and in New Zealand where they're an introduced species. The venison is said to be excellent in flavor and texture, but alas, I didn't get a chance to prove it.
3. Vienna, in winter, is gray and drab, but the Austrian people are warm and friendly even when the weather's cold. The blue Danube is a muddy brown, but several Viennese went blocks out of their way to direct me to the Hotel Sacher, where I stayed because I like *Sachertorte*, a chocolate cake named after the hotel a century ago and famous the world over among sweet-toothed overweight guys like me. (Actually the *Sachertorte* at the Sacher Hotel is nothing special, but the coffee may be the best in the world outside Cuba.)
4. Rubber-bottom boots are not the ideal footwear for climbing around in deep snow on steep, slippery mountains.
5. Salzburg is one of the most beautiful cities in the world, with perhaps the greatest musical tradition. (Mozart was born there, and a summer Mozart festival annually attracts music lovers from hundreds of countries. Winter's the off season, but when I asked a bearded youngster, obviously American, sitting next to me at breakfast one morning whether there were any concerts that evening, he said no, but if I'd hang around until next week I could hear him conduct a concert of his own chamber music. I was sorry I couldn't stay.)
6. About 16,000 chamois are shot annually in Austria, of which a percentage are old, deformed, or diseased animals culled to upgrade the herd. There are no limits except the cost, although when a specified number of animals have been taken from a particular section, no further kills may be made there that season. Prices vary from about $100 to $250 for a doe to $150 to $400 for a male, depending on size of horns and the going rates for that neck of *die Walder*. You won't need a permit to bring firearms into Austria, and for chamois a .243 is sufficient rifle (I carried my 30-06 because it's nearly a pound lighter than my .243).
7. European sportsmen rate the chamois high, I think, because hunting it takes them into superbly scenic mountain country (the animals are seldom found below 4,000 feet or above 8,000) in pursuit of a wary quarry that must be skillfully stalked and whose killing usually requires a fairly high degree of marksmanship, under conditions that may range from late-summery to mid-wintry (but are seldom too rugged for even the out-of-condition hunter, as

would be higher-altitude sheep hunting). Under normal circumstances, much of the hunter's satisfaction comes from locating and comparing several trophy specimens before choosing one to stalk, and a friend told me of sitting on a mountainside in mid-August studying three bucks half a mile away, holding his binoculars in one hand and stuffing wild Austrian blueberries into his face with the other. He said by the time he decided which *gamsbocke* was best he was too full of berries to walk half a mile.

Also in favor of the chamois is its abundance, and the ritualistic formalities surrounding the kill. Because I wasn't able to get to my chamois I missed out on this fol-de-rol, which involves dipping evergreen twigs in the animal's blood and presenting them to the successful hunter, and placing a green twig in its mouth as a symbol of its final meal and a sentimental salute to its spirit. I didn't mind skipping this, but to the tradition-minded European sportsman these rituals are important, and give him a sense of kinship and community with hunters past and present. (Walking through the crowded railway station in Vienna, carrying a cased rifle, I was politely greeted with the traditional "Waidmannsheil!" three times by strangers, and returned the traditional reply, "Waidmannsdank!" Literally these mean "Hunter, I salute you!" and "Fellow hunter, I thank you!")

8. Never try to hurry up an Alp.

Meet Ireland's "Mr. Woodcock"

Last November while shooting driven pheasants at Lord Dunsany's castle a few miles north of Dublin—a private shoot run by a syndicate of Dublin sportsmen which accepts visiting Americans as paying guests, not because they really need the money[*] but because most of the syndicate members have both patriotic and business interests in promoting tourism—I noticed that while both the shooter and the beater were fairly casual about pheasants, of which the average bag at a day's shoot is about 200 for eight guns, the real excitement came when the beaters cried " 'Cock up!" or " 'Cock for'rd!" as they shuffled in line through the woods driving the game ahead of them. The " 'cock" in Ireland as in England and Scotland is the woodcock, and because it's a comparatively rare avis and darkly mysterious in its comings and goings, most sportsmen in those countries regard this kingsize snipe as a sort of welcome bonus which sometimes befalls them as they're shooting other, more commonplace species: grouse, partridges, pheasants, snipe, and even woodpigeons.

For example, the count on the two days I shot at the Dunsany estate (4,000-odd acres, teeming with both wild and pen-reared-to-six-weeks pheasants) was 316 pheasants, eight woodcock and three woodpigeons the first day and 176 pheasants, five woodcock, four woodpigeons and a bantam chicken the second day. (The bantam was one of a flock that roams wild around the estate except when being used to hatch out wild pheasant eggs each spring, and made the mistake of flying out of a copse along with a dozen or so pheasants on the last drive of the day, when the light was poor.)

[*]Charges are $140 per gun for a day of driven shooting, $28 per gun for a day of walk-up shooting, including guide, dog, transportation and lunch with drinks at the castle. For information on available dates (between November 1st and January 31st) write to Mr. Arthur Williams, 17 Dawson Street, Dublin.

At lunch in the gun room of the Dunsany castle on the second day, I overheard some of the syndicate members talking about woodcock, and when they began swapping stories about a man named John Buckley, who specializes in shooting 'cock in the area around his County Galway home and who was reputed to kill upwards of four hundred a season and to own the best woodcock dogs in the country, I asked Arthur Williams, the Dublin realtor who captains the syndicate, what the chances were of my catching up with Buckley and persuading him to show me some of his secrets. Williams said he'd try to arrange it, and asked if I could come back the first week in January, when the weather should be "hard" enough to freeze the birds out of the mountain tops and high bogs and concentrate them in the lowland thickets and forests, where they'd be reasonably accessible.

I said I could and would, and went back to New York. Shortly after the holidays I boarded an Irish International Airlines jet at Kennedy Airport, had an Irish whiskey, had another, had dinner, had an Irish coffee, fell asleep. woke up a few minutes out of Shannon Airport next morning, had breakfast, disembarked, rented a car and drove sixty miles due north to Galway, where I admired again the strange gray beauty of that city, checked in at the Great Southern Hotel, drank a quick pint of Guinness to get the taste of typewriter out of my mouth, and found a message from Williams: John Buckley wasn't available, and he himself was deep in some urgent real-estate negotiations, but he had arranged for another man to take me woodcock shooting.

He had, too. The man was a large, genial Galwegian named Sean Murphy who had hunted woodcock in the area all his life but who, it developed, had been so distraught at the loss of a favorite setter two years before that the shooting heart had mostly gone out of him; to oblige his friend Williams and me, a guest in his land, he took his gun down off the pegs, borrowed a handsome if addle-pated Irish setter, and took me wood-cocking. But although I liked Sean and enjoyed his company, whether we were slogging through boggy meadows or helping each other buttress the bars at every country pub we passed, and although he found woodcock, he wasn't the man I had come for. And by this time, I sensed that John Buckley, for reasons of his own, had no interest in going along with my project; when I tried to work up some resentment about this, I discovered that I couldn't think of a single reason why he should.

On the contrary, I thought of lifelong friends and old college roommates who would unhesitatingly go my bail or give me the button-down shirts off their backs but who would no more reveal their favorite woodcock covers to me than they'd suck eggs or shake a martini.

And so, when at the Great Southern bar that evening I heard that John Huston, who lives not far from Galway City and is now an Irish citizen, and about whom I had been asked to write an article, was back from Rome and at his house at Craughwell for a few days, I thought to hell with the woodcock story, telephoned Huston, made an appointment to see him the next day, and did so.

When I told Huston I had hoped to do a story about Ireland's "Mr. Woodcock" but hadn't had much luck with it, Huston said, "I don't know whom you had in mind, but there's a chap lives the other side of Galway who's a friend of mine and knows an awful lot about woodcock. If you'd like, I could put you onto him." "What's his name?" I asked, and when Huston said "Buckley" I asked if he could arrange a meeting. "No trouble at all," said Huston, and picked up a telephone; ten minutes later I had a date to shoot woodcock with John Buckley the next morning.

While waiting the next morning for the legendary Mr. B. to come by and pick me up, I ran over in my mind what I already knew about woodcock. I had hunted them in New York, New Jersey, Pennsylvania, and New Hampshire, where there are some resident birds but where the shooting is mainly at migrating woodcock as they drift down each fall from Maine and from Canada's maritime provinces, where they nest and breed, to the wintering grounds in Louisiana, Texas, and the Gulf area. Because they depend for food almost entirely on worms, which they pluck from the depths of soft mud with their long, flexible beaks, a sudden hard freeze can send them barreling southward overnight, pausing to rest during daylight and flying from dusk to dawn. A nocturnal species, they may dawdle for a week or more at favorite spots along the migratory route if the weather doesn't push them, laying up in thick cover during the daytime and feeding by night.

Because woodcock frequent the same covers year after year, until the vegetation or trees undergo a change through growth, fire or cutting, and because these patches of cover may be no more than a few yards in diameter and no different, to the human eye, than a score of similar places along the same hillside, a woodcock hunter who stumbles onto one of these hot spots seldom gets up and announces its location at the next meeting of his rod-and-gun club. On the contrary he locks the secret in his heart along with perhaps a dozen other such covers, and damned well *keeps* it locked.

Thus the hard-core, card-carrying woodcock hunter in the eastern United States will, when seeking this species, usually go from cover to cover and waste no time in "hunting blind"; he may park his car, walk a quarter mile up the hillside to an alder clump, kick around it, flush a woodcock, shoot (or shoot at) it, walk back to the car and drive a mile or two or ten to the next cover on his itinerary.

Interestingly, when he repeats the circuit a day or two later the same covers will hold replacements, if the birds are still migrating through the area; nobody knows for sure why a specific cover will always attract them but it does, and obviously the woodcock is able to spot it from the air and settle in, as easily as you recognize a motel sign when you're migrating by car and know it means food and shelter.

I knew, too, that the European woodcock is roughly twice as large and heavy as its North American counterpart (twelve to fourteen ounces, on an average, against five to seven ounces), and that in its migratory pattern Ireland is the terminus for a large number of 'cock that summer in Finland, northern Russia, Norway and Sweden, just as Louisiana is the end of the line for vast numbers of woodcock that nest in Canada and the northern United States. Other Scandinavian and Russian birds winter in the south of France and keep going into Spain and Portugal; some cross the Mediterranean into Africa, and in southern Morocco one time I was told that during the ferocious winter of 1962–63 large numbers of woodcock arrived there in November and sat out the winter in the cork-oak forests.

Although some woodcock-banding was done in Europe as far back as the 1890s, there has not been enough to provide any solid information on migration routes. No one knows for sure what proportion of the migration comes directly from Norway to Scotland across

300 miles of storm-swept North Sea and what proportion follows the European land-mass through Denmark, Germany, Holland, Belgium, and France before crossing the Channel to England (in which case they're going north for the last leg of their journey). No one knows how many of the migrants to Ireland come through, or from, Scotland, and for that matter no one can say what percentage of the woodcock wintering in Ireland are permanent, nonmigratory residents.

In short, the European woodcock, *Scolopax rusticola*, is a first-flight, full-fledged, fine-feathered mystery even to professional ornithologists, and until coordinated, cooperative banding and band-collecting programs are set up in all nesting and wintering countries it's likely to remain so. Even when the verdict is finally in on migration routes and by-routes, the woodcock hunter will still find bafflement in the way all woodcock in an area seem to vanish into thin air at times, and their uncanny predilections for certain spots of cover or even for a particular bush or shrub.

Buckley had said he would pick me up at ten o'clock, and at 9:59 he popped through the lobby door and greeted me cordially. A husky, medium-height, clean-shaven man who looked as though he might have captained a small midwestern college football team in the early forties, he was wearing a well-tailored shooting jacket and knickers of thorn-proof tweeds, with canvas leggings over high-topped waterproof shooting shoes, and looked fitter than a fiftyish business man is supposed to. When he had loaded my cartridge bag, lunch, flask, binoculars, camera, sweater and 12-gauge skeet-bored Winchester Model 21 into his small station wagon, Buckley drove east along the north shore of Galway Bay, then south toward Kinvara and the mountains beyond.

On the way, he explained that he had first hunted woodcock when living as a business man in France after World War II, and that the French *becassiers*, or woodcock hunters, were among the world's most dedicated; it was there he had learned much of the lore and methodology that he now applied in pursuit of the Irish birds.

The first big flights of 'cock generally arrive in the west of Ireland on the first full moon in November, Buckley said, and depart on the first full moon in March. On arriving they settle in the high hills and mountains, and are scattered so widely and thinly that hunting is unproductive, although a man with a good dog might find a few birds in a day's walking through high country. After the first frosts the 'cock move into the swales and valleys, where the ground is still soft, but it's only after a really hard freeze that they concentrate in the forests and thickets, where by scraping away a layer of leaves and duff they can still get their beaks into the unfrozen ground. (This beak, incidentally, is equipped with a flexible tip that can open to grasp a worm or grub while the entire apparatus is buried to the hilt in mud, and has its own nervous system that detects insect movements in the ground. Because the woodcock spends so much time with its beak plunged deep into soft earth its eyes are located near the top of its head and set back toward the rear; when flying, the woodcock has to point its beak toward the ground in order to see where it's going.)

We were in high, wild, mountainous country now, looking out over thousands of acres of low-growing gorse and heather and grass punctuated with outcrops of weathered limestone and an occasional clump of rhododendron and scrub oak; near the top of the hill Buckley parked the car and we unloaded guns and dogs. One thing woodcock detest,

Buckley said, is being dripped upon, and when a thaw sets in after a frost, as it had the previous day, the birds clear out of the thick stuff to avoid the drip of melting frost and spread out through the open fields and moorland; this place, he said, was a bit on the hairy side for walking but sometimes produced well after a thaw and was worth a try.

John let the dogs out of the back: two small English setters, a dog and a bitch, each with a bronze bell on its collar, and a Labrador retriever. As we swung out across the moor, with the setters working ahead of us and the Lab staying closely at heel, he explained that the bells were obtainable only in France, where they are made for that purpose; they differed slightly in tone, so that in heavy cover he could tell by the bells which dog was where.

The dog had been trained to work wide, John said, and the bitch to work fairly close; when either of the bells stopped jangling he knew instantly that the wearer was on point, and knowing which general direction the bell had last been heard from he would whistle the other setter in with a "silent" high-frequency whistle and send it in that direction. When the second bell stopped as the dog honored its mate's point he was able to judge the bird's position fairly accurately, and knowing which way the 'cock was likely to fly he would station his companions and himself so as to have the best chance for a fair shot. *Then, with guns in position, he would send the Labrador retriever to flush the bird.*

"A woodcock," John said, "will almost always fly to light—toward the sun, usually, but sometimes toward the most open spot in the woods. This means you can have a pretty good idea which way he'll fly when flushed, and can place yourself and any other guns accordingly." I recalled hearing the same thing from veteran woodcock hunters about the North American bird, and having boned up before leaving for Ireland I recalled that the American woodcock's scientific handle is *Philohela minor*, and that most people think "philohela" means "sun-lover," an odd name for a nocturnal bird. Actually, the Greek "hela" means bog, which makes better sense.

We had been walking and climbing up and down steep, slippery hillsides and weather-worn limestone outcrops so rough and rutted that each step was an adventure—twice I had stumbled into ancient potholes and was lucky not to have dented either my gun barrels or skull—and after two hours of steady plodding and scrambling we had seen one lone woodcock go out ahead of us; even the dogs were beginning to be discouraged. Topping a rise I saw the station wagon ahead; we had walked a wide but birdless circle.

Over a tailgate lunch of cold chicken, Irish brown bread, and Irish ale I asked John whose land we were on, and learned it was one of a number of so-called "shooting lettings" he leases from the Irish Land Commission; yearly rentals are low enough that almost any serious shooter of moderate means can afford to lease a few hundred acres of game-producing land, and it's possible to rent the shooting rights to four or five thousand acres, in some remote sections, for under $100 a year. (Having rented it you're entitled to keep other shooters the hell off of it, but in practice this would mean hiring a bailiff or gamekeeper, as there are always a few local patriots who feel that poaching helps to maintain a national tradition.)

Through a mouthful of chicken I asked John if many serious 'cock shooters used cocker spaniels today, since this breed was originally developed to cope with the woodcock (by picking the runts from springer spaniel litters and mating them with other runts until they bred true). Buckley said that a few traditionalists still favored cockers but that in his mind there was no substitute for a pointing dog, nor any doubt that in general the best pointing breed for the purpose was the English setter. I told him that in my own upland hunting, for whatever species, I let my Labrador retrievers work out in front of me and tried to get up close enough for a shot when I saw them making game, or hoped the bird would flush in my direction, and that John Ward and Norman Slade, perhaps the leading woodcock connoisseurs in the American Midwest, used the same system. Buckley nodded politely, as if I had said I always put a little chocolate syrup in my whiskey highballs, and suggested we get back to hunting.

(By this time, probably, a few readers will have planned to write indignant letters pointing out that "hunting," in Ireland as in England, means fox hunting, and that the correct term for my activity is "shooting." They're wrong. Much gamebird shooting in both countries consists of stationary shooters with birds being driven over them, and it would be incorrect and inaccurate to describe this as "hunting." But when gunners tramp around the British Isles searching for (i.e., hunting) game, the term "hunting" is properly used, even though the British prefer "rough-shooting" or "walking up." On the other hand, when an Irishman says he's going hunting or refers to hunting clothes, he means fox hunting.)

Four hours, a lot of miles and no woodcock later we were back at the car. I was tired and disappointed, especially as Buckley had indicated earlier that one day was all he'd be able to take off from his busy schedule; although I had picked up a good bit of information I had yet to see those setters find a woodcock or John Buckley fire a shot from his 12-gauge detachable-sidelock Purdey. Then, while we were casing our guns, John said, "I think we may do better tomorrow," and I felt better.

On the way back to Galway we stopped at Paddy Burke's in Clarenbridge for a plate of the best oysters I've ever eaten and a pint of Guinness. Patrick A. Burke, the fifth generation of Patrick Burkes to be hosts at this fine pub, greeted us (and explained, when I asked about it, that the bottle of black-labeled Tennessee sour-mash whiskey on the bar was kept there because it's a favorite of John Huston, who stops in frequently). Over the oysters (which come out of Galway Bay a few hundred feet from the pub) I asked John Buckley what makes a good woodcock hunter, and he said it was partly a knowledge of the birds, partly an ability to snap-shoot, and mostly having good dogs and knowing how to work them. When I asked what kind of knowledge he meant, John said it was knowing, for example, that after woodcock settle in for the winter they won't tolerate much disturbance, and will clear out of a cover if it's hunted more than once or twice in a season (which is why he leases enough land to eliminate the need to over-shoot any one part of it); it was knowing that usually after trees in a cover have grown much higher than twelve feet the 'cock look for more congenial habitat; it was knowing that 'cock usually lie along the edges of a wood rather than deep inside, especially in the evening as they're preparing to move out to feed in the meadows or cow pastures, where worms are easy to come by; it was knowing that after a night of bright moonlight woodcock are likely to have fed heavily and to be logey, close-setting, and slower-flying than usual.

But the really important thing, John said, is to have good pointing dogs, keen of nose and willing to work cover thoroughly, since the 'cock is ordinarily a staunch-holding bird that may let you actually step on him before he'll flush. As woodcock are virtually invisible on the ground, blending their rich brown-and-black coloration into almost any woodland flooring, the gunner without dogs may walk miles through cover that is filthy with woodcock and flush only an occasional bird, or none.

The next morning we headed in another direction; half an hour after leaving the city we turned off the main road into a trail that struggled through forest so lush it reminded me of tropical jungle. There were signs of logging, and John said this was Forest Department land to which he leases the shooting rights. When the trail petered out we parked the car, turned the dogs loose and started down one of the "rides," or cleared lanes, that traverse the heavy growth.

Less than a hundred feet from the car the bitch stiffened in a point near the edge of the tangle; John motioned me on down the ride to cover one flank while he backed off to cover the other. I noticed he had positioned me so that the 'cock, if it flew toward the clouded sun, would give me the shot. The retriever had stayed close at heel; at a wave of John's hand he plunged into the thicket and the bird jumped and flew over my head, giving me a perfect station-eight skeet shot, which I missed a good two feet behind. I heard John's gun, and swung around to see the 'cock tumbling into the woods behind me.

While the Lab was retrieving the dead bird, John told me the dog setter's bell had gone silent while we had been getting in position; he whistled the bitch to his side and sent her into the woods. We could judge her progress roughly by the bell, and when it too went silent we had a good fix on the bird. This time he sent me on down the path to an intersecting ride, with instructions to cover both clearings from the corner. Then, having backtracked to put more room between us, he sent the retriever in the direction of the bird. A few seconds later it came over me high, and I connected with a load of 8's; while retrieving the downed bird I heard John shoot, and in a minute he came down the ride carrying a dead woodcock.

Each setter must have been on point on a separate bird, John said, and my shot had turned the second 'cock in his direction; at any rate it was evident we had hit a woodcock jackpot, and before we went back to the car for lunch John had five birds in his gamebag and I had three (and should have had five or six others, as John had consistently given me the choicest stand; unfortunately he couldn't do much about my shooting). In all we had flown nearly twenty woodcock in two hours, and had had shots at all but five or six.

During another tailgate lunch John told me there are several gun clubs up and down the west coast that hold driven woodcock shoots during the season (September 1st to January 31st); at these affairs, ten guns might account for a hundred 'cock in a day, or the figure might be as low as twenty. I mentioned that Sean Murphy had taken me flighting one evening: because woodcock flying out of a woods at dusk to feed in open fields will follow the same route night after night (and year after year), local shooters know these spots and may take up positions along the flyway at dusk, snap-shooting as the birds pass overhead in the near darkness. Later I learned that some European sportsmen disapprove of flighting as being too easy; this bemused me, as I hadn't been able to see the birds, much less hit them.

After lunch we walked in another direction, coming out on a half-acre outcrop of bare limestone in the midst of thick scrub oak, laurel, and birch. While the setters worked the edges of the thickets we stood on the table of rock; when they went on point the retriever was sent to flush and almost always the 'cock flew toward us, since we were in a clear and therefore lighter section. But the shooting was tricky, as the bird usually flew directly at us and a shot would have endangered the dogs; they had to be taken after they had passed and were going away. I snap-shot at one as it zipped behind a holly tree, and was surprised to find it dead, although only a few pellets could have got through the thick leafage. In all, the odd outcrop produced ten birds flown and six killed. As we walked back to the car, in the early dusk, two 'cocks got up in front of me from the edge of the ride and I killed both; as John had predicted they were coming to the edge of the woods preparatory to flying to feed, preferring to take off from open ground rather than through the heavy foliage of the woods.

When I thanked John that evening over an Irish whiskey for a grand day of sport and for all his kindness, I couldn't refrain from one parting and inevitable question: Is it true that woodcock sometimes carry their young in flight between their legs, as so many qualified observers claim to have witnessed, or is this a superstition, as so many equally qualified observers profess to believe. "I've been waiting for that one," John said. "And my answer is: let's have another whiskey."

That night, while I was having a nightcap at the Great Southern bar, a man standing beside me said he understood I had been shooting with John Buckley, and I said I had. "He's a great man for the woodcock, all right," the man said. "I've heard tell that when strangers want to go shootin' with him and learn all his secrets, he takes them up in the hills and runs them so ragged they mostly decide that no woodcock is worth it. Sort of a test, you might say, that not many pass. I suppose it might be a true story." I said I supposed it might be, bade him goodnight, went to bed, and dreamed of woodcock as big as turkeys.

For the U.S. sportsman wanting to try his hand and his gun at this great wingshooting sport, there are several approaches. Simplest is to sign up with one of the travel agencies that specialize in neatly packaged shooting trips. You may pay a few dollars more in this case but if your time's worth much more than the Wages and Hours minimum you'll likely end up dollars ahead over do-it-yourself arrangements. (Bear in mind that in Ireland, as in most of Europe, there is no such thing as free shooting; game is the private—and valuable—property of the landowner; you won't see any posted land because it's understood that permission to shoot or fish is required.)

Another worthwhile procedure is to write to the Irish Tourist Board, 590 Fifth Avenue New York City, telling them what type of shooting you're most interested in and the dates you plan to be in Ireland; they'll send you a list of shoots open to visiting sportsmen, with information and rates. They'll also provide a list of "sporting hotels" which either own shooting rights in their areas or have arrangements with local gun clubs, landowners or ghillies (guides).

Still another procedure, if you're adventuresome and extroverted, is to come without making arrangements of any kind; bring rough clothes and a gun or two (but no dogs, unless you're willing to wait while they sweat out six months of compulsory quarantine), and check into any good hotel in the west of Ireland; having checked in, head for the nearest pub. You'll be spotted for an American as soon as you order a drink, and asked why you've come to Ireland; when you say it's to shoot woodcock, it's even money someone will offer to take you out shooting, or at least to introduce you to his cousin Mick who knows more about woodcock than any man in the parish and wouldn't mind to be taking the day off tomorrow. This is risky, since in their high-voltage hospitality and with the best of intentions your benefactors may lead you up a few woodcock-less alleys; on the other hand you'll meet some interesting people, hear a lot of splendid talk and perhaps even luck your way into some first-rate shooting. But it's not for the man on a tight schedule.

One last tip: legal closing time for Irish pubs is eleven o'clock; and it's usually strictly observed. (But not always. In a country pub in County Clare one time, after a day of snipe shooting, I realized it was after one A.M. When the publican came by with an armload of peat for the fire I asked him when he closed. "Ah," he said thoughtfully, "sometimes for a week in December.")

—*True Magazine*, 1967

Jungle Stuff

While wheezing and choking on the mixture of fly ash and carbon monoxide that passes for air in New York City, I read recently that one-fifth of all the oxygen in the earth's atmosphere is generated by the 575 million acres of tropical forest in the Amazon basin. Or maybe it was one-fiftieth. At any rate it was a lot of O_2, and I recall hoping that some of it might seep up to Manhattan. Then, by Jorge, a friend telephoned to ask if I'd like to fly down to Brazil and spend a few days on a houseboat on the Araguaia River, fishing and birdwatching and loafing. And even if the air in the Great Metropolis hadn't been lumpier than usual that day, I'd have said yes.

Quickly getting together my passport and Kaopectate, I hurried aboard a Braniff DC-8 late the next night, and after sleeping through a Miami stop, woke up in Panama City's airport at first daylight; another stop at Lima, and we flew south along the spectacular coast, then almost due east, across Lake Titicaca and the Andes, to Rio de Janeiro. At the airport, awaiting my luggage, I was startled by a mass howl of anguish and horror so shattering that I thought the other end of the airport building had collapsed, mashing thousands into a bloody pulp. Not so, it developed, but something almost as tragic: underdog Czechoslovakia had just scored the first goal against Brazil in the World Cup *futbol* eliminations in Mexico. Happily, *Futboler* Pele and his mates rallied to win handily, or footily, and all through that night delirious fans whooped and cavorted outside my hotel room facing the Copacabana Beach (where, before turning in, I had found votive candles burning in pits dug in the sand, sometimes with licorice sticks and chocolate bars arranged decoratively around the flickering, untended flame; "Offerings to the water gods for today's victory," a Brazilian told me. "We are a people of many deities.").

The next morning, to Brasilia on a Varig Boeing 737. From the air it appears to be an artificial city surrounded by genuine slums, but the bush pilot who met us said we had no time for sightseeing; it was a three-and-a-half-hour flight northwestward to the

145

landing strip machete'd out of the jungle alongside the houseboat's mooring, and he would have to return that same day, before dark. He had a German name and a thin, handsomely Teutonic face, and read Mickey Mouse comic books intently as soon as the single-engine Piper Cherokee reached altitude.

The houseboat, I had been told, was usually tied up at the northern end of a 200-mile-long, 50-mile-wide island in the Rio Araguaia, and the pilot set aside his reading to point it out to me on a detail map. The world's largest river island, with its own system of rivers, it has been set aside as the Isla Bananal National Park and Indian Reserve. By studying the map carefully, I finally found its southern end, where the north-flowing river splits to create the island. But this is flat, heavily forested flood plain, with water heights that vary as much as fifteen feet between rainy and dry seasons, where channels and meanders and horseshoe lakes make a pattern so complex that the river may have five or six island-separated channels at low water, and be a five-mile-wide watery expanse in the rainy season.

Long before the houseboat came in sight, I had seen enough forest to convince me that Brazil has to be a prime producer of oxygen, even though part of our flight was over treeless hills and broad expanses of wetland; some of that splendid gas was being consumed, however, by vast brush fires in the hills, probably set deliberately to help clear ground or improve grazing; as we moved north into the heavy stuff, the true "Mato Grosso," or thick forest, there were fewer fires, then none. We picked up the Araguaia River and followed it for an hour; finally Fritz folded a half-read Donald Duck and skillfully plunked the Piper down on a rutted mud runway at the river's edge, taxiing us almost to the gangplank of the houseboat.

The 75-foot-long Jungle Queen, looking like an enormous white floating shoe box topped by a pilothouse, was tied to some trees on a mud bank at the end of the airstrip. I teetered down the gangplank and was greeted by the craft's owner, Andre Rakowitsch, a fiftyish, mustachioed, Austrian-born, English-speaking Brazilian. Andre showed me my room, one of eight double-bunked cubicles, each sharing a shower and washbasin with another room, and asked if I played chess; he seemed pleased when I said I did. He took me aft to show me the houseboat's engine room: three smallish Swedish outboard motors hooked to a bar between the two welded-steel pontoons that support the superstructure (and draw twenty inches under full loading).

"Twenty-four horsepower!" Andre said, pointing at the engines. "Each?" I asked, hardly believing a piddling 72-horsepower could propel the hulking vessel. "Altogether!" Andre replied, beaming at my astonishment. "Eight horses each! Wait and see—we go downriver pretty soon." He hurried off to mobilize the crew of ten, all recruited from river villages in the area, while I slipped into something comfortable. Informality was the watchword, and a blond young Englishman named Rodney, who seemed a sort of social director and chief bos'n combined, padded about in bare feet night and day.

By the time I had changed into shorts and sandals, the Jungle Queen was under way. "She makes six knots with all motors," Andre told me in the wheelhouse, "but even on one motor, she goes nicely. How I get into houseboat business? Ha! I use to be in white hunter business: four tents that must be set up every night and taken down every morning because we move every day. Clients that get angry when I am unable to produce a world-record jaguar in five days and even angrier when I don't produce any jaguars at all. *Senhor*, you would be surprise how difficult it is to find a jaguar in this jungle when you need one! Finally, I figure must be easier way to make a living. Such as houseboat. You don't take it down in the morning and carry it around all day and set it up again at night. And instead of crawling around in scratchy jungle looking for unexisting jaguars, you lie in sun, or fish, or drink, or read or count birds, or watch porpoises. That is how I got in the houseboat business. Excuse me, I go and see the cook so we don't have blue food.''

Later I learned that the cook, capable but recruited locally, was under the impression that all foreigners adored the color blue, and on several occasions, using vegetable dyes, had tinted meat, potatoes and vegetables a rich cerulean to welcome guests aboard. I wondered about the porpoises, too, since we were nearly a thousand miles from salt water, but on going topside as we slid down the river, I saw three cavorting alongside, and the pilot, another local river man, told me they were one of two fresh-water species found in the Amazon basin.

There are also, of course, piranhas, those savage predators of the Amazonian water-world. Fishing with a casting rod and ordinary bass plugs and spoons, I caught scores of them. They weighed from a few ounces up to three pounds and were of three different species. Any of the piranhas will assault a lure cast into still or slow-moving water in eddies, bayous and backwaters, and I soon learned that a wooden plug lasted for only four or five fish before it was savaged to splinters. Plastic plugs lasted longer, but the larger fish crunched treble hooks into twisted tangles. Even the enamel finish of metal lures was soon chipped off by the scalpel-sharp teeth, and wire or braided-wire traces proved essential.

The prize sport fish of the area is the tukunare, or peacock bass, a gaudily handsome, perch-like fish that averages three or four pounds and grows to ten or twelve. These coexist peacefully with the piranhas, but if one takes a lure and gets tangled in the roots or vines along the bank, there's an explosive flurry that lasts five to ten seconds, and the lure comes back with only the tukunare's head remaining. Piranhas generally came to the boat untouched by their brethren and, with the help of a pair of pliers to avoid having one's fingers amputated, were released more or less intact.

Yet that evening, when we had pulled up to a sandbank and moored the Jungle Queen to some stakes driven into the sand, most of us—there were five other guests—went swimming, on assurances that piranhas never frequent water with any substantial current. As we swam every day and none of us was even partially devoured, the information may have been correct.

There were other fish, of course. One evening, casting a floating bass plug into an eddy the size of a supermarket parking lot, I hooked into a 45-pound pirarara, a spectacularly ugly catfish that rose to the three-inch plug like a trout to a dry fly. I boated it after a half-hour of strenuous work; the same eddy produced a 10-pound bicuda, a pike-like fish that leaps like an Atlantic salmon, and in addition, the usual dozen or so piranhas. There are also air-breathing lungfish, called pirarucu, and a catfish called piratinga, both of which occasionally grow to 500 pounds (I was informed), but nothing so ostentatious took my lures. Generally these monsters are fished for at night, with heavy saltwater tackle baited with whole dead fish or chunks of fish.

To get bait, the crew would take two or three of the fishing boats after dark, cruise around the shallows until they located a school of herring-like fish each about 10 inches long, then run the boat back and forth through the school at high speed until enough bait-fish, scattering to escape what they probably mistook for a porpoise, had jumped into the boat. I found this as much fun as the fishing, and one night two boats came back, after 20 minutes, with more than 60 baits.

Some visiting sportsmen, I was told, sleep all day and fish all night for the really big pirarucu and piratinga, considering anything under 100 pounds a dwarf. One method is to bait with a half-pound chunk of catfish or a brace of herrings on a single hook and drift with the current for a mile or two, then run back upriver and drift down again. When a fish is hooked, it's permitted to tow the boat around until it's exhausted or breaks off. Another procedure is to tie up to the bank or a snag, chuck a large bait into an eddy and let it soak until something happens. (Generally what happens is that smaller fish nibble it to nothing, and rebaiting is necessary every 10 or 15 minutes.) I spent two evenings at this latter gambit but couldn't connect with anything larger than my previous 45-pounder, and gave up just about the time (probably) things were hotting up.

In addition to the two outsize catfish species, I saw an enormous black animal surface twice along the edge of the river, and later heard it—or something—chasing bait-fish back in the flooded brush along the banks. This, I was told by the excited crewman with me, was not a porpoise, although about the same size, but a "devil fish"; it seemed to breathe air, had a hump on its back and looked something like a manatee, but Andre assured me the devil fish was a myth, so I may not have really seen and heard it.

Monkeys chattered in the trees along the river but couldn't be seen in the lush jungle growth. Tapir tracks criss-crossed most sandbars, and we spotted one tapir about the size of a baby hippo swimming in the river, and watched it scramble up the bank. Capybaras, the world's largest rodents, were seen twice on sandbars, and alligators could be "shined" along the river's edge every night with a strong flashlight; the only 'gator I saw in daylight came charging out of a clump of roots toward a plug I had cast in toward shore, but thought better of it when he saw the boat. (All fishing was done from a fleet of eight 15-foot aluminum boats with 10-horsepower outboard motors; these were towed behind the houseboat while we cruised each day to a new location.)

There are Indians back in the bush, but none showed while we were there. Bird life was abundant, and I regretted not having brought a field guide. Parrots flew over the forest roof in squawking flocks, and I counted what seemed to be five species of kingfisher. Herons, skimmers, tern, plovers and other aquatic species abounded. Binoculars are essential for the traveler here.

One morning, after we had tied up overnight alongside an overgrown bank, I jumped ashore and walked into the jungle to see what it was like in there. The going was rough, through vines and thorny brush, and a few feet back from the river there was no visible indication of the water's direction, although I could hear one of the crew singing. I went further back, and when I came to a dry stream bed, the undergrowth thinned so I could see fresh tapir tracks in the sand. Then it occurred to me that nobody had seen me come ashore, and if Andre decided to move the Jungle Queen, they might think I had fallen overboard; between the piranhas and the alligators, there would be little point in their looking for my body, and after some no-doubt interesting experiences, I would end up as a shrunken head in a São Paulo curio shop. So I got the hell back to the boat.

The Jungle Queen had a bar stocked with what in Portuguese are called *wheeskey, jeen, room* and Coca-Cola (for mixing with the *room*), as well as soft drinks. The upper deck is ideal for sunbathing, and I was assured that during the Queen's mid-May to mid-October season, even a light shower is a rarity. Normally the boat makes Monday-to-Monday cruises of the river with up to sixteen passengers. The fare is $550, including the air taxis from Brasilia to the river base and return. There are modest rental fees for fishing tackle and individual fishing boats, but you can bring your own tackle: a bait-casting rod and reel, with 20-pound-test line, and a few dozen plastic plugs and metal spoons are all you'll need.

Just before the cruise ended, Andre remembered I played chess, and hauled out a battered set. He clobbered me in two quick games, with some sort of sneaky Viennese gambit, and when he was called away to fix the generator, I hid the board and got one of the crew to take me fishing. I'm pretty good at outwitting fish.

—Sunday *New York Times*, 1971

The Great James Bay
Goose Factory

If you're a goose hunter, a dozen football-sized lumps of blue clay with a piece of white paper stuck on each look like a dozen lumps of blue clay with pieces of white paper stuck on them. But if you're a blue or a snow goose, those lumps sitting in a northern Quebec marsh look like blue or snow geese, and when you spot them from the air you may decide to pay them a visit—after all, where there's a goose, there's likely to be goose food, and you may be ready for lunch.

If you do decide to drop in on them, it may be the last decision you'll make. Because just about the time you're setting your wings to 'chute in among that flimflam flock, a couple of guys are going to rise up from behind those willow branches stuck in the mud, each with a strange black stick in his hands pointing right at you.

And when the sticks go bang, you're dead. Then, from behind another curtain of willow branches, a Cree Indian will stand up, walk out, retrieve you and go back to wait for another gullible goose.

Since you're reading this, you're no goose, so let me tell about what's surely the best and fastest goose shooting in North America—possibly the best anywhere. Some hunters say it's *too* good. The Canadian limit is five geese a day and, in that area, ten in possession, which means that you must give some geese to the Crees if you shoot for three days or longer. And if you get your day's five geese by 9 a.m.—as is likely at the Cabbage Willows Club on James Bay (a part of Hudson Bay in northern Quebec)—you'll have a lot of time on your hands for gin rummy, gin rickeys or simply meditating on your sins. And the opportunities for committing any new ones in that remote and watery neck of the woods are awfully slim.

One clear, cool morning last September when three blue geese spotted a bunch of fraudulent wildfowl on the marsh, heard what seemed to be the high-pitched voices of the bunch urging, "Come on down—goose goodies galore here!" and set their wings to glide into the scene, I was one of the two guys who stood up and pointed black sticks at them. The other gunner was Charles Lee of Gladwynne, Pennsylvania. When Lee said, "Let's take 'em!" I shot the lead bird and missed the second in line when it flared. Lee then bagged the pair before they could climb out of range.

Reggie Hester, one of the two Cree Indians who had "talked" the high-flyers into the rig with an astonishing demonstration of calling—using only his vocal chords and cupped hands—walked out and picked up the birds. Reggie Hester's uncle, Pat, stayed crouched in the skimpy blind they had shared, scanning the skies for more geese that might come within his calling range.

Calling, the way the James Bay Crees do it, is almost always a two-man operation, with one caller barking the high falsetto notes and the other hitting the low notes, until they blend into what sounds like a good-sized flock of excited blue or snow geese. When geese in the air answer the callers the conversation is one of the most thrilling sounds in the world of sport.

For more than a century, blue geese were the mystery waterfowl of North America. Each autumn blues arrived in Louisiana by the hundreds of thousands and spent the winter on the mud flats of the Mississippi delta, gorging themselves on the grasses that grow there. But when they departed in early spring and headed north, nobody knew where they went, although several teams of waterfowl scientists spent years searching for them in northern Canada. Not until June 26, 1929, after a dedicated six-year search covering more than 30,000 Arctic and sub-Arctic miles, did a Canadian biologist named Soper find blue geese nesting on the western end of Baffin Island, "a gloomy land, haunted by leaden skies and harassed by chilling gales of rain and snow."

But Soper and most of his fellow biologists believed that blue geese, although usually found flying and sometimes mating with lesser snow geese, were a distinct species, and only in recent years have ornithologists agreed that blue and lesser snow geese are simply color phases of the same species, and may even occur in the same clutch of eggs, just as yellow and black Labrador retrievers may occur in a single litter. And because the blue goose seems to have the dominant genes, as well as the better protective coloration, some scientists believe that eventually the pure-white lesser snow goose will be phased out in a process of natural selection, although it won't be next week or even in the next century.

While Lee and I waited for more geese to come in, huddled on upturned wooden boxes behind our screen of willow cuttings, I told him what I had learned about James Bay shooting on a trip to the Cabbage Willows camp the previous year. The drill is almost invariable: up in predawn darkness; breakfast; into 21-foot guideboats with ten-hp outboards, two hunters and two guides to a boat; down the Cabbage Willows River to the open waters of Rupert Bay and up one of the scores of tidal creeks that lace the marsh, while the tide's still high enough to get 'way back in. Then walk (sometimes a mile or more) to a spot where geese are likely to feed; set up precut willow branches to form screen blinds; watch guides expertly spade up lumps of mud and decorate each with pieces of white paper or white feathers to make decoys. Shoot; eat lunch; shoot some more; when the tide is high again walk back to boats for the run back to camp; happy hour; dinner; nightcap; bed.

The thirty-two square miles of marsh leased by the club, oldest of twenty-one goose-shooting camps in the James Bay area, is covered with wild celery, widgeon grass, glasswort, sedges, pondweeds and other waterfowl-nourishing plant life. When the blues and snows have nested and raised their young to flying size on the barren breeding grounds several hundred miles further north, they fly south each September to the rich feeding on the James Bay flats. This large marsh is in effect a vast staging area, with hundreds of thousands of geese feeding day and night in preparation for their 3,000-mile migration to Louisiana's Gulf Coast. And when you consider that some of these birds will fly the entire distance nonstop, you'll know why they need all the nourishment they can get before takeoff.

(In recent years a lot of blues and snows have stopped migrating all the way down to Louisiana. They've discovered that huge, man-made lakes and reservoirs along the route provide adequate wintering facilities, and age-old migrating patterns, long thought to be as unchangeable as the tides, have altered radically in a few decades. Also, say some biologists, a slight warming of the temperate zones may have helped to modify migration routes.)

Suddenly the Crees began calling frantically—uh-HOO, uh-HOO, uh-HOO!—and Lee and I crouched lower, watching a bunch of five blues and one all-white lesser snow, a hundred yards up and heading past us toward a huge concentration of birds a mile away, change course and swing about to investigate the almost-hysterical goose talk. When the geese were 30 feet above the decoys and had put down their landing gear Pat Hester called, "Shoot!" and we jumped to our feet and fired. I dumped the two blues on my side of the bunch, Lee took a blue and the white goose. (It was the only snow in our limit of ten birds that day; thirty years ago the ratio would have been closer to fifty-fifty.) While Reggie Hester was picking up the birds, a trio of juveniles—always less wary than the older birds—flew almost directly over us a hundred feet up, perhaps to investigate the strange goings-on, and when Lee bagged the lead bird I scored a lucky double on the others. It wasn't quite 9 a.m. and we had our limits.

But the tide on which we ran up a narrow creek three hours ago had gone out, leaving our boat high on a mud bank, and we were stuck for another three hours. No problem— you're also entitled to a daily limit of six ducks apiece, and since the spot we were in wasn't especially ducky, the Hesters gathered up geese, gear and willow branches and we trudged half a mile across the marsh and rebuilt our blinds between two small ponds crammed with pondweed and other duck food. Before our guides had finished trimming up the blinds a pair of mallards buzzed the pond in front of us, and we each dropped one as they spotted us and started climbing. Reggie Hester propped them on tufts of mud in the shallows, as decoys, and finished his blind-building chores.

Incidentally, walking the marshes is fairly hard work, especially when the tide's in with two or three inches of water overlying several inches of mud. A mile, when you're slogging through this stuff, seems like three or four unless you're in top physical condition.

There's a school of James Bay gunners that maintains the Crees deliberately walk your ass ragged for any of a number of reasons: simple sadism; revenge on white men; a belief that you'll not appreciate the shooting unless it's difficult; an established management policy of making the customers so tired they won't stay up all night drinking, playing cards and making passes at the Crees' womenfolk.

In special cases, however, exceptions are made. Last fall, one elderly hunter confined to a wheelchair got his limit of geese from a strategically placed guideboat.

Two hours later our duck limit was filled, and we slogged back across the seemingly endless wetland to our boat. Walking back I had felt the same deep, atavistic sense of involvement with nature that I always feel when hunting a marsh—perhaps because it was from a marsh that life first crawled onto dry land. I had been fulfilling primitive man's ancient role as a meat-eating predator while observing civilized man's rules of limited kills and his self-imposed code of sportsmanship. (The Crees, living too close to the edge of survival to care about the fine points of field-sport ethics, feel that shooting a flying bird instead of waiting for it to light is a piece of white man's idiocy; it may be.) I had killed my own meat, honestly and cleanly, instead of having it killed for me by strangers in a slaughterhouse; it was a good feeling.

For the indefatigable gunner who gets his limit of geese *and* ducks early, there are snipe, those elusive little game birds of legend and fact. If all the ducks and geese disappeared, James Bay would still be a paradise for the dedicated sniper, and it's possible to have sport as good as any you'll find in Ireland, where all good snipe shooters go when they die. And if geese stop flying for an hour or two you can always leave the blind and try walking up some snipe in the grass.

An hour later we were back at camp, putting ourselves around a generous slug of single-malt whiskey and comparing notes with the eight other hunters in residence. Of the fifty geese taken, forty-four were blues, three were snows, two were Canadas and one was a white-fronted or "specklebelly" goose. All but seven were adult birds; later parties would find a higher percentage of juveniles, since the young birds are usually last to leave the nesting grounds, especially if early clutches of eggs are wiped out by weather. Some years the young birds never do show up and are assumed to have perished in severe Arctic storms shortly after the hatch.

Looking at the limit of geese laid out for counting in front of the clubhouse, I did some simple mental arithmetic and figured they had cost us about $50 per goose, or roughly fifteen times what we'd have paid for the same amount of goose meat at home markets. The Cabbage Willows tab for a three-day shoot is $550, including everything except transportation to and from your home to Val-d'Or, Quebec, and tips to guides and camp staff. Depending on how far you live from Val-d'Or, the total tab would be between $650 and $750.

What makes a man spend that kind of money for three days of no-guarantee shooting, knowing he may be eaten by mosquitoes if it's warm and windless, or frozen if a norther howls out of the Arctic Circle, and that he'll probably walk himself ragged through muddy marsh getting to and from the shooting area each day? I think it's more than the shooting—more than the adventure—more than the remoteness from any kind of pollution or man-made eyesores.

I think it's the chance to take part in an ancient tableau of nature: to hear what may be the most exciting dialogue-without-words in all creation, when Crees and geese call back and forth across the marsh in a chorus as wild and primeval as the howling of wolves; to see geese rise from a marsh in numbers that literally blacken the sky, with the beating of their wings sounding like a thousand kettledrums, the way men crouching in caves saw and heard them 50,000 years ago. Once I asked Tom Wheeler, who founded the camp nearly thirty years ago, if anyone came just to see and listen to the geese. He named five "regulars" he was sure would come back every year even if all shooting were forbidden. I suspect there would be a lot more than five.

Wheeler, a pioneer in the airline industry, loves wildfowling as much as he loves flying. When he sold Wheeler Airlines in 1964 he enlarged the camp to accommodate eighteen gunners, offered a cuisine unusual for a hunting camp (*escargots à la bourguignonne* as a prelude to your *coq au vin*, for example, and wine with every evening meal), brought in the best Cree callers and guides in the district and generally made the place a byword among North American goose hunters.

Last season there were nine Cree families camped near the clubhouse in their wood-framed oval tents: eleven guides, nine squaws, sixteen kids. When the hunters leave in mid-October the Indians start hunting for themselves, drying and smoking as many geese and ducks as they can kill to tide them over the long, cold winter. Entrails are made into soup, and even heads and feet are boiled to extract the last smidgeon of nourishment; down and feathers are used to make quilted winter clothing.

Last year Wheeler sold Cabbage Willows Camp to Manny Wilson, a pleasant-mannered PR man for Canadian International Paper Company who plans to continue the tradition of good living. My understanding is that the paper company has a piece of the action, but Cabbage Willows will still be run as a public camp. Instead of the complicated bus and bush plane procedure previously used to get hunters into the camp, they will fly this year from Toronto, Ottawa or Montreal to Val-d'Or by Air Canada, from Val-d'Or to Moosonee on James Bay by a local airline, and from Moosonee to camp by float planes.

But if you'd like to experience this grand sporting adventure, you had better not delay too long. Last fall the James Bay Development Corporation, created overnight by the Quebec provincial legislature, announced plans to throw dams across every major river flowing westward into James Bay, to eventually generate ten million kilowatts of electricity and create thousands of jobs in the area. Nobody knows how much this will alter the salinity of the water and the growth of plants that now attract the huge concentrations of waterfowl—but everybody knows that when the Crees have their choice of working at a power plant or dam in comfortable conditions with year-round job security and fringe benefits, most are going to prefer it to the part-time, highly uncomfortable, totally insecure life of a goose guide. It's an odds-on bet that in a few years goose calling and goose guiding will be lost arts in that part of the world; even if the geese stay, it won't be the same ball game.

There's no doctor at Cabbage Willows, but a short-wave radio can bring one in by float plane from Moosonee or Matagami in less time, probably, than it takes your family doctor to make a house call. When I learned that elderly and even invalid sportsmen frequently come to Cabbage Willows and manage to get their fill of goose shooting, I asked Wheeler about medical facilities.

He told me one of his sportsmen had been taken so ill his friends wanted to send him by air to the hospital at Matagami, but the sick man insisted he'd feel better in a few hours. When they learned that a man in another party was a veterinarian, they asked if he'd have a look at their stricken friend. The vet refused, explaining he could lose his license by treating a person, and besides, he wasn't trained in people-type medicine.

When the others insisted, pointing out the nature of the emergency, the vet reluctantly agreed to examine the patient. He sat beside the man's bunk, looked at his tongue, rolled back his eyelids, took his pulse and felt his forehead. Then he stood up and said, "Gentlemen, if this is a human being I'm not qualified to pass an opinion on his condition. But, brother, if this is a springer spaniel he is one sick son-of-a-bitch."

—True Magazine, 1972

The Caribou
Went Thataway

Well, there was this big, lanky, fourteen-year-old California ranch kid, and he went into the rodeo manager's office and said, "Mister, I want to sign up for the calf-roping but my paw says I ain't allowed to. So I can't use my right name." And the manager said, "Son, no matter what name you use, it'll be slim pickin's out there today."

So the boy said, "That's as good a name as any, I reckon—put me down as Slim Pickin's." The manager spelled it "Pickens," and the boy won $400 that afternoon. The money didn't last long, but the name has stuck for forty years, while the boy grew into a top professional rodeo rider and then lucked his way into an acting career when a movie talent scout saw him on a newsreel. Slim liked being an actor because it wasn't as strenuous as bulldogging steers and paid well enough that he could do a lot of hunting and fishing, all over the world.

I met Slim the first time a few years ago in Arizona. We were both guests at a Winchester-Western wing-ding in Phoenix, and we snuck off with some of the W-W people to celebrate the opening of the dove season at a field a few miles out of town. Between doves, Slim told some of the funniest stories I've ever heard, mostly about his rodeo career. Some of them may have been true.

So last September, when I was loitering around the airport at Fort Chimo on Ungava Bay in northernmost Quebec, waiting for a thirty-year-old PBY to fly a group of ten hunters, including me, into an Eskimo-owned-and-operated caribou hunting camp on the Ford River, and saw Slim loping across the runway toward the same airplane, I was what Slim would call right pleased. When he said he was going to the same camp to make a TV short with "Red" Fisher, a Canadian producer of outdoor films, it suited me fine, because what I wanted was (a) a story and (b) a caribou, but mostly (a), and I figured with Slim there I had a sure-fire story, even if he didn't fill his license (HOLLYWOOD ACTOR BOMBS, CARIBOUWISE). Slim said they would have only three days, so I'd be able to tag along with him and still have time, after his party had left, to try for my own deer. ("Caribou" comes from a Micmac Indian word meaning "shoveller," but the several North American subspecies of this deer are larger, with bigger, heavier antlers

156

than their European cousin the reindeer. And the Ungava region of Quebec, where we were to hunt, has produced the highest-scoring antlers listed in the current Boone and Crockett Club records, and should yield even bigger trophies in the future.)

We were headed for an outpost camp of Ilkalu Lodge, on a tributary of the George River (which flows north into Ungava Bay, due south of Baffin Island). The camp's season, sandwiched between the appearance of the migrating caribou and the freezing of the lake—actually a wide part of the river—is so short that only three parties of eight to twenty hunters can come in for a week each, and even then the last group may have trouble getting out on schedule. The camp is Eskimo-owned, and proprietor Willie Imudluk, a former Hudson Bay Company employee, is an enthusiastic hunter as well as a pioneer in a Canadian Government program to provide new sources of income for the native peoples of the far-northern areas.

At the camp, after an hour's flight in the lumbering amphibian, we were welcomed aboard by John MacDonald, a young Scot who lives with his wife at the George River Settlement, speaks fluent Eskimo and works for the Department of Indian Affairs as an interpreter and counselor. (Most of the Eskimo guides understand some English, but are too shy to try speaking it.) John's wife, 100 miles away at the 200-Eskimo settlement, relayed radio messages to Fort Chimo and gave us daily weather reports when we couldn't get through with our smaller transmitter.

Squatting beside the fire that Joshua Ananak had coaxed into life in the lee of a huge boulder, out of the wind that whipped across the empty tundra—using pine sticks he had carried all morning in his knapsack, since there's not enough wood to make a match stick in an acre of this land—I now helped Joshua watch the battered teakettle, and could see there was something on his mind.

John MacDonald had told me Joshua spoke a little English—very little—and would probably be too shy to use it; he was right, and our conversation for the three days of hunting since Slim's party had left had consisted of some eight or ten words. I knew Joshua was twenty-four years old, lived at George River Settlement, wasn't married, and had been one time to the big city (Fort Chimo, pop. 700), but only because John had told me. Otherwise I would occasionally point to an outsize hoofprint and say "Tuk-tuk!" and Joshua would say "Cah-ree-boo!", and we would thus demonstrate our re-markable fluency in each other's language.

But now, with the natural curiosity of these friendly, extroverted people and perhaps appreciating my effort to communicate and wanting to reciprocate, Joshua looked up and said carefully, *"How . . . old . . . you?"* I told him, and he smiled shyly and said, *"You . . . old . . . man."* (Among Eskimos, whose life expectancy even today is still low, anyone over fifty is venerable, and "old man" is a term of respect.) I agreed, and emboldened by his communications breakthrough Joshua said, *"Where . . . you . . . live?"* "New York," I said, and Joshua said, *"Noo . . . Yock."* "That's right," I said. "New York."

Then Joshua asked me a question, and to this day I don't know the answer. He frowned in puzzlement and said, *"Where . . . that . . . near?"*

Slim Pickens, durn his ornery hide, had snuck off with Willie Imudluk and a cameraman the first morning after we got there, intending simply to have a look around, but had stumbled on to a very respectable caribou bull and had killed it, on the theory that a caribou in the hand is worth several hundred in the tundra. Slim had wanted to stalk it, he told me, but Willie had made him wait behind a boulder for what seemed hours (and may have been nearly an hour) while the upwind animal grazed to within easy range. Aeons ago the Eskimos, who until recently killed their game with spear or bow and arrow or harpoon, learned to let the animals come to them; on the treeless, even shrubless tundra stalking is difficult, and time is one thing an Eskimo generally has plenty of. I went back with Slim that afternoon to take some pictures, and watched the three guides with us butcher the caribou swiftly and efficiently, then demonstrate why you're not likely to get rich selling refrigerators to Eskimos.

On top of a table-sized boulder they spread a layer of small flat stones; on the stones, they laid a layer of meat; then a layer of stones, and a layer of meat, until all the meat was in the pile. Then the entire mound was covered with rocks as heavy as a man could lift, and the spaces between them chinked with smaller stones, until the cache looked like a random pile of rocks, or a trail-marking cairn. Wolf-proof, fox-proof, and even wolverine-proof (polar bears never intrude this far inland), the cache would keep the meat in good condition until winter, when the men would come on their snowmobiles to run traplines for otter, mink, fox, wolf, and wolverine. Without the layers of stones to separate the layers of meat, the whole pile would freeze into one solid lump.

When I got back and told John about this, he was surprised that the Eskimos hadn't included the greenish, half-digested stomach contents, which he said they almost always did. "Sometimes they think a white man might find it offensive," John said, and I remembered, then, that after we had left the cache two of the men had left us and gone back, perhaps to add the stomach contents, which are rich in vitamins and make up a large part of the vegetable matter in the diet of nomadic Eskimos.

When Slim and his crew flew out, I started to hunt myself. By now I had learned that several of the party had shot their caribou swimming in the lake; they had been brought alongside the deer in outboard-powered freight canoes, shot the swimming animals, and that was that. When I suggested to one of them, a Pennsylvania lumber mill owner, that this didn't seem the height of pure sport, he said, "Look, friend, I came here to get caribou, and I got one." Another man, owner of a New Jersey garden supply company, had his guide shoot a swimming caribou for him.

For some reason, shooting caribou in the water is legal; although it's illegal to shoot swimming whitetail deer or moose; probably it's because the Eskimos, before they had firearms, were only able to kill caribou in the numbers needed for their winter food and clothing when the animals were migrating across rivers and lakes, and could be easily speared from canoes. But Vivian Sleight, my tent-mate, a retired businessman from Honeoye Falls, New York, in his middle sixties, stalked and killed a splendid bull with a 62-inch spread between beam tips, and I see no reason why, even if the Eskimos, whose survival depends on caribou meat and hides, are permitted to kill them swimming, the sport hunter should not be forbidden to shoot these deer within, say, 100 yards of a lake or river. (This would prevent having the guides post a visiting hunter beside the water and then, in their canoes, swimming one or more animals virtually into his lap; I had to decline this arrangement myself, after making it clear I would not shoot a swimming caribou.)

And so, for four days I walked the hilly tundra with Joshua, hoping to come across one or several of the bigger, older bulls which keep to themselves, scorning the large mixed herds, until they're ready to move in and gather a harem. Usually this happens about the latter part of September or early October, when their antlers are not only free of velvet but are no longer pink with blood and too soft for fighting. We walked from ridge to ridge, stopping atop each to glass the broad valleys below until satisfied there were no big bulls within sight. Three times we stalked mixed groups to check out the bulls in the herd, and each time agreed there was nothing worth shooting. One time we saw three enormous white-caped bulls walking briskly across the tundra about a mile away, but were unable to catch up to them despite an hour of on-the-double, sweat-drenched stalking.

(The barren-grounds tundra is mostly six to eighteen inches of shrubs, mosses, and dwarf bushes overlaying rock or shale or clay, and walking on it is like marching on a gigantic mattress, with each step involving almost as much vertical movement as horizontal. Since you're dressed for protection against brisk winds and temperatures not far above freezing, a ten- or fifteen-mile up-and-downhill hike is guaranteed to knock some of the longitude off your equator, and I lost eight pounds in six days, despite seconds at every meal.)

But at the end of our scheduled five-day stay I still had no caribou, and although I asked John MacDonald to assure Willie that I didn't really mind, and that I could have killed any of a half-a-dozen fair-to-good bulls during the week, I knew that Willie and the guides were distressed to think that for the first time a hunter might leave their camp without a trophy. I turned in the night before the PBY was to come for us feeling a little disappointed that I hadn't found the caribou I wanted but pleased to have seen a part of the world and its wildlife that were new to me, and glad to have a good excuse to come back.

Next morning I peered through the tent-cabin door across the lake, but couldn't see the far shore for haze; a heavy roof of low cloud hung a few hundred feet over the land, decapitating the higher hills and making it impossible for a plane to get in. When John got through to Fort Chimo and learned the weather was bad throughout the area and unlikely to clear that day, I changed back into hunting clothes and spent another day with Joshua and another guide, Sandy Unatuinak. Sandy's cheek was scarred and he walked with a limp; I learned later he had barely survived an attack by half-crazed sled dogs as a child. Attacks by these normally friendly near-wolves occur occasionally in Eskimo settlements, and it's no rarity for a child or even an adult to be killed by them. "Sandy's lucky to be alive," John assured me, but I noticed that even with one leg permanently lamed he covered ground faster than I could. Once again, we saw scattered bands of caribou cows and young bulls, but none of the massive-antlered loners we were looking for.

Next morning the weather was still thick, but at breakfast John asked us to stay close to camp, as it might clear in time for a plane to come in. An hour later I was packing my sleeping bag when John stuck his head into the cabin. "If you want to try for a big bull,'' he said, ''here's your last chance. Josh and Sandy went scouting in a canoe this morning and they've located two good bulls about a mile down the lake. But you'll have to hurry.'' Five minutes later I was in the canoe; when we neared the bulls, which were grazing 400 or 500 yards back from the shoreline at the foot of a steep slope, the guides cut the motor lest it spook them, and paddled until well downwind of the caribou.

A mile below them we went ashore and hurried up the slope to the shelter of a boulder. When Joshua indicated we were to wait for the bulls to graze within shooting range I loaded the .270, checked the 4X sight against fogging, and leaned back to wait—but not for long. Sandy had snaked his way across the tundra to a rise, and now came running; the caribou had turned up a draw and might be on their way up the hill and into the hinterland. The three of us ran, crouching (and one panting), for what seemed a mile and may have been a third of that, until Sandy signaled for us to lie down and start crawling. When we topped a rise the bulls were 300 yards away and feeding slowly up the hill.

We backed off the rise, crawled nearly 100 yards closer and cautiously peered over another rise: the bulls were still there, but alert, heads raised and ready for flight. ''Shoot!'' Joshua whispered, and I slid the rifle into position, fixed the crosshairs on the biggest bull's brisket—he had turned and was almost directly facing me—and pulled the trigger. In those *Field & Stream* stories deer drop dead when you do that, but in this case the caribou was startled but otherwise fit as a fiddle. (Later I realized there had been a stiff crosswind blowing, which I hadn't allowed for; that's the best I can do, alibi-wise.)

But now, both animals were running up the hillside; I stood up, found the bigger buck in the scope, led him slightly and fired offhand; to my astonishment he collapsed, and was stone dead by the time we ran up to him. (The 130-grain bullet had hit about three inches below the spine and just behind the rib cage, expanding to deliver its full cargo of shock inside the carcass.)

Fewer than one in three caribou bulls have the double brow palm (or ''double shovel''), but this one did; with both beams over fifty inches and good symmetry it came within a few points of making the Boone and Crockett Club record book (and for a while I thought it was well up among the top trophies, until I learned that the tip-to-tip spread doesn't count in the scoring). And pleased as I was, my pleasure wasn't more than Willie's, Sandy's, and Joshua's; they had kept me from sullying the camp record by going home emptyhanded, and although they may have thought I was foolish to pass up swimming bulls, they had worked enthusiastically, cheerfully, and skillfully once they knew what I wanted.

Next morning the cloud lifted, and the PBY splashed onto the lake not long after noon; after a night at Jimmy Grist's Arctic Adventurers Hotel in Fort Chimo, a sleek Nordair jet whooshed us 1,000 miles south to Montreal, and the Air Canada connection to New York had me home in time for dinner. (There are advantages to living an hour from JFK Airport, as I keep telling Trueblood out there in Idaho.)

—Field & Stream, 1975

A Very Short
History of the BB Gun

Simply because Anna Sten invented the Sten gun, a lot of ill-informed people are under the impression that Brigitte Bardot invented the BB gun. (To the best of my knowledge Miss Bardot never actually invented anything. But she did make some improvements in stuff other people had invented.)

Other people who didn't invent the BB gun were Bebe Daniels, William Beebe and Bebe Reboza, although any one of them might have done so if he or she had put his or her mind to it and it had not already been invented by Professor Charles W. Daisy, a somewhat eccentric genius who also invented the chain.

Daisy was fooling around in his lab one day with some air he had found in a desk drawer; some time before that, he had theorized that air could be used to blow up balloons and alleviate flatness in bicycle tires, and while conducting experiments in this area he had noticed that if you stuffed a lot of air into a can and clapped the lid on quickly enough, it would later make a hissing sound when you punched a hole in the lid. Professor Daisy thought this invention could be sold to theater audiences attending plays featuring a villain, and intended to patent it.

Earlier, however, Professor Daisy had invented the BB (so called because it resembled a very small base-ball), but hadn't figured out any particular use for it. Then he used one to plug a hole in one of his hiss-pots, as he called them, the pressure inside blew it out and into the 9-ring of a target which the Professor had hung on his wall to hide an old diploma. Ever a perfectionist, he decided to make a device that would put the BB in the 10-ring, and in no time at all had invented the *Daisy Air Flier*. (Daisy called it an "Air Flier" because the BBs flew through the air. In the official announcement, however, a drunken printer accidentally rearranged the letters in "flier" so it came out "rifle," and it was decided to leave it that way, as the printer had gone home to sleep it off and anyway the Professor sort of liked the sound of it. "Anyway I sort of like the sound of it," was the way he put it.)

Another version of the story of the invention of the BB gun has it that Professor Daisy was dozing under an apple tree one day, and a BB fell out of the tree onto his head. "I wonder what made that BB fall out of the tree," the Professor mused. (No doubt *you* would have wondered what the BB was doing up in the tree, which is one of the differences between you and a genius.) (And not the most important one.)

Then it occurred to the Professor that someone up in the tree might have *shot* the BB at him, and he decided to invent something to shoot back with: ergo, the Daisy Air Rifle. (Actually his work was in vain, as after he had invented it he realized you should never, under any circumstances, which was where he happened to be at the time, even point a BB gun at any other person, much less shoot it at him.) (Never.)

Whichever version you prefer, the fact is that throughout the ages man has used air for many things—inflating volleyballs, flying kites, drying damp socks, cooling hot borscht, inhaling, fluffing up down pillows (up down?), playing bagpipes, and blowing up paper bags and bursting them to frighten old ladies. It remained for Professor D. to discover that air could also be used to shoot pellets or BBs at targets or tin cans or aspirin tablets, and I think I'll go and take a couple right now.

—Daisy Shooting Annual, 1976

Life in a Log Cabin

I grew up in a small suburban town near Pittsburgh, and like most of the kids in town I belonged to one of three, or it might have been four, Boy Scout troops in the village. Mine, Troop 1, met in the basement of the Episcopal church every Thursday evening. Most of the meetings were devoted to lightly supervised violence including boxing, rassling, tugs of war and other minor forms of mayhem. The basement floors were bare concrete, and it was considered a dull meeting when nobody got even a mild concussion, much less a skull fracture.

Most of us in our troop were sort of embarrassed at being Boy Scouts, and made a point of never showing up at a meeting wearing more than one article of the uniform, usually a shirt with the insignia worn off, and anyone who had appeared wearing the full, official regalia would have been severely manhandled, or boyhandled. Merit badges were regarded as a form of show-boating, although some of us, under the prodding of whoever happened to be our Scout Master at the moment, picked up one or two. (Alpha Bowser, in Troop Three, got enough merit badges to qualify as an Eagle Scout, and went on to become a Marine Corps general, which shows what collecting merit badges can lead to.)

Like most of the members of Troop 1, I had joined not in order to help old ladies across the street but because Troop 1 had a genu-wine log cabin in the woods a few miles out the Steubenville Pike. It had been built largely by the kids themselves, with a lot of advice and a little assistance from the fathers of some of them, although a mason had been hired to direct the construction of the stone fireplace and chimney. The logs had come from local trees, mostly slippery ellum, and had been trimmed and notched with axes and adzes before being dragged into place by a rented mule. For several years a picture of the cabin was printed on the front cover of the Boy Scout handbook, and the battered snapshot shown here was taken several years after the cabin had begun to

deteriorate. (Elm, slippery or otherwise, isn't the ideal tree for building log cabins, but this one lasted 20-odd years.)

I had turned twelve, old enough to join the troop, just as the cabin was being finished, and was permitted to lay a few stones in the chimney and help set the window frames. For the next several years I spent a good many weekends and a lot of weekday nights there, usually with three or four other kids but occasionally, when the weather was bad or unusually cold, I would be alone overnight (and it's a measure of that pre-Little League era that there was rarely an adult with us, yet although our parents, so far as I know, had all the feelings toward us that normal adult humans have for their get, no one worried about us, even after Ossie Dunlap shot himself in the toe with his Model 07 Winchester single-shot bolt-action .22 rifle. The general feeling seemed to be that Ossie was sort of a smart-ass kid anyway, and that having only nine toes would be a settling influence on him.) There was something called the Winchester Junior Rifle Corps within the troop, and a 75-foot shooting range in the church basement, on which we shot up enough ammunition twice a month to enable the Winchester people to dole out bunches of medals that said "Junior Marksman" and "Junior Sharpshooter" and still show a substantial profit on the operation. The shooting was supervised, with a lot of emphasis, properly, on safety.

The woods around the cabin were infested with gray squirrels, and it was the in thing to arrive there—a three-mile hike for most of us—with a blanket bed-roll, a hand axe, a .22 rifle and four or five pounds of potatoes, carrots, onions and celery, then to sneak off into the woods and shoot a squirrel, or two if possible, which, when dressed out and combined with the vegetables, could be made into a more-or-less edible concoction which we called Brunswick stew. We had only a hazy notion of legal hunting seasons but knew enough not to shoot squirrels or rabbits in the spring or early summer lest a nest or den or hollow tree full of young be left to starve. Naturally after a few years of this the squirrel population in the immediate vicinity was considerably thinned out, and also the squirrels were smarter since the dumb ones had been made into stews, and some of the kids began bringing hamburger or hot dogs and beans, although others felt that this was cheating. But even the kids who brought hamburger brought their .22's too.

I suppose that nowadays if anybody saw a fourteen-year-old kid wandering around town with a sure-enough rifle under his arm she, or even he, might put in a hysterical call to the fuzz. In those happier and more innocent times it was assumed by most right-thinking citizens that a boy should have a gun and learn how to use and respect it, and so long as we didn't shoot up the town or each other our having the rifles was accepted as normal and unobjectionable. (I got my first .22 as a twelfth birthday gift.)

Although most of us came from reasonably well-off or well-to-do middle-class white-collar or professional families, I can't recall ever seeing anyone arrive with a sleeping bag. There were ticks (the canvas kind, not the biting kind) in the loft at the rear of the cabin, and a bale of hay with which to stuff them; in cold weather we simply took off our boots, put on an extra pair of woolen socks and crawled into one or two blankets laid on top of a tick and pinned into a sort of rough "bag" with blanket pins. The hay got pretty lumpy after the first few hours of sleeping, and if it got too cold one of the three or four of us in the loft might climb down the ladder to the main floor and put another log on the fire, which would flame up and crackle for a while, creating an illusory warming effect until we fell asleep again.

Cooking was done, mostly, indoors on the large open fireplace, which had metal arms that swung out on which to hang pots. We learned to use a Dutch oven to bake what we laughingly called bread, setting the cast-iron pot in the hot ashes and piling live coals on the rimmed lid, but mostly we relied on one of the three or four communal pots in the kitchen. Most of us had Boy Scout cooking kits which nested together and fit into a canvas case; after a while the canvas absorbed enough bacon grease and baked-bean juice to acquire a rich, overripe pungency, and could probably have been boiled into a nutritious soup in an emergency. Pots and pans were washed in a small stream not far from the cabin, and if the washing was perfunctory and largely ritualistic, I can't recall any cases of ptomaine poisoning, or at least no fatal ones. Our drinking water came from a small spring near the cabin; it disappeared under fallen leaves each autumn and had to be re-excavated each weekend, but from it came water more delicious than any I've tasted since.

Most of our time at the cabin was spent on chores, which seemed endless because they were. We buck-sawed logs into fireplace length and split them with wedges and a sledge hammer. There was usually loose chinking between the logs to be replaced, or water to be brought from the spring, or bedding to be aired, or pots to be scoured, or meals to be cooked, or squirrels to be hunted, or ashes to be hauled from the fireplace, or a new hole to be dug for the outhouse, and when someone asked me one time what on earth we *did* there, I couldn't think of anything that would normally be considered fun. But taken altogether it *was* fun, and gave me a sense of adventure as rich and real as any I've felt in the Amazon jungle or the African plains.

Today, of course, there are a lot more people than there were then, and probably anyone wanting to go out into the woods and build a real log cabin out of real trees would have to file an environmental impact statement and install an approved septic tank, and the project would be overrun with Little-League type parents wanting to make the rules and run the show; it's almost enough to make a man glad he grew up before Coleman made the outdoors so comfortable. But not quite.

—*Coleman Camping Annual*, 1977

I Am a Hunter

When I wrote an angry note to Les Line, the editor of *Audubon*, the handsome publication of the National Audubon Society, about what I felt was an unwarranted condemnation of hunters in the magazine, Les invited me to present a hunter's point of view. I'm afraid my anger shows in the piece, and I might not be as aggressive about it today, although I stand by my point that meat-eating man lives by killing or having it done for him, and that nature is essentially a food chain in which man is one link.

There were 400-odd letters to the editor regarding the piece, almost all of them denunciatory. One woman wrote, "I hope you are shot in the gut and lie in a cold wet ditch and die slowly," and several others were similar. A number of people wrote that it wasn't my killing of wildlife they objected to, it was my enjoying it. (I don't know any hunters who enjoy killing. What they enjoy is hunting, of which killing is often a component.)

I gave the letters to a woman at Yale University, who wanted to write a doctoral thesis based on them. I don't know if she ever did. The text appeared opposite a beautiful color photograph of several dead game birds.

I didn't kill those lovely birds on the opposite page. But I've killed a great many birds just as lovely, and have spent long and happy hours in an effort to kill not only ruffed grouse and woodcock but partridge and pheasant, ducks and geese, doves and quail, not out of any need other than psychic.

How, then, am I able to feel (as indeed I do) that I revere life at least as much as, and probably more than, those good men and women of America who abhor hunting and hunters? Let me try to tell you.

In 1955 I attended the annual meeting of the National Audubon Society to present a conservation award to Robert Porter Allen, the society's research director, who had done important field studies on West Indian flamingoes and roseate spoonbills and who had, a few months previously, discovered the long-sought nesting grounds of the whooping crane. The award was part of a corporation-sponsored program of which I am the director, and whose selection committee has always included persons prominent in Audubon affairs.

At the dinner, to my astonishment, I learned that the society's *own* highest award would be—and was—presented to Walt Disney. Until that moment it had not occurred to me that anyone seriously concerned with defending nature and the environment could hold Disney in anything but mild contempt for his anthropomorphistic, lily-gilding, nature-faking exploitation of wildlife and, indeed, all outdoors. Disney had, even then, convinced a whole generation that nature was something set to cornball-clever musical accompaniment and consisting largely of cobras fighting mongooses, sidewinders fighting road-runners, tarantulas fighting scorpions, eagles stooping on gophers that always escaped, and other contrived and staged episodes designed to titillate an audience of sentimental make-believers and urban ignoramuses, and intended not to educate or edify but to realize the largest possible profit to Disney and his stockholders.

I realized then that the National Audubon Society, or at least a dominant group within it, took a view of renewable resource conservation quite different from my own and that of the professionals—foresters, wildlife managers, fisheries researchers, soil conserva-tionists, hydrologists, and other dedicated specialists—I knew and admired. But since, as a spokesman for nearly twenty million licensed American hunters (and for a minority group of hunters holding memberships in the society), I've been invited to defend my view in these pages, let me in turn invite those who decry and condemn hunting to join me—briefly and invisibly—in a duckblind on the edge of a New Jersey marsh not far from Barnegat inlet.

It's 3 p.m of a bitterly cold, bright December day, and I've been sitting on a plank bench in a sunken box, with Joe, a middle-aged Labrador retriever, since shortly before the sun rose at about 7 a.m. My booted feet are in icy water, and ache with cold. (I spent half an hour in darkness pumping water out of the blind and arranging the decoys, which I lugged across a quarter-mile of ice-crusted marsh from my boat, but the water leaks back in.) I'm dressed for cold weather, and except for my feet I'm not too painfully uncomfortable. Nor is Joe, who is at least as happy to be here as I am.

I hold a double-barreled 12-gauge shotgun across my lap, and for nearly ten hours I have been waiting for a black duck or ducks—wariest of all waterfowl in these parts—to come into the rig of a dozen decoys floating in the shallow water in front of me. So far none have come, although a few have flown round the blind out of gun range, looked it over, and decided not to drop in. If any should, I would try to kill two of them, which is all the black ducks the law permits a shooter in any one day. (The law is slightly more generous with other, more abundant, species, but none of these is as challenging a quarry, nor as much a part of this region's tradition of waterfowling, nor as good to eat.) If I had killed my two blacks early in the day I would have dawdled awhile—perhaps ten minutes—and then picked up my decoys and gone home.

And so for ten hours I have sat here—cold, cramped, hungry despite the sandwiches

I shared with Joe, and happy. Happy in a way the nonhunter can't ever know. Oh, I've been out of the blind a few times, to rearrange the decoys when the wind shifted and when the tide changed, to let Joe stretch his legs, to stretch mine and stomp some feeling into my numb feet. But mostly I've sat and watched for ducks, or watched Joe, who usually sees ducks long before I do, and gets tense and excited when he does. (We watch through a screen of marsh grasses, so that ducks won't see my too-pale face and flare off.)

Although this is an unusually windless and consequently duckless day, it hasn't been an uneventful one. A lot of life goes on in a marsh, and every bit of it, at this time of year, concerns food—and therefore death. And I've been observing it, while waiting for ducks: the schools of killies being chased by bigger fish, the wintering marsh hawk (I think, although it may be a migrating roughleg) patrolling the far side of the marsh looking for a rat or rabbit, the skunk prowling so near I hope Joe doesn't catch his pungent scent and try to investigate.

I'm not enough of a naturalist, of course, to see all of it, but I see enough to know, if I hadn't known before, that a marsh teems with life, even in winter. And with death, as life feeds on death. My 7x35s are around my neck, but I seldom need them to see and savor this day's episode in an eternal drama of survival.

After a while the sun sets, and I wade out into the shallow flats and pick up the decoys. I'm disappointed, and so is Joe, but we're still happy in the special, elemental way that hunters feel happiness. I don't analyze it or articulate it, and it doesn't occur to me to try doing either until the next evening, when I'm at a dinner and sitting next to a nice (*really* nice) white-haired lady whom I don't know, but who notices that my tiepin is a miniature duck in flight.

"Are you interested in ducks?" she asks, and I tell her how I spent the previous day. "But if you enjoyed it, and saw so many interesting things, why couldn't you have left your gun at home, and just gone and sat in the blind all day, with your dog and your binoculars?" she said.

"Because," I said, "I don't regard nature as a spectator sport. If I were to leave the gun at home, or to bring it without the intention of using it, I'd be in that marsh as a spectator, or a peeping tom, or a bystander. But nature, to all animals, including the human, is essentially one big food chain. And when I go into the marsh with a gun, prepared to kill ducks and take them home and eat them, I'm there as a predator, as part of the food chain, with as much right to be there as the hunting marsh hawk or the skunk.

"Granted," I continued, "I've got a top spot on the chain, with no man-eating predators to cope with, but the worms will get me sooner or later, and I'll start again at the bottom. But when I'm there as a predator, I'm there as part of the natural scene, and I feel a oneness with nature that I never feel except when hunting, and that no nonhunter, much less an antihunter, can possibly experience. I become involved. I become not a student of nature, or a lover of nature, as though nature were a bug on a pin or a box of chocolates— I become a *part* of nature, in a way I don't experience even when backpacking into the wilderness or canoeing down a white-water river. Even in the woods or on the river I'm extraneous, an interloper, an outsider. But with a gun in the duck marsh, or in a woodcock thicket, or walking a hillside for ruffed grouse, I'm there as a predator—not as ruthless, perhaps, as a goshawk or a weasel or a Siberian tiger, but just as intent on killing.''

"My goodness!" says the nice lady, who had not meant to do more than make polite conversation. "Personally, I'm content to *watch* birds, and I think killing is, well, if you'll forgive me, reprehensible, and I'm very much opposed to it.'' She smiles to show she means nothing personal, and goes back to her lamb chop, which six weeks ago was part of a cuddly lamb with large brown pleading eyes that did it no good when the man came to cut its throat. I notice she doesn't have to force herself to eat it, and that she is, like everyone else at the table, a natural-born carnivore, with jaws and teeth designed for eating meat.

To that nice lady, of course, nature is a mildly amusing spectacle, and she would no more actively participate in that very basic and natural activity of mankind, the killing of other animals for food, than she would climb up on the stage at the Philharmonic and sit in with the woodwinds. She cannot even associate a lamb chop with killing, because in her plasticized, technicolor world, animals don't die unless they are cruelly slain by wicked hunters.

I think it is this refusal to accept death as an essential aspect of life, and man as a carnivore and therefore by deed or fiat a killer, that leads the antihunting sentimentalist into the idiocies of which he is frequently guilty. I don't mean the nonhunter who says, in effect, "Yes, I'm a meat-eater, but I prefer to have someone else do my killing for me.'' This is a matter of choice, or of esthetics, and I'm pleased that there'll be one less person intruding on my favorite woodcock covers or poking about my marshes. It is those who attempt to make a moral issue of lawful hunting who make fools of themselves, even if their foolishness is currently fashionable.

Foolishness? I don't mean the lady president of an antihunting organization who proclaims on a national television show that she delights in hearing of the number of hunters killed each season, and wishes the numbers were much larger. That kind of sickness is possibly curable. I do mean, for example, my well-meaning, kind-hearted, antihunting, nitwitted neighbor who "rescued" six mallard ducklings from a nearby pond last spring to raise in her bathtub, because five others of the clutch of eleven had been killed, probably by a large snapping turtle or perhaps a fox or skunk. It was her idea that the mallard hen was a white, Protestant, Anglo-Saxon lady who had somehow been transformed into a duck, and who felt as grief-stricken as any such lady should when five of her children had been destroyed.

When I explained to her that a pair of mallards begins breeding at one year of age, hatches an average of eight ducklings or four pairs each year, each of which pairs starts producing ducklings after one year, and that the original pair may live and breed for at least ten years, and that by this sort of geometric progression, if not for turtles and hunters and such, would have produced, at the end of ten years, a total of 19,531,250 ducks, and that if, at the end of those ten years, three of those 19,531,250 ducks are alive there has been, in effect, a 50-percent increase in the mallard population, she said, "Oh, Mr. Zern, you're just trying to confuse me." The ducklings died of applied Disneyism. Unmolested, one or two might have survived.

I mean, too, the foolishness of the antihunter who has never seen a deeryard strewn with the starved corpses of whitetails—killed not by hunters but by the namby-Bambi sentimentalists (including some hunters) who had successfully opposed the shooting of does. And so when man, whom nature designed as a predator, failed to substitute for the wolves and mountain lions nature had intended to help him keep the herds in balance with their food supply, the result was the virtual wiping out of all, not just a few, of the deer in that area. (I've never killed a North American deer, as a matter of preference, but when on several occasions I've seen the grisly results of underkilling, I've felt guilty at not having tried.)

Reverence for life? I think not, in the case of the antihunters. At least I've never met one who felt strongly, or at all, on the subjects of fishing, or logging, or farming, or other forms of life-destroying human activity. (Trout and trees and turnips are forms of life, even though unsanctified by Disney.) No, the antihunter is curiously selective in his solicitude for life, as though he had only a tiny amount and must ration it sparingly. I have had the unsettling experience, during one evening, of being attacked by a small but ferocious lady who accused me, within the same hour, of (a) condoning the hunting of wild birds and mammals, and (b) opposing the killing of people, even those with whose politics I disagreed, in Vietnam. I pleaded guilty on both counts.

And that, rather clumsily stated, is my position. Nature designed me as a meat-eating predator, and I accept nature on its own terms, acknowledging death, including my own (and yours, madam) as an essential aspect of life, not to be euphemized or Disneyfied or otherwise denied. When I kill a wild duck or pheasant cleanly and instantly, in the fullness of its wild beauty and strong flight, I save the life of a domestic duck or chicken, which would be killed in abject, squawking terror. When I kill a sharp-tailed grouse or bobwhite quail I become part of the process of life, accepting and fulfilling my role as predator and rejecting the destructive Old Testament concept of man as something separate from nature.

That the pheasant was introduced by hunters to be hunted, and that America's wildfowl would probably have vanished years ago if not for the efforts of hunters to save their habitat, is perhaps beside the point. But my friend the late Ralf Coykendall, with whom I sat in marsh blinds and trudged New England woodcock thickets, once observed that if the bald eagle were only good to eat and came readily to decoys it would no longer be in danger of extinction; he was less than half-serious, of course, but it *was* hunters who demanded and got the compulsory duck stamp to provide money for waterfowl refuges and who raised millions of dollars through Ducks Unlimited to restore duck-breeding marshes.

And so I ask not that you join me in hunting—I'd much prefer you didn't—but that you understand, in part at least, why I hunt.

—*Audubon*, 1972

PART

III

AD
FINITUM

In 1950 George W. Mason was chairman of the corporation that became American Motors, and I was an agency copywriter on the account. He was a keen sportsman, one of the founders and first treasurer of Ducks Unlimited, and when he died left many miles of river-front property along Michigan's Au Sable to the state, to ensure perpetual angler-access to that lovely river. When on three or four occasions he invited me to fish with him at his six-bedroom, four-bath "cabin" on the river, I felt it my bounden duty to accept.

George was a brusque, outspoken man, and one day, as we floated down the river casting dry flies and deer-hair 'hoppers in against the banks, he said, "Ed, why is the stuff you write about fishing and shooting so much fun to read, and the stuff you write about Nash cars so dull?"

"That's an easy question," I said. "Your advertising department doesn't have to approve the stuff I write about shooting and fishing."

"Given a free hand," George said, "could you write copy about the cars that would be fun to read?"—and I said I thought so but wasn't sure. "Try it," George said, "and if you get something you like, don't send it to the advertising department. Send it to me."

I went back to my Madison Avenue office and fooled around and finally sent copy and layouts for six full-page magazine advertisements directly to Mason. I illustrated them with home-made cartoons because I'm a frustrated cartoonist, and signed them because I wanted to make it clear they were written by a human being and not a corporation. Mason sent them back with orders to run one each month in the major outdoor and men's magazines. The campaign lasted for nine years and more than a hundred advertisements, some of which were, I hope, fun to read.

Readership surveys showed the ads were read thoroughly by from four to seven times as many readers-per-dollar as the "straight" Nash advertising. I had two drawers full of letters from owners professing to have bought their Nash cars because of the ads, and a special folder of letters from total strangers apologizing for having bought other makes. Perhaps the ads were more fun to write than to read, but I've chosen a handful of my own favorites, and a silly booklet for fishing lines that's now a collector's item, I'm told by a sporting-book dealer.

I think they prove something about advertising, but I'm not sure what.

TEAL TALE!

No. 22 in a series of NASH AIRFLYTE ads by ED ZERN

ONCE there was a flock of green-winged teal sitting around on a marsh pond.

"Kids," said the oldest and wisest duck, "I got some advice for you. *Beware of Nash Airflytes!*"

"Why?" said the other ducks.

"Because," said the leader, "when you see a Nash Airflyte parked near a blind, you can figure the sportsman is a pretty smart Joe, and a better-than-average wingshot."

"I don't get it," said a young duck.

"It's simple," said the leader. "It's a lot easier for an Airflyte owner to go gunning. He can drive long dis-tances without getting all pooped out, because the Airflyte handles so easily and rides so smoothly, even on back-country roads. He can afford to get out often, because the Airflyte's so economical. With the Weather Eye Conditioned Air System he doesn't mind driving in sub-zero weather, be-cause inside the car it's like summer. So he gets a lot of chances to sharpen up his shooting eye."

"I hear them Airflytes even got Twin Beds," said another duck.

"That's correct," said the leader. "Not to mention the 5-position re-clining seat, and Hydra-Matic Drive, and the biggest darn luggage com-partment you ever saw!"

While the ducks were all gabbling at once about the other features of the 1951 Nashes, like good road clear-ance and all-welded Airflyte Construc-tion, and making so much racket they couldn't hear anything else, a farmer with an old beat-up pump gun snuck up on them and knocked down his limit before they could fly out of range.

After gathering them up, he walked back to his buckboard, said "Giddap!" to his team, and drove home.

MORAL: *Well, horses have pretty good road clearance, too.*

Nash Motors Division Nash-Kelvinator Corporation, Detroit, Michigan.

See all three Nash Airflytes for 1951: The Ambassador, the Statesman and the Rambler (in Convertible, Station Wagon and Suburban models.)

FABLE FOR FAMILY MEN

This is No. 29 in a series of NASH AIRFLYTE ads by ED ZERN

ONCE there was a weak, skinny little guy whose wife was always giving him unsolicited advice.

"Why don't you trade our car on one that has an Airliner Reclining Seat, stupid?" she kept saying. "I'm entitled to a *little* consideration!"

At other times she would say, "Horace, you must be out of your mind, so-called. The idea of driving a car without a Weather Eye Conditioned Air System! And only a boob, totally lacking in appreciation of comparative values, would tolerate an automobile that doesn't even have seats that turn into Twin Beds, or a one-piece curved windshield on all models, or all-welded unitized construction for added strength and safety—you knucklehead!"

Of course, Horace had a ready answer for all these suggestions. It was, "Yes, dear."

So he went down to his Nash Dealer's and ordered a 1951 Nash Airflyte with an Airliner Reclining Seat, Weather Eye Conditioned Air System, Twin Beds, one-piece curved windshield, all-welded Airflyte Construction and many other exclusive features.

"I suppose you're aware that this car has many important advantages for outdoor sportsmen?" said the salesman.

"You don't say?" said Horace, and in order to get the full benefits of his Nash Airflyte, he took up hunting and fishing. In no time at all he became so musclebound that his wife was afraid to make any further suggestions, and they lived happily ever after.

MORAL:

You, too, can have big biceps! See your Nash Dealer!

Nash Motors Division, Nash-Kelvinator Corporation, Detroit 32, Michigan

1951 MOBILGAS ECONOMY RUN: Nash Ambassador 25.92 M.P.G., Statesman 26.12 M.P.G., Rambler 31.05 M.P.G. (with overdrive)!

Musky Fisherman MAROONED!

No. 32 in a series of NASH AIRFLYTE ads by ED ZERN

ONCE there was a sportsman who started out on a musky-fishing trip in his Nash Airflyte, and when he got out of town on the state highway a farmer thumbed a ride with him.

"Right nice car you got," said the farmer as they drove down the highway. "One of them Nash Airflytes, ain't it?"

"Yes sir!" said the sportsman. "Finest car ever made for people who hunt and fish. Twin Beds for overnight sleeping, or for snoozing while your partner drives on long trips. Weather Eye Conditioned Air System—finest heating and ventilating in the world! Unbelievable fuel economy! Biggest luggage compartment you ever saw! And that seat you're sitting on adjusts to five different positions—a wonderful comfort feature!"

"Sounds purty good," said the farmer. "How's she ride on rough roads?"

"Ha!" said the sportsman. "This car has coil springs on all four wheels!"

"You don't say," said the farmer, skeptically. "Down here there's a dirt road off to the left. Bet she'd fall apart before you'd git five miles on that road."

"We'll just see about that!" said the sportsman. So he turned off on the dirt road and drove five miles.

"Not bad, mister," said the farmer. "But y'see that side road goin' up the mountain? That there's a humdinger fer bumps—bet you couldn't git halfway up there without bustin' wide open!"

"No?" said the sportsman. "Watch this!" So he drove four miles up the mountain, until the road petered out beside a big red barn.

"Well, dog my cats!" said the farmer. "She sure sailed right over them bumps! Well, thanks a lot, mister—by a strange quirk of fate, this here is where I live."

"Hey, wait a minute!" said the sportsman. "At least you might admit you were wrong about the Nash Airflyte!"

"Only about the *blue* ones, bub," said the farmer. "I knowed all along my *maroon* Airflyte takes them rough roads slick as a whistle! If my wife wasn't usin' it to visit her folks, I'd show you."

MORAL:
Be careful about picking up hitchhikers.

Nash Motors Division, Nash-Kelvinator Corporation, Detroit 32, Michigan

1951 Mobilgas Economy Run: Nash Ambassador 25.92 m.p.g., Statesman 26.12 m.p.g., Rambler 31.05 m.p.g. (with overdrive)

THERE AIN'T NOBODY IN HERE BUT US LUGGAGE

ONCE there was a sportsman whose mind came unglued from trying to cram all his gear into the luggage compartment of his Ajax Eight. As a result he got the impression he was an outboard motor, and went around complaining that his mixture was too lean.

At the rest home where they sent him he met another sportsman who thought he was a .30-06 carbine and complained that he hadn't been properly sighted-in. They got along fine, especially since the director was a veteran hunter and fisherman and understood their problem.

One day the whole staff rushed into the director's office and announced that both men were missing. "We've looked high and low, Doc," they said. "They must of flew the coop."

"H-m-m," said the director. "The question is—where would you go if you were an outboard motor? Aha—that's it! Come with me!"

The director then led the staff out to the driveway where his Nash Ambassador Airflyte was parked and said, "Gentleman, this car has many exclusive features that appeal to sportsmen especially.

"A Wonderful Twin Bed. arrangement. An Airliner Reclining Seat. A Weather Eye Conditioned Air System—pressurized and thermostatically controlled. All-welded Airflyte Construction—stronger, safer and smoother-riding.

"But the important feature in *this* case," said the director, walking around to the back of the Airflyte, "is the luggage compartment—so spacious that even an outboard motor hardly takes up any room at all!"

"Right you are, Doc," said the sportsman (who was sitting inside the luggage compartment with his friend the .30-06). "I feel comfortable for the first time since I got here! In fact, I hardly feel like an outboard motor any more."

"Splendid!" said the director. "What *do* you feel like?"

"I feel like a guy who has come to his senses and is about to order a Nash Airflyte," said the sportsman. "And so does my friend here, I'll bet."

"Not me!" said the .30-06. "I already *got* a Nash Statesman Airflyte! I went off my rocker trying to figure how a car that big gets 25 miles to the gallon of gas at average highway speeds."

So the sportsman traded his Ajax Eight (which got 14 miles to the gallon coasting downhill) for the Nash Airflyte, and they both got released in time for the opening of the duck season.

No. 33 in a series of NASH AIRFLYTE ads by ED ZERN

OGDEN NASH DEALER'S DILEMMA

ONCE there was a man who opened a Nash Dealership in Ogden, Ute.,

And when people who weren't bona fide hunters and fishermen came in to buy a car, he gave them the boot.

Well, one day a little fat guy with white whiskers and a red suit walked in and said, "How much trade-in allowance can I get on six reindeer and a sleigh?",

And the Nash Dealer said, "Hey!

"Don't be ridiculous!

"I suppose next you'll be telling me you're St. Niculous!"

"Yep!" said the roly-poly gent, "And I'm tired of living like it was still the horse-and-buggy age.

"What I need is a car with a huge compartment for luggiage!

"And instead of fooling around with Donner and Blitzen and such obsolete creatures,

"I want a Nash Airflyte, with Twin Beds and a Reclining Airliner Seat and Weather Eye Conditioned Air and all those elegant Nash features!

"Why should I be playing nurse-maid to reindeer by the squadron

"When I could be driving the car that is, according to what I've heard, the world's most modren?"

"That's a good question," the dealer said. "But while I dislike to appear capricious,

"I got a personal policy against selling a car to someone unless he hunts or ficious.

"And if I should violate this policy just once,

"This showroom would soon be cluttered up with a lot of characters that neither fishes nor honce.

"So naturally I can't go selling a Nash Airflyte to every Tom, Harry and Dick

"Who wanders in here claiming to be St. Nick.

"Then there's a problem about trade-in, too:

"I refuse to turn my used-car lot into a zoo!

"I'll admit I got a couple of used cars that are ready for the dismantlers,

"But at least they don't have antlers.

"However," said the Nash Dealer, "in view of the fact that you have been handing out gifts to all deserving parties from the goose-shooting flats of James Bay to the marlin grounds of Bimini,

"I figure it is high time somebody climbed down *your* chimini!

"So, in order that you can make your rounds in greater comfort, not to mention more economically and faster,

"Here, with my compliments, are the keys to this new four-door Nash Airflyte Ambaster.

"And if anybody should ask you why I violated my long-standing policy, it's because

"It's a mighty poor policy that doesn't have a Santa clause."

MORAL:

For your hunting and fishing friends, a Nash Airflyte would make a Christmas gift positively de luxe.

(Or, if they already have a Nash, how about a copy of *How To Catch Fishermen* by Ed Zern, on sale at all stores that sell buxe?)

Number 34 in a series of NASH ads by ED ZERN (with abject apologies to Mr. Ogden Nash, who has kindly agreed not to sue)

Nash Motors Division,
Nash-Kelvinator Corporation,
Detroit 32, Michigan

LOVE CONQUERS AUL!

No. 41 IN A SERIES OF NASH AIRFLYTE ADS BY ED ZERN

ONCE there was a sportsman named George B. Aul, who was unmarried. He figured a bachelor was a man who never made the same mistake once. But on account of it being Leap Year, he was awfully nervous.

"Stop worrying, George," said a fishing companion. "Trade in your car on a Nash Ambassador 'Golden Airflyte'. Then if some gal gets after you, you can jump in the car and head for the hills. She can't catch you, because the new Super-Jetfire engine is even hotter than the one that set the stock-car speed record of 102.4 miles an hour last year. And with that wonderful Twin Bed arrangement, and that huge luggage compartment for supplies, you can drive the car back in some old logging trail and live in it until it's safe to come out!"

"Great idea!" said George. "Been meaning to get a Nash anyway." So he bought an Ambassador Airflyte with Dual-Range Hydra-Matic Drive, glare-free Solex glass, Twin Beds and Airliner Reclining Seats.

Up to this time none of the unattached females in town had paid much attention to George, because he was sort of inconspicuous, and besides he was usually off somewhere hunting or fishing. But as soon as he started driving around in the first American car designed by Pinin Farina, the girls let the air out of his tires, drew lots to see who got him, and before you could say "Weather Eye Conditioned Air System" he was standing in front of a parson saying "I do".

*   *   *

MORAL: *If you're already married, it's safe to buy a 1952 Nash Airflyte.*

Nash Motors Division,
Nash-Kelvinator Corporation
Detroit 32, Michigan

SEE ALL 17 MODELS OF THE NASH GOLDEN AIRFLYTES AT YOUR NASH DEALER'S NOW

BIRD-DOGGEREL!

A Nash-owning hunter named Bristom
Put up seventeen grouse, but he missed 'em;
    He said, "I don't care—
    I can still breathe the air
From that wonderful Weather Eye system!"

Said bartender Angus McCass,
"Hoot mon! My Nash Statesman's got class!
    It's amazing how far
    You can go in that car
On a wee one-ounce jigger of gas!"

There was a quail-shooter named Bower
Whose outlook was dreadfully sour;
    To a Nash salesman, he
    Said, "It's not for me;
It has Twin Beds—but how come no shower?"

A coon-hunting sportsman named Fife
Said, "Roominess? You bet your life!
    Those Nash seats are so wide
    My nine hounds ride inside
And there's still some room left for my wife!"

A writer of ads exclaimed, "Durn!
I wonder if I'll ever learn
    That when writing in rhyme
    It's a chore, every time,
To make the stuff scan—especially on things
like safer, stronger, all-welded Airflyte
Construction, and the fact that this is
No. 45 in a series of Nash ads by Ed Zern."

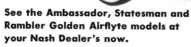

See the Ambassador, Statesman and Rambler Golden Airflyte models at your Nash Dealer's now.

Nash Motors, Division of Nash-Kelvinator Corp., Detroit 32, Michigan

LAME DUCK LAYS AN EGG!

No. 49 in a series of *Nash* ads by Ed Zern

WELL, these ducks were sitting around the bayou and this lame duck swam up. "Howdy, stranger," said a pintail. "How'd you get crippled up like that?"

"Yeh," said the other ducks, eagerly. "Let's hear about it!"

"Well, sir, it's quite a story," said the lame duck. "I was coming down the Mississippi flyway and just south of Vicksburg I saw these gunners in a blind. There was a Nash Airflyte parked not far away, so I figured—"

"What model?" asked a mallard.

"'52 Ambassador," said the lame duck. "Well, I figured them guys in the blind owned the Airflyte, so I—"

"I hear that *new* Ambassador, the 1953, is simply terrific," said a gadwall. "It's got *power steering*, for one thing!"

"They got a new 100-horsepower *Powerflyte Engine* in the Statesman models," said the pintail. "And the same swell Twin Bed deal, with Reclining Seats."

"You don't say?" said the lame duck. "Well, as I was saying—"

"It's the hottest-looking car on the road," said a greenwing teal, "with that Pinin Farina styling and all."

"Okay, okay!" said the lame duck. "So I figured I'd buzz the blind, and—"

"Look, bub," said the mallard. "How come you keep butting in all the time? If you're not interested in the new Airflytes, at least you can keep your trap shut!"

"Yeh!" said the pintail. "Get lost, Limpy!"

So the lame duck swam away, and the next time he told the story he was careful to leave out the part about the Nash.

MORAL: *If you're a duck, don't go around buzzing blinds. If you're not a duck, see the 1953 Ambassador and Statesman Airflytes at your Nash Dealer's showroom.*

Nash Motors, Division of Nash-Kelvinator Corp., Detroit 32, Michigan

THE CASE OF THE CLEVER COYOTE!

No. 53 in a series of *Nash* ads by Ed Zern

ONCE there was a coyote who was being pursued by a pack of hounds. When he'd outrun all but one hound, the coyote called back to his pursuer: "How come you're still going strong, Fido?"

"My boss drives a 1953 Nash Airflyte," said the hound. "That car rides so smooth that I slept all the way out from town. So I was well rested."

"Aren't you getting winded?" called the coyote.

"Not at all," said the hound. "I think it's because of the Nash's Weather Eye—seems like breathing that fresh, filtered air builds up a guy's lungs, sort of! It's a great car, that Airflyte!"

"Hmmm," thought the coyote, "if I can keep this pooch gabbing about his boss's car, he'll soon be out of breath and call it quits." So he called back, "Tell me *more* about that Nash, kiddo!"

"Gosh, I hardly know where to begin," said the hound. "It's styled by Pinin Farina, the greatest custom-car designer. It's all-welded construction, for greater strength, safety and

quiet. Power steering's available on the Ambassador, and all models have Dual-Range Hydra-Matic Drive. And I mustn't forget to mention the capacious luggage compartment."

"The *what* luggage compartment?" said the coyote, who had a limited vocabulary, even for a coyote.

"Capacious," said the hound. "Means roomy. And of course, there's the famous Twin Bed arrangement, and the Airliner Reclining Seats—my goodness, I seem to be all . . . out of . . . *breath!*"

"Ha!" said the coyote. "I counted on that, you foolish mutt!"

"Oh, I almost forgot one thing," said the hound. "Namely and to wit, the terrific reserve of power in that Nash Ambassador's Super Jetfire Engine!"

So saying, he put on a burst of speed, caught the coyote and cooked his goose before you could say, "See your Nash Airflyte Dealer today!"

MORAL : *Don't kid around with hounds that use words like "capacious."*

Nash Motors, Division Nash-Kelvinator Corporation, Detroit 32, Michigan

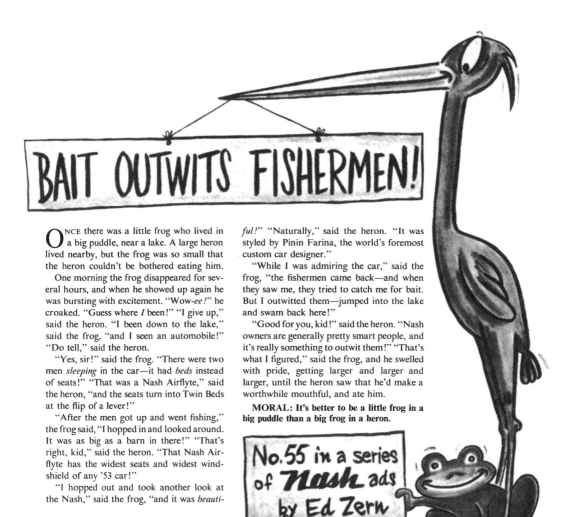

BAIT OUTWITS FISHERMEN!

ONCE there was a little frog who lived in a big puddle, near a lake. A large heron lived nearby, but the frog was so small that the heron couldn't be bothered eating him.

One morning the frog disappeared for several hours, and when he showed up again he was bursting with excitement. "Wow-*ee!*" he croaked. "Guess where *I* been!" "I give up," said the heron. "I been down to the lake," said the frog, "and I seen an automobile!" "Do tell," said the heron.

"Yes, sir!" said the frog. "There were two men *sleeping* in the car—it had *beds* instead of seats!" "That was a Nash Airflyte," said the heron, "and the seats turn into Twin Beds at the flip of a lever!"

"After the men got up and went fishing," the frog said, "I hopped in and looked around. It was as big as a barn in there!" "That's right, kid," said the heron. "That Nash Airflyte has the widest seats and widest windshield of any '53 car!"

"I hopped out and took another look at the Nash," said the frog, "and it was *beautiful!*" "Naturally," said the heron. "It was styled by Pinin Farina, the world's foremost custom car designer."

"While I was admiring the car," said the frog, "the fishermen came back—and when they saw me, they tried to catch me for bait. But I outwitted them—jumped into the lake and swam back here!"

"Good for you, kid!" said the heron. "Nash owners are generally pretty smart people, and it's really something to outwit them!" "That's what I figured," said the frog, and he swelled with pride, getting larger and larger and larger, until the heron saw that he'd make a worthwhile mouthful, and ate him.

MORAL: It's better to be a little frog in a big puddle than a big frog in a heron.

No. 55 in a series of *Nash* ads by Ed Zern

Nash Motors, Division Nash-Kelvinator Corporation, Detroit 32, Michigan

Judge Joins Mob!

68th in a series of Nash ads by Ed Zern

WELL, THIS COP hauled this pickpocket into court and said, "Your Honor, I just caught him working a crowd down the street."

"What kind of a crowd?" said the judge.

"There's a big mob of people at an auto dealer's showroom," said the cop, "but I didn't stay to find out why."

"Durned if I know why people hang around them places," said the judge. "Did you catch this bird with the loot on him?"

"You bet!" said the cop. "Four wallets, seven shotgun shells, three gold watches, two hunting knives, a cherry bobber, a dog-training collar, six fountain pens, a dozen snelled hooks, five—"

"Yike!" said the judge. "*The new Nashes!* Court's dismissed—gangway!"

And so everybody including the prisoner rushed down to the Nash Dealer's to see the 1955 Ambassador V-8 and Statesman models with sensational new styling, new air conditioning and a whole slew of other exciting features plus Twin Travel Beds, Airliner Reclining Seats, huge luggage compartment and all the rest of Nash's famous special-for-sportsmen advantages.

This time the pickpocket got five wallets, a popper plug and the judge's crow call.

MORAL
If at first you don't succeed, try, try again.

Nash Motors Division,
American Motors Corporation,
Detroit 32, Michigan

ONCE THERE WAS A DUCK-HUNTER driving through the west in his 1951 Nash Airflyte with Hydra-Matic Drive. When he came to a town way back in the hills where they were holding a Lying Contest, he parked his car and entered the contest.

After the local talent had told about the windstorm that blew the wagon tracks off the hayfield onto the courthouse lawn, and the gopher that burrowed into the side of a dust storm, and the fast-growing vine that wore out the pumpkins dragging them around on the ground, it came the duck-hunter's turn.

"Friends," he said, "I drive a 1951 Nash Airflyte, with Twin Beds and an Airliner Reclining Seat. On account of having coil springs all around, and super-

rigid, all-welded Airflyte Construction, it's just about the smoothest-riding car on the market. In fact, one night I was driving through a town at 50 miles an hour and ran over three hogs and the mayor, and never even felt a bump.

"And the next day," the duck-hunter said, "I crawled back into that enormous Airflyte luggage compartment to look for a sack of decoys I had mislaid in there, and got lost. I wandered around in that luggage compartment for three days and three nights, and if I hadn't flushed a covey of quail and shot one with my pistol I'd have starved to death before I found my way out."

The Judges Committee then declared a brief recess, and when it was over the chairman rapped his gavel. "Gents," he

said, his voice quivering with rage and indignation, "durin' the recess, me and the boys done some checkin' up. This here stranger left the keys in his Nash Airflyte—so we lined up three hogs and the mayor, and throwed in a deputy sheriff for good measure, and run over 'em at 50 miles an hour.

"Then we opened up the luggage compartment to see how big it really is. And folks, I got somethin' to tell you! *This lop-eared, low-down, no-good, ornery, double-crossin' coyote was tellin' th' TRUTH!*"

So everybody jumped on the duck-hunter and beat him black and blue and took him out and flang him into the horse-trough.

MORAL: *Never leave the keys in your car.*

Nash Motors Division, Nash-Kelvinator Corporation, Detroit, Michigan.

See all three Nash Airflytes for 1951: The Ambassador, the Statesman and the Rambler (in Convertible, Station Wagon and Suburban models.)

Three Mermaid Stories

(A Booklet for Western Fishing Line Company, 1959)

Once there was a man named Wilmer B. Wipps, who wanted to catch a mermaid. So he went down to Angleworm & Fish, a sporting-goods store, and explained his problem to the clerk.

"What kind of a mermaid did you want to catch, sir?" asked the clerk. "Gosh," said Wilmer, "you mean there's more than one kind?" "There are lots of kinds," said the clerk. "There are speckled mermaids, and walleyed mermaids, and smallmouth mermaids, and sockeye mermaids to name a few. There are also mer**men**, of course." "Is that so?" said Wilmer. "Do they ever, well, sort of get friendly, like, with mermaids?" "Certainly," said the clerk, "and when they do, it's called a merger. What kind of mermaid would you like to fish for?"

"Well," said Wilmer, "I think I'd like to catch a smallmouth mermaid. How do I go about it?"

"First of all," said the clerk, "you'll want a spinning rod, and a spinning reel, and some lures, and some 'W-40' Monofilament, the monofilament that's famous for its combination of high strength, low stretch and resistance to fatigue. Also—"

"Never mind that 'W-40' spiel," said Wilmer. "I already got some monofilament that's plenty good enough."

The next weekend Wipps hooked a mermaid on his spinning tackle, but the monofilament he was using wasn't famous for its combination of high strength, low stretch and resistance to fatigue—consequently it busted, and the mermaid got away.

Moral: **People who use "W-40" Monofilament are smarter than Wipps.**

Once there were two fly fishermen who went into a sporting-goods store. "What I want," said the first fisherman, "is a dry-fly line that will float all day, without dressing."

"Brother," said the salesman, "you sure come to the right place! What you want is a 'W-40' Floating Fly Line. Man, it really **floats!** I remember one time an excursion boat loaded with women and children started to sink ninety feet from shore. I was on the bank with my fly rod and a 'W-40' Floating Fly Line. The Tufcote finish on that line is so smooth it shoots right through the guides, and so I easily cast ninety feet to the sinking boat. Well, sir, every last man, woman and child tight-rope-walked to safety on that 'W-40' Floating Line—and some made several trips, to carry their belongings."

"Okay," said the first fisherman, "I'll take one."

"What I want," said the second fisherman, "is a line that **sinks.** One that will take a wet fly down to where the lunkers lay, and not take all day about it."

"Brother," said the salesman, "you sure come to the right place! What you want is the 'W-40' Sinking Fly Line. Man, it really **sinks!** I remember one time I was fishing from a boat and the current was so strong the anchor started to drag, and I was rapidly being swept over a falls. Fortunately I had a 'W-40' Sinking Fly Line on my rod, and—"

"Okay," said the second fisherman, "I'll take one."

Then both fishermen went to a famous trout lake, rented rowboats and rowed out to the middle of the lake. While the first fisherman was putting his rod together a beautiful young mermaid popped up beside his boat. "Kiddo," she said, "I like your looks! Come on down and spend a few minutes with me and I'll give you a gunnysack full of pearls, and a lard pail full of gold nuggets. You'll be rich as Croesus! Just a few minutes—come on!"

"It's a deal!" said the first fisherman, and hopped over the side into the water. Unfortunately, though, he had the "W-40" Floating Fly Line in his pocket, and couldn't sink, and the mermaid, who thought he was stalling, called the deal off and swam away in a huff.

And when the second fisherman saw the first fisherman floundering in the water he thought he was in trouble, and jumped in to save him. Unfortunately, though, he had the new "W-40" Sinking Fly Line in his pocket, and naturally he sank like a stone, and was never heard of again.

Moral: **Sometimes you're better off without a "W-40" Fly Line.**

Once there was a man named Gus, who was bait-casting in a lake and foul-hooked a mermaid. When he reeled in and saw what was on his plug, he was furious. "Beat it, sister," he hollered. "G'wan, scram! Can't a guy fish in peace without some dizzy fish-tail dame butting in? Take off!"

"I can't, stupid," said the mermaid, "I'm hooked right in the—well, see for yourself." "Gosh," said Gus, blushing, "you sure are! Here, take my pliers." While the mermaid was unhooking herself, Gus said, "Don't you know no better than to fall for a bass plug, dopey?" "Sure I know better," said the mermaid, "but this one was chugging along without a line on it! When I swam over to investigate, I accidentally got hooked. How can you fish a plug without a line?"

"I got a line, blondie," said Gus, "but it's one of them 'W-40' Bait Casting Lines, with the new scientific camouflage color that makes it practically invisible to fish. Also, 'W-40' Bait Casting Lines are smaller-diameter than other lines of the same test, so they're less visible on that score, too. It's on account of Western's exclusive 'Hot Stretch' process that removes surpl—hey, come back with them pliers, toots!" "In a minute, mac," said the mermaid, and sure enough she was back in a minute with an armload of bass. "Here," she said, throwing a couple of dozen big bass into the boat, "this is to make up for spoiling your fishing. So long!"

As the mermaid was disappearing into the depths of the lake a warden came by, found the big mess of bass in Gus's boat and hauled him off to a magistrate, who fined him fifty dollars for exceeding the creel limit. When Gus explained about the mermaid the judge fined him another ten bucks for being drunk.

Moral: **When you stop and think about it, maybe that guy Wipps wasn't so dumb.**

PART

IV

EXIT
LAUGHING

Sometime in 1958 Hugh Grey, then the editor of *Field & Stream*, asked if I'd like to write a department to be called "Exit Laughing" to run each month on the last page of the magazine, with the understanding that I could write on any subject provided it didn't violate the postal laws and had some relevance to hunting and fishing, or at least to the out-of-doors, and I said yes.

The first "Exit Laughing" ran in the November, 1958 issue and the column has appeared in each issue since then. I think this was the first magazine feature that required the reader to turn backward instead of forward when the piece was continued on page so-and-so.

Not surprisingly, some "Exits" are sillier than others, and I've picked out some of the ones I liked best to be in this book. If I left out your favorite I'm sorry.

Two years ago at a fishing camp in Alaska another fisherman said to me, "Mr. Zern, I thought you'd like to know that I always start reading *Field & Stream* at the front of the magazine." I bought him a drink.

These are not in any particular order, but then neither am I.

Recently I learned that Mr. George Plimpton's book *Paper Lion*, in which he describes his experiences with a professional football team while disguised as an athlete, was still selling briskly; as this had been going on for a year or so it was patent that Plimpton must be wallowing in pâté de foie gras, vintage Puligny and matched Purdey shotguns, while I am barely able to afford pastrami, off-year sneaky pete and a beat-up pump-gun. At about the same time I read an article in a weekly sports magazine in which Sam Baker of the Philadelphia Eagles was quoted as saying, when telling of an unsuccessful try for a fifty-yard field goal in a driving rain, "It was like kicking a wet duck."

While I was assimilating that simile it occurred to me that although temperamentally unsuited to being abrased by linemen or contused by red-doggers, I could nevertheless experience in some degree the sensations of a pro-footballer without the discomfort and inconvenience of being maimed, and thus might, perhaps, qualify for some of the crumbs from Plimpton's platter. Hurrying to the telephone I called Duncan Dunn, whose commercial shooting preserve near Princeton raises several thousand mallards every year, and asked if I might borrow a duck.

"What do you want it for?" Duncan asked, and when I said I wanted to kick it he thought for a minute. "By George," he said, "you've finally hit on a technique—I recall last year you tried a shotgun without much success. I presume you want a low-flying duck?" "I don't give a hoot how it flies," I said. "I'm going to kick it on the ground." "A true sportsman," mused Duncan, and told me I could have one of his ducks for experimental purposes the next day.

Arriving the next morning I found him puttering with the pheasant pens, but he came back to the clubhouse with me and produced a drake mallard in a wooden cage. "Knowing you're a gentleman as well as a sportsman I assumed you wouldn't want to kick a female," he said; I agreed, and asked him where I'd find a faucet. "If you're thirsty," Duncan said, "there's beer in the game-cooler." "I'm no thirstier than usual," I said. "I need the faucet to wet the duck." "You can't wet a duck," Duncan said. "If you pour water on a duck it runs off like water off a duck. You'll have to make do with a dry duck."

"Look, Duncan," I said. "If Sam Baker had meant a dry duck he'd have said so.

Whereas he specifically said a wet duck. If you think I drove seventy miles to kick a dry duck you've got another think coming. Where's the faucet?" "I don't think you drove seventy miles to kick any kind of a duck," Duncan said. "I don't think, period. In this business, I can't afford to. On the other hand, though, I don't go around kicking ducks. There's a faucet right behind you, by the bench."

I took the mallard out of the cage, turned the faucet on and held the duck under it. It didn't seem to be getting very wet, but after a while it began to feel heavier, and while I was trying to decide if it was just my arm getting tired a car pulled into the yard and a skinny little bald-headed man got out. "My name's Pritchert," he said to Duncan. "I'm an inspector for the New Jersey League Against Cruelty to Animals. We check on shooting preserves, and if you don't mind I'll look around."

"Help yourself," Duncan said. "Be my guest. What I'd like to see, though, is some-body from the New Jersey League Against Cruelty to Shooting Preserve Operators." While Duncan was explaining some of the cruelties inflicted on him by various types of shooters, Mr. Pritchert came over and watched me for a minute. "What are you doing to that duck?" he asked.

"I'm wetting it," I said. "That's what *he* thinks," Duncan said. "He's been holding it under there for ten minutes, and it's no wetter now than when he started. The only thing he's wetting is the property. Why don't you pinch him?" "Why are you wetting it?" Pritchert asked, more suspicious than ever. "So I can kick it," I said, changing the duck to the other hand as my arm was about to drop off. "Ha!" said Pritchert triumphantly, and then he stopped and thought a minute and said, "*Kick* it?" "That's right," I said. "I suppose that sounds kind of kooky to somebody who isn't a writer."

"Why in the world would you suppose a thing like that?" Duncan said, and Pritchert said, "Kicking a duck is cruelty, mister. I'm obliged to warn you. You kick that duck and we've got an airtight case against you." "If he can't kick any better than he shoots," Duncan said, "you wouldn't have a snowball's case in hell." "*Chance* in hell," I said. "Good Lord. Snowball's *chance* in hell. Case in hell doesn't make sense."

"Well, now," Duncan said. "That's very good. You stand there holding a duck under a faucet that you drove seventy miles so you could kick it, and you're saying I don't make sense. Mama mia!" "What's that?" Pritchert asked. "Italian," I said. "It means his mother. It's an expression." "Not that," Pritchert said. "That cage. Is that what you keep your ducks in? That little bitty thing?"

"What do you keep yours in," Duncan said, miffed. "A suite at the Waldorf Astoria?" "He doesn't keep them in that," I said. "That cage was just for the one I needed for kicking." "Look," said Duncan, "are you going to run that faucet all day? This place is a quagmire already, and that duck's still dry as a bone." It was, too, and my arms were so tired I turned off the water and put the duck back in the cage.

"Keeping a duck in that thing is cruelty," Pritchert said, "and no two ways about it." "I agree," Duncan said. "Why don't you arrest him and take him into Trenton. Or anyway get him the hell out of here so I can get some work done." I figured things were getting out of hand, and even if the duck had been sopping wet I had sort of lost interest, and so I let it out of the cage. It hopped out and waddled over and stood under the faucet, which was still dripping. Pritchert took out a notebook and asked me my name; I told him and he wrote it in the book. Duncan said, "My name's Duncan Dunn. The duck's name is Marvin. I wish both you guys would go away." "Marvin what?" Pritchert said, and while he and Duncan were having some sort of a discussion I got in the car and drove home. Who needs Purdeys?

FREAK FISH FORESEEN!

At the last meeting of the Madison Avenue Rod, Gun, Bloody Mary and Labrador Retriever Benevolent Association the following business was transacted:

Mr. Marvin Chase inquired what had become of a certain member who had not showed up at the last several meetings. Mr. Gene Hill reported that this member had recently bought one of those beer-can throwers at Abercrombie & Fitch, to be used for wing-shooting practice, and that in order to have enough empty cans to provide decent shooting the member had taken to drinking large quantities of beer. Within two months he had become a hopeless alcoholic, had quit his job and deserted his wife and family, and was now a Bowery bum. Mr. James Rikhof proposed that a Bowery chapter of the MARGBM&LRBA should be organized, as there would probably be other cases of this sort, but the motion was defeated.

Mr. Ralston Martin, chairman of the science committee, reported that the latest hydrogen bomb would wipe out an estimated fifteen million people in the New York City area, and that this would undoubtedly reduce fishing pressure on the Beaverkill, Esopus, and other Catskill area trout streams. He further said that many biologists predict that strontium-90 and other fallout materials would produce a number of two-headed creatures, and that in the case of trout this would greatly increase the chances of catching them, as if one head was not in a feeding mood the other might be.

Mr. Whiting Hall, chairman of the committee on truth in advertising, said that he had personally supervised efforts to check the accuracy of an advertisement which stated that the Winchester Model 59 barrel is wound with 500 miles of glass fiber, but that the committee was unable to unravel the test barrel, and in fact could not even find the end. However, he said that Winchester had given permission to have somebody come up to the plant with a tape measure.

Mr. Vance Morton, chairman of the poetry committee, reported that he had planned to read a poem about natural-resources conservation at the meeting, but would have to ask for a postponement as he had been unable to think of anything that rhymed with "ecologically disoriented." However, he offered to recite an ode that the committee had composed jointly on the subject of the Dingell-Johnson bill. The offer was declined.

Mr. Harold Mersey reported that in the Sportsman's Notebook feature of the September *Field & Stream* a formula for waterproofing tents started with instructions to "dissolve

½ lb. powdered alum in 2 qt. boiling rainwater. Pour solution into 2 gal. cold rainwater.''
Mr. Mersey said he had been anxious to waterproof a tent to use on his vacation but had
been unable to find a store in New York City that sold rainwater. As a result he planned
to open a rainwater bottling plant, and had even thought of an advertising slogan, ''The
quality of Mersey's is not strained.'' He said a formula for preserving pork-rind lures in
the same article required a salt-brine solution strong enough to float a raw potato, but
that all he could find in the kitchen of his apartment was a package of instant potatoes,
so that in addition to a leaky tent he had had to put up with perishable pork rind.

Mr. Ted Rogowski, chairman of the research committee, reported that a psychiatrist
friend of his had psychoanalyzed fifteen fishermen during the last two years, and had
cured each one of them of all interest in fishing by revealing the compulsively masochistic
irrationality of their behavior, which was essentially an unconscious effort to resolve their
inner guilt-tensions by acting out an infantile rejection of reality through fishing. As a
result, Ted said, all fifteen patients had given up fishing and turned to civic welfare work,
getting ahead in business, and other emotionally mature activities, and the psychiatrist
had been able to buy a luxurious camp on one of the best salmon rivers in New Brunswick.

Mr. Ken Booth reported that his wife had come across a $70 curly-maple blank that
he had been saving to make a new stock for his 16-gauge Parker, and had had the gardener
split it up for peony stakes. He said it had made very poor stakes, as they were too wavy.

He said the amount of alimony had not yet been decided but that he was hopeful, as the judge was known to be a handloader.

There being no further business to transact, the meeting was adjourned.

How To Shoot Quail

Some of the outlying chapters of the Madison Avenue Rod, Gun, Bloody Mary and Labrador Retriever Association have been grossly tardy in filing their quarterly reports; in fact, last fall's report has just arrived from attorney John S. Daily, chairman of the Fort Smith, Arkansas, chapter. It reads as follows:

"Recently was in Oklahoma visiting old friend whom I hadn't seen in many years. Invited me to go quail hunting. Accepted with alacrity and pleasure. After loading his station wagon with lunch, shells, guns, and rain gear, friend carefully folded and placed in rear of wagon a quilted mattress pad, smoothing it gently. Then whistled softly, whereupon appeared elderly black-and-white English setter. Dog large for breed, with massive head and oversized jaws. Looked him over carefully, thought I detected faintly

hostile gleam in eye. Host gently lifted him into back of car and onto mattress pad. After under way, inquired dog's name. 'Butch,' answered friend.

" 'How old?' I inquired. 'Some say 14, some say 16,' answered friend. High hopes for day afield began to wane.

"After few minutes of traveling, Butch arose from mattress pad, climbed over back of seat, snuggled self on my hunting jacket. Pretended not to notice this flagrant breach of canine manners, but friend did. He reached back and patted old dog's head. On arrival at hunting ground, host lifted Butch from my jacket and gently placed him on ground. We loaded guns, he parted barbed wire of fence and assisted Butch through strands. In field, Butch bestirred self into slow, tottering trot. Maintained this pace fifty to seventy-five yards ahead of us. Although dog wasn't covering much ground, host gave him no commands, never called him in, urged him on, or signaled change of direction. Merely followed Butch. I followed him.

"After ten minutes, Butch stopped at edge of brier thicket. Didn't point. Just stopped and stood still, tail limp, nose slightly lowered, expression thoughtful. Host and I walked silently up behind him. As came abreast, nice covey flushed from briers directly in front of dog's nose. Friend killed two, I killed one. Butch shuffled out, retrieved all three quail faultlessly, with gentle mouth.

"Rest of covey had flown about hundred yards straight away, then veered to right over patch of scrub oaks. Butch ambled ahead to about point where covey had veered right, then turned left and moseyed over hill. About 200 yards from where I estimated singles should be, Butch stopped again in small creek bottom. Again just stood still, sagging slightly. Single bird rose, I fired and missed. Host killed it. Butch's retrieve leisurely but otherwise faultless. Thirty yards farther, Butch again stood still. When walked up beside him, dog absentmindedly lifted leg against mine, wet canvas pants leg slightly but held point, if that's proper word. Two singles rose. I missed mine, host killed his with second barrel. Butch stopped for third single which flew my way. Missed it twice.

"Butch then quit singles, went in new direction up small steep hill. At top, stopped again but this time laid down. Host walked up, sat down beside him, bid me do same. After five minutes' rest, Butch rose slowly to his feet, resumed ambling trot. Second covey and third followed much same pattern as first, including singles, with never word of command or instruction from master to dog.

"After working over singles of third covey, tallied score mentally and realized host had eight birds, I had three but had missed more than he had shot at. Further recalled he had not missed bird at which he fired, although in two cases had required second shot when first missed. Embarrassed at being outclassed, fired three shots but failed to touch a feather on fourth covey rise. Butch retrieved nice right and left for friend. Alibied apologetically, 'You're shooting so well I'm plumb flustered, can't hit a thing.'

"Host replied, 'Ah, but difference is I have to kill birds, you don't.' Seemed odd statement, as friend surely didn't need quail to feed family.

" 'What do you mean,' I asked, 'you have to kill birds?' Friend embarrassed. Pointed to Butch. "When I miss one," he said, 'he wets *my* leg.'

"Otherwise not much activity this chapter."

HOW TO GET A BEAGLE BLOTTO

If I had my single-trigger, detachable sidelock, full-and-modified druthers I would spend most of my waking hours loitering in the vicinity of Montana trout streams, Alberta duck sloughs, and Maine woodcock covers, with occasional forays to chase a flock of chukars up an Idaho coulee or brandish a Garrison rod at a New Brunswick salmon. But the day they divvied up druthers I was out behind the barn smoking corn-silk and studying corset ads; as a result I am obliged to work in New York City, dodging crosstown buses instead of charging bull moose and wishing the local fish weren't quite so gefilte.

And when occasionally I do escape to the boondocks I'm obliged to endure the well-meant commiseration of camp operators, guides, and local sportsmen who persist in telling me how unfortunate I am to live in that meretricious metropolis, instead of telling me where to find a 4-pound brown trout. They have a point, of course, but they're usually so busy making it that I seldom get a chance to tell them that New York City has a kind of sporting life all its own.

I'm not referring to the fact that it's not merely possible but probable to catch 20-pound stripers, shoot a limit of ducks, and kill ten-point whitetail deer literally within sight of the Manhattan skyline. On the contrary, the sporting life I refer to is almost entirely a conversational one, existing haphazardly on street corners, at luncheon restaurants, in gin mills, and around the counters of the town's few bona fide sporting-goods stores, as a sort of furtive lunatic fringe on what literary historians sometimes call "the oral tradition."

Thus a man hurrying back from a hasty lunch to attend a meeting of his company's marketing committee meets a friend who's already late for an appointment with his accountant, and although both of them have just risked death and a jay-walking ticket by crossing the street against the don't-walk warning in order to save 15 seconds, they pause while the first man tells the second about his plans to fly to James Bay for the goose shooting next fall, and the second reports the highlights of a weekend on the Ausable River. Or, to be more specific, take the case of my own sporting life last week:

On Monday in Grand Central Station I ran into Wally Sherman, who asked if I remembered a conversation we'd once had about the tendency of advertising men to say "production-wise" or "gross national product-wise" or "cost per thousand women between the ages of 18 and 34-wise," and I said I did. He then explained that he had asked a high-powered advertising executive for suggestions on how to fish a certain trout stream in New Hampshire's White Mountains, and had just received a cryptic note in reply. It merely said, "Advise dries, flies-wise."

On Tuesday, while walking down 44th Street, I met Gene Hill and learned he had spent the morning with his lawyer, revising his will. He said it now named Abercrombie & Fitch as his executor, as he figured nobody else would be able to make head or tail of his estate.

On Wednesday while coming out of the subway at 59th Street and Lexington I ran into Gordon Hurd. He said that some time ago he had bought one of those beer-can launchers that utilize a .22 blank cartridge to propel an empty beer can as a practice target for wingshooters. He said he didn't especially like it, but that at an outdoor office beer party it had come in handy when several of the waiters failed to show up. He said that once he had got the hang of the ballistics he had been able to lob a can of beer from the ice tubs clear across the lawn into the lap of a thirsty colleague, and that except for a couple of misfires and a can that ricocheted off a tree and clobbered the firm's best customer, it had been a bang-up success. He said that before the next beer party, however, he would take it out to the gun-club range and sight it in.

On Thursday I had lunch with Harry Throckmorton, who said he had got awfully tired of meeting fishermen and hearing how they had just taken a 22-inch 4-pound brown trout on a size 20 nymph tied on a 6X tippet, and that he had finally perfected a portable and fully transistorized lie detector which could be carried in the pocket of a fishing jacket. He said he had tried it out on five fishermen on the Housatonic the previous Saturday, and that three of them had taken the Fifth Amendment, one had demanded to be permitted to call his attorney, and the other had tried to shove him into a deep pool.

On Friday I met Harry Merck on Fifth Avenue, and learned that since making a fortune selling tiny cocktail sausages, which he called Marteenie-weenies, he had become deeply interested in dogs. He said that many of today's dogs, particularly if they ran in field trials, lived lives of great anxiety and tension, and that just as a before-dinner cocktail could improve a tired businessman's disposition and calm his nerves, so a small snort of booze could relax a springer spaniel or an English setter after a hard day afield. As a result, he said, he would soon put on the market an alcoholic beverage known as Pooch Hooch, from which considerate dog owners could concoct canine cocktails. While he was telling me that he would even provide special drinking dishes, to be known as Pup Cups, I ducked into a doorway and lost him in the noontime crowd.

All the same, it's nice to think that soon this stuff will be on the market, and that my Labrador retrievers won't have to face the new migratory waterfoul regulations cold sober.

HOW TO RUN A SPORTING-GOODS STORE

At last month's meeting of the Madison Avenue Rod, Gun, Bloody Mary, and Labrador Retriever Association the following business was transacted: Treasurer Gene Smith reported that he had not had a chance to balance the books, as he had had to take his children to the doctor to have them wormed or something of that sort. Mr. Richard Wolters, on a point of order, said that to the best of his knowledge children were never wormed, and that they had probably merely had distemper shots. Mr. Smith said that whatever it was, it had prevented him from finishing the treasurer's report but that perhaps it was just as well, as the association was currently running a deficit.

Mr. Robert Rose said that since the members spent most of their money on sporting goods, maybe the association should start its own retail store and use the profits to finance the club. He said he felt certain that by applying up-to-date, scientific merchandising principles to a sporting-goods store the members could undoubtedly make a lot of money. Mr. Carl Vance said what kind of principles, for instance, and Mr. Rose said well, for instance it was a well-known fact that the only reason most sportsmen didn't buy more sporting goods was for fear of their wives. He said that if he were running a sporting-goods store in New York City he would set up a Special Confidential Delivery Service; for an additional charge of $2 any purchased item would be delivered by plainclothes delivery men driving unmarked cars, and would be wrapped in old newspapers or—if a rod or gun—would be contained in an old beat-up rod tube or gun case.

Mr. Rose said he could probably get unemployed character actors for this work, and that when a housewife came to answer the doorbell the delivery man would say, "How do you do, Mrs. Johnson—I don't believe we've ever met. I live over on the other side of town, and I want to return this fly rod your husband lent me some time ago. Tell him thanks a million. 'Bye now.''

Mr. Gene Hill suggested that a suspicious wife might inspect the merchandise, and that for an additional $2 the store could buff most of the blueing off a new shotgun and scuff up the stock, and take similar measures with a new rod—dirty up the cork grip, knock off a guide and, possibly as a last resort, put a slight set in one of the tips.

Mr. Jim Henshall said that if the store gave trading stamps, it might solve the entire problem. "If Abercrombie & Fitch gave green stamps with shotgun shells," Mr. Henshall declared, "my wife would have the freezer full of them. And the refrigerator would be full of cardboard shell boxes, each with one or two shells in it."

Mr. Whiting Hall said he had noticed that all fishermen pick up fly rods, when shopping for a new one, and wiggle them briskly. He said this can get pretty tiring, especially if the fisherman is out of condition, and suggested that the store should have an automatic rod wiggler. He said it would be simple to build, using a small electric motor, and that the customer would merely set up the rod, insert the butt into the holder and push a button, whereupon the machine would wiggle the rod while the customer stood by and admired the tip action.

Mr. Hall said he had also noticed that browsing hunters invariably pick up double-barreled shotguns, break the action, and look through the barrels. He suggested that a certain percentage of these guns should have pictures of attractive young ladies wearing bikinis or less in the barrel, to stimulate interest in the shotgun department. "Anyway," Mr. Hall said, "when a man does all that looking he's entitled to see something."

Mr. Karl Oswald said he agreed that wives were the key to the problem of selling more sporting goods, and said the store should have a special gift department where sportsmen could buy presents for their womenfolk. He said that for their anniversary, for instance, he had given his wife a new hand trap with a special spring arrangement, and that she had been very grateful, as with the old one she kept throwing her elbow out.

Mr. Harold Martin said he was not sure women really appreciated such thoughtfulness, as his own wife was being unreasonable at the moment. He said he had persuaded her to rub her face with boiled linseed oil instead of her regular vanishing cream, since it worked so successfully with gunstocks, but that unfortunately the results had not been favorable. Mr. Dick Decker said that most women's faces were more porous than walnut, and that probably she should have used a sealer first. Mr. Gene Hill offered to lend Mr. Martin some of his checkering tools, but the offer was declined.

There being no further business to transact, the meeting was declared adjourned.

TEST YOURSELF

In the August issue of *Trout*, official publication of Trout Unlimited, there's a quiz-type test for fly fishermen. Without exception, the questions deal with such matters as proper hook sizes, differences between spentwing and upright patterns, proper uses of the double haul in casting, and other purely technical considerations.

It has always seemed to this department that the really important and fundamental problems of fishing cannot be, or at least should not be, reduced to mere technical know-how or mechanical skills; rather, that they are essentially moral and ethical in nature, and that such efforts as this to despiritualize the sport are a sad reflection of the materialistic world in which we live today.

I have, therefore, drawn up a quiz of my own with the thought that if all trout fishermen were forced to take a test of this sort, only those who achieved a certain minimum grade would be granted licenses and the pressure on our streams and lakes might thus be substantially reduced. Here are the questions:

1. You are engaged to marry your beautiful and charming childhood sweetheart, whose family has no money but who loves you devotedly. Two weeks before the wedding date you meet a homely, bowlegged, pigeon-toed girl whose father owns two miles of excellent trout fishing near his home, has a shooting and fishing lodge in western Montana, and owns both banks of three topnotch pools on the Miramichi in New Brunswick. She is an only child, and is obviously attracted to you. What do you do about your engagement?

2. After spending considerable time and money learning to tie flies, you collect a magnificent assortment of natural blue dun and other high-grade hackle, furs for dubbing, fine-wire hooks, and other materials. Shortly after you install a fully-equipped fly-tying table in your den, your six-year-old son develops a violent allergy to feathers. What action do you take?

3. While fishing the lower Brodheads in Pennsylvania you notice an enormous brown trout rising steadily to a hatch of green drakes. Just about the time you have tied a No. 12 Green Drake to your leader and spent ten minutes carefully working your way across the current into casting position, you notice that the hatch is beginning to taper off. At the same time you hear a cry from the railroad track alongside the stream and see that a beautiful damsel in a low-cut gingham dress has caught her foot in a switch and is calling to you that the express train from Stroudsburg to Scranton is due in three minutes. What do you do?

4. While fishing from a boat with a wealthy uncle who owns a number of custom-built Payne, Garrison, and Orvis rods with matched reels and lines, not to mention several best-grade Parker shotguns and a brace of matched Model 21 Winchesters, he tells you that as his own children have no interest in outdoor sports he has recently revised his will to leave all his fishing tackle and guns to you. When he stands up to play a fish in deep water, you recall that he's unable to swim a stroke. What's your next move?

These are, admittedly, difficult questions, and while I don't propose to reveal the correct answers, these hints may be in order:

1. It may help your thinking on this question to bear in mind that while beauty fades and mortal love may turn to ashes, the Miramichi has been a pretty good salmon river for several thousand years.

2. Frankly, you may not get full credit on this if you suggest putting the boy up for adoption. There are several good boarding schools that accept boys of this age, or you could send him to live with relatives. Adoption is a lengthy, bothersome process.

3. Some fairly expert sportsmen have been tripped up by this one. We suggest you ask yourself which is more difficult to come by, a four-pound brown trout or a pretty girl.

4. Well, there's that proverb about casting your bread upon the waters.

I would propose that anyone flunking this test should be obliged henceforth to stop taking up space on trout streams and confine himself to some other pastime. There's not enough good water today for even the truly dedicated anglers, and if a man doesn't have a sense of proportion and a feeling for relative values, he doesn't deserve a license.

HOW TO TIE FLIES

Well, there was this handsome, happy-go-lucky young prince who spent all his time fishing except between seasons when he repaired rods and tied flies, and one day his father the king called him into the throne room and said, "Son, I just got word my ticker's on the blink, and it may not be long before you'll be taking over this job. It's time you started thinking of getting married and settling down."

"Okay, Pa," the prince said, "but right now I'm in the midst of tying up a batch of Quill Gordons for opening day—it's next Saturday, and I promised some of the guys around the palace I'd furnish each of them a dozen. Thank goodness my cousins Ethelbert and Halmred don't fish, or I'd never get finished. As a matter of fact I'm running out of natural blue dun hackle already, and there's not a decent neck in the kingdom. I may even have to dye some."

"Frankly, son," said the king, "it's Ethelbert and Halmred I'm worried about. They're going around saying you're a scatterbrain and a pipsqueak, and talking about how if you were king the country would go to pot every trout season. I think they figure if you were out of the picture they'd be next in line for the royal throne."

"Gosh, Pa," said the prince, "I wouldn't want that to happen. They're always talking about what a waste of time and manpower fishing is, and how much bigger the GNP would be if all fishing were abolished. By the way, Pa, what does GNP mean?"

"It means gross national product," said the king, "and it's kind of complicated. Better

ask the Grand Vizier to explain it to you. But before you do, I want you to look over this list of eligible princesses and decide which one you'd like to start courting. Any one but the Princess Angelina.''

"What's wrong with Angie, besides those thick ankles?" the prince asked.

"My goodness," said the king, "haven't you heard? She offended the West Wood Witch, who has promised to transform any suitor of Angelina into a beast of some sort. Last week she turned Lord Grumby's son into an aardvark just for taking her to the movies, so I guess she means business.''

"Golly, Pa," said the prince, "do you mean this witch can transform anybody into any kind of animal or bird or fish?"

"Not fish," said the king, "this spell doesn't work under water. Here's that list.''

"Okay, Pa," said the prince, "I'll check it over." So saying, he headed for the West Wood, and knocked on the witch's door. When she opened it the prince said, "Good morning, ma'am. I hear you can turn people into aardvarks.''

"You ain't just whistling *The Sorcerer's Apprentice*," said the witch proudly. "What about it?"

"Nothing," said the prince, "only from what I've heard, aardvarks are easy. I was wondering if you could turn people into something really difficult?"

"Such as?" said the witch.

"Well, let's see," said the prince. "Well, maybe such as an Old English Gamecock?''

"Nothing to it, buster," said the witch, "gamecocks are kid stuff.''

"Not the kind I meant," said the prince. "The kind I had in mind have feathers that are sort of a dirty blue-gray color, with very stiff, glassy barbules and hardly any web. From what I hear there isn't a witch in the kingdom can turn a man into one of those."

"What lamebrain told you *that* cock-and-bull story?" sneered the witch.

"Gracious, I don't remember," said the prince. "Let me think a minute. Oh yes, of course—it was my cousin Ethelbert. I asked him to explain it to me, but he was in a hurry to go courting some dizzy princess—said his brother Halmred was courting her too and he wanted to get there first. That Angelina must be *some*thing."

"Well, well, well!" said the witch. "Ethelbert, eh? And his creepy brother? You sure you really meant a dirty blue-gray, not a nice, bright, jazzy blue?"

"Gray-blue, with just a touch of rusty red," said the prince, "and be sure there's no web in the neck feathers."

A few weeks later, right after the king died, the prince issued an edict that from henceforth GNP stood for great northern pike, and declared a day of mourning for Ethelbert and Halmred, who were missing. As fishing was considered bad form during periods of mourning the prince spent the day tying up a batch of Quill Gordons—using natural blue dun hackle with a touch of rusty red—and the next day had his limit before noon.

There were eighty-seven entrants in the contest to translate the motto of the Madison Avenue Rod, Gun, Bloody Mary & Labrador Retriever Benevolent Association (''Keep your powder, your trout flies and your martinis dry'') into Latin; in addition, seven readers submitted translations into French, Norwegian, Pennsylvania Dutch, and pig Latin. Five entries were from college professors and three were from high-school Latin teachers. There were eight entries from Ohio, seven from New York State, and four each from Massachusetts, Minnesota, and Wisconsin.

No two of the translations were exactly alike, and most had only a slight resemblance to any of the others. Five people included suggestions for coats of arms with their translations. Four entrants included self-addressed stamped envelopes, from which we steamed the stamps to help defray the expense of running the contest. Six entrants misspelled one or more English words in their letters of submission, and one of these, a high-school senior, misspelled eleven words out of a possible fifty-five; one high-school teacher spelled it ''Feild & Stream.''

When the entries closed on February 15, the problem of judging arose. My wife, a devout egalitarian, felt that as one's intelligence and to a certain extent one's educational opportunities are matters of luck and inheritance, and as it would therefore be unfair to penalize the more ignorant and stupid entrants for something over which they had no control, the only democratic way to select the winning entries would be to draw them out of a hat.

This posed another problem, as the writer, who has a tendency to pinheadedness, found that none of his hats would hold more than a third of the entries, and that even his wife's sombrero-type beach hat would accommodate fewer than half. (My daughter suggested that the beach hat would be inappropriate for anything except littoral translations, and was sent to bed without any supper.)

It was finally decided to select the winning entries on a basis of neo-pragmatic opportunism, plus one point each for neatness, witty side remarks and flattering references to any of the writer's books. On this basis the winners are as follows:

First prize: Jaroslav Jan Pelikan, Titus Street Professor of Ecclesiastical History, Yale University Divinity School, New Haven, Connecticut. Professor Pelikan, whose somewhat impressionistic entry was distinguished by its nifty combination of classical Latin meter with two triple alliterations and a tolerable rhyme, was obliged to put the martini before the powder and the trout flies in order to bring this off, but explained that it seemed no less than fitting to have the aperitif come first. His version:

> *Semper siccandae sunt: potio*
> *Pulvis, et pelliculatio.*

Second prize: John H. Moss, President, Consultants in Operations Research for Public Service, Inc., Bethesda, Maryland. Mr. Moss's translation, "*Cave ne tuus pulvis pyrius, tuae muscae piscatoriae, et tui martinii non sicci sunt,*" is solidly constructed, and Mr. Moss received two extra points for using the word "aetiology" in his scholarly letter of transmittal.

Third prize: F. F. Murphy, Denver, Colorado. Mr. Murphy's translation, "*Semper siccus pulvis, salaris setae, et martinii vestri fiant,*" is not especially skillful, but he gets a prize because in order to produce it he used a Latin-English dictionary published by Ginn & Co.

Among a number of close contenders for the three prizes were high-school student William Bloxson of Riverhead, Long Island, who wrote, "This is the first time in two years I've had any use for my education"; Bill Laurent of Fishing Tackle Trade News, whose accompanying note was written in Latin; Miss Eleanor Adams of Albany, California, whose entry was on a postcard of the Christian Brothers wine cellars; and the Reverend Father E. T. of a seminary faculty who requested that his initials only be used, lest he be reassigned from the philosophy department to teaching Latin again.

Special Certificates of Merit go to Richard Wolters, because his wife's name is Olive; G. Norman Slade of White Bear Lake, Minnesota, whose entry was in an obscure Skoweegian dialect but who offered to put the writer into some good woodcock cover; and to Harvard student Walter Nichipor, to help offset the prize to a Yale teacher. And to all the others who entered, my thanks for your concern, effort, and (in a number of instances) scholarship. I've sent checks for fifteen, ten, and five dollars to the three prizewinners, and as this leaves me with a rather neat profit of ten dollars on the page, I think I'll trot on down to the corner tavern and have a martinus or two.

TROUT FISHERMAN'S NARROW ESCAPE

Once upon a time a beautiful young princess, with cheeks like primrose petals and hair like spun gold, went for a walk in the forest. When she saw a toad hopping along the path, the princess said, "Oh, you ugly, warty creature—how hideous you look!" It happened that two witches, one of whom was pretty ugly and warty, were passing nearby, and thinking that the princess was commenting on her appearance the ugly, warty one immediately cast a spell over the fair maiden, who thereupon fell into a deep sleep.

"Insolent snippet!" screamed the ugly witch. "You shall sleep until doomsday, unless perchance a handsome young prince shall kiss your ruby lips!"

"You're letting her off pretty easy, aren't you?" asked the second witch. "You know how them handsome young princes are—the first one that finds her is going to figure he might as well kiss her, and bingo—there goes the spell."

"You're right!" said the ugly witch. "How's this: you shall sleep until a handsome young prince *with three legs* shall kiss your ruby lips! That ought to hold her!"

"Don't be too sure, toots," said the second witch. "I'll admit most handsome young princes only got two legs. But just last week at the county fair I seen a chicken with three legs, and if it can happen to a pullet it can happen to a prince."

"That's a fact," agreed the warty witch. "Let's see now, how about this: you shall sleep until a handsome young prince *with three legs and rabbit ears* shall kiss your ruby lips! There, if that doesn't keep blondie out of circulation for a couple of aeons, I'll turn in my broom!" And the witches hobbled on through the woods, leaving the lovely young princess deep in sleep.

Pretty soon who should come along but a handsome young prince and his companion, a tall young duke. Both of them carried fishing rods, for they were on their way to angle for trout, and the prince carried a stout wading staff, as the stream to which they were going was swift and treacherous. "Hey, prince," said the tall young duke, "you know what that staff reminds me of? A third leg, that's what! It's like you got three legs! Waddya know—a handsome young prince with three legs! Haw, haw!"

But the prince paid no heed to his companion's jest, for he suddenly realized he had forgotten to bring his fly box. "Woe is me," he said sadly. "But perhaps I can find at least one fly stuck in my vest. Ah, yes—sure enough! Here's a No. 12 Hare's Ear—and by the Lord Harry, here's another!"

"Hare's ear?" said the tall young duke, who was a worm fisherman. "You got two hare's ears? Haw, haw! A handsome young prince with three legs and rabbit ears! Ho, ho, that's a hot—Hey! Get a load of the dame!"

"Get a load of what dame?" said the prince.

"That one there," said the duke, pointing to the beautiful princess asleep on a couch of ferns and sweet grasses.

"My word, she's sound asleep!" said the prince. "By George, I've got a good notion to slip her a kiss! Here, hold my rod a minute."

So saying, he was about to plant a lusty smooch on the princess's lips when the tall young duke, who was nobody's fool, shouted, "Hold it, Romeo! Don't do it!"

"For heaven's sake," said the prince, unpuckering his lips, "why not?"

"I'll *tell* you why not," said the duke. "I figure any time you find a good-looking chick in a deep snooze it's even money some witch has slapped a spell on her. Them witches are hell on good-looking dames—especially princesses, and take a look at that royal signet ring on her pinky. You go bussin' this blonde, buster, you're liable to break the spell."

"Well, why not?" said the h.y.p.

"Prince," said the duke, "you're a nice guy and all, but sometimes you don't *think* good. Lemme spell it out for you. You bust the spell, and Nembutal Nellie wakes up—she's grateful—she insists you gotta come to dinner and meet her old man—the first thing you know you're engaged—and all of a sudden you're married. After that, no more trout fishing—you got to stay home and put up the screens. No more deer hunting—your wife thinks they got such nice eyes. And besides, she don't approve of the guys you hunt with. No more beagles and bird dogs in the palace—she can't stand dog hair on the sofa. Pretty soon she'll be throwing out all your broadbill decoys to make room for a playpen. Get the picture, kiddo?"

"Holy smokes," said the prince, "that sure was a narrow escape! Let's get on down to the crick before the trout quit jumping." So they hurried on down to the Junction Pool, where they each caught their limit of browns.

NEW BOON FOR SHOOTERS!

In Ireland last October with Warren Page to shoot snipe, I woke one morning at the Shamrock Hotel in Athlone to find the thermometer at an unseasonal 38 degrees instead of the normal 60 or 65, and so after breakfast I stopped at a men's clothing store on the main street, bought a pair of inexpensive knitted woolen gloves, and asked for a pair of scissors. When the storekeeper produced them I cut the fingers off the gloves to make them into shooting mitts and—not wishing to litter up the obliging merchant's counter—put the amputated fingers into the pocket of my shooting jacket.

That evening, standing at the bar in the combination pub and tackle shop of F. Browne in Athlone, I got to talking with a local sportsman about the uncanny ability of the common snipe to zig when the shooter zagged, and absentmindedly pulled one of the woolen glove fingers out of my shooting-jacket pocket. "What's that?" asked the Athlonian. As at that moment I also felt a few leftover cartridges in another pocket, I explained that because the combustion rate of gunpowder varied according to the temperature, decreasing in speed when it was colder and thus affecting the muzzle velocity of the shot

and changing the forward-lead requirements on a crossing bird, many American shooters protected their cartridges from chills and wintry blasts by means of knitted covers, and I slipped the glove finger over the shell to show him how it worked. After finishing a third pint of Guinness it occurred to me that such an essential article of field equipment would have a name, and so I further explained that because the principle was the same as that embodied in an ordinary tea cozy, these articles, manufactured by an enterprising gentleman named Kincaid, were called Kincaid Kartridge Kozies, and that no serious, self-respecting American shotgunner would think of walking around in cold weather with a pocketful of stark-naked shells.

I don't know whether my companion took this explanation unsalted, but I observed that he seemed to be edging farther and farther away from me right up to closing time, and the next morning as we walked down the street I noticed several local people staring at me and whispering among themselves, with someone occasionally pointing his finger at his forehead and twirling it meaningfully. All in all I began to feel a bit of a bounder, and have since lain awake several nights brooding over the arrant caddishness of this effort to pull the leg of a kindly, courteous fellow sportsman.

In the future, however, I shall sleep like a log, thanks to a recent issue of *Winchester Proof*, a monthly bulletin of news for shooters. According to an item in that interesting publication, cold cartridges in cold chambers actually do perform at appreciably less than warm-weather power, and trajectories drop along with the mercury. In short, not only had I spoken truthfully to my fine Hibernian friend about the effect of temperature on ammunition, but I had also inadvertently invented a sorely needed item of shooting equipment.

In consequence I have just organized the Knickerbocker Knitted Knickknack Kompany to manufacture a variety of models of the Kounty Kerry Kartridge Kozy, so called in recognition of the birthplace of the idea. (I believe Athlone actually lies a considerable distance from County Kerry, but I've taken the position that all's fair in love and alliteration.) K. K. K. Kozies will be available in all popular gauges from .410 to 12, and magnum models may be had at a slight surcharge. The standard Kozy will be made of a good grade of wool, but there will be cashmere and alpaca models for wealthy sportsmen, tropical-worsted models for use in mild weather, and a special tweed model for use while shooting driven grouse.

Admittedly it may take some persuasive selling to put this new product across, but I have already engaged an advertising agency and will embark on an all-out campaign when the shooting season opens. The agency has come up with a theme song you'll be hearing shortly on your local radio station; set to the tune of "K-K-K-Katie," it goes:

> K.K.K.Kozies, sanforized Kozies,
> You're the only k-k-k-kartridge koat for me;
> When a-a-ammo
> Doesn't go whammo
> Kount on Kozies to restore trajectoree!

And as soon as large numbers of sportsmen are made aware of the disadvantage of cold ammunition we also plan to manufacture and market a cartridge belt with an electrical heating element, similar to that used in electric blankets, that can be plugged into any outlet. This will be priced at $3.75 for the upland-bird shooters' model, with an additional charge of $499.50 for the extension cord.

While walking down Fifth Avenue the other day I ran into Archie Mercer, a former advertising executive. When I asked where he'd been keeping himself for the ten years since I'd last seen him, he said that after making a fairly substantial killing on the stock market in 1950 he had quit his job and become an anthropologist.

"It was what I'd always wanted to do," he said, "and after sweating out a doctorate at Penn, I managed to get assigned to some expeditions, and have been pretty much on the go ever since. Just got back, in fact, from six months on the Bweti Islands, a last stronghold of cannibalism and other fascinating customs."

"You mean that the natives actually eat people?" I said.

"Yes, indeed," said Archie, "the Sengi tribe kills and eats rival tribesmen regularly. Actually they *trap* their human prey, in pitfalls baited with food—dig a deep pit, cover it with mats, camouflage it with grass and stuff, then set a dish of whatever food is in season on the mat and wait for a Goora or a Maati or some other tribesman to come along and fall for it—literally!"

"My word!" I said.

"However," said Archie, "the Sengi are rather queer ducks, and for some remote reason—probably something to do with religous taboos—they don't bait the pitfalls with real food. Instead, they make imitation bananas and yams and breadfruit and whatever else happens to be in season—it's considered very bad form to use the real article. Oh, of course some of the Sengi cheat a bit—pretend they're using imitation stuff, but sneak a real pawpaw onto the mat if they think nobody's looking.''

"It must be awfully interesting," I said.

"It is indeed," said Archie, "and I hope to get back there and dig much deeper into the whole mysterious business. For example, there are shops in the villages that sell nothing but the materials from which the imitation foods are made—dried leaves, balsa wood, kapok, pebbles that look like berries when they're painted, macaw feathers, monkey hides. God knows what all. And most of the men of the village hang out there, arguing about which natural foods are in season, and which are best for baiting a particular jungle path or a particular tribe—they say there's one tribe, the Pakkos, whose members get to be seven feet tall and weigh three hundred pounds, but they feed only at night, and the Sengis will argue all day about whether it's best to use light-colored artificial food, so the Pakkos can see it better, or dark food, since the Pakkos are supposed to be able to see as well by night as by day."

"I hope you're able to get back there," I said.

"So do I," said Archie, "especially because I hope to study the differences between the various victim-tribes. The Sengi can't agree on this—some say the Gooras are so easy to trap it's no fun, and others hate the Maatis because they're too wary, and also they're reputed to drive out the rather stupid Gooras. Some say the Maatis jump higher and oftener, trying to get out of the pits. Also there are some who claim the Gooras are much tenderer and tastier, although personally I found—oops, sorry, just noticed that clock! I'm ten minutes late for a meeting of the Natural Science Society—see you around!''

A few blocks down the Avenue I spotted Dick Morgen wearing a happy smile, and as he usually looks haggard and distressed I asked him what was up.

"I'm glad you asked," he said, beaming. "Remember how upset I was the last time I saw you, about all this pollution of the atmosphere—atomic bombs, Fifth Avenue buses, industrial smoke and all that? Well, this morning it occurred to me that probably the greatest single source of air pollution is people breathing. Think of it—almost four billion human beings inhaling good clean oxygen all day long and exhaling crummy carbon dioxide! And then I realized that if only everybody in the world would hold his breath for one minute twice a day—say once in the morning and once at night—it would conserve a total of 100,000,000,000 cubic feet of oxygen every day, or 36,500,000,000,000 cubic feet of the stuff every year! I'm on my way right now to talk to a man at the World Health Organization—see you later.''

"So long," I said, but when I tried holding my breath that evening I got all black in the face and my wife made me stop, as she said it was frightening the dogs.

TRUCK STUFF

I had lunch the other day with my filthy-rich friend Charley Throckmorton, and would have outfumbled him when the check came except that he couldn't be bothered competing. (It was Charley, you may recall, who, when he got interested in handloading, constructed his own private shot tower.) While he was riffling through his credit cards I noticed what seemed to be an absurd number of New Jersey automobile registrations, even for Charley (who lives there), and asked him about them.

"There are only seven," Charley said, "one each for the Aston Martin, the two station wagons, the beach buggy, the Land-Rover, the camper outfit, and the hatchery truck." "You have a *hatchery?*" I said. "No," said Charley, "I have a hatchery *truck.*" "Why?" I said. "Well," said Charley, "last year I drove out to California, and stopped at a diner somewhere in Kansas. Ordinarily I'm wary of diner food, especially in that part of the country, but there were several big, shiny trucks parked outside as well as a lot of passenger cars, and I'd always heard that this was a reliable indication of good, or at least edible, food.

"Pulling into the parking area, I bumped into a truck and broke one of its taillights, and so when I went inside I tried to find the driver to tell him what I'd done and pay for the damage. And I couldn't find him. Checked every customer in the joint, looked in the men's room, and finally asked a waitress to help me. She got rather flustered and turned me over to the proprietor, who told me a fancy yarn about the driver having been taken ill. But when I insisted on knowing how to get in touch with him, he shrugged and said okay, I'll level with you. Then he explained that after putting most of his life savings into building and equipping the diner about a year previously, he had been unable, during the first six months, to break even, much less show a profit. Motorists looked for diners with trucks parked in front, and the truckdrivers already had their regular eating stops.

"Then one day, he said, he read about a bankrupt sale in the city, with a fleet of tractor-trailer jobs among the assets being liquidated. The next morning he went into town, bought two of the outfits with his last capital, drove them home one at a time, and parked them in front of the diner. In no time at all, he said, he was getting so much transient trade that he'd had to enlarge the kitchen and put on two extra waitresses, and had even invested in two more trucks. I paid him for the taillight, ate a leathery T-bone steak, and went on my way.

"I forgot all about it," Charley said, "until this spring. As you know, I live not far from some pretty good trout water—Flatbrook and the Gorge of the Raritan—but as usual all the good pools were terribly crowded. Then I remembered that Kansas operator, and so I went into town, bought a tank truck, had it painted to look like a state hatchery truck, and took it back to the place.

"Nowadays, when I fish the Gorge, I have one of the hired men park it behind some bushes about a mile away, with a walkie-talkie in the cab, and when the water gets too crowded I call in the code word. In a couple of minutes my man drives by in what seems to be an official hatchery truck, asks one of the fishermen along the river how to get to another stream about ten miles away, and drives off in that direction. And before you can say 'Musconetcong' almost every, ah, sportsman in sight will have jumped in his car and hightailed it down the road after the truck.

"They never catch it, though, because it ducks into a side road just around the bend and circles back to wait for another call. I must say I've had the least crowded fishing this year since you and I fished the Gorge with Ken Lockwood nearly thirty years ago. Does that answer your question?" I said it did.

HOW TO SHOOT PIGEONS

While in Yucatan several years ago, to shoot pintail ducks and poke around Mayan ruins, I met an American resident in Merida whose only serious complaint about the country was his inability to maintain hubcaps on his Buick sedan; he said they were removed so swiftly and efficiently, after each replacement, that he marveled at the mechanical genius of the Mayas, and said that if they had been remiss in their failure to invent the wheel they were far in front of all other races in their agility at de-hubcapping it. "Actually," he said, "they're a charming and dignified people, and I'd cheerfully forgive their swiping of the 'caps if they'd only let me know where to go to buy them back."

A few days later I jeeped far back along a jungle trail that finally petered out in a Maya village of wattled huts and impoverished but proud and pleasant Indians who spoke no English or Spanish but knew the language of hospitality, and who welcomed Shaun Viguerie, my guide and mentor, and myself with gourds of home-grown, home-brewed chocolate and heaping platters of food. Or, to be more precise, with heaping Buick hubcaps of food. I tried to find the Yanqui automobilist again, with the thought that he might wish to visit the village and try to ransom his hubcaps with payments of pots and pans, but my airplane left before I could locate him.

Some time ago I read of a midwestern city that had been plagued with pigeons and had finally, in desperation, called on some of the local shotgunners to come downtown each Sunday and shoot the pests in a roped-off office-building area. I'm not sure how effective this was, but it undoubtedly helped the shooters kill a Sunday afternoon, and I think of it every time I walk through the south end of New York's Central Park, which could probably provide faster pigeon-shooting action than any place this side of Venice's Piazza San Marco.

Unfortunately New York elects to cope with its pigeons by less direct means, and according to my friend Les Henderson, whom I met on Fifth Avenue recently, the city authorities have secretly sent out crews to net the birds by the thousands; they are put— 20,000 at a time—into huge vans with crosswise perches, driven at least a hundred miles into the country, and released.

Les said that a friend of his was assigned to drive the truck into the Catskills, and had invited him to come along. Having nothing better to do he accepted, and was enjoying the trip until they turned off the main road and headed up a steep mountain road, as the driver's instructions were to release the birds in an isolated area. Halfway up the mountain, Les said, the truck stalled repeatedly on account of the gradient, but was unable to turn on the narrow road or even to back down. The driver, meanwhile, insisted that his orders were to release the birds at least a hundred miles from city limits as the pigeon flies, and he was short of this distance by ten or twelve miles.

"For a while," Les said, "I thought we were stuck, and then I had an idea. I got out and walked beside the truck, pounding on the side of it with a heavy stick, and my friend Charley had no trouble driving up the rest of the mountain. Because, of course, as soon as those 20,000 pigeons started flying around it reduced the truck's load by several tons."

I considered pounding on Les's side with a heavy stick but had none handy, and so proceeded on my way as he on his.

How To Find True North

One of the pleasures to which I look forward each month is the arrival of *Winchester Proof*, a publication having to do with matters of interest to outdoor writers. Representing the combined talents of Winchester-Western's research biologists, ballistics experts, and public-relations geniuses, this lively bulletin is almost always worth careful perusal and sometimes—as I am about to reveal—it contains nuggets of information that are, quite literally, life-savers.

Thus, in one of last winter's issues I came across the following: "It can get mighty cold in the woods this time of year. . . . If you lose your compass and can't find the North Star, don't despair. You can still find true north, which should be a great help. Prop a stick into the ground at a 45-degree angle and hang a rock from the end of the stick. Just before noon, mark the spot where the rock's shadow falls (*a*), and again about six hours later (*b*). Starting directly under the suspended rock, draw a line to a point midway between the morning (*a*) and the afternoon (*b*) marks. This line points to within three degrees of true north.''

Shortly after reading this I chanced to be hunting partridge in New York's Sullivan County and became hopelessly lost in a heavily forested area. Recalling the instructions in *Winchester Proof*, I stuck a stick into the ground at a 45-degree angle and hung a rock from it, using the lace from one of my boots as a cord. Unfortunately it was considerably after noon when I realized I was lost, so I was obliged to build a crude lean-to and spend the night huddled in it, to be on hand for the following noontime.

At five minutes before twelve the next day I marked the shadow of the stone (*a*), and as I had nothing to do until 6 o'clock I decided to take a short nap. (I first tried going for a walk, but kept stumbling over my unlaced boot and gave it up.) Unfortunately I fell into a sound sleep, and by the time I awoke the sun had gone down and it was again necessary to spend the night in the lean-to.

The next day at noon I once more marked the spot (*a*) and carefully refrained from falling asleep lest I repeat the previous day's fiasco. Unfortunately at about 4:30 P.M. a heavy rain began to fall and softened the ground to such an extent that the stick fell down.

The following day I again arranged the stick at a 45-degree angle, being careful to prop it with stones so that it couldn't collapse, and just before noon I marked the stone's shadow (*a*). At 5:45 a large cloud came up and obscured the sun so thoroughly that the stone cast no shadow (*b*), and I again spent the night in the lean-to.

The next afternoon the cord, no doubt weakened by prolonged exposure to the elements and the weight of the stone, broke in two shortly before 6 o'clock, and by the time I could remove my other bootlace and hang the rock from it, being considerably weakened by hunger and cold, it was 6:15. Realizing that Rome wasn't built in a day, I shrugged philosophically and crawled back into the lean-to.

Unfortunately during this period the days had been getting shorter, and on the sixth day, although everything else went swimmingly, the sun set at 5:52.

By this time I was growing desperate as well as hungry, and might have panicked or gone off my rocker and stumbled about in the woods babbling incoherently and tearing holes in my good Burberry shooting jacket, if a party of Girl Scouts had not come by on a Nature Hike and, after reviving me with cookies, led me back to civilization.

Once upon a time there stood, in the middle of an enchanted forest, a tower one hundred feet high. In a locked room at the top of the tower was a beautiful young princess who had been imprisoned there by her wicked uncle, the king, who feared she would claim the throne he had seized when the former king, her father, had died. To prevent her rescue, a fierce firebreathing dragon had been tethered beside the main gate of the tower, while at various landings on the stairs that ascended to the princess's chamber were chained a maneating tiger, a ravenous lion and a ferocious leopard, each eager to dine on anyone foolhardy enough to defy the false king's will.

One balmy April day a handsome young man rode up to the clearing in which the tower stood, dismounted from his charger, unsheathed his sword, and advanced resolutely toward the entrance to the tower. When the dragon rose to bar his way, the young man swung his mighty sword and lopped its head from its body. Stepping over the prostrate corpse the fearless youth smashed the padlock on the door, opened it, and stepped inside. There he was confronted by the maneating tiger, but one swift blow of his sword put an end to the creature's carnivoracity.

Advancing up the stairs, the young man next came upon the hunger-maddened lion, but again a single sweep of the steel sufficed to write finis to the savage monster's life, and when the leopard rushed snarling to devour him, it too was mortally smitten.

Then the reckless youth advanced to the top of the stairs, and when he saw that the way was barred by an iron door he once again swung his great broadsword and cleft the lock in twain, so that the door swung open. When the young man stepped into the forbidden room the beautiful princess rushed forward and threw her arms around him. "My hero!" she cried. "My gallant savior! How brave and strong and noble you are!"

"Lay off, toots," cried the young man in alarm. "You're crushing the fly box in my jacket! Take it easy! And besides, who are you and what are you doing here?"

"Silly boy," said the princess, "I'm imprisoned here by my wicked uncle, the false king. But you must have known, for else why would you have slain those frightful beasts and fought your way to this tower?"

"Honey," said the young man, "you got me wrong. I knew there was a dragon downstairs because I seen him every time I came past, and I knew there was some other livestock inside because I heard them roaring and snarling and whooping it up every time I rode by. But I sure didn't figure there was any dames on the premises."

"In that case," said the princess angrily, "why did you force your way to the tower?"

"Because where else," said the young man, "can a guy get the kinks out of a fly line?"

When he saw that the princess was mystified, the youth continued, "Lemme spell it out for you, sis. Last fall my dopey brother-in-law used my best double-tapered fly line to troll for walleyed pike with a June-bug spinner. Well, next week is the opening of trout season, and the line's full of kinks and twists. So I come up here so I could dangle the line out of the top window and let it untwist itself—after all, this is the only building in the whole crummy kingdom that's a hundred feet high."

So saying, the youth drew a fly-rod reel from his pocket. Stepping to the window, he quickly paid out all the line, letting it dangle in the breeze, where it soon worked out its twists. While the young man was winding the line back onto the reel the princess said, "Well, perhaps your gallantry was unwitting, but in any case I am overjoyed to have my freedom, and will follow you in gratitude and devotion."

"You will in a pig's eye," said the youth. "You'll stay right here while I go round up another dragon and some maneaters. If you think I'm going to get mixed up in some big political deal just when the trout season's about to bust open, you're off your noodle. Furthermore, if the king stuck you in the brig he must of had a pretty good reason, and little Charley don't aim to cross him. So long, blondie—see you around."

After the young man had repaired the lock he closed the door on the princess, bought a second-hand dragon and staked it out beside the tower, live-trapped a lion, a tiger, and a leopard to replace the ones he had slain, and had everything back in apple-pie order by opening day.

How To Cook A Caribou

At the last meeting of the Madison Avenue Rod, Gun, Bloody Mary and Labrador Retriever Benevolent Association the following business was transacted:

Mr. Tex Brockett, chairman of the Chicago Chapter, reported that thanks to important advances in the development of sodium pentothal, this so-called "truth serum" could now be administered orally, and being virtually tasteless could be slipped into a fellow woodcock hunter's martini, muscatel, or milkshake much in the manner of a mickey. As a result, he said, he had acquired a long list of excellent coverts and had enjoyed sensational shooting last season. But by the same token, he added, he had thought it wise to pass up a number of free drinks proffered by gunning friends, and as probably not more than one drink in five or six had actually been drugged, he calculated that each woodcock in his bag had cost him a sizable slug of sourmash bourbon, and he sometimes wondered if the game was worth the candle.

Mr. Sam Blake, chairman of the Aberdeen, Washington, Chapter, reported that upon hearing that the *SFI Bulletin* for September had included a section titled "Stripper Symposium" the chapter had ordered one hundred copies from the Sport Fishing Institute. He said by the time they learned that the article dealt with strip mining in Ohio it was too late to cancel the order.

Mr. Stan Combes, chairman of the Accounting Committee, reported that at the close of the 1964 trout season he had added up the cost of transportation, new tackle and depreciation, meals, licenses, liquor, club dues and so forth, and had found that his trout fishing had cost him $117.95 per day. He had therefore arranged to hire a man who had agreed to do all his trout fishing for him during the 1965 season, at a charge of only $75 per day. He estimated that this would result in a total saving of more than five hundred dollars, with which he planned to buy a new shotgun.

Mr. Ted Burns reported that he had taken his wife and three children on a 2,000-mile salmon-fishing trip to Labrador, by car, and that he had made the mistake of buying a bushel of eating apples at the beginning of the journey. Because of his intense feeling about littering highways the children had been forbidden to throw anything from the car, and he said that the vehicle was so filled with the remains of apples that it was impossible to describe. Mr. Tom Innes, chairman of the Nomenclature Committee, on a point of order inquired if it could not have been described as a corey Ford, and was ejected from the meeting.

There being no further business to transact, the meeting was adjourned.

Upon receiving the following letter from a North Dakota reader—"Dear Mr. Zern: How come you never give us any useful information? Like you take Trueblood or Tapply, they explain how to repair busted fly rods or cook a meal while camping. Don't you know no recipes or something?"—it occurred to me that I have indeed been remiss in this respect. I therefore hasten to pass on to readers this suggestion for a tasty and nourishing dish especially suitable when camping in caribou country.

Côtellettes de Caribou à la Sangue Veritable. Sauté 6 caribou cutlets lightly in fresh creamery butter, then arrange in a circle in an earthenware baking dish lined with prosciutto ham sliced paper-thin. Garnish with Brussels sprouts, half-roasted chestnuts, tiny glazed onions, a tablespoon of chopped shallots, 6 sliced mushrooms, and 1 cup of *petits pois à l'ognon* mixed with shredded lettuce. Slice 3 white truffles very thin and cover the garnish with these. Add ½ cup of white wine of a good year. Bake at 400 degrees for 40 minutes, then baste with a sauce made of Madeira, fresh thick cream, beef stock, brandy, and purée of tomato. Continue baking for 10 minutes. Arrange cutlets in a rosette, cover with *Sauce Perigueux*, garnish with parsley, and serve with a 1955 or '59 Chambolle-Musigny.

I omit directions for making *Sauce Perigueux,* as this subject was thoroughly covered in my article in a recent issue entitled "Wilderness Survival." *Bon appétit!*

ALL ABOUT WORM-FISHING

I met Malcolm Wheatley on 45th Street the other day, and when the subject of trout fishing came up, I found him no less vehement on the matter of worm fishing than he has been, more or less, for the past thirty years. "Mal," I said finally, "I think you exaggerate. Personally I'm a fly fisherman, and think it's the best way to fish for trout, but I can't believe that worm fishermen do as much damage to streams as *you* seem to believe."

"Ye gods, man!" shouted Mal, who's excitable. "You can't be serious! I can cite you dozens of cases where streams have been RUINED by worm fishermen!" "Name one," I said. Mal sputtered for a moment, then dragged me into a coffee-shop and flung me into a booth. "All right, buster," he snarled, "you asked for it. Just one case? Okay, you know the Lackawaxen, in Pennsylvania?" "Certainly," I said. "Well, sir," said Mal, "just about five years ago this month a worm fisherman from New Jersey went there fishing with his fiancée. It so happened she was from Barnegat, and had an almost

insane passion for orderliness. One of those people who go around straightening pictures that are already straight and emptying ashtrays with one burnt match in them.'' ''I know the type,'' I said, ''but what about worm fishing?''

''I'm coming to that,'' Mal snarled at me. ''When this worm-fishing s.o.b. asked her to pick him out a wiggler from his bait can, where he had them in sphagnum moss, she opened up the can and then let out a helluva shriek. 'THE KELP!' she yelled. 'IT'S ALL TANGLED!' It wasn't kelp, of course, but to anybody from Barnegat it looked like seaweed. And naturally it was kind of messed up, which on account of this thing she had about orderliness caused her to scream.'' ''Naturally,'' I had to admit.

''Well,'' said Mal, ''a native walking by on the road alongside the river heard her scream—matter of fact, he'd seen them going down the bank and had figured they were up to no good—and then heard her holler what he thought was 'HELP! I'M BEING STRANGLED!' '' ''That figures,'' I conceded.

''Okay,'' said Mal. ''When the native heard that, he ran out in front of a passing car to stop it and get help. Unfortunately he jumped right in front of the car and it hit him and killed him stone-dead.'' ''For goodness' sakes,'' I said. ''What a pity.'' ''Ha!'' said Mal. ''That's nothing! True, the guy was penniless and had an invalid wife and no insurance—but the lady driving the car that hit him jammed on her brakes, and the truck behind her hit *her*. It so happened she was a destitute widow with seven children, and the whiplash injury she got when the truck slammed into her left her paralyzed from the eyeballs down—a hopeless case. The children were all farmed out to orphanages, and are growing up bitter and neurotic at the trick fate played on them.'' ''It *was* a tough break,'' I agreed.

''You ain't heard *nothin'*, pal,'' Mal said darkly. ''The bird driving the truck bumped his head into the windshield, and although nobody thought much about it at the time, he complained of pains in his head for six months afterwards, and then went berserk one day and killed six people with a meat cleaver before they gunned him down like a dog.'' ''You can't blame them too much,'' I said. ''After all, six—''

''Never mind them!'' Mal screeched, his face contorted with fury. ''I haven't even come to the bad part! While the truck was standing there a deputy sheriff with a wife and five children came roaring down the road in a high-powered car—he'd had a call from a nearby farmhouse—and smashed into the truck, kapow! In fact, he hit the truck so hard that the car bounced off it and down the bank into the creek, drowning the driver.'' ''Gosh,'' I said, ''what a terrible tragedy!''

''Listen!'' yelled Mal. ''Here's the payoff! This deputy had a house and a rose garden and a nice lawn and all that, and loved gardening, and when he took off to answer the accident call he had a gallon jar of weedkiller in the back seat, and when the car rolled down into the creek the jar broke and the weedkiller ran out into the current. Every last drop—right into the river!'' ''What about it?'' I said.

''Great balls of fire!'' Mal screamed. ''Holy saints in heaven! *That gallon of poison killed nearly one hundred trout in the next quarter mile of river—including a dozen or so that would go over three pounds!* AND YOU ASK WHETHER WORM FISHING DAMAGES A TROUT STREAM? HA!''

I had to admit he had a point, and so I paid for the coffee.

HOW TO CAST A FLY

At the last meeting of the Madison Avenue Rod, Gun, Bloody Mary and Labrador Retriever Beneficial Association the following business was transacted:

Mr. Martin Matthews, chairman of the Committee to Save America's Trout Streams, said he had recently visited the Beaverkill to observe progress of the highway construction that threatens to destroy the river. He said he had been touched to notice another member, Mr. John Candless, standing beside an enormous bulldozer as it moved toward the stream, with tears streaming down his cheeks and convulsive sobs racking his frame. Mr. Candless, on a point of order, said it was true that he had shed tears and sobbed, as the bulldozer had run over his foot.

Mr. Dick Forley, a new member, said he had just recently been taught to cast a fly by the clock method, in which the caster thinks of his casting arm as the hour hand of a clock as he faces left, and is trained to stop his arm and rod at the 10-o'clock position on the forward cast and at the 1-o'clock position on the back cast. Mr. Forley said he had been making fine progress all during last winter and spring, but that after daylight-saving time began he could never remember whether to stop his back cast at 12 o'clock or 2 o'clock, and had nearly had a nervous breakdown.

There being no further order of business, the meeting was, on motion duly made and seconded, adjourned.

HOW TO HAVE BANG-UP TROUT FISHING!

While in Eugene, Oregon, last June to attend the organizational meeting of a national federation of fly-fishing clubs, at which I helped Lee Wulff and Gene Anderegg represent the Theodore Gordon Fly Fishers of New York, I overheard considerable talk as to the most sporting way of taking trout, and it was the consensus of the group that this meant fly fishing. However, nobody asked my opinion.

Actually I am prepared to concede that fly fishing is somewhat more sporting than most other rod-and-reel techniques, although for sheer skill and delicacy, upstream worming in low water can hardly be upstaged; however, it seems to me that when using the word "sporting" we imply more than mere cunning and craft.

Who, for example, would hold that it's not more sporting to stalk a ravening Bengal tiger, on foot in heavy jungle, than to boot a bunny from a brush pile in the back pasture? What outdoorsman would deny that it's more sporting to shinny up K-22 or even the Matterhorn than to go for a hike in the woods, no matter how briskly? And why? *Because one essential element in the highest order of sport is DANGER—the matching of physical, mental, and emotional fitness and skill against the possibility of injury or death.*

For this reason it has long been obvious to me that by far the most sporting method of taking trout from streams is by means of dynamite (or, in the case of small streams, dynamite caps); in fact, in the hard-coal regions of Pennsylvania you may still hear a stick of the stuff referred to as a Lithuanian fly rod. The element of danger is enhanced by the necessarily nocturnal nature of the sport and the likelihood that even if a premature explosion doesn't delete some essential part of your anatomy, an alert game protector may arrange to have you stashed away for several months, causing you to miss the woodcock season.

And just as Lee Wulff finds the epitome of sport in the short, superlight rod, so does the dedicated dynamiter (or *bangler*, if I may suggest an apter appellation) carry his avocation to dizzier sporting heights by means of the short, fast-burning fuse. Some years ago, in fact, I predicted that as the sporting appetites of Americans grew jaded the popularity of this method would almost certainly burgeon; I announced this sociological foresight in an article entitled "The Coming Boom in Trout Fishing," but so far the fly-fishers have held their own, and at the last meeting of the American Fishing Tackle Manufacturers Association (AFTMA), the Hercules Powder Company wasn't even represented.

HOW TO USE A WADING STAFF

Defendant: May I say a few words, your honor? Thank you. First, I didn't really mean to damage the plaintiff that much. Those teeth couldn't have been in there very firmly in the first place, or they wouldn't have popped out like that. And it's a medical fact that some people bleed easier than other people. But let me tell you exactly what happened.

Well sir, I got up that morning at 3:15. It takes me just under two hours to drive to Cooper Creek, and I had promised my wife I'd carry some trash out of the basement before I left. And since Larry Kane had been with me the week before and seen that enormous brownie in the Trestle Pool, I figured he'd be trying to get there ahead of me. What I didn't figure was that my wife would hear me pussyfooting around in the basement trying to get that trash out without waking her, think it was burglars, and call the cops.

Also it was pure coincidence that just as Officer Gus Boyle came around the corner of the house I was reaching for my handkerchief rather hastily on account of not having been able to blow my nose while lugging an armload of old velocipedes and stuff up the basement stairs, and that in the moonlight he thought I was going for a gun and whacked me across the side of the head with his night stick.

So after my head had stopped ringing and Gus had given me some aspirin from his first-aid kit, I told him no hard feelings and went into the house to explain to my wife that there weren't any burglars, never dreaming she would have looked for me, found me gone, figured she was alone and defenseless and taken up a position just inside the bedroom door armed with a footstool. Fortunately my wife isn't much on muscle, and when my head had stopped ringing again I gave her a tranquilizer, took a couple myself, got in the car and headed for Cooper Creek. A few miles north of Newtonville, on the expressway, I saw a car coming up behind me fast and recognized it as Larry Kane's new blue sedan, so rather than have him beat me to the Trestle Pool I gave Old Ironsides the gas and got her up to eighty before the new blue sedan pulled up alongside me and a guy in a matching blue uniform waved me over to the side of the road. After thanking him for not hitting me on the head I put the ticket in the glove compartment and went on my way, arriving at the Trestle Pool about 7 A.M.

This trestle pool is called Trestle Pool because there's a single-track railroad trestle goes across it, and as there's only one milk train a day it's safe to walk across it. I was doing just that when I looked down and saw that monster trout cruising around a few yards upstream and inhaling some kind of stone-fly on the water, and since I already had a large dry-fly on my leader I stood on the trestle, about fifteen feet above the water, and cast a long line upstream, letting the fly come down over the fish. When he took it I lifted the rod and was into him solidly.

Well sir, I let out a whoop, and when something whooped back I looked up and saw the milk train coming around the bend, whistling. There wasn't time to get off the trestle so I tossed the rod into the creek and hung from a cross-tie by my fingertips until the train had gone by, and had just enough strength left to pull myself back up, what with chest-high waders, hobnailed mule-skin wading shoes and all.

I could see the rod going down through the fast run below the pool and so I crawled through a barbed-wire fence and started after it, forgetting there's a bad bull in the lower field, and had just retrieved the rod with the fish on it and was backing up onto the bank when this hopped-up Holstein came charging across the meadow bellowing bloody murder, and so I skipped back into the deepest run in the creek, discovering as soon as I got in over my backside that the barbed wire had ripped a large hole in my waders. It didn't matter, though, because the water was over my waders anyhow, and also the current knocked me down and swept me downstream about a hundred yards into an eddy, where I climbed out onto the bank more or less intact except that my hat had washed away. But I still had the rod and the trout was still on, and still strong.

As a matter of fact I had to scramble downstream another quarter-mile or so to keep up with it, and kept falling down and banging myself on account of my head started ringing again and making me dizzy, and when I finally slid this four-pound, 20-inch brown trout up on the bank a warden stepped out of the bushes and said, "That's a nice fish, mister. Let's see your license." When I explained that my license tag was on my hat and the license was inside the hatband and the hat was somewhere downriver, he said the law was the law and that he'd have to release the trout, which he did, and confiscate my tackle until I could prove that I really had a license, which he did.

I walked back to the car, found a tire flat, changed it, and drove home. When I pulled into the driveway the plaintiff, who lives down the street a piece, strolled up the driveway and said, "Howdy. Been fishing again?" I said yes, and he said, "Well, everyone to his own taste. Personally I don't fish—just don't have the *patience*." Well, your honor, there was this wading staff in the back of the car and I guess I must have picked it up and—beg pardon? You are? And you tie your own flies? And the case is what? Dismissed? No sir, the wading staff wasn't damaged. Yes sir, I understand about trespass, but I'd rather not prefer charges. Shucks, it was nothing, your honor. Tight lines to you, too.

HOW TO BE AN INDIAN CHIEF

While in Scotland last May I lashed the River Spey to a rich, creamy lather without raising a single salmon or, in fact, so much as a stickleback, and in order to keep my spirits up after several days of this I retired one evening to the bar of the Ben Mhor Hotel in Grantown-on-Spey and ordered a wee drap of malt whisky. (Actually I ordered a double wee drap, as not only had my spirits drooped but also it had begun to snow.)

I recognized the gnarled and gnomish townsman standing next to me as a gillie I had seen on the river that day, and when we had commiserated on the state of the fishing, the weather, and the world, I commented that at least it was good to be surrounded, as we were, by renowned distilleries and suggested that if one had to have a pain, so to speak, it was best to have it in an aspirin factory. And when I praised the Scots for their skill in the making of whisky and their readiness to help dispose of it once it had been bottled, the old man agreed. However, he said, it would be a mistake to assume that the Scots were foremost among appreciators of the juice of the barleycorn. There was, he assured me, a tribe of South American Indians living in the wilds of the Andes Mountains whose passion for *uisquebeatha* exceeded even that sometimes attributed to their North American cousins.

"Och, mon, I know o' it fair-r-rst-hand," he assured me, "ha'in' spent mair than foor-r-r years o' my life in that far-r-r-away place, sair-r-rchin' for the Sooth Amer-r-rican emeralds that I'd hair-r-rd aboot in my travels. An' d'ye ken hoo many o' them infair-r-rnal stones I foond in a' them years o' luikin'? Na' a one, mon—na' a seengle one!" He paused to examine his glass, which seemed to be empty, and when I had signaled the bartender to take appropriate action, he continued.

"Aye," he said sadly, "I sair-r-rched th' Amazon Reever fra' th' mooth o' it ta th' haidwaters, nae t' mention th' Oorinoco and ithers too noomerous t' recall. I luiked i' th' hielands an' I luiked i' th' lowlands, but ne'er once did I set eyes on an emerald— na' 'til I coom ta th' tair-r-ritory o' th' Blancos Manos!"

"The territory of the what?" I said. "Th' Blancos Manos," the old man said, staring in astonishment at his glass, which was empty again. I flagged the bartender. "Them's th' wild Payr-r-roovian Indians I was tellin' ye aboot—th' ones wi' th' eensatiable cr-r-ravin' f'r whusky!" "Of coorse," I said. "I mean, of course."

"Aye," said the old man, staring reminiscently into space. "I was campin' oot near a wee village i' th' Andes, an' a' th' toonspeople tellin' me t' be wary, lest I fa' inta th' clootches o' them hor-r-rible sahvages, th' Blancos Manos. But I was yoong, then, an' i' guid health an' a', wi' a map I'd brought f'r a hondred guineas that shooed plain as day where th' emeralds was thick as pebbles on th' beach, an' so I headed f'r th' secret canyon where them green stones was lyin' aboot, free f'r th' takin'.

"When I'd walked f'r ten days, slippin' an' scrabblin' o'er boolders as beeg as hooses, wadin' through bogs up to my sporran and swimmin' reevers fu' o' melted snoo, I r-r-realized I was lost—th' bluidy map wasna' wair-r-rth a teenker's damn! Aye, an' naught f'r it but ta try as best I cuid ta fin' my wa' back t' ceevilization.

"Weel, sair," said the old one, "I hadna' barely got tair-r-rned ar-r-roond than *whackety!* It was an arrow, mind ye, that smashed inta th' rocks o'er my head, and I kenned richt off it was them bluidy wild Indians wha' I'd been warned aboot. When anither arrow coom wheestlin' by my bonnet, I spied a wee cave i' th' side o' th' hill an' ran inta it. I had a pair-r-rl-handled peestol i' my knapsack an' a box o' ammunition, an' I feegured t' gae doon fichtin', as a Scotsman shuid." He sighed, and there were tears in his eyes; I followed the line of his melancholy stare, and saw that it focused on his glass, which was dry as a bone.

When the glass was full and the old man had taken a tentative sip to be sure it was real, he squared his ancient shoulders and went on. "F'r three days an' nichts," he said, "I held them bluid-thair-r-rsty sahvages at bay. True, I didna' wing but twa o' th' heathenish fiends, an' sent them howlin', but th' rest o' them stayed fair back and waited me oot. Finally, mind ye, when I couldna' keep my eyes open nae mair, I dozed off—an' woke up wi' five or maybe seex o' them divvils settin' on me, whilst anither pack o' them stude by luikin' on.

" 'Och, ye bluidy redskins!' I says to them. 'It's nae use t' rob me, I dinna hae a seengle emerald!' Wi' that, one o' th' sahvages steps up and says, 'No want emeralds. Got plenty emeralds. No want gold. Got plenty gold. Want whisky. You got whisky?' 'Aye, that I do,' I told him.

"Weel," said the old man, "ye micht na' believe it, but that Indian tuik a dooble handfu' o' emeralds oot o' his robe, an' a guid-sized sack o' gold noogets t' boot. Then he says they're na' oonly giein' me th' emeralds an' th' gold, in exchange f'r the whusky, they're a'so giein' me th' head mon's twa bonny daughters f'r wives an' makin' me th' chief o' th' tribe, wi' a palace ta leeve in an' a hondred sair-r-rvents t' wait on me hand an' fute. *An' a' f'r a bottle o' whusky, d'ya ken?*"

"My goodness," I said. "What in the world did you do with all those emeralds. And those gold nuggets? And those daughters?" The old man looked at me sadly. "Och, mon, I didna' do naught wi' them," he said. " 'Twas th' oonly bottle o' whusky I had left, and th' nearest replacement ten days distant—I couldna' conseeder th' offer, na' f'r a meenit!

"But it eelustr-r-rates," the old man said, draining his glass, "t' wha' lengths them sahvages will gae f'r a bottle o' whusky!"

HOW TO BUY AIRPLANES!

Last July, while fishing the Big Hole River in Montana, I ran into Fred Weiler, an erstwhile dove-shooting companion and presently head of the Bureau of Land Management in Arizona. Fred said he was on vacation, and as the morning hatch of little yellow stoneflies had petered out we retired to a saloon at Twin Bridges and took up positions at the bar, as it's a well-known fact that the act of fly-casting generates substantial amounts of static electricity within an angler, and that by placing one foot on a brass rail or other conductor and the other on the floor, as a sort of ground wire, this dangerous buildup of amperage can be drained off safely in an hour or so.

While we were being deactivated, Fred got to talking about the years he had spent with the BLM in Alaska and remarked on the role of the airplane in that rugged, roadless country; the Bureau, he said, maintained a small fleet of them, and favored the Grumman Goose for certain types of amphibious service. Fred said that when it was decided to use the Grumman product for Alaska, the Bureau's purchasing agent had sat down at his typewriter, inserted a sheet of letterhead paper, and written on it:

> Grumman Aircraft Company
> Long Island, N.Y.
> Gentlemen:
> Please send three Grumman Gooses immediately.
> Sincerely yours,
> (signed) Bureau of Land Management

After having sat and stared at this for a while, the p.a. had ripped the paper from the typewriter and inserted a fresh sheet, on which he wrote:

> Grumman Aircraft Company
> Long Island, N.Y.
> Gentlemen:
> Please send three Grumman Geese immediately.
> Sincerely yours,
> (signed) Bureau of Land Management

When the p.a. had sat and looked at this for several minutes, he tore it from the machine and inserted a third sheet, on which he typed:

> Grumman Aircraft Company
> Long Island, N.Y.
> Gentlemen:
> Please send a Grumman Goose immediately.
> Sincerely yours,
> (signed) Bureau of Land Management
> P.S.: Hell, make it three.

I had the feeling that the story might be untrue, but not knowing if it should be checked with an ornithologist or an etymologist I kept my peace, and we ordered two more martinuses.

EVERY LITTER BIT HELPS

Walking one time through *Sierpes*, that truly serpentine shop-street of Seville, on my way to the bullring with my son who then lived in that city, I was surprsed to see him toss the outer wrapper of a candybar onto the paving. Having brought him up to feel that littering is morally one with incest, arson, and keeping trout, I asked him how come.

"Thoughtfulness, Pop," he said, tossing the inner wrapper too. "One day last year I stood not far from here waiting for the light to change. When I took the last cigarette out of a pack and crumpled it and put it in my pocket, an old man carrying a streetsweeper's broom tapped my arm. 'How am I to make a living, senor,' he said sadly, 'if you don't throw stuff in the street? If there's nothing to be swept up, I'll be out of a job and my sick wife will starve. What do you have against us poor sweepers, to act so heartlessly?' So I fished the pack out of my pocket and threw it in the gutter, and hope you'll do the same while you're here. Things are looking up in Spain, but jobs are still hard for older people to come by."

Thereafter in Seville I dutifully dumped all my litter on the street, in the name of full employment and international solidarity, but it was always with an uncomfortable furtive feeling, and when the *feria* ended and I went up to the Pyrenees to fish for trout it was a relief to find there were no streetsweepers, for whose welfare I was somehow responsible, in the small mountain village where I stayed. (And no litter either, it was pleasing to note.)

What this brings to mind, of course, is the responsibility of all of us, in this complex economic jigsaw puzzle of a world, to help provide employment for each other. Years ago, for example, I was taught (by Liz Greig, that wee bonnie lassie) to tie trout flies, both wet and dry, in my fingers, without benefit of vise. And twenty years ago I found it far easier to pick up trout, bass, or salmon by hand, after properly playing them out, than to carry a net. Even before that I had given up lugging a creel, as I almost never killed fish unless needful of protein and far from a T-bone.

Then about five years ago I began to have difficulty in sleeping, and when all physical causes had been ruled out, my doctor suggested, as tactfully as possible, that it might be something on my conscience. I assured him this was impossible, as during my lifetime I had never indulged even in minor vices, much less major ones. Having learned as a youth that tobacco stunts the growth and alcohol dissolves the protective coating of mucous membrane in the entrails, I had shunned these evils, and had not once ever sneaked a peek at my opponent's cards while playing spit-in-the-ocean (for fun, of course, and not

for stakes), not falsified an expense account, or had improper thoughts. And when a friend had given me two salmon flies after I helped him gaff a 30-pounder on the Matane, I had had them appraised and declared their full value on my income tax return for that year, as I had received them, even though unsolicited, in return for services rendered and they were therefore taxable as income.

"But there must be something," the doctor said, and I assured him that except for a recurring dream I had no symptoms of any emotional disturbance whatsoever. "What kind of a recurring dream?" the doc asked, and when I said it was always of gaunt, unhappy people standing in a breadline, he sent me off to a psychiatrist. The psychiatrist was rather young, but after I had explained to him what a breadline was, it took him only a thousand-odd dollars worth of treatment to discover that all the people in my dream were unemployed makers of creels, nets, and fly-tying vises.

Since then, of course, I have tied all my flies in a vise, and carried a creel and net even though I don't use them. As a result I now sleep so soundly that I frequently miss important engagements with editors and agents, and as a further result may soon be on a breadline myself, if I can find one.

JOIN YOUR LOCAL ROD & GUN CLUB!

Once upon a time in a far-off land, there lived a rich and noble king whose young daughter, the princess Hermyonthe, was so beautiful that suitors swarmed around her like New Jersey fishermen around a hatchery truck. Young men came from near and far to seek the fair Hermyonthe's hand, but only a fortunate few were permitted into the castle grounds, and only after they had been interviewed by the Royal Physician, the Royal Philosopher, and the Royal Genealogist, and had satisfied these examiners that their physical endowments, ancestral antecedents, and intellectual attainments were of exceptional quality, and that in nobility of character and devotion to high ideals they ranked foremost among all their peers.

When, occasionally, a suitor would be ruled eligible by the Royal Screening Committee, the applicant would thereupon be ushered into the presence of Hermyonthe's father, the king, who would address him thusly: "Young man, my advisers have spoken highly of you. But because the demand for the hand of my beautiful and talented daughter far exceeds the supply, I find it necessary to subject you to a further test.

"To the north of my country lies a vast Enchanted Forest guarded by a fire-breathing dragon, in which roam fearsome monsters and bloodthirsty beasts. Deep in this wicked wilderness is a lake in which dwell creatures of savage strength and finny fury, well known to be devourers of men. And into this lake there flows a rushing river in which abides a magical fish of solid gold.

"You must go to this forest, slay the Fire-Breathing Dragon, and catch the Golden Fish. When you bring it to me, you may have my daughter's hand in marriage—aye, and half my kingdom for your personal fief! But I must warn you—*full half a hundred suitors have gone before you, and not one has returned, with· or without the Golden Fish!*"

"Sire," said the fifty-first eligible suitor, "I fear not. Wish me godspeed!" On arriving at the edge of the Enchanted Forest the young suitor, whose name was Alvedrias, was approached by an enormous fire-breathing dragon, which he promptly smote to the ground, and proceeding through the forest he came to a lake, in which swirled and swam strange creatures of frightening size. On spying a rushing river that flowed into the lake, the suitor extracted a fishing line and hook from his pocket, and having cut a stout pole and fastened the line to it, he dug a fat earthworm and impaled it upon the hook.

But no sooner had he dangled the worm in the edge of the stream than forth from the bushes sprang two young men of angry countenances, crying "Hold!"

"Hold what?" asked the startled Alvedrias.

"This is fly-fishing-only-water," declared one of the accosters, "and worm-dunkers aren't welcome. As a member of the Stocking Committee I'll have to report—but say, I don't recognize you!"

"Gus," said the second accoster, "I'll bet this is the creep who cold-cocked Wimpy—listen, friend, did you bash a dragon this morning, at the edge of the wood?"

"I did," said Alvedrias proudly, "and left his corpse in the copse."

"Fortunately," said the first accoster, "he's recovering nicely—old Wimpy's made of pretty tough stuff. I take it you're another suitor of the princess, come to catch the Golden Fish, just as we came?"

"You're right," said Alvedrias, "and I intend to catch it."

"Not with that nightcrawler you don't," said the second accoster. "No bait fishing permitted in the river. And no Golden Fish under eight inches."

"You mean there's more than one?" asked Alvedrias.

"There are so many," said the first accoster, "they're getting stunted."

"In that case," inquired Alvedrias, "why hasn't one of you caught one, taken it back to the king, and claimed the princess's hand?"

"Are you kidding?" asked the first accoster. "This forest is crawling with game—deer, elk, wild boar, wild turkey, ruffed grouse, and bobwhite quail. We're on a major flyway, and this lake is stiff with mallards and pintails every fall. Come October, there are flighting woodcock in here as thick as dead leaves, and lots of resident birds at other times. We've stocked ringnecks in the swamps and they're already propagating nicely."

"Those swirls in the lake," explained the second accoster, "are made by fifty-pound muskies chasing five-pound smallmouths—and we plan to poison out those crummy

Golden Fish and restock the river with browns and rainbows. In short, pal, we got it made here, all fifty of us. If you'd like to join the Enchanted Forest Rod & Gun Club, I'll refer your application to the membership committee.''

"What about that fire-breathing dragon?" asked Alvedrias.

"Shucks, he's the club mascot," said the first accoster. "We use him to burn off brush sometimes, and he helps to scare off poachers.''

"What about fearsome monsters?" asked Alvedrias.

"They're mostly protected species," said the second accoster, "although there's a special-permit season on unicorn.''

"Mmmm," said Alvedrias thoughtfully, "come to think of it, that's a pretty silly name, Hermyonthe—I'm not even sure how to pronounce it. Better put me down for a permanent resident membership—my name's Alvedrias.''

"Welcome, Al," said the first accoster. "Let's go on back to the clubhouse and meet the gang.''

"Okay," said Alvedrias, "I'm with you. And by the way, can either of you tell me exactly what the devil is a fief?''

At a Federation of Fly Fishermen's dinner at Jackson Hole, Wyoming, I sat next to Arnold Gingrich, who fills in those hours not occupied with publishing *Esquire* by writing delightful reminiscenses of a fascinating and fishful life, and when he commented on my birdlike appetite I explained that I had taken an appetite-reducing pill that morning, and that it hadn't yet worn off. "A great invention, those pills," Arnold said, and told me a story.

Some months previously, he said, he had been doing research for an article on early angling books, and had arranged to spend a day in the rare-books room of the New York Public Library. Because of the redtape involved in checking into and out of this carefully guarded sanctum he wanted to work straight through the lunch hour; on the other hand,

Arnold said, he knew by experience that come lunchtime he'd be too hungry to concentrate on anything but thoughts of food. So he had telephoned his doctor, who prescribed some sort of appetite-inhibiting drug and arranged to have it sent to his home.

The next morning, Arnold said, he had started out the door before remembering the capsules, and although late for his commuter train had rushed back in and gulped one down. At the library he worked straight through the lunch hour without so much as a twinge of hunger, and even when he left at 5 o'clock felt no interest in eating. "We had guests for dinner," Arnold said, "but despite two martinis I had no appetite whatsoever, and had to force myself to eat a small portion of a superb coquille St. Jacques. When someone commented on my magnificent self-discipline I explained it was a purely pharmaceutical phenomenon, and when another guest asked the name of the drug I said I only knew that the capsule was dull gray in color, and suggested that anyone sufficiently interested was welcome to look in the medicine cabinet."

In a minute one of the guests had come back and said, "The only capsules in the medicine cabinet are bright yellow. There aren't any gray capsules there." "He was right, too," Arnold said. "It took a call to the druggist to establish that what I had gulped down in the morning was a little plastic capsule full of silica gel, a chemical that absorbs moisture and was meant to keep the medicine dry. Even after the phone call it took me several hours to work up any interest in food."

By this time I was getting my appetite back, but before I could do anything about it the waiters came and took away my steak.

LOST WEEKEND

On Saturday I fished for trout.
I hunted woodcock Sunday.
But all good things must peter out.
Sic transit gloria Monday.

HOW TO SHOOT TRAP

While in Detroit last winter I had a pleasantly vinous dinner with Lee Smits, an outdoor writer and sportsman who celebrated his 80th birthday several years ago and who still cavorts around a duck marsh or deer meadow like a kid of 60. When we got on the subject of wingshooting I told him of the time when, at my first bigtime trapshoot, with nerves taut as banjo strings, I broke seventeen clays on my first round and while slinking off the line was approached by an elderly gent who said, "Follow me, bub." The old-timer then led me out behind the clubhouse and poured me a stiff slug of Jack Daniels' finest, after which I shot two 22's and a 23 (even Old Man Motlow can't work miracles);

it was the first time I had had-a drink while shooting, and the last, but it taught me something about the importance of relaxation.

"That reminds me," Lee said, "that in some English sporting magazine, recently, I read a letter-to-the-editor from a retired army man who had served in India for thirty years. He claimed they all shot considerably better while suffering from a mild touch of fever, which most of them had off and on while out there."

I mentioned this to Gene Hill at a New Jersey trapshoot last month, and he phoned me yesterday to say that by bribing an attendant at the Philadelphia Institute of Tropical Diseases he had managed to get a dozen *Anopheles* mosquitoes guaranteed to be malaria carriers and that a week before the next big registered trapshoot at Travers Island he planned to stick his bare arm into the cage and let the mosquitoes chew on it long enough to insure himself a small siege of fever.

For a box of nickel-plated pigeon loads, he said, he would let me stick my arm into the cage too, but I declined, as I'm still recuperating from hip dysplasia contracted, I think, while trying to put body-English on a station wagon that my wife was backing out of the driveway.

HOW TO FISH WITH A PRIEST

I was telling my friend Eddie Edmonds about fishing with a priest one time, and was explaining that while the fishing hadn't been sensational the day had been a pleasantly ecumenical one when Eddie interrupted. "I'd never go fishing with any kind of a clergyman again," he said. "Not after the experience *I* had." "What experience was that?" I said.

"Well sir," Eddie said, "I've never been much of a churchgoer, but Anne takes it pretty seriously, and one time she told me the parson at the church she attends had heard I was a trout fisherman and wanted me to invite him along some weekend. I refused, and we had a bit of a scene, and finally to keep the peace I said I'd do it. So the next Friday afternoon I picked him up and we drove up to Roscoe on the Beaverkill.

"That night at the Antrim Lodge the parson said he appreciated what I was doing for him, but wondered if he could make one small request. I said of course, and he said he had a real hang-up about bad language—said that even the mildest bit of profanity gave him a terrible chill up and down his spine. He said it was like a piece of ice between his shoulder blades every time he heard a four-letter word or the name of God taken in vain, and he asked if I'd try to avoid using any rough language. I said okay, Rev, I'll sure keep it in mind, and besides I've never been a real big-league cusser anyway.

"Next morning we drove downriver to the Wagon Wheel Pool and fished our way down through the fast water to the head of the Culvert Pool, and I said, 'Rev, there ought to be a real good brown trout lying just this side of that boulder that splits the main current there—go ahead, let's see you catch him.' 'No sir,' he said, 'I wouldn't know how to get a fly in there without drag—you show me how it's done.'

"So I stepped into the fast water and laid a big Rat-face MacDougal alongside the rock and whammo! A hook-jawed brownie a good two feet long came charging out from under that rock, inhaled that big dry fly, and took off downriver until most of my backing was off the reel. I started running after him, hollering at a spin-fisherman to get out of my way, but by that time the fish had changed its mind and was coming back up, and the idiot spin-fisherman got confused and waded into the loop of the line, and I had to run back down and unwrap the line from his leg. While I was doing that the treble hook on his lure got caught in my vest and the only way I could follow the big trout was to wiggle out of my vest one arm at a time and leave it hanging on his lure, dragging in the water so I knew all my fly-boxes would be flooded.

"By some miracle the trout was still on when I got free of the spin-fisherman, and had obviously begun to tire, so I started reeling it in when suddenly the reel dropped off the rod and the current washed it downstream. When I made a lunge for it my feet slipped and I fell felt-soles over tincups into the river, and when I finally got onto my feet again I saw that A, the trout was long gone and B, my favorite Winston rod was busted into two separate and distinct pieces. So I turned and waded back to where I'd left the preacher, and there he was stretched out on the bank, dead as a mackerel.

"I figured it was a simple case of heart attack from all the excitement, but the doctor who made out the death certificate said no. He said he couldn't even try to explain it, but somehow on a warm day in June that poor guy had frozen to death.''

While fishing the upper Miramichi one time I bet a companion 25 cents that a grilse I had on the end of my line would go over five pounds, and when it weighed in at an ounce or two under four I complained to Charley Norrad, my guide, mentor, and friend, that I had a remarkable flair for losing wagers. Charley said some people were that way, and declared that in days past a local doctor by the name of Twembley had a virtually unsullied record of lost bets. People would come for miles around, he said, to bet with the doctor on football and hockey games, elections, ice-out day, and almost anything that involved an element of chance, as it was known up and down the river that a wager with the doc was money in the bank.

"On the other hand," Charley said, "I used to know a fella named Lucky Louie, who worked in the woods winters and over at the sawmill summers, and who was famous for never having voluntarily taken a bath, although once as a boy he had fell into the river. This Louie was the luckiest fella in creation at cards and betting, although he was generally obliged to play cards or make bets downwind from his chums, as other gamblers complained that one whiff of Louie would make their eyes water so they couldn't read the spots on their cards. But Louie, he claimed his luck was on account of his unwashed condition—said most people soap away all their natural good-luck oils by taking a bath every couple of months, whether they need it or not.

"One time this Lucky Louie," said Charley, "accidentally jabbed a hole in his foot with a peavey—point went clean through his boot—and when he started limping pretty bad the boss ordered Louie to go into town and have it treated. Louie said okay, but when he started to put his sock back on, that he hadn't had off since coming to the camp six weeks before and maybe six weeks before that, the boss said he'd have to take a bath before going to the doctor.

"Well sir, Louie argued and hollered and moaned, but finally took a hunk of soap and headed for the river. When he came back he looked pretty shook up, and a bunch of the other jacks tried to make bets with him, figuring maybe he was really right about people washing away their luck and hoping to catch him whilst he was still under the influence of water—although several that got downwind of him said he was still unjeezly fragrant.

"Anyhow," said Charley, "Louie was too upset by his ordeal to make any bets, and when the boss assigned me to go with him to town, I was happy to get out of the woods for a day, and down the river we went—with me doing most of the poling on account of Louie still being in a state of shock. When we got to town I herded him up the street to the doc's place and waited with him until Twembley called him into the office. When he got inside, the doc asked him to take off his boots, and when Louie had kicked off his boot and peeled off his sock, the doc looked at it and said, 'Holy saints in heaven! I'll bet five dollars that's the filthiest foot in New Brunswick!' And Louie said, 'Doc, you got yourself a bet—looky here!'"

"And before you could say aye, yea, or nay, he had shucked off his other boot and sock. Well sir, there wasn't nothing for the doc to do except pay him the five dollars, because when Louie had snuck off to the river he'd only washed that one foot, and the other probably hadn't touched water since that time he'd fell in the river, thirty years previous. Maybe it's like Louie used to say—some people win bets, and other people bathe."

"Whatever became of that doctor?" I asked, and Charley said, "He made a bet one February he could walk clear across Moose Bay on the ice without falling through, and naturally he lost the bet. When they found his body in the spring it was full of eels, and they sent a telegram to his wife that said—"

"Never mind," I said, "I know that one from away back," and Charley said, "Okay, let's go fishing." Which we did.

Not long after this story appeared in *Field & Stream*, I had a letter from A. W. Weidemann of Hendersonville, North Carolina. Mr. Weidemann wrote that he had been born near Trondheim, Norway, some 80 years previously, and that he regularly sent his copies of *Field & Stream*, after reading them himself, to his brother, a medical doctor in Trondheim.

Mr. Weidemann reported that when his brother, a student of early Norse history and literature, had heard Charley's story about Dirty Louie it had rung a faint bell in his memory. He had accordingly looked into the sagas of the Norse kings collected by Snorre Sturlasson about the year 1200, and had found virtually the same story in the saga of King Olav Haraldsson, better known as "Olav the Sacred." He had then translated it into English and sent it to his brother, who sent it to me. Dr. Weidemann's translation included this portion:

One early morning the king was awake, but the other men were all sleeping. The sun had just risen and daylight come into the room. The king chanced to see that one of Toraren's feet was uncovered by the bedding, and he regarded the foot for a while. Then he awakened the other men in the room, and said to Toraren, "I have been awake for a while, and I have seen a strange sight, and that is a foot so ugly that I do not believe there is a foot more ugly in this town." He asked the others what they were thinking, and all agreed with him. The king then said, "I am willing to wager there is no foot so ugly as that one."

Toraren said, "And I am going to bet that I will show you a foot that is more ugly." And then he showed his other foot, and that was by no means prettier, for one of the toes was cut off. Toraren said, "Now I have won the bet."

But the king said, "The first foot was ugliest, because it had five ugly toes, and the other foot only four ugly toes. Thus I have won the bet."

Mr. Weidemann suggested that Leif Ericson may have brought the story with him to America sometime around the year 1025, as he was a friend of Toraren, and that the anecdote had probably been kicking around Iceland, Greenland and Canada's maritime provinces ever since, in one form or another. My own feeling is that anyone wishing to berate me for telling old jokes in this book has an airtight case.

THE CASE OF THE BOOKISH FLY FISHERMAN

It was a June day some twenty years ago, on the Brodheads Creek in Pennsylvania, that I met an elderly gentleman fly-fishing the flat water below Charley Rethoret's Hotel Rapids. He was elegantly dressed, with stocking-foot English waders and twenty-dollar muleskin brogues over them, and he was one of the first men I ever saw who used a store-boughten wading staff. I had been sitting on the bank gutting a brace of breakfast-size browns and watching him work his way downstream with a wet fly. He was fishing

a short straight line in the precise, almost mechanical way that good wet-fly fishermen often employ, and it wasn't until he was nearly on top of me that I noticed the book under his right arm, held close to his side by the pressure of his elbow. When he saw me, he stepped up on the bank and sat down beside me.

"Not much doing today, is there?" he said, filling his pipe, and I noticed that he still kept the book under his arm.

"Not much," I said, "but it may pick up around four-thirty. Yesterday a nice hatch of Light Cahills came about that time. Do you mind if I ask why you carry that book under your arm, instead of in your jacket or your creel, where it can't fall into the water?"

"Not at all," said the old man. "I carry it under my arm because I've been carrying it under my arm, while fishing, for forty years. Not the same book, of course—they wear out, and I replace them."

"Do you read them when the fishing's slow, or what?" I asked.

"My dear boy," said the man, "I have never read a book in my life—make it a point never to read a word. Strains the eyes, and a true fly fisherman needs to keep his eyesight absolutely keen. A worm fisherman, of course, could be blind as a bat and still catch trout—but I see you're a fly fisherman, and understand these matters. But although I never read books I sometimes look at the pictures, and one time in a book on fly fishing I saw a photograph of a man holding a book under the upper part of his casting arm while he cast. I was just learning to fish with flies, and hadn't had much luck. So the next time I went trout fishing I put a book under my arm, the way the photograph had showed, and, sure enough, on my first cast I hooked a trout. Since then I've always held a book under my arm—guess I always will."

"I've seen those photographs too," I said. "If you had read the text, it would have explained that holding the book under your arm is just an exercise to train you to hold your arm in close to your body, so you'll use your forearm and wrist properly. You're not supposed to hold a book there while you're actually fishing.''

"Maybe not," said the man, "but that's the way I do it, and I manage to catch a trout now and then." He went on to say that because the books wore out, or occasionally fell into the water, he bought them by the dozen—when he found one that felt just right, he would order twelve copies. And occasionally on his lunch hour he would visit several bookstores, trying out the new books for feel and fit; it's amazing, he said, how few books are suitable for carrying under one's arm.

When I asked him why he didn't use a piece of wood cut to the shape of a book, which would have been cheaper and wouldn't have worn out or been damaged by water, he said curtly, "A glass rod would be cheap, and wouldn't wear out, but I noticed that you're using a split-bamboo Payne. Good day, sir!''

After he had gone on down the river I walked back to the hotel to get some lunch, and Charley Rethoret came over to the table and sat down for a minute. "Funny thing happened a little while ago," he said. "An elderly gent came in here, in fishing clothes, sat down in a booth and when I went to take his order he asked me to read the menu to him. Said he couldn't afford to risk straining his eyes, or some such nonsense. He had a book under his arm, and kept it there even while he was eating.''

"I know," I said. "I met him downstream, book and all.''

"Did you notice the title of the book?" Charley asked.

"No," I said, "did you?''

"He left it on the table while he went to wash up," Charley said, "and I saw that the title was something about Alsace-Lorraine. Since that's where I lived as a child, I opened it up and saw it was hollowed out inside, like one of those old books made into a cigarette case. Only there weren't cigarettes in it—just a tin box. So as long as I'd already snooped, I looked in the box, too.''

"What was in it?" I asked. "Heroin?''

"Worse than that," said Charley. "Angleworms.''

HOW TO SHOOT DOVES

While in Tucson last September to attend the annual conference of the International Association of Game, Fish and Conservation Commissioners, I managed to get in a morning of dove shooting, and although I had my limit of ten birds by 8 o'clock I somehow missed one. This mystified me, and I was inclined to charge off the baffling incident to a blown pattern, but on returning to New York I found a letter from Mr. Fred Farr, a meteorologist and chairman of the Flushing, New York, chapter of the Madison Avenue Rod, Gun, Bloody Mary & Labrador Retriever Benevolent Association.

Mr. Farr pointed out that in my recent scholarly analysis of the thermodynamics of fly casting I had overlooked a factor which he felt should be taken into account, along with the centrifugal forces generated by the earth's rotation on its axis, various lunar and sidereal juxtapositions affecting the planet's gravitational field, the expansion of the universe, precession, and so forth. This factor, which I must confess I had completely disregarded, is the rather mysterious Coriolis Force, which tends to push any moving object in the northern hemisphere to the right, regardless of the direction in which the object is moving and regardless of the medium—air, water, old crankcase oil, pistachio ice cream, or whatever—through which it is moving.

Immediately it dawned on me that this was the explanation for my incredible lapse—an explanation that jibed perfectly with the fact that in Arizona I had deliberately been shooting doves—as I do all game birds—with the merest edge of the pattern, in order not to have more than two or three pellets in the bird. Ordinarily I shoot doves on the right edge of the pattern, but in this case, in order to avoid looking directly into the early-morning sun I had several times shot so as to bring down the doves with the left edge of the pattern. Thus the slightest shift of my shotstring to the right would cause a clean miss, and in the future I shall bear this in mind, as it may explain why, during the season of 1961 or perhaps it was '62 I missed a ruffed grouse.

I had intended to think up a very short story to fill up the rest of this space, but after refereeing the 15th Annual Duck-shooting Championship of the World at Duncan Dunn's Amwell Shooting Preserve in New Jersey, which my friend Dave Crosby won handily, I stopped for some Crazy-Quail shooting and whiskey drinking (in the order named) at Gene Hill's country place near Princeton. While Gene was pouring I got to talking with his 4-year-old daughter Jennifer, and figuring the best defense is a good offense I asked her to tell me a story.

"What kind of story?" Jennifer said. "Hmmm," I said. "How about a bear story?" "Well," said Jennifer, "once there was a little girl bear and she was hungry and she was thirsty. So she ate herself and she drank herself and she tasted like lemons. That's the end."

As it is clearly out of the question to top this for Balzacian brilliance of plot, Proustian subtlety of character delineation, and Truebloodian narrative pace, I have given up the idea of fictionalizing my way out of this monthly dilemma and instead shall clear up one of the more difficult questions with which various other editors have been unable to cope. To wit:

Dear Sir: Although my husband has hunted and fished at every opportunity since our marriage seventeen years ago, he has never once taken me with him, despite my pleas. I am sure I could learn to love these sports as much as he does, and that sharing experiences afield would make our marriage more meaningful to both of us. But when I beg him to take me along, he turns on his heel and walks away. What is the reason for this? Mrs. R. L. C., Calif.

Dear Mrs. C.: The heel, lying as it does directly underneath the columnar leg-bones which support the body's weight, is a natural pivot. E.Z.

If any of you other readers have hard-to-answer questions about the outdoors, don't hesitate to send them in.

When I asked my friend Knox Robertson if he believed in ghosts, he snorted and said he most certainly did not. "I'll tell you why," he said, "if you'll fill up those glasses again. And not so much water this time."

"You'll remember I went to England on business last year," he said, "and as I have a second cousin in Scotland, with fishing rights to several pools on a first-rate salmon river, I took along a pair of rods and some reels and flies and whatnot. When I called cousin Hamish from London—I'd never met the man, although we'd corresponded a bit—he invited me up for a week's fishing, and as soon as I'd finished my business in the city, off I went to the ancestral village.

"I found my cousin living in a sort of small castle that had obviously been going downhill since Bonnie Prince Charlie's time, with not much in the way of plumbing and absolutely nothing in the way of heating except for a small fireplace in each room and a large one in the main hall. But Hamish made me as comfortable as possible in a guest bedchamber, and as we spent most of our time fishing the river, I didn't much mind the clamminess of the castle. In the evening, after dinner, we'd sit before a crackling fire with a decanter of malt whisky to ward off chills and vapors, and talk—mostly about why there were no salmon in the river. Neither of us had had so much as a touch after five days of hard fishing.

"Hamish said it was most unusual—the salmon simply hadn't come up from the tidewater, although the river had plenty of flow and the holding pools should have been full of bright fish. I knew that he, as the host, felt even more disappointed than I did, and so to change the subject I told him about the elderly guide—gillie, I mean—he'd furnished me with, and how solicitous the old man was of my well-being, always asking me how I'd slept and what kind of dreams I'd had. But instead of amusing Hamish, this seemed to distress him and finally he blurted out, 'See here, old chap, there's something I should have told you. This castle is—well, dammit, it's haunted. That's why old Donald kept asking how you'd slept. Perhaps I shouldn't have told you even now, but you *are* part of the family, y'know. Don't worry, though, it's only Mother, and she's never bothered a soul, except to give them a bit of a start when she's gadding about the premises.'

"Then he told me that his mother—I suppose she'd have been my great-aunt or something of the sort—had died some twenty years before, when he was a young man, and had taken to haunting the castle shortly afterward. There was nothing anyone could do about it, Hamish said; as a matter of fact, the old girl was actually useful, in a way— it seems she turned up sometimes wearing costumes that foretold coming events. Naturally I listened to this cock-and-bull story with a perfectly straight face—I might have resented his pulling my leg if I hadn't realized he was simply trying to provide a bit of atmosphere for a visiting cousin—sort of haunts across the sea, you might say. And I must admit it helped to take my mind off the rotten fishing.

"Well, it finally came to be Friday evening, with still never a salmon, and I had to leave for London the next day at noon. That night after dinner Hamish and I sat before the hall fireplace having a nightcap, and we agreed that even though I might squeeze in a few more hours of fishing in the morning, it wouldn't be worth the trouble. The truth is, my arm and shoulder were worn out from five days of fruitless fly casting, and I figured I'd had it for this trip. Just then Hamish nudged my arm and nodded toward a balcony at the end of the hall. I looked up just in time to see a haughtily handsome white-haired lady walking slowly across the balcony. She was wearing a sort of tweedy suit and a green felt fedora hat, and looking straight ahead.

"It wasn't until she floated right through the closed door at the end of the balcony that I realized who she was, but before I could say anything Hamish let out a whoop. 'By George!' he said, 'we're in luck! She's wearing her fishing clothes—keen angler, she was—and that's a sure sign there'll be fish in the river tomorrow. Never fails! Let's be streamside at daybreak tomorrow, and make up for lost time!' And of course we were.''

"But I thought you didn't take any stock in ghosts," I replied.

"I don't," Knox said. "We flogged that river to a froth the next morning and didn't raise a single fish."

HARD QUESTIONS ANSWERED

Once again it's the season when all the editors of *Field & Stream* try to tidy up for year's end, and find they have accumulated some hard-to-answer questions from readers; as usual when stumped for answers, they call on me, knowing I'll be able to draw on my vast fund of woodsy wisdom and outdoor expertise to get them off the hook. Here, then, are some of the queries:

Q: I have recently moved to a coastal town, and have never fished except in fresh water. I hear local anglers referring to something called a "jig." What is it? L.B.P., Stamford, Conn.

A: Fish are not abundant in Long Island Sound, and frequently fishermen go for weeks without hooking anything. When they do, it makes them so happy that they do a little dance, or "jig," out of sheer joy. Are you sure you heard properly? Many Long Island Sound fishermen refer to a "jug," which is something else. E.Z.

Q: When I became engaged, my fiancee said she understood how much I loved to hunt and fish, and promised never to interfere. Now we're married, and she nags me night and day to give up outdoor sports altogether. She says if I loved her I'd gladly stay home. If this keeps on I'm going to blow my brains out. Please give me whatever advice you can. J.R.Y., Akron, Ohio.

A: Since trajectory isn't important here, our recommendation would be a .35 Remington with 200-grain soft-nose bullet. E.Z.

Q: My husband is a deer hunter, and I frequently hear him use the expression "in rut." But when I ask him what it means, he stutters and stammers and changes the subject. Please tell me the meaning of this term. Mrs. R.N.O'B., Seattle, Wash.

A: Deer hunters are not generally awfully literate, and "in rut" is simply a misspelling of "en route." A deer going from one part of the forest to another is said to be "in rut" or "en route." In the case of mature bucks this constant traveling back and forth causes their necks to swell up, or vice versa. E.Z.

GOOD NEWS FOR ANGLERS

By and large I have no bone (*os*) to pick with professional biologists, beyond the fact that they tend to be limited in the scope of their thinking and rigid in their interpretation of data. But this, alas, seems to be a crucially *central* fact.

Thus, we find a recent issue of *SFI Bulletin,* the generally excellent publication of the Sport Fishing Institute, bewailing the spread of the so-called "walking catfish" throughout Florida waters and warning beneath scare-headlines that the "plague" would soon spread across the entire South if not somehow checked. Plague indeed! Let's take a really objective look at this finny phenomenon and see what it actually portends for anglers everywhere.

The "walking catfish," or Asian catfish, or (to the biologist) *Clarias,* was imported by dealers in exotic species for home aquariums a few years ago, and raised in outdoor ponds in Florida. Not surprisingly, since the ability to "walk" on dry land on their pectoral fins at the rate of about a mile in four hours is the reason they were imported in the first place, some of the catfish soon climbed out of the ponds and took off across country in quest of greener pastures, or perhaps wetter water. By now the species has made itself at home in hundreds of Florida's lakes, canals, ponds, and rivers, and is rumored to be turning up in Georgia and Alabama. When a pond or ditch dries up or is poisoned or polluted, the ambulatory Asian simply shrugs a slimy shoulder and shuffles off across the countryside until he comes to a more congenial body of water.

This spectre of a landscape literally crawling with millions of migrating fish throws the fisheries biologists into a tizzy, simply because they have pigeonhole mentalities: rabbits belong in brier patches, partridges belong in pear trees, fish belong in water. And any slight deviation in the textbook pattern upsets them so much that they lose all perspective and start fumbling for the panic button.

What, in reality, are the implications of this piscine perambulation? Well, sir, in point of fact every farsighted sportsman should be rejoicing! Since by now it is painfully clear that the Reagan administration has no intention of making a serious effort to combat water pollution, and that most of industry is as unwilling as most local governments to spend the money necessary to halt or repair the damage already done, we face the almost certain prospect that shortly we shall have little or no water in which a decent, self-respecting fish would care to live, even if it could.

What, then, could be more agreeable than a fish that doesn't *need* water? We can all go on fishing pretty much as usual, except that we need no longer be bothered with boots and waders, boats and outboard motors, floating fly lines, sinking fly lines, wet flies, split shot, and a lot of other accessories that won't be needed when all our fishing is done on dry land. And of course, while it may become monotonous fishing for the same kind of fish, it's quite possible that the walking catfish can be successfully hybridized with other species, so that if the biologists get on the ball right away we may soon have walking walleyes, strolling sturgeon, crawling crappies, trotting trout, marching muskies, and a dozen other varieties of footloose fish. Angler, count your blessings!

When I told a folk-singing friend about this last summer, he grabbed a guitar, and sang a song of celebration, to the tune of "Boll Weevil." It went something like this:

> *Oh, de angler say to de catfish,*
> > *"Who kickin' up all dat dust?"*
> *De catfish say to de angler, "I does*
> > *it 'cause I must,*
> > > *Jus' lookin' for a home, jus'*
> > > *lookin' for a home!"*
>
> *Well, de Fish an' Game Depart-*
> > *ment say to de catfish, "We bet-*
> > *ter hab a liddle talk."*
> *De catfish say to de F&GD, "Sorry,*
> > *but I gwine for a walk,*
> > > *Jus' lookin' for a home, jus'*
> > > *lookin' for a home."*
>
> *Den de catfish say to de policeman,*
> > *"What dat sign say I jus' pass?"*
> *De fuzz, he say to de catfish, "It*
> > *say Keep Off De Grass,*
> > > *While lookin' for a home,*
> > > *while lookin' for a home!"*

There was more, but a hatch of brown drakes came on just then and I hurried off to find my tackle.

BOOK NOTE

Irish Bogs was written by J. W. Seigne, an English sportsman, and was published in London in 1928 by Longmans, Green. I first saw it while browsing in the library of an Irish manor house, where I had been invited to shoot pheasants, and decided not to steal it as I was going on to London and knew I'd be able to find a copy in one of the several excellent secondhand bookstores there.

At Foyles, the shop on Charing Cross Road that prides itself on being able to produce for sale any volume ever published in England, I hunted up a clerk and told him what I wanted. He said, "*Irish Bogs*, J. W. Seigne, Longmans, Green, 1928—just a moment, sir." In a few minutes he came back and said, "Sir, that book was published in a small edition and has never been reprinted. We had a copy in here two years ago, and no doubt others will turn up. But there's a waiting list of four persons ahead of you wanting the same book. If you'll give me your name and address, I'm sure we'll have a copy for you in a few years time.'' I said no thanks, and after trying several other book stores with the same results, decided I could probably get along, somehow, without a copy of *Irish Bogs*, and forgot it.

About a year later I went into a secondhand bookstore on 59th Street in New York, to have a look around, and when a salesgirl approached and asked if she could help me, I was so annoyed at this violation of bookstore etiquette (which forbids a salesman to disturb a browsing customer) that I snapped a curt ''No!'' She went back and sat down at a table, and when I saw she was young and pretty I thought perhaps I had been ruder than absolutely necessary, and so I went over and said, ''As a matter of fact, miss, you *can* help me. I'd like a copy of a book called *Irish Bogs*, by J. W. Seigne, published in London by Longmans, Green in 1928.''

The young lady's face lit up and she said, ''Yes, sir—here you are, sir!'' There was one book lying on the table, and she handed it to me. It was a copy, in mint condition, of *Irish Bogs* by J. W. Seigne. When I had pinched both myself and it to make sure it was real, I asked the girl why she had had the book on the table. She blushed prettily and said, ''Well, you see, sir, I just started working here this morning, and it's my first job ever, and Mr. Abrams showed me a big pile of books in the back room and asked me to sort them out. He said to put all the fiction in one pile and all the poetry in another pile and the biographies and history books and technical books and so forth each in separate piles. It was my first assignment and I wanted to do it perfectly, but when I got all through I had this one left over. What kind of a pile do you put a book about Irish bogs in? I'm just waiting for Mr. Abrams to get back from lunch and I do hope he won't be angry with me.''

Just then Mr. Abrams came in, and I solved the young lady's problem by buying the book.

DIFFICULT QUESTIONS ANSWERED

One of the advantages of being 80 is that one accumulates a vast fund of knowledge which, tempered by the wisdom that comes with having bobbed and weaved, or woven, through 4/5ths of a century and successfully slipped most of the roundhouse punches that Destiny had aimed at one's kisser, enables one to cope with most of the difficult questions one encounters. For example:

Dear Mr. Zern: In a recent ''Exit Laughing'' in which you wrote about Ted Trueblood and his Dutch oven, you mentioned a Baked Alaska. What is it? J. R. C., Okla.

Dear Mr. C.: That was a typographical error, of course, and should have read ''Baked

Alaskan.'' During the early days of that 51st State conditions were primitive, life was hazardous, and cannibalism was sometimes necessary for survival. And anyone who has ever tried eating a raw Alaskan will understand why those who survived learned a number of recipes for just such emergencies.

Dear Mr. Zern: I was interested in your recent reference to Tom Wheeler's goose-shooting camp on James Bay, and to the Cree Indian guides. Are the Crees a particular tribe, or what? A. K. L., Mo.

Dear Mr. L.: The Crees are a tribe inhabiting large areas of Quebec, Ontario and parts of the Maritime Provinces. They are a branch of the Algonquins, and are noted for their woodsmanship. One Cree encampment, on the now-deserted Isle Bois Brule in the Gulf of St. Lawrence, was also famous for the elaborate and ornate costumes and finery worn by its members. When this tribe died out the last surviving member moved to Trois Rivieres, where he used to parade down the main street wearing the latest Algonquin fashions. He was known far and wide as the Dernier Cree.

HOW TO GIVE YOUR WIFE A VACATION

I've heard about husbands who thought only of themselves when planning family vacations, and no doubt a few such self-centered, selfish men actually exist.

But in my own case I try always to bear in mind that my wife doesn't care about fishing or shooting, and so when she reminded me last spring that I had had several trips to Africa, South America, and Canada since she had been anywhere interesting, I said, ''Dear, you're quite right. You deserve a vacation, and by the lord Harry you shall have it. Where would you like to go?'' And when she said she'd like to go to the south of France, I said, ''And so you shall!'' and set about making the arrangements.

It occurred to me while doing so that in order to get to France one is more or less obliged to pass the British Isles, and as Keith Davis, erstwhile president of the Ruffed Grouse Society of America, had called me from Michigan a few days before to invite me to fish a week on the Aboyne Castle water on the Dee, which he had leased for the month of May, I hastily called him back to accept. I explained to Evelyn that it would be silly to fly over Scotland and all those salmon without stopping, and she readily conceded my point.

And so on May 15 we boarded an Icelandic Airlines flight for Glasgow, and shortly after renting a car there were snugly ensconced in an inn beside the Dee, where for seven days I fished that lovely river and even managed to extract a few salmon from it, from 10 to 19 pounds.

''It would be ridiculous,'' I said to Evelyn as we packed to depart from Aboyne, ''to be this close to Edinburgh and not stop by to see Michael and Evelyn Brander, especially as Mike mentioned one time he could probably wangle me a day on the Tweed.'' Unable to fault the logic of this she agreed, and so we drove to Haddington where Mike, who has written a number of books on shooting, dog-training, horses, hunting, and the Scottish Highlands, and his family greeted us. After Mike and I had fished the Tweed, shot some wood pigeon, and run some in-depth consumer tests on several brands of single-malt whiskey—oops, whisky—and as we were preparing to take our leave a few days later, I said to Evelyn (Z.), "According to my road map we're just a couple of hours north of Wisbech, which is near Elm, which is where David and Marjorie Barr live, and I promised Dave if we were ever in his neighborhood we'd stop by and I'd help him fish a river in Norfolkshire that's stiff with trout, and also play some golf.

"Also," I pointed out, "when not being a barrister David writes for *The Field* and *Country Life*, and it's important to keep in touch with other writers—swap trade secrets on margin widths, that sort of thing." And so after we had taken our leave of the Branders, with Mike's affable father providing a stirrup cup of Glenlivet before we drove off, we headed for Elm, and the following day I fished the Babingley with David and arranged to play golf the following morning with him and a friend, which we did.

By now we were barely 200 miles from France, and I felt we were making excellent progress; then, just before starting out next morning for London, I looked through my wallet for a fishing snapshot I wanted to show David, and what should I come across but a folder Dermot Wilson had sent me, explaining his set-up at Nether Wallop, in Hampshire, where for a reasonable figure he can arrange for fishing on several private stretches of the Test and the Itchen, no doubt the two best-known trout rivers in the world and richly deserving of their fame.

A call to Dermot established that he could find accommodations and a piece of river to fish, and so, after Evelyn had admitted that Hampshire was in the direction of France, off we went Nether Wallopward, and for the next two days I had fabulous fishing, taking a 3-pound brown and two 2-pounders from the Test on one of George Harvey's #20 Light Cahills, and a few nice rainbows from the Itchen on Partridge Tail nymphs. (I also derricked a 6-pound rainbow from the spring-fed pond behind the old mill that houses Dermot's mail-order tackle business, but as Leigh Perkins of Orvis had dredged a 7-pounder from the same pond a few weeks previously and Lee Wulff, or perhaps it was Joan, had had a 9-pounder, my feat wasn't mentioned in despatches.)

Then to London, where as a special treat for Evelyn I took her to Hardy's illustrious tackle shop to see their salmon-fly pins, and thence to Paris, where I learned that Charles Ritz was off fishing but was expected back any day, and although I was tempted to suggest that we wait for him, in hopes he might put me onto some good water, I told Evelyn, "No, this is your vacation, not mine! Let's drive right down to Entrevaux!"

"Where's Entrevaux?" Evelyn said.

"You said you wanted to go to the south of France," I explained, "and Entrevaux is smack in the middle of the south of France. It's also where George Yamaoka—remember, you met him at a Theodore Gordon Flyfishers dinner—has a trout fishing lodge. He's there now, and invited us to fish his water when I saw him just before we left New York. You don't want to go to the south of France and just stand around with your teeth in your mouth, do you?"

"As a matter of fact," Evelyn said thoughtfully, "I don't want to go to the south of

France at all. I want to go to the Loire valley and look at chateaux and then go to Brittany and look at Mont St. Michel and eat *moules farcis* and drink Muscadet.'' And so we did, because my wife doesn't get many vacations and I wanted this to be one she'd remember.

And so, after a week of gaping at Mont St. Michel, an island with a chapel on it surrounded by water too shallow for good fishing, and some other old buildings at Chartres and Chambord, we drove to Luxembourg and flew to Iceland, where I made arrangements to come back the following month for some of that splendid little country's superb salmon fishing, and back to New York and home.

Since then Evelyn has remarked several times on how much she appreciated my complete and utter unselfishness in taking her to France—but in all honesty I must admit there was a motive behind it. Because now I'll feel free to spend next vacation doing what *I* want.

HOW TO FORGET FISH

I was recently pleased to learn that Dr. David Starr Jordan, the famous authority on freshwater and saltwater fishes who for a number of years was president of Leland Stanford University, was notorious for his inability to remember the names of even close associates. Finally, when during an important ceremony involving the dedication of some new buildings he had risen to introduce the university chancellor and had been unable to recall his name, a committee of the administrative faculty called upon him to respectfully urge that he make an effort to learn the names of at least the most important of his colleagues. ''Gentlemen,'' Dr. Jordan is reported to have said, ''I shall certainly make such an effort, as I have many times in the past. The trouble is, every time I remember a name I forget a fish.''

I have not forgotten Mr. C. L. Strohmeyer's name, because I have it in front of me, on a letter from him received last week. He writes: ''Dear Mr. Zern: In the January issue you say you welcome difficult questions. I have one. A group of us here in Erie have a deer camp in the Allegheny National Forest, where electricity is unavailable and we use oil lamps for light. We notice that every cowboy in every horse opera on TV or in the movies comes into a pitch-dark cabin or shack, strikes a stove match on the table and touches it to the wick of an oil lantern. Instantly the whole room lights up like the grand ballroom at the Waldorf Astoria. My question is, where can we buy a couple of those lanterns. The ones we have don't seem to work that way. Sincerely yours.'' I have referred this to the Lighting Fixtures Editor, as everyone around here has been reading Ardrey and Lorenz and is feeling territorial.

Nor do I have trouble recollecting the name of Billy Joe Johnstone of Little Rock, Arkansas, whose signed letter is before me: ''Dear Sir: I can figure out Mr. Trueblood and Mr. McClane and Mr. Tapply and those gentlemen because I think they are trying to tell me something that will maybe be useful in my life. But I can't figure you out. I read your column every month but most of the time it don't make very good sense to me. What exactly is the purpose of your column? Yours truly.'' Would that all questions were as easy to answer, Billy Joe. The purpose of this column is to cast a gleam of light, however flickering and feeble, into the dark recesses of the human spirit, and to bring to all mankind except the United States Army Corps of Engineers a vision and a message of hope and inspiration for the future. Any time, Billy Joe, any time.

I know Mr. Harold McBride's name because it's right here on this tear-sheet from the November 18, 1971, issue of the Humble, Texas, *Humble Echo*, which includes the following classified ad:

> *THE HUNTER who left his shotgun and shoes in the creek bed in my pasture may reclaim these articles if he will tell me what he was after, or possibly what was after him. Phone 446-2021.*

In an effort to find out what *was* after the shotgunner and in accordance with my policy of sparing no expense in my efforts to keep my readers well-informed on vital issues I telephoned 446-2021 in Humble and got a very nice lady on the line who said no, she had never heard of the ad and in fact didn't even have a pasture, much less a creek bed, and yes, this is 446-2021 in Humble, Texas. She even told me her name, but I forgot it.

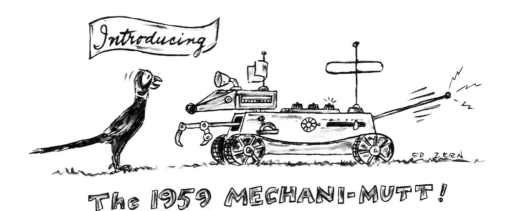

Introducing

The 1959 MECHANI-MUTT!

SAFARI NOTE

When Michael Woodford, an Englishman with the FAO in Kenya, invited me one time to fish one of the better trout streams that come down off Mt. Kenya, I accepted instantly; although Mike's main thing is falconry, on which he has written several books. He's a keen fly fisherman as well, and pleasant company.

With his son John we drove out from Nairobi, and during the 100-mile run Mike explained that there was little danger, while fishing, of confrontations with elephants, as they seldom come down to the streams until darkness sets in. However, in the event of such a meeting, Mike advised me, I should graciously let the elephant have the right of way. "The only wildlife you're likely to run into," Mike said, "is a pack of baboons on the upper water. They'll sometimes make threatening noises and gestures, but I can't imagine they'd actually attack anyone."

So later that day, when I stopped to chat with an elderly and elegantly dressed English angler who said he had previously fished only on a few famous chalk streams in the south of England, and discovered that this was his first week in Kenya and his first day of African trout fishing, I asked him how he found it. "Interesting," he said, and went on to say that while fishing further up the gorge he had been harassed by some nasty, hairy creatures which had snarled at him from the bushes. Quite unpleasant, he said, and when I told him they were baboons, he looked astonished.

"Baboons!" he said. "My word! So that's what they were!"

"What had you thought they were?" I asked.

"Well, quite frankly," he said, "I had assumed they were some type of worm fishermen."

HOW TO SHOOT DUCKS

When a friend of mine was in Kenya on safari early this year he noticed one of the numerous Africans of the entourage puzzling over what seemed to my friend to be a fairly simple problem in arithmetic. And so later, when the African's name came up at the dinner table that evening, my friend said something about the man's stupidity.

"What makes you think he's stupid?" the professional hunter asked, and my friend told him.

"That stupid man speaks fluent English, Swahili, Kikuyu, Masai, and Kamba," the hunter said gently, "and he can get along pretty well in Arabic, Italian, and Turkana. How many languages do you speak, doctor?" My friend, who flunked high-school French before going on to a fairly brilliant career in his field, told me he had seldom heard a point made more succinctly, and said he had apologized in the only language he knew.

It reminded me that a couple of years ago I had gone to Czechoslovakia to do a story on bird shooting there, which is excellent as well as relatively inexpensive, and after taking part in several driven-pheasant shoots I told the guy in charge of me that I'd like to get in a day of duck shooting, since the season had just opened.

So that evening we flew from Prague to Bratislava, the chief city of eastern Czechoslovakia, arriving in time to visit a number of wine cellars deep beneath the medieval buildings of that ancient settlement on the Danube. It was late October, the new wine had just come in as fresh and heady as young love, and somehow it was 5 A.M. before we got back to the hotel. That afternoon we drove through pleasantly hilly countryside for several hours until we arrived at Palarikova, formerly the shooting preserve of a Count Karoly and presently an elegant shooting lodge for visiting foreigners, with ducks, geese, pheasant, partridge, hares, roebuck, and wild boar abounding on its several thousand acres. I was shown to a room that looked like the set for a lavish production of a Franz Lehar operetta, with a bed the size of a badminton court. After a simple supper with more new wine I retired to it, and was just beginning to get accustomed to it when the guide hammered on the door and said it was time to get up and go duck shooting.

At breakfast the guide introduced me to Josef Kisary, a young, enthusiastic wildlife-management expert in charge of running the estate; Kisary, the guide said, speaks no English, and asked if he should come along to interpret. "Hunters speak a universal language," I assured him. "Go back to bed." The guide looked grateful in a hung-over way and went back to bed.

Half an hour and two fried eggs later I was sneaking through a cold, wet field, gun in hand, with Kisary; we could hear ducks gabbling in the pond beyond the field, and by sign language Josef let me know we would try to jump them. Unfortunately, several dozens of pheasants were skulking ahead of us in the high grass; when we were almost within gunshot of the pond they panicked and took off in a cackling chaos that spooked every duck within five hundred yards, and we watched flocks of mallards, pintail, and pochard departing in all directions. A pair of mallards swung 'round and headed for us, and I was just about to take what should have been an easy left and right when Josef tapped me sharply on the shoulder and said, "No!"

I put my gun down and watched the birds pass overhead, thinking maybe they don't shoot mallards on this pond. Josef shrugged, motioned me to follow and led me to a blind made of woven twigs. Pointing up he let me know that some of the ducks would be flying over the blind, but when a brace of pintail came over and I stood up to shoot he hissed "No!" again, and again I put the gun down. When he said "No!" the third time and I let another pair of mallards fly past, I could see he looked awfully unhappy, and asked him in what I hoped was German why he said "No!" each time I started to shoot.

He took a pencil and pad from his pocket, wrote something, and handed the pad to me, pointing to the pad and saying "No! No! No!" I looked at the pad and the word he had written: N-O-W! It was the only English word he knew; he had learned it for the occasion, and being a logical man he pronounced it to rhyme with blow, throw, slow, snow, crow, and low. Somehow I explained what "No!" meant, and we walked a mile to another pond. There were still a few ducks trading between ponds but the morning flight was over and except for a brace of pochard which I scratched down after a long wait, so was my chance at Czechoslovakian duck shooting.

Back at the castle, when my guide said something about the universal language of hunters, I fetched him a whack on the skull with a cleaning rod.

ALL ABOUT MOUNTAIN LIONS

Even if Theodore Roosevelt had not been a great President, he would have been known today as a pioneer in natural-resource conservation, especially in the fields of wildlife and national parks. But in T.R.'s day the science of wildlife management was little understood even by biologists, and so when Teddy, while President, saw at first hand the "ravages" of mountain lions on the herds of mule deer that made the Kaibab Forest a deer hunter's paradise, he ordered an extensive campaign of shooting and trapping the big cats.

When the mountain lions had been virtually exterminated in the Kaibab, the deer herd increased tremendously for a few years. Then, because the vast herds of deer had eaten not only the normal increment of browse and grass but also, in their desperate hunger, the branches and roots that would have provided the next year's forage, they finally became so undernourished that disease killed them by the thousands. Today we realize that the lions, wolves, and wildcats that preyed on the herds were performing an important function, and by preventing overpopulation had kept the deer in balance with their food supply, and healthy.

The deer, in short, needed the lions and wolves as much as the carnivores needed the deer. In recent years we have recognized that one way, and perhaps the best way, to maintain a healthy population of deer, elk, antelope, or even wildfowl and game birds is to permit enough predation to cull the weak, diseased, deformed, and otherwise substandard members from the herd or flock, so that only the fittest survive to breed.

Unfortunately we haven't yet applied the same common-sense approach to management of the human animal. For example, it's well known (to me, at any rate) that one reason for this country's greatness was the multitude of dangers that beset the early pioneers and ensured that only the hardiest would survive. What with rampaging Comanches, trigger-happy vigilantes, stampeding cattle, grizzly bears, tarantulas, bad whiskey, ornery mules, train wrecks, prairie fires, blizzards, drunken cowhands, stagecoach robbers, cyclones, runaway horses, rattlesnakes, and an almost total lack of doctors, surgeons, hospitals or even Band Aids, it was no wonder that only the strongest, toughest, nimblest citizens survived long enough to beget progeny. The result was a systematic weeding-out of the weaklings, and a fine, upstanding breed of men to populate the West.

You may imagine my consternation, then, when on a recent trip to Denver I was severely reprimanded by a uniformed agent of the local fuzz for crossing the street against a red light—this, mind you, at 1 A.M. on a nearly deserted street with not an automobile, bus, or taxi within mangling distance. Ye gods and little Dolly Vardens! No wonder we New Yorkers are smarter, quicker thinking, faster on our feet, and generally the all-around superiors of people in Denver, St. Louis, Nebraska, Cincinnati, and other Western cities. The internal-combustion engine is to New Yorkers, thank heaven, as wolves are to caribou and mountain lions to mule deer—a means of eliminating the feeble and unfit.

Walking down Fifth Avenue last summer I was constantly overhearing visitors from Omaha, Ohio, and other Western states exclaim, "My, how these New Yorkers scurry and rush about!" If I hadn't been in such a hurry I'd have stopped to explain to them that New Yorkers who don't scurry and rush about, at least while crossing streets, are soon ground to a bloody pulp beneath the wheels of crosstown buses, or tossed several stories high by taxicabs, or clobbered by a paddywagon full of mobsters, muggers, Mafiosi, malefactors, murderers, and other miscreant Manhattanites.

It is this constant culling of the hesitant, the slow-reflexed, the clumsy and the astigmatic that has, through generations of evolution, made New Yorkers so sure-footed, agile, and alert, and has kept them in balance with their food supply. And if ever they were to be required to cross streets only at intersections, and only when the DON'T WALK sign had stopped blinking, it would be just a matter of a few years until the city would be populated by fuzzy-brained, slew-footed, maladroit nincompoops and bumbling, myopic dullards, all of them producing at least one litter a year.

I don't know if Denver is electing a mayor this fall, but if so I hope that city's thinking citizens will draft a man pledged not merely to encourage jay-walking but to abolish safety zones, pedestrian signals, and other sops to the sentimental old ladies who keep yammering, "How could you have the heart to run over a pedestrian? They have such big, soft, beautiful eyes!"

Otherwise, it's just a matter of time until Denverites are soft all over.

AMAZING DEER-HUNTING ADVENTURE

While hurrying down Madison Avenue last week, I ran into Mike Lonergan, whom I hadn't seen for some time. "How's with you, Mike?" I said, and he said, "Ed, you're just the man I've wanted to see. I had a most remarkable experience while deer-hunting last winter, and I want to tell you about it. Buy me a drink and I'll fill you in!"

When we had found ourselves a booth in a side-street saloon and ordered a brace of bourbons, Mike said, "Remember that little dirt road we discovered that time we hunted woodcock in the Bald Eagle Valley while you were at Penn State? The one that ran back into a hollow, and you said it looked like there had to be at least one moonshine still not too far up it?"

I said I remembered it was somewhere near Hannah Furnace, and Mike said, "Well, I drove up that road the first day of the Pennsylvania deer season, in that old olive-drab jeep of mine, the one I always have trouble starting in cold weather. Had to get out and haul some tree trunks off the road a few times but I got about a mile back from the highway before the road petered out in brush.

"I didn't see any stills," Mike said, "but I did see a lot of deer sign, so I parked the vehicle back in under a clump of rhododendron and threw a brown blanket over the hood. Jerry Parks had told me a blanket over the hood might make it easier to start, although I couldn't see how it would hold enough heat to make a difference, but I'd grabbed an old brown blanket on the way out of the house and I put it over the hood.

"Well sir," Mike said, "there were deer trails every hundred yards or so, and when I saw one that looked like it got a lot of traffic I hunted downwind from it to where it ran into a couple of other trails below a limestone ledge.

"So I walked around and got on top of the ledge, where I could spot anything coming up or down, and sat there for over an hour. Saw seven or eight does and a spike buck, but the buck got wind of me too soon for a shot even if I had wanted to take it, which I didn't. There was a good bit of shooting going on up and down the valley, and I figured the deer would be moving pretty well, but after an hour I got too cold to sit still and started hunting my way back toward where I had left the car.

"Finally, when I figured I was just about back to where I'd started I caught a glimpse of what looked like a deer in a clump of rhododendron. I stood real still and watched that spot of brown for a long time, but couldn't even tell which end was head and which was tail, much less if it was a legal buck. Finally my eyes could just barely make out the outline of the animal, and then I was pretty sure I could see antlers. In fact, I was positive!"

Mike took a long pull at his bourbon and water, and I said, "Yes, yes. What then?" (I have this flair for repartee.)

"Well," Mike said, "when I was positive—absolutely *positive*, mind you—that it was a buck with legal antlers, I slowly raised Old Betsy—I was shooting my old reliable thutty-thutty, and that 180-grain slug sort of elbows its way through shrubbery, so I wasn't much concerned about the brush—held where I figured that buck's boiler-room ought to be, and pulled the trigger. Kaboom!"

"Keep talking, for heaven's sake!" I said. "What happened?"

"Well," said Mike, "I was sort of surprised that that deer didn't come swarming out of the rhododendrons, because of course a lung shot doesn't nail 'em down right away. So I walked on down there, and what do you think I found in that clump of rhododendron?"

"Tell me!" I said. "For Pete's sake, what did you find?"

"A dandy little four-point buck," Mike said proudly, "as dead as Rutherford B. Hayes. That bullet had caught him in the neck, and I doubt he had even twitched. I dressed him out, hauled him over to the jeep—it was less than a hundred yards away—and was back home that same evening with a hundred pounds of prime venison!"

"Very nice," I said. "But tell me, exactly what was so remarkable about this experience?"

"Oh, yes!" Mike said. "Almost forgot! That blanket trick really works. Engine started right off—barely touched the starter! Thanks for the drink, Ed—see you around."

"Not if I see you first," I said.

Or would have if I had thought of it.

ALL ABOUT EAGLES

Now that *Field & Stream* has a woman's editor, it occurred to me that all too many outdoorsmen are unable to communicate effectively with their wives, and that Maggie Nichols' column may help to correct this. And as faulty communications are known to be responsible for more divorces than any other cause, this could well lead to improved domestic relations in the homes of *Field & Stream* readers, and a lower divorce rate than among the underprivileged, non-communicating readers of *Sp-rts -f--ld and --td--r L-f-*.

Mulling this over at breakfast yesterday I said to Evelyn, "What do you think of Maggie's column, now that you've had a chance to evaluate it? I mean, what's your net impression?"

"I think it's great," Evelyn said, "and speaking of nets, you were going to put that bird-net over the strawberries before the starlings eat them like they did last year."

"I was going to," I said, "but there's a hole in that net a bald eagle could get through. But I wanted to know how you felt about *Field & Stream*'s woman's page."

"I don't have to read a woman's page in *Field & Stream* to know that bald eagles don't eat strawberries," Evelyn said, "and if Maggie Nichols says they do, she takes from a different ornithologist than I do."

"Maggie hasn't ever written anything about eagles eating strawberries," I said. "At least I don't think she has. What do you think of her column otherwise?"

"Even if bald eagles did eat strawberries," Evelyn said, "there hasn't ever been a bald eagle in Scarsdale except that one with a broken wing at the Nature Center."

"That was a horned owl," I said.

"Whatever it was," Evelyn said, "I'll bet a pretty penny it didn't eat strawberries. I've never heard such silly talk. First Duncan Barnes says bald eagles eat strawberries, and now you say owls . . ."

"It wasn't Duncan Barnes," I interrupted, "it was Maggie Nichols."

"You told me Duncan's responsible for everything in the magazine," Evelyn said, "and now you're trying to make that nice girl take the rap. And anyway, it was *you* that said horned owls eat strawberries, not Maggie. Where are you going?"

"Out to put up the net," I said. While I was mending the hole my neighbor George Dee came along and I asked him what time it was. He told me, and went on his way. Actually I knew what time it was, but wanted to make sure I could communicate with somebody.

There has been a lot of crank mail coming in here addressed to somebody named Wilbur Duckfoot or Duickenfoos or something, and the mailroom boy has been dumping it on my desk. I have read some of the letters and must confess I'm unable to make head or tail of them, although my name seems to crop up in most of them. What I want to know is, what goes on here? There is a smartass kid named Wilmer or Wilbur who loiters around the hallways here and whom I occasionally permit to retype my column, especially

on those mornings when my hand is unsteady from having drunk too much milk the previous evening, but I've never heard his last name and hope I never have occasion to. (Milk contains lactic acid, which corrodes the central nervous system, but I love the stuff and drink it despite doctor's warnings.)

Anyway I have had to throw this creepy kid out of my office on a number of occasions, as he keeps leaving pieces of model airplanes around the office, not to mention bottles of airplane glue which I suspect he sniffs, and also because he keeps asking me questions about girls when he isn't whining and snivelling that he wants to be a humorist. I keep explaining to him that he can humor me by clearing out of the office, and I confess I sometimes give him a fatherly pat on the head in order to get his attention. But I most emphatically deny I have ever been really rough with him. He just happens to be one of those people who bleed at the least little tap.

Actually I don't bleed easier than other people, but Mr. Zern was watching over my shoulder and he has just left to get a glass of milk, he says. He only gave me $5 for last month's piece because he said I typed it too slow, which was because my thumbs hurt on account of him having hung me up by them after he found out I had written about our professional relationship in the January issue, but when you are 14 you heal pretty fast. I don't know how old Mr. Zern is. The only time I asked him he hit me with his cane.

I have to go now and write Mrs. Nichols' column.

HOW TO SHOOT CROWS

Over the years a number of readers have written, asking me to provide them with my crow-shooting system as it appeared here a decade or so ago. As both of them are regular subscribers I can hardly afford to ignore their request, and hasten to comply.

The system is based on a study of crow behavior conducted by research biologists at Phelps University which showed that crows have a relatively high level of intelligence and are actually able to count, but only in multiples of three or less, so that the conventional procedure for fooling crows—by sending several men into a blind, then having all but one of them leave—is not likely to work except with very young birds, if at all. Thus, even if six crow hunters go into a cornstalk blind and only five come out, the crows probably won't be fooled, as they will have counted off the hunters in trios and will realize that one of the groups is short a man; as a result they will stay the hell away from there until the frustrated gunner gives up and emerges.

My system for successful crow hunting is childishly simple, and consists of the following steps:

1. Build a blind overlooking a cornfield frequented by crows.

2. Assemble a group of twenty-five hunters, all dressed more or less alike and of nearly equal height, build, and facial characteristics. All the hunters should be clean-shaven, but *twelve of them should be wearing false mustaches*. The group should assemble in a barn or some sort of building not less than 350 yards from the field. (It would be prudent to have a few spare hunters on hand, to substitute in cases of pulled muscles, heart attacks or other contingencies.)

3. All of the hunters should be equipped with 12-gauge shotguns, but it is advisable that these be fairly light in weight, as it is important that *all hunters going to and from the blind must travel at a dead run*, so that the crows will not have sufficient time for their calculations.

4. As soon as a flock of crows comes into the area, eleven of the hunters are dispatched from the old barn to the blind, running at top speed. The instant they arrive, seven of them turn around and rush back to the barn.

5. When the seven hunters get back to the barn, they are joined by six other hunters and the thirteen of them sprint back to the blind as fast as possible; on arrival there, ten of them immediately turn around and dash back to the barn.

6. Before the ten arrive, eight more hunters are sent from the barn to the blind. When they meet the ten returning from the blind all of them switch hats and false mustaches while milling around in a tight huddle, then break it up and resume running to their respective destinations.

7. As soon as the eight hunters arrive at the blind, five of them turn around and rush back toward the barn; on the way they meet nine hunters running from the barn toward the blind, whereupon the hunters divide themselves into two groups of seven, one of which runs back to the barn while the other rushes to the blind, changes hats and mustaches, leaves two of its members there and dashes back to the barn.

8. Of the twelve hunters now in the blind, nine rush across the fields to the barn while twelve of the thirteen hunters in the barn charge en masse from the barn to the blind; on arrival they immediately turn and sashay back to the barn taking two of the three hunters still in the blind with them, *leaving a single hunter.*

9. It is, of course, essential that all this be done at the highest possible speed, so that the crows will fall hopelessly behind in their arithmetic and in the consequent corvine confusion fail to realize that a hunter is concealed in the blind.

10. Eventually the crows will learn to count faster, so that the system must be modified occasionally to keep ahead of them. In addition to having the hunters run faster, it may be necessary to introduce false beards and quick-change toupees as well as false mustaches, and to build a second blind on another side of the field so that the traffic will be triangular instead of simply linear, requiring the crows to start working on trigonometric permutations and geometric progressions in order to cope. In severe cases the hunters may be equipped with numbered jerseys from 1 TO 25 *but with the number 17 omitted and two number 21s.* (This can also be done with roman numerals, when birds are very wary.)

Watch this space next month for an equally simple, foolproof system for outwitting that wily old woodchuck in the back pasture, requiring no special equipment other than a stuffed Guernsey cow and a milkmaid's costume.

BUG INTERRED

Lately people have begun to notice us outdoor writers whipping around in our Isotta-Fraschinis and Apperson Jack rabbits, smoking our cork-tipped Melachrinos and English Ovals, stuffing ourselves with fresh beluga caviar, drinking Dom Perignon '59 out of the slippers of ladies who are probably no better than they should be, buying if not sirloin steaks at least the better grades of chuck, and otherwise employing the bundles of C-notes thrust upon us by eager editors of outdoor magazines. As a result, a lot of those observers are trying to get into the act, and hardly a day goes by that I fail to receive a manuscript from some banker or bishop or burglar who is thinking of giving up a perfectly good livelihood to become an outdoor writer.

The trouble with almost all these efforts is that they lack the professional touch, and to illustrate, let me quote one in full, as submitted by my friend Mr. Lyle H. Banks of Bend, Oregon. Mr. Banks is 85 years old, and as a youth in Atchison, Kansas, he horsed around with another kid named Ray Holland; it occurred to him recently that this might be a good time to start a new career in the outdoor-writing field, since Ray had done pretty well at it, and accordingly he sent me the following short story, which I reproduce here in its unexpurgated entirety: *While crawling around in the grass a bug was swallowed by a cow. It was warm and snug inside the cow, and the bug fell asleep. When he woke up, the cow was gone.*

Here, in one handy package, are perfect examples of many of the mistakes made frequently by nonprofessional outdoor writers. For one thing, the author completely neglects to establish the dominant character traits of the main characters; we finish the story knowing little or nothing of their hopes and ambitions, their secret fears and innermost sorrows, their frustrations and despair. Hell, we don't even know their names, much less the real nature of the relationship which, although short-lived, must have touched one or both of their hearts and at least one of their lower intestines.

And dialogue, which is the life-blood of an outdoor story (*"Joe, come quick, I am being eaten by a bear!" exclaimed Charley, which reminded me of the evening last winter when Charley had dropped by the house to borrow a cup of Hoppe's No. 9 and we had first talked about a trip into the grizzly-infested wilds of Alaska, and the many evenings we had spent planning this adventure. And so, just a week ago, we had landed at the Anchorage airport and so forth and so on.* Of course that's only half a dialogue, but eventually Joe gets around to acknowledging Charley's request, only to find that he is about 1,500 words too late and that Charley is already partially digested. Let's see now, where were we? Ah, yes), is totally lacking. You would expect that the bug, undergoing an experience not unrelated to the catharsis of Greek dramatic tragedy, would have a few words of comment, if only, "Boy, it sure is stuffy in here. Dark, too."

Then, too, Mr. Banks should know that outdoor writers are usually paid by the word, and that for beginners ten cents a word is considered fair recompense. At that rate Mr. Banks would get $3.40 for his story, and if he sold one a month, which is about average output for outdoor writers, he would make $40.80 a year before taxes, which might see him through one week at the Bend Diner, leaving fifty-one weeks to cope with, or with which to cope. Or with which to cope with. (Grammar, as Mr. Banks will learn if he pursues his new bent, is a tricky thing to get the hang of. Or of which to get the hang.) And at Peter Kriendler's boarding house at 21 West 52nd Street in New York City, a favorite beanery of both outdoor and indoor writers, $40.80 would barely get him through one lunch, and a very light lunch it would be at that.

In short, and much as it grieves me to pan the work of a fellow sportsman and especially one who was a friend of the late Ray Holland, who bought the first story I ever sold, I am obliged to say that in my opinion Mr. Banks's story is a flop.

CULINARY STORY

Once again it's that time of year when the calendar runs out, and the editors find themselves with letters-from-readers that are difficult to answer and that are therefore passed on to me, as my fund of outdoor knowledge seems well-nigh inexhaustible. Here's a letter from a man in Philadelphia:

"Dear Field & Stream: I am a lifelong subscriber to your fine magazine, and have always insisted that my children read it as well. In fact, I have striven to inculcate in them my own, and your own, ideals of outdoor competence and sportsmanship. Recently, however, my daughter—a graduate of Miss Spence's and Wellesley, and an accomplished performer on the 'cello and harpsichord—broke her engagement to a brilliant young banker and a few days later eloped with a short-order cook, on the grounds that he was a fine wingshot and a skillful fly fisherman whereas the banker had been a poor shot and an indifferent angler. I am distressed and confused by this, and for that matter do not even know exactly what a short-order cook is, although I gather it is not one of the higher-paying professions and my daughter has expensive tastes. Can you offer any advice in this unfortunate—or so it seems to me—situation? E.K.McW., Merion, Pa."

Dear McW.: I must confess that the term "short-order cook" is unknown to me, and it's possible that you misunderstood your daughter. Several years ago I heard about a somewhat eccentric chap who lived in a pigsty because, he said, he preferred the company of young pigs to young people; as a result he could be smelled several blocks away. He was frequently referred to as a shoat-odor kook, and for all I know this may be the same chap. Tell your daughter to try to stay upwind of him at all times.

ALL ABOUT ROOSTERFISH, PUBLIC SPEAKING, STUFF LIKE THAT

Awhile back my wife and I went to Mazatlan on the west coast of Mayheeko to attend a conference of the Outdoor Writers of America, virtually none of whom actually write outdoors, and while there listened to Secretary of the Interior Rogers C. B. Morton speak on the problem of preserving tidal estuaries and estuarial ecosystems as recreational areas and more importantly as ecological necessities, since many species of saltwater fishes are dependent on estuarial marshes as sources of essential nutrients in the food chain.

Mr. Morton gave a good talk, which he prefaced by saying he had a keen interest in estuaries, and that in fact his two middle initials stood for "Chesapeake Bay." The more I thought about this later the more it seemed likely that Mr. Morton had been pulling our collective leg, and that in fact he probably doesn't have two genuine middle initials but invented them as a public-speaking ploy, since he spends a good bit of his time making speeches at various charity balls, clam bakes, church bazaars, community bar-becues, cotillion balls, and centennial banquets, at any of which his phoney initials would provide a nifty lead to his remarks.

At a gourmet society, for example, he could proclaim his middle initials stood for Cook Book, or Cordon Bleu, or Cinnamon Bun, or Charcoal Broiled, or Cake Batter,

or Canadian Bacon, or Crab Bisque, or Cheese Burger, or Corn Bread, or Continental Breakfast. At a meeting of architects or building-trades people it would be Cinder Block; at a Panther convention, Coal Black; at the Iowa State Chamber of Commerce convention, Council Bluffs; at a brewer's convention, Cold Beer; for an antiquarians' meeting, Covered Bridge; for gunsmiths, Cylinder Bore; for Adderley addicts, Cannon Ball; for bankers, Corporate Bond; for fitness freaks, Cold Bath; for marlin fishermen, Cabo Blanco; for law officers, Cat Burglar or perhaps Cell Block; for lip readers, Comic Book; for newspaper editors, Copy Boy; for assassins, Cold Blood; for people with large feet, Canal Boat; for misers, Cash Box; for confectioners, Candy Bar; for romanticists, Captain Blood; for winos, California Burgundy or Christian Brothers; for surf anglers, Channel Bass; for Easter Islanders, Captain Bligh; for war-mongers, Casus Belli; for homespun philosophers, Cracker Barrel; for pool hustlers, Cue Ball; for office workers, Coffee Break; for students, College Boards; and so, as the fellow said, forth.

After figuring that one out we flew across the Sea of Cortez to Cabo de San Lucas, where we spent two days at the Hotel Finisterra, which may be the most spectacularly beautiful resort hotel in this hemisphere. The hotel, which is carved out of a solid-stone cliff overlooking the Pacific and surrounded on three sides by billfish and roosterfish, not to mention dolphin (or dorado) up to 50 pounds, had few guests because of its newness and the off-season, but after coming in from catching and releasing two marlin and four roosterfish I met a man at the bar who told me he had spent most of the morning and part of the afternoon battling a monstrous fish of some kind that had never showed, and that when it seemed as strong after five hours as it had in the beginning, and he had been unable to gain line and his arms had started coming out of their sockets he had reluctantly let the mate cut the line.

His hands were badly blistered, one thumb was dislocated, and he could barely lift his creaking frame onto a bar stool; his fingers were swollen from gripping the rod and his bald head was raw with sunburn; he had pulled a tendon in his shoulder and had banged his knee against the fighting chair when he jumped into it; in addition he had become seasick and violently ill during the final half-hour of the fray. When I suggested he might consider giving up marlin fishing for good, he looked at me in astonishment. "And miss all that fun?" he said.

When I reported this to my wife I noticed she seemed bemused, and I asked her why. "I was just wondering," she said, "if Mr. Morton ever got asked to speak to a convention of Sea Bees." I went back to the bar.

HOW TO AVOID SPLITS

Once there were a couple of fishermen, one elderly and the other middle-aged, standing on a bridge peering into the river 50 feet below. Suddenly a young man rushed out onto the bridge, took off his coat and climbed up onto the railing. "What's going on, bub?" asked the elderly angler.

"I'll tell you what's going on," said the young man bitterly. "I'm about to jump into the river and end it all, that's what's going on."

"My goodness," said the elderly angler, "why would you want to do that?"

"I'll tell you why, pop," said the young man. "For years my girl used to go fishing with me, and said she was crazy about it. She even put her own worms on the hook. So last winter we got married—and now the season's open, and she says she hates fishing and can't stand worms. She says I got to give up fishing entirely and take up bowling, so we can have fun together. So stand aside, gents—I'm going to jump!"

"Hold it just a minute, son," said the elderly angler. "Let's not be hasty. I think your bride has a valid point. After all, fishing *is* pretty much a waste of time and a constant source of frustration and irritation. It's a wrecker of hopes and dreams. When I was your age I was on the verge of a brilliant career as a paleontologist, but I frittered away so much time and energy on trout streams and bass ponds that I never got anywhere. My good, sweet wife, may she rest in peace, tried to warn me, but I wouldn't listen. All I could think of was fishing, and after years of shameful neglect she died of a broken heart. Today my children shun and despise me, and I can't say I blame them.''

While the elderly angler was wiping a tear from his eye, the young man got down off the railing and said, ''Gosh, pop, maybe you've got a point. But doggonit, I *enjoy* fishing. What could be as great a thrill as catching a whopping big smallmouth bass or a granddaddy walleyed pike?''

''Son,'' said the elderly angler. ''I'll tell you what can be an even *greater* thrill! It's seeing that trusty old bowling ball take a nifty hook right into the 1-3 pocket, and watching all ten of those maples go flying! It's seeing delight in your lovely wife's eyes when she scores a spare, God bless her! It's being together with her every Tuesday night and Saturday afternoon, sharing the splits and strikes alike as you go through life hand in hand!

''Also,'' said the elderly angler, ''it's seeing your score improve every time you visit the alleys, and knowing you're the master of your own destiny, and not at the mercy of some stupid fish or inconsiderate weatherman. It's feeling your body grow stronger with the healthful exercise of rolling that splendid sphere down those gleaming boards, and knowing you won't ever be crippled up with rheumatism and arthritis and God knows w/ at all from years of falling into cold, damp trout streams. It's not having to worry about leaky waders and knotty leaders and sand in your reel. It's thumbing your nose at the population explosion—after all, there'll still be room to build more bowling alleys even when the last rivers and lakes are clogged with silt and waterskiers. Believe me, son, your wife knows best, and you should thank her and bless her for steering you away from a dismal, dead-end existence.''

''Well,'' said the young man, ''maybe I *was* being hasty. You really think I should give bowling a try?''

''Of course you should!'' cried the elderly angler. ''You'll love it! Now hurry on home and give that little woman a great big smooch and tell her you're on your way to get fitted for a pair of bowling shoes. Toodle-oo!''

When the young man had hurried off, the middle-aged angler said, ''Okay, Harry, what's the big idea? You know you never had a career as a paleontologist. Hell, you just barely scraped through eighth grade. And what's this about a wife and children— you've never even looked at a woman unless she was wearing some kind of fur you figured you might pinch for fly-tying. And the only thing you despise more than bowling is toe-dancing. Right?''

''Right, stupid,'' said the elderly angler, ''but there's a brown trout as long as your leg lying right below us, alongside that old wagon wheel. If that poor schnook had jumped he'd have scared it into the next county, and I figure to try for it this evening.''

''Oh,'' said the middle-aged angler. ''Well, there's no trout there now—that goof standing there on the rail must have scared it.''

''By George, you're right,'' said the elderly angler, peering into the water. ''And to think I told that poor kid a pack of lies—what a sinful, cynical, selfish thing to do! But it's not too late to make amends. Let's go!''

''Yes indeed,'' said the middle-aged angler, and so they ran after the young man, dragged him back to the bridge, and flung him into the river.

HOW TO WIN A PIN

Once there was a beautiful blonde princess who was very proud of her fair, unblemished complexion and didn't care who knew it. "Get a load of my epidermis, buster," she would murmur to each prince who came courting her. "Some cute cuticle, wot?" And she would hurry off to find a mirror and admire herself some more, until the suitor sighed and went away defeated.

One day while sitting on a bench beside a flowing brook the princess looked up and beheld a hideous hag, whose face was covered with warts and wens and blotches, hobbling along the path. "Well, waddaya know!" jeered the princess. "It's Spotty Dotty, the dermatologist's dream girl! Hiya, Horrible!"

"Hiya yourself," said the hag, whipping out a magic wand and waving it at the princess, who was instantly transformed into a 5-pound brown trout with black spots as big as half dollars and who lay flopping about the grass. "How do you like *them* freckles, Freda?" cackled the hag, kicking the trout into the brook, where it swam away and hid under a rock. Then the witch replaced her magic wand in her handbag and hobbled off down the path.

Sometime later a handsome young prince came to the brook, which had just been leased by the rod and gun club to which he belonged, and you may imagine his delight

when he hooked and finally landed a 5-pound brown trout. "Wow!" said the noble youth. "What a walloper! Mmm-MMM!" And scooping the trout up in his net, he gave it a smacking kiss. At that instant the trout leaped from the net and became the same beautiful blonde princess who had suffered the witch's wrath.

"Your royal kiss has broken the spell!" said the grateful damsel, flinging herself into the prince's arms. "From henceforth I am yours, to do with as you will. For I have repented of my arrogant, vain ways and my unbearably narcissistic egocentricity, and will never again speak unkindly to one less favored by nature than myself!"

"Okay, dearie," said the hag, hobbling out from behind a bush, "since you seem to have learned your lesson, you may resume your true form, and God bless you."

As the witch turned to go the prince raised his staff and cried, "Halt! Not so fast, my gruesome granny! And don't reach for that wand or I'll bust your ugly skull wide open!"

"What does this mean, handsome one?" whined the witch, eyeing the prince's cudgel apprehensively.

"It means," said the prince, "that for nearly ten years I've been trying to catch a trout big enough to win one of them *Field & Stream* buttons to wear on my crown. Unless this dizzy blonde is turned back into a brown trout by the time I count three, I'm going to hammer you into the ground like a tent peg. One—two—ah, that's more like it!"

After the prince had got his *Field & Stream* button he mentioned the circumstances to the chairman of the club's Stream Stocking Committee. "A five-pound brown trout?" said the chairman. "You don't say! And all because she made fun of that witch who comes by there once in a while? Hmmm, very interesting. By the way, have you seen our last few bills from the local hatchery? We may have to raise the dues."

And so ends the story, except that on frequent occasions the chairman was seen pointing toward the stream and whispering in the ears of a number of traveling salesmen, tramps, transients, tinkers, tourists, and tax collectors, and it was observed that although the club's dues were not raised in the slightest the fishing improved tremendously.

ALL ABOUT DOLLS

Recently I read of a meeting of representatives from such various groups as Help Our Wildlife (HOW), Citizens United Regarding Environment (CURE), Save Our American Resources (SOAR), Franco-American Museum Of Underwater Studies (FAMOUS), the Group Against Smog & Pollution (GASP), and Save America's Vital Environment (SAVE), among others. I forget the purpose of the meeting, which I'm sure was commendable, but I was distressed that the Madison Avenue Rod, Gun, Bloody Mary & Labrador Retriever Benevolent Association (MARGBM&LRBA) had not been invited to participate.

When I complained, in my high, whiny voice, that not only was, or is, the MARGBM&LRBA a classy organization, with a motto ("Keep Your Powder, Your Trout Flies, and Your Martinis Dry"), which has been translated into genuine Latin, but that hardly any of its members have ever been convicted of more than one felony in any twelve-month period, one of the organizers of the meeting said it was because nobody could pronounce "MARGBM&LRBA" and also it was not a real word, like "SOAR," "CURE," and "GASP."

This seemed probable, and I was quick to point out that there is, in fact, a group closely allied with MARGBM&LRBA which calls itself the American National Trout Institute Dedicated In Sundry Elementary Specifics To A Better Life, Including Stiffer Hackles, Modern Equipment, Nifty Tackle, Also Reasonably Imaginative And New, Improved, Scientific Methods (ANTIDISESTABLISHMENTARIANISM). When I called attention to the fact that the new group seemed eminently eligible on the basis of its high ideals, noble objectives, and easily pronounceable initials, I was advised that unfortunately they had already invited the Associated Naturalists Translating Ichthyological Data Into Scientific Educational Statistical Tables Albeit Limited In Scope, Having Monitored Elementary Natural Trivia Apparently Relevant In A Normally Idiosyncratic Social Milieu (ANTIDISESTABLISHMENTARIANISM), and that to admit both organizations would invite confusion.

Thus frustrated, I went on home and found a few interesting items among the letters from creditors (they might at least send me *blue* duns), including a note from Mr. Philip Chancey, who lives close by the ill-starred Cross-Florida Barge Canal, commenting on my reference some months ago to sticking pins in my Army Corps of Engineers doll. Mr. Chancey says he, too, has an Army Corps of Engineers doll, but that instead of sticking pins in it he rents a bulldozer and runs back and forth across it.

HOW TO SPEND $100,000.00

Last September I went up to Martha's Vineyard to fish for striped bass with Nelson Bryant, who writes the outdoor column for *The New York Times*. I felt pretty good about the 25-pound bass I caught from Nelson's boat, and would have felt even better if someone hadn't hauled a 49-pounder from the same spot a few minutes later.

Waiting for the return ferry to Vineyard Haven I found a brant decoy in an antique-shop window and recognized it as the handiwork of Ira Hudson, who built boats at Chincoteague in Virginia around the turn of the century and caulked the chinks of time between boat-building chores by carving excellent decoys. On the ferry, with time to kill, I got to recalling the last time I was on Chincoteague, and how I had gone from there to Wachapreague to shoot clapper rail with Bill and Harold Burton and George

Killmon, and how after some fine sport we had come back to Bill's house, where his wife, a handsome, kindly lady, plied me with freshly baked brownies.

After Bill, a retired coastguardsman, explained that any stick or pole used by baymen to take soundings at night is known locally as a Chincoteague compass and that someone had once tried to sell them by mail under that designation at ten dollars apiece, we got to talking about ways to make money, since all of us had already figured out a number of ways to spend it.

George told about a free-enterprise advocate down in Currituck County who had invented a special kind of whiskey for elderly people and had called it Old Fitzgeritol, and was doing a land-office business until the Feds busted him. Through a mouthful of brownies I sputtered the story of my boyhood chum Andy Martinson, who kept himself in jawbreakers and other luxuries by letting the rest of us plink away at the caged family canary with his BB gun, three shots for a penny the length of the Martinson front porch, and it wasn't for several months, during which Andy amassed well over two bits, that somebody actually hit the canary and killed it.

Mrs. Burton came back just then with more brownies, and said money was a nice thing to have, all right, and she just wished she had a hundred thousand dollars. "Now what in the world," Bill said, "would you do with a hundred thousand dollars if you had it?" Mrs. Burton had just been making small talk, but when Bill asked, she stopped and reflected.

"Well," she said thoughtfully, "I know how much you like gunning on Cedar Island, and I know how some city folks are trying to buy it and turn it into a private club. So I reckon the first thing I'd do is buy Cedar Island for you, so's nobody could ever keep you off of it. And I'd hire Amos Cullen to build a nice shack for you, with bunks and a stove and all for when you wanted to stay overnight. Let's see, that would be about forty thousand dollars, so I'd still have sixty thousand.

"And then," she said, "I know just what I'd do! I'd buy you a brand-new fishing boat, with a flying bridge just like those fancy boats from Norfolk and Philadelphia. I know you like that old boat of yours, but it's time you had a real good one, and you deserve it. And I guess that would cost about thirty thousand dollars, so I'd still have thirty thousand left.

"And then," she said, "I'd buy you a new duck gun, one of those real good ones with two sets of barrels, one for just geese, and a good leg-of-mutton case with solid brass buckles and all. And I'd get myself a fur coat."

Bill had been paring an apple with his jackknife, but he slammed them both down on the table, turned indignant eyes on Mrs. Burton and demanded, "What in the name of Sam Hill do you need with a fur coat?"

And the cold weather reminds me of an item in the English *Shooting Times*, about a farmer whose donkey died in the dead of winter and who spent several hours trying to dig a hole in the hard-frozen meadow to bury it. Finally he was obliged to bury the beast on its back, with its legs sticking out of the shallow grave, and when the correspondent last saw him he was on his way back to the meadow with a saw in order, he explained, to cut the legs off flush with the ground.

HOW TO CURE A HIDE-BOUND HOG

I was staying at Dana McNally's fishing camp on Fourth Musquacook Lake in northern Maine, hoping to derrick some of those monster squaretails out of the famous Barrel Hole, and when Dana asked if I'd like to go along while he flew his floatplane over to Long Lake where his 80-year-old father, the legendary Wild Willy McNally, was building a new cabin, I said yes indeed, and off we flew.

When we had landed, if that's the word for it (watered, maybe?), taxied a quarter mile up the Chemquasabamticook Stream, and beached the aircraft on a sandy bank, we went ashore and found Willy. He looked to be a well-preserved 65, pointed out without eyeglasses a deer I could barely make out with binoculars, and asked if I was from New York. I admitted I was, and asked if he had ever been there.

"Once," he said, and when I asked if he had liked it, he said he had not liked it worth a damn. "What didn't you like about New York?" I asked, and he said, well, it was a lot of things, but mostly it was the noise. "My hotel room was on the second floor, and the traffic was something awful, even after dark. Couldn't sleep a wink."

"It's pretty bad, all right," I agreed.

"Bad?" he snorted. "It was terrible! All night long, that *clop, clop, clop!*" I mulled this over for a minute, then said, "Mr. McNally, exactly when were you in New York?"

"Well, sir," said the old man, "it must have been about 1908 or thereabouts. I suppose it's changed some." I allowed it had, and said new buildings were going up all over the place.

"Same thing here," said Willy, pointing to the nearly completed log cabin. He said he had run a trapline along the Chemquasabamticook when he was 17 years old, and had thought then it would be a fine place for a camp. "And now I'm eighty, and we're building it," he said. "I've never been one for rushing into something." We agreed this was prudent procedure, and after Willy had told me about a hide-bound hog he had once owned that couldn't grow or gain weight until he had rubbed it all over with neat's-foot oil, Dana and I crawled back into the plane and flew back to Fourth Musquacook.

HOW TO REPAIR A CHIMNEY

I'd been wondering why Ollie Rogers hadn't shown up at the last several meetings of the MARGBM&LRBA, and now have a letter of explanation from him. "Dear Ed," he writes. "You may recall when you were up here for grouse last fall I showed you where Hurricane Donna had knocked the top 4 feet off the chimney, and when the weather turned really cold I had to do something about it, as the fireplace wouldn't draw. So I rigged a platform on the roof beside the chimney, fastened a pulley to it and hauled up a couple of barrels of bricks and a lot of mortar. When I got the chimney built up about 3 feet the fireplace drew better than it ever had before, so after finishing off I hoisted the barrel up alongside the platform, secured the rope to a lilac bush near the base of the chimney, then climbed up to the platform and filled the barrel with all the leftover bricks and mortar. Then I went back down and untied the rope to let the barrel down. Unfortunately the barrel and bricks weighed a good bit more than I did, and when I cast off the rope the barrel came plummeting down, yanking me off the ground and into the air. I didn't know what to do so I hung on, and halfway up to the roof met the barrel coming down, getting banged up considerably in passing. When the barrel hit the ground it landed so hard that the bottom fell out, spilling the bricks and making the barrel a lot lighter, so that I started right back down, meeting the barrel coming up and getting clobbered again. When I landed on the pile of bricks it stunned me so that I released the rope, letting the barrel fall down on my head. This knocked me unconscious for several minutes, and while lying on those cold bricks I caught a slight cold. As soon as it clears up I'll be coming around to weekly meetings. Regards, Ollie."

HOW TO RENT AN ATLANTIC SALMON

A number of years ago, during a drought so severe that the mayor of New York City was urging householders to put bricks in the tanks of their flush toilets, I was lunching with the editor of a well-known men's magazine, and remarked when the subject of the drought came up that the only people who really knew how to use water properly were the Scots, who used it first to make malt whiskey, or whisky, and then, if they had any left over, to provide fishing for salmon. (I recall Wilson Stephens, the recently retired editor of that fine English publication *The Field*, telling me of his first, long-ago visit to the Spey, when he took a train to Elgin and hired a taxicab to take him upriver to the lodge where he would be staying; when the taxi arrived at the top of a hill overlooking a vast panorama of the Spey valley, the driver pulled off the road, switched off the engine, and stared solemnly at the distant hills. "Why are we stopping?" Wilson asked, and the driver said, "Och, mon, because from this point, on a clear day like today, y'can see twenty-six distilleries—and every one o' them in wairrkin' order!")

When the editor asked if I would do a piece on the symbiotic relationship of malt whiskey and *Salmo salar*, I said I would, since I already had plans to go to Grantown-on-Spey, the heart of the *uisgebeatha* belt, for a fortnight of fishing. He asked me to try to get at least one unusual photograph for illustration, and as soon as I arrived at Grantown and had checked into my hotel I loped over to the village grog shop and bought a flat pint flask of Glen Grant, a single-malt whiskey distinguished not only by its potability but also by its almost total lack of color.

My plan was to arrange a freshly caught Spey salmon surrounded by open clip-boxes of salmon flies against a backdrop of one of the several stone-arch bridges across the river, and to shoot the scene through the clear-glass flask of gin-clear whiskey. So now I had the whiskey, and the salmon flies, and the bridge, and the river, and lacked only a salmon. But not for long, I thought, and the next morning found me sloshing happily down the river, flinging Durham Rangers and Cossebooms and Blue Charms into some of the most salmon-free water this side of Central Park Reservoir. Two days later, when neither I nor anyone else at the two top fishing hotels had killed a salmon or even lost one, or had a touch—it was low, warm water and what few fish were in the river weren't moving—I decided to rest the river for a few days and do my homework on the distilleries.

Five days later, having visited and photographed some of Scotland's most famous whiskey-works inside and out, I came back to Grantown and found the river still low, warm, and fishless. That evening I sat at the hotel bar and laid my predicament on the bartender, who said, "Well, sir, if I were in need of a fish, I should drive down the river a few miles to the place of a man named MacPhergus, who is a dealer in game. If there's a salmon to be had in this part of Scotland, he'll have it. But I've heard he's a dour sort and not over-fond of Americans, so he may be a difficult customer."

Next morning I drove down the river road and found MacPhergus's place. At the end of his driveway was a one-story building, and inside I could see several roedeer hanging, and a number of hares. In front of the building there were six salmon from 8 to 15 pounds lying on a large concrete slab, and a man I presumed to be MacPhergus, from the surly glare he gave me, was hosing them down. When he laid the hose aside and asked what he might do for me, I told him I wanted to rent a salmon for one hour.

"Not a chance," said MacPhergus grimly. "The lorry'll be coming by in an hour, and won't be back this way until Friday. It's out of the question. Why would you want to rent a salmon, anyhow?" I told him I wanted to take a photograph of it through a pint of whiskey, and when he looked puzzled I showed him the flask.

"It's a daft idea," he said sourly, "and I want no part of it. I'm a hard-working, Christian man, and I don't approve of tomfoolery. What were you planning to do with the whiskey when you finished taking the picture?"

"I was planning to give it to you, for the rent of the fish," I said.

"Take your pick of the fish," he said moodily, "but try to get it back before the lorry comes."

I got some interesting photographs and had the salmon back in time for the lorry. When I got back to New York the editor said he was sorry but the business manager had vetoed the piece because all their whiskey advertisers sold blended Scotch, and could I make it a blended whiskey story, which I declined to do. If you hear of anybody who is in the market for a photograph of a rented salmon taken through a pint of white malt Scotch, please get in touch with me at once.

ALL ABOUT DARKEST AFRICA

Twenty-odd years ago I was sitting in a Third Avenue saloon with some assorted characters and somehow we got to talking about the most frightening experience of our lives. There was one man there who had spent three sleet-soaked days and two bitter-cold nights on a ledge in the Italian Alps, until a rescue party had come and taken him to safety. There was a guy who had been treed by a wounded (but not by him) Cape buffalo while shooting guinea fowl in Kenya, and still limped slightly because the buffalo had bit his heel as he scrambled up the barely adequate fever-tree. There was a man who said he had been through typhoons and train wrecks and muggings, but that nothing had ever frightened him as much as the sound of a dentist's drill when he was 10.

There was another man there, a quiet, balding little guy named Carl something, who was, as I recall, some sort of designer, and when we asked him if he had ever been really, completely frightened, he said yes, he had, but didn't like to talk or even think about it. When we insisted, he finally said okay, he'd tell about it.

"It was in North Africa," he said, "and the Germans were still in control of a lot of real estate. I was in a Ranger outfit headquartered in Oran, and ten of us were assigned to raid a couple of enemy command posts in the mountains. We were to go by Jeep to a certain spot, on an absolutely jet-black, moonless, overcast night, then walk seven miles over a mountain trail that might or might not be land-mined. When we got to the post we were to destroy it and its equipment with explosives, kill as many Germans as possible, then re-group at a ravine about a mile away.

"From there," he said, "if there were more than four of us left, we were to proceed about four miles along another trail to a second post and destroy it as well. Then we were to get back to the Jeeps as best we could. And as all this was going to take place in total darkness, the group of us spent nearly a month studying detailed blowups of aerial recon maps of the trails we'd be using and the layout of the German posts, until we knew every rock and bush and stump along the way; as a matter of fact we even learned alternate trails, and I think any one of us could have gone the whole distance blindfolded, if necessary.

"Finally," Carl said, "there came a dark enough night for the mission, and after a final briefing we blacked our faces and hands, piled in our Jeeps, and an hour later were on our way along the mountain trail. We found the German post without much trouble, killed five Germans when they resisted—although at least one got away in the darkness—destroyed the buildings and equipment with explosives, and felt pretty good about the whole thing when all ten of us showed up at the regrouping spot.

"By this time, of course," Carl said, "we were deep in enemy territory, so we walked as quietly as possible, single file, along the narrow footpath that would take us to our second objective. Not a word was spoken, and we moved as carefully as possible. In the darkness we couldn't see the man ahead of us or behind us, but tried to keep a proper distance by the sound of shuffling footsteps, and the faint sounds of breathing.

"And then," Carl said, "something began troubling me. For a while I couldn't figure what it was. And suddenly, I knew. There was too much shuffling of feet, and too much breathing. *There were more than ten men in that procession—a lot more.*

"I realized what had happened," Carl said. "The Germans had sent out a patrol, probably, when we burned the buildings—it would have been visible for a long distance—and we had fallen in with them in the darkness, or they with us. And somehow, I sensed that I wasn't the only one who realized what had happened. We *all* knew—but we all, friend and foe, kept on shuffling along in the blackness. Because if you stopped, the man behind would catch up to you, see by your insignia you were an enemy, and kill you. So for the next five minutes we kept shuffling along the trail, while the tension got thicker and thicker and my heart was pounding like a kettle drum.

"Then somebody tripped and cursed in German," Carl said, "and all hell broke loose. You couldn't see, so you lashed out with your combat dagger at anyone who came near. It was a pretty nasty business, and of course we never got to the second target. Six of us got back."

It was the scariest true-life adventure story I had ever heard, but Carl was obviously so upset by the ordeal of recalling the experience that nobody asked him any questions, and it wasn't until a year or so later that I learned he had spent the entire war at a quartermaster's desk at Fort Hamilton.

HOW TO WIN AT POKER

Steve Ferber and I once spent two splendid days floating and fishing the Snake under the expert supervision of Paul Bruun, who combines guiding with writing a highly readable outdoors column for the local newspaper, and Jay Buchner, a young but able and affable outfitter. When we took the rafts out of the river at Moose one evening Paul reminded me that I had once included in this department the official rules of Dave Bascom's patented poker game called Seven-Card Hi-Middle-Lo Moose, and asked if I'd send them to him. I've located the rules, but rather than plunk down the 22¢ it would cost to mail them to him I shall list them here, where Bruun is likely to see them at no expense to me.

I should explain, perhaps, that Bascom, editor and publisher of *The Wretched Mess News*, devised the game as the result of a number of complaints from his fishing cronies, including this one, about his predilection for wild-card games when playing dealer's-choice poker; herewith the rules.

1: The game is exactly the same as conventional seven-card high-low stud except as otherwise specified. 2: In addition to a high and low winner there shall be a middle winner based entirely on the five cards in the six-spot through ten-spot range. 3: Any player who is dealt a four, whether up or down, may take one card of his own choosing from the player on his left, who must then play with his reduced hand. 4: Any player who is dealt a trey face-up must exchange a card with the player on his right, each being free to select from his own hand the card he prefers to swap. 5: Any player who is dealt a nine face-up must contribute $2.75 to the pot or drop out. 6: Any player who is dealt a seven face-up must donate a card of his own choosing to the player two places to his right. 7: Any player who is dealt a red queen face-up is entitled to moose privileges. To avail himself of this option he first contributes four bits to the kitty, then goes outside and looks for a moose. At the end of two minutes he returns to the table and calls out "Moose!" or "No moose!" If he calls "Moose!", the dealer must give him two extra cards, one face-up and one face-down. If his call is "No moose!" he gets one additional card face-up. However, if his call is "Moose!", any other player may challenge him by contributing 50 cents to the pot. All players then go outside and look for moose. If a simple majority of players agrees that the moose-caller actually saw a moose (as evidenced by sighting a moose or by fresh tracks or droppings), the challenger, on returning to the table, must forfeit a card to the player two places to his left on Mondays, Wednesdays and Fridays, and two places to his right on other days of the week. If the decision is that the call was deceitful, the moose caller must surrender his bonus cards and forfeit a card of his selection to the player sitting three places to his right.

8: In areas where moose are not indigenous one of the following animals may be substituted: armadillo; dugong; coata mundi; tapir; sita-tunga; Marco Polo sheep. 9: Any player who is dealt a one-eyed jack together with a black ace, whether up or down, may demand a re-deal and a new game at any time up to the placing of his final bet, in which case the pot remains and a new hand is dealt to those who had not dropped out at that point. 10: Any player who is dealt an ace face-up must freshen the drinks of all players who so desire, and in his absence the player on his left will play his hand for him but without looking at his down cards. 11: The last player to bet or raise (but not call) at the hand's end is entitled to be last to declare whether he is going for (a) high, (b) middle, (c) low, (d) both middle and low, (e) both middle and high, (f) both high and low or (g) all three. Thus, the player on his left must be the first card player to declare.

12: POSITIVELY NO WILD CARDS.

PHONY STORY

Last June, while in La Grange, Georgia, to fish the nearby West Point Reservoir, I lunched with Larry Daniel of that area's development commission. When the subject of bird dogs came up, as it frequently does in that state, Larry said he had once worked as a serviceman for the Southeastern Bell Telephone Company in western Georgia, and had been sent to investigate a faulty telephone in a backwoods farmhouse. The only inhabitant of the house, an elderly lady, complained to him that the telephone bell didn't ring when people called her. "Maybe nobody calls you," Larry suggested, and the old lady said, "Of course people call me. I get five or six calls every day."

"How do you know when to answer the phone, if the bell doesn't ring?" Larry asked, and the lady said, "When I hear the dog howling, I know there's somebody on the phone." When Larry asked how the dog knew there was somebody on the phone, the lady said she didn't know *how* the dog knew, but it knew. When Larry called the operator and asked her to ring him back, the phone didn't ring but the dog howled bloody murder.

"Where *is* the dog?" Larry asked, and when the lady said it was under the porch, Larry went to see for himself. He found the dog, an aged setter bitch, tied up under the porch with a length of copper wire for a leash; when he traced the wire he found it was the ground wire from the telephone, and that somehow the bell mechanism had developed a short-circuit, which gave the setter a mild jolt of juice every time the phone should have rung.

Larry said the setter's name was Belle, but he disconnected her anyhow, fixed the short, and went about his business.

HEREFORD TODAY—GUN TOMORROW

Students of venery, which does not mean what you think it means, or more accurately does not mean what I think you think (because of its superficial resemblance to a group of words deriving from the name of the Roman goddess of love, although in fact it derives from the Latin verb *venari*) it means, will no doubt recall that a few years ago Mr. Rochester Haddaway of Texas suggested, in his capacity as regional director of the Madison Avenue Rod, Gun, Bloody Mary & Labrador Retriever Benevolent Association, that cows should be made legal game, and that this matter was referred to the Association's Committee on Advanced Thinking for further study.

I am happy to report that the Committee, after having been sunk in deep thought since the matter was brought to their attention in late 1966, has surfaced with a strong recommendation that Mr. Haddaway's proposal should be regarded favorably and if possible transmitted into law. The Committee cited the following considerations:

A: Farmers would no longer be able to sit around making knee-slapper jokes about hunters mistaking cows for deer or elk, and as presumably some of them, lacking this outlet for their creative impulses, would devote that portion of their time and energy to threshing wheat or gelding pigs or whatever it is that farmers do when not lolling about beating their gums, the result would be a substantial increase in agricultural productivity and in the Gross National Product.

B: Cows are, as a rule, tastier and tenderer than deer or elk.

C: Cows are, in most parts of the country, more abundant than deer, and occur closer to towns; in a time of fossil-fuel crisis this would mean shorter distances driven by hunters and a considerable saving of gasoline.

D: Cows generally do not skulk about in the woods like deer and elk, but stand around in the open and are therefore easier to shoot. This would result in a considerable number of man-hours (or person-hours if you prefer, although in this and similar instances I personally find the entire rationale behind such semantic shenanigans highly irrational) being saved, and a net gain in hunter efficiency.

E: Outdoor writers would have an entirely new field of opportunity; with the subject of deer-hunting having been worked over for several centuries, writers could turn to such bright new topics as "Steer-stalking Strategy," "The Phantom Holstein of Sunnydale Farms," "Don't Use That Sidelock Boss on Bossy!," "How To Pasture-ize Your .30/30," "South Forty Safari," "Field-Dressing The Friesian," "Still-Hunting the Santa Gertrudis," "Choose Your Game: Moo or Moose?," "Belted Cartridges For Belted Swiss," "Charged By a Charolais," and perhaps even a column called "Cattle Prattle."

F: Business would boom for taxidermists as steer-slayers rushed to have a Boone and Crockett Milking Shorthorn or Ayrshire mounted.

G: In the event a hunter actually did mistake a cow for a deer and shoot it, he could pretend he knew all along it was a registered Guernsey, and avoid painful embarrassment.

H: The arms and ammunition industry would benefit through the manufacture and sale of new cartridges (Dogie Duster, Cow Kapow, etc.) and new, specially designed firearms (Elsie Smith, Stampede Stopper, etc.).

I: The Disney Studios would be able to produce a full-length color-cartoon film about a Hereford calf whose daddy was killed by hunters. The calf, named Spami, would have big, soft, soulful eyes, and millions of Disney disciples would almost certainly stop eating beef and start picketing MacDonalds.

The recommendation has been turned over to the Committee on Fast Foods, for further study.

A FLAGON OF FABLES

The Ugly Princess

Once there was a princess who was ugly as sin. Her old lady, the queen, used to shake her head and say, "Sure, she's a sweet kid. But boy, she is some ugly!" One day her old man, the king, said, "Kiddo, you ain't never going to make it on sheer pulchritude. What you got to do is take up some sport where guys and gals do something together, preferably where the light isn't too good—that way you'll meet some men, and maybe they won't notice you ain't a raving beauty until it's too late. So get moving."

"Yes, papa," said the princess, and hurried down to the local sporting-goods store. When she told the clerk her problem he looked her over and said, "Princess, you got the build of a natural-born shotgun-shooter. It just happens I got this pigeon-grade Perrazzi with gold inlays and three sets of barrels in stock—let's see how it fits."

After the clerk had sawed a half-inch off the stock it fitted fine, and after buying a shooting vest, a cartridge belt, and a case of trap loads the princess wrote a check for the stuff, drove to the local gun club, and signed up for a course of lessons from the pro. In a week she was busting clay birds like crazy, went 100 straight at skeet her second week, and was smoking the blue rocks from 22 yards.

Sure enough, along came a handsome but somewhat astigmatic duck hunter, who watched the princess powdering clays from all stations, then sidled up to her, and proposed a liaison. "A *what*?" said the princess, partly from starting to go deaf and partly because her vocabulary was not extensive.

"A liaison," said the handsome young duck hunter. "You know, like Shacksville."

"Oh, that," said the princess. "Okay, but only with, you know, legal documents and a ring and like that."

"Fair enough," said the h.y.d.h., and a few days later they were married and moved into an apartment.

When the duck season opened the h.y.d.h. took the princess to his duck club, set out a rig of decoys and joined her in his blind. When the ducks started to come into the rig and saw the princess, they flared off, and when this happened several times the handsome young duck hunter said, "Sorry, sweety-pie, I got my priorities," and filed suit for divorce.

Moral: Ugliness is only skin deep, but if it flares ducks, that's deep enough.

Charley Fox and the Grapes

Once there was a trout fisherman named Charley Fox, and one day when he was walking through the woods on his way to the Letort he spied some wild grapes growing on a vine overhead. "Man, them grapes surely do look edible," said Fox to himself. "I do believe I will just reach up there and grab me a handful, especially as I forgot to bring my lunch." But when he reached for the grapes he found they were so high he was unable to pick any. "Oh well," muttered Charley, "they probably aren't very good anyway." So he started to go on his way, but suddenly thought, "Hey, I got an idea!" So he put his rod together, made a loop of line at the tip, reached up and pulled down a big bunch of grapes.

When he bit into one of the grapes it was so sour he spit it out. While he was doing so, several hornets flew out of a nest, which had been disturbed when he pulled the vine, and stung him.

Moral: Not everything that flies is a Pale Evening Dun.

The Dog and Its Reflection

Once there was a Chesapeake Bay retriever who was not overly bright even for a Chesapeake Bay retriever. One day he managed to scrounge a large beef bone from a soft-hearted butcher, and decided to go off somewhere where no other dogs would hassle him while he chewed the bone. *I know what,* he thought to himself, *I'll go over to the other side of the creek and hole up in that patch of alders.*

As he crossed a plank bridge over the creek he chanced to look over the side, and what did he spy but his reflection in the water, beef bone and all. *Hey, that's some bone that homely mutt's got in his mouth,* the foolish dog thought. *I think I'll grab it.* But when he opened his mouth to snatch the reflected bone, the real bone fell out of his mouth into the creek, where it hit a 22-inch, 5-pound brown trout on the head and killed it. When the Chessie retrieved the trout, an unscrupulous angler came by and, wishing to win the local fishing contest by fair means or foul, quickly traded him a standing rib roast for it.

Moral: Sometimes it's better not to have too much grey matter.

DUYKENFOOS DISAPPEARS!

It's true—that cruddy Duykenfoos kid has mysteriously disappeared. At the time of this writing he has been gone for a week, and failed to show up last Friday to have his bandages changed, although actually it was a superficial contusion that didn't even require stitches, caused when he banged his skull into a desk corner when I playfully reached out to tousle his unkempt hair with a perfectly harmless paperweight, and I've never seen anybody who bleeds as easily as that scrawny ingrate, who has never been able to get it through his pointy little noggin that money isn't everything, and constantly bellyaches about having his allowance raised, so that his room in the basement behind the furnace was referred to the other day by Managing Editor Dave Petzal as the whine cellar, because Petzal is capable of almost anything.

Maybe I should have seen it coming, because for quite some time Wilbur has been acting moody and withdrawn, muttering to himself and failing to address me as "sir" or "boss man," which I have always good-naturedly insisted he do in order to instill in him a sense of respect for his elders, but the tip-off should have been the envelope I found in his wallet while checking to make sure he was actually as short of funds as he claimed, as I did not want to misjudge the kid, and just as I had suspected there was still a dollar of his weekly allowance, which I took to teach him a lesson.

How the fuzz got into this I don't know, but when this guy from the Missing Persons Bureau came into my office and sat down, I kept my cool and said, "Have a chair, officer."

"I already got one," he said. "Where's Duykenfoos?"

"You got me," I said.

"I don't want you," the detective said. "I want the Duykenfoos kid."

"So do I," I said. "I got an 'Exit Laughing' due tomorrow, and I've been counting on his, ah, well, assistance. To help the grubby little urchin prepare himself for a life of literary fulfillment I sometimes permit him to sort of rough out a column. Sometimes, if I'm feeling especially kindly toward him, I let him polish it up a bit. There's a lot of talk going around about job-training for youth, but by George, I'm actually doing something about it."

"That's really quite touching," the dick was obliged to admit. "But where is he?"

"Officer," I said, "I don't know. The only clue is an envelope with this piece of paper, with 'Field' and 'Stream' written on it. I don't know what it means."

"Possibly," the fuzz said, "it's some kind of code—maybe an anagram." He studied it for a minute and then said, "By the saints above, it *is* an anagram! 'Field' is obviously 'I fled,' and 'Stream' is just as obviously 'master'! He fled his cruel master! That's you, buster!"

"Cruel my foot," I protested. "Unless, of course, you meant it for an anagram of 'lucre'—after all, I've been giving the ungrateful twerp an allowance of $3.75 a week every blessed week except when I was a bit strapped for cash. Hey, here's another clue—

this slip of paper was in his wallet. It has writing on it—'Only those of proper hgt. apply'—perhaps he was trying to get a job as a midget.''

The missing-persons guy studied the slip and said, ''I think not. I think this is some kind of hidden-clue message, a call for help. Like why would he abbreviate 'height'— 'hgt. apply'—unless you got somebody on the magazine named H. G. Tapply. Is that possible?''

''It's not only possible,'' I said, ''it's probable. Tapply writes 'Tap's Tips' every month, about how to make slingshots out of old garter belts and like that. He's very nice.''

''That's it!'' the dick said. ''He's fled his master and is trying to get a job writing Tapply's stuff instead of your monthly material.''

''This guy Tapply,'' I said, ''lives away the hell and gone up in the New Hampshire boonies, and only comes into New York once a year, to trade muskrat skins and ginseng for salt and flour—Wilbur wouldn't last long in that set-up. And all that fooling around with garter belts might put ideas in his head. But wait—let's look in his office. There may be other clues there.'' I got the shoe box Wilbur uses for an office—actually it's a fine shoe box, Johnston & Murphy 9½E, and a bit of Scotch tape keeps it together nicely— and found another slip of paper with some writing on it: ''To troubled ed.'' ''Hey, here's a note addressed to me,'' I said, handing it to the cop.

''I doubt it,'' he said. ''I suspect this is another anagram, maybe for one of your other editors with whom Duykenfoos contemplates collaborating with. 'To troubled ed'—got any ideas?''

''How about Patrick F. McManus?'' I said. ''Or Gene Hill? George Reiger, maybe? Bob Brister?''

''Sorry, bub,'' said the man, ''they don't none of them fit. But how about this—any of you *Field & Stream* guys got girl twins?''

''Not that I know of,'' I said. ''Why do you ask?''

''Because I just worked out the anagram,'' the dick said. ''It's 'double dotter.' That's twin girls in my book.''

''In mine,'' I said, ''it's a guy who's hooked on umlauts.''

''To each his own,'' the cop said. ''Well, I got to be going. Incidentally, if you come across an elderly geezer named Crater, wearing a black robe, give me a ring at the precinct. Toodle-oo.''

''Crater?'' I said. ''Why don't you put a *tracer* on him?'' But the government guy was gone.

HOW TO SIGHT IN A RIFLE

Last July I floated the Smith River in Montana with assorted other members of the Axolotl Society, a highly disorganized group of fly fishermen and bon vivants, or at least vivants. Axolotl is a Nahuatl Indian word meaning "servant of water," according to my dictionary. Actually all servants are about 97 percent water, the other 3 percent consisting of calcium, carbon, iron, phosphorus, and dandruff, and an axolotl is a small lizard of the genus *Ambystona* which never gets beyond the larval stage and occurs in Mexico and in a few lakes in the western United States. I don't know why the Axolotl Society is named after a lizard but I suppose they had to name it after something, and perhaps by the time Bill Miller, its founder, founded it, all the less slimy animals had been taken.

While waiting in a saloon in Helena for the others to show up, I got to talking with a local angler on the stool next to me. He told me he was temporarily short of funds, but that if I'd buy him a drink he'd tell me the secret of successful trout fishing in Montana, a secret he had learned from a physics professor who was also a full-blooded Shoshone Indian. I bought him a double whiskey and he told me that on account of the earth spinning from west to east, the fish in north-and-south-running streams tended to get pushed to the west bank of the river, and that I could catch more trout and save a lot of time by ignoring the east banks of such streams altogether, and concentrate on the west banks.

I thanked him kindly and asked, if this principle would also apply to streams in other states, and he said he had never fished anywhere but Montana and couldn't speak authoritatively about fishing elsewhere. After he finished the double, the local said he had just saved me from wasting a lot of time, and that in America time is money, and the law says an ordinary man's time is worth a minimum of $3.75 an hour. He sized me up carefully, seeming to have some difficulty focusing (or perhaps it was the dim light) and finally said he reckoned my time would be worth about $1.25 an hour, and that as he had just saved me at least 10 hours of time which I might have frittered away fishing the east banks of rivers, he figured I still owed him several drinks.

He said he had gone to a lot of trouble to extract that secret from the only full-blooded Shoshone Indian in the world with a Ph.D. in physics who was also a good fly tyer, and that I was exploiting him by buying only one lousy drink for a secret that could assure me of one hell of a lot of trout. While I was explaining that it had been a double whiskey and also I had let him have some of my potato chips, several Axolotl Society members came in and I said I would have to go, and I joined them.

Later, on the river, I got to thinking about the secret tip and wondering how it might jibe with a theory recently sent to me by Joseph G. Brown, a fly fisherman and professional engineer from Westport, Connecticut. Mr. Brown, who is right-handed, says he had trouble taking trout on flies tied by left-handed tyers, and feels this may relate to the rotation of the earth from left to right when one is facing north. He thinks it may be possible or even likely that flies tied by left-handed tyers *in the southern hemisphere* might work for him, but *only if fished in the northern hemisphere*. Conversely, flies tied by right-handed tyers in the northern hemisphere should produce well for left-handed anglers in the southern hemisphere. I discussed this with Dick Carlsberg and Matt Byrne while we waited on the riverbank for the helicopter that flew us out of the canyon and to the Great Falls airport, and it was agreed we would do some field work to establish the validity, if any, of the theory. Left-handed fly tyers wishing to participate in this important scientific project are invited to send flies, preferably tied with natural rather than dyed hackle, to this writer c/o *Field & Stream*, 1515 Broadway, New York, N.Y. 10036. Right-handed fly-tyers may also participate in this historic investigation, and should send flies, in sizes 10 to 22, to the same address. Dry flies and nymphs are preferred, but terrestrials, streamers, and bucktails are also acceptable.

And while I'm up, and the locale is western, let me report a letter from Dick Rinker of San Antonio, Texas. Mr. Rinker deposes that a few years ago he was invited by the brother of the owner to shoot antelope on a ranch in northern Colorado, during the absence of the owner and his wife and while the brother was ranch-sitting for his sibling. When they arrived at the ranch about noon the owners had already left, and the brother suggested they sight in their rifles right away. He hung an old license plate from a nail on the side of a sagging, weather-beaten shed 100 yards from the ranch house, as a target, and when Dick asked if the owner might not object to having holes shot in his building, the brother said it was not being used and was slated to be destroyed and torn down any day now.

It took only one round each, from Dick's .270 and the brother's .243, to verify their zeros, and by evening they each had a 15-inch pronghorn hanging in the barn. A few days later the owner and his wife returned, and at dinner the wife was delightfully cordial but the owner seemed strangely morose. Finally, when the wife left to refill a platter of elk steaks, the rancher said he was sure glad it had taken the hunters only one round apiece to sight in. That way, he said, there were only two holes in the new Cadillac he was keeping in the shed to surprise his wife with.

NEW METHOD FOR SQUIRRELS

While I was standing in a slow-moving line for theater tickets the other day the man in front of me, a soothsayer, said he had to go to the bathroom and would I hold his crystal ball until he got back. I said of course I would. "Please don't look in it," he said, and I promised I wouldn't. As soon as he left I looked into the ball, and this is what I saw:

In the spring of 1988, to celebrate the 40th anniversary of their highly profitable movie *Bambi*, and in hopes of creating another box-office bonanza, the Disney Studios decided to make a sort of sequel to that all-time favorite. The new animated-cartoon film, about the adventures of a beautiful Hereford heifer with big brown eyes, was called *Spambi*, and upon completion a year later was an instant success.

"Now I know why they're called *MOOvies!*" gushed Rex Reed, and most other critics, and the public, agreed with him.

The plot of the picture was disarmingly simple. Spambi's father, a syringe, had been kidnapped by a gang of anti-artificial inseminationists and brutally smashed. Her widowed mother, a registered Hereford cow, tried to raise her and her brothers Nambi and Pambi, to be good law-abiding livestock, but life on the range was filled with such perils as locoweed, rustlers, red-hot branding irons, and people making Marlboro commercials.

But the greatest danger was the cruel-hearted cowboys who came every year to round up the animals to be sent to the stockyards and then kay eye ell ell ee dee. That's what happened to Spambi's two brothers, and even to her mother when she got old, and also to her friends Hambi the pig and Lambi the sheep. The villainous assassins who ran the big meat-packing houses were shown wallowing in the gore of innocent calves and steers and hogs. It was a very sad picture, and thousands of tons of popcorn were rendered soggy and oversalted by the tears of millions of movie goers. But the waterlogged popcorn wasn't the only casualty.

Within a few months of the picture's release, hundreds of local chapters of such fast-growing new organizations as SOS (Save Our Steers), FOB (Friends of Bovines), POP (Pals of Pigs), and several others had sprung up across the country. Slogans appeared on car bumpers; "Don't baste a lamb—lambaste a butcher!" and "I brake for steak!" were typical. Schoolchildren marched on the Kansas City and Chicago stockyards, tearing down the fences and releasing thousands of livestock into the streets, where they created traffic havoc and a sanitation problem. Abattoirs were burnt to the ground. Butcher shops were picketed, and their windows smashed. Angry mobs stripped supermarket shelves of A-1 Sauce.

In a few months the agricultural world was a shambles. Cattlemen, unable to market their steers or hogs or sheep, cancelled their orders for new farm machinery. Steel mills closed down. Unemployment figures soared. There were mud slides in California. Just then the soothsayer came back and snatched his crystal ball away from me, so I don't know what happened after that.

*   *   *

Dr. Arthur V. Brown, Assistant Professor of Aquatic Ecology at the University of Arkansas and chairman of the Fayetteville chapter of the Madison Avenue Rod, Gun, Bloody Mary & Labrador Retriever Benevolent Association, reports that while driving along a backwoods road in the Ozark National Forest not long ago he spied a local resident sitting under a tree not far from the road. When he stopped and asked the man what he was doing, the man said he had been hunting squirrels until the car had scared them off. When he asked the man where was his gun, the man said he didn't have a gun with him, as he was uglying them to death.

When Brown expressed skepticism, the native offered to demonstrate. After a few minutes a gray squirrel ran along a white-oak limb nearby, the hunter whistled to get the squirrel's attention, then made a hideous face at it, and the squirrel dropped stone dead.

After the native had picked up the squirrel and stuffed it into a gunny sack containing several other dead squirrels and an oppossum, Professor Brown said he had told the man it had been a truly astounding performance, but that he doubted anyone else could look ugly enough to kill a squirrel. The native assured him he was wrong. He said he used to send his wife out to do the hunting, but when she got older and uglier she tore up the critters so bad they weren't fit to eat, although he still sent her out when geese were flying so high they were out of his range.

DUYKENFOOS RETURNS

With mixed feelings I am obliged to report that Wilbur Duykenfoos is back. It appears he was at the bottom of that old well in my back lot all the time, which I had for some time considered to be a possibility, as I had heard what seemed to be muffled shrieks and moans from that general direction several times and had meant to check on the well at my first opportunity, but the weather has been a bit unsettled and I've been feeling a bit peaked. (One time I did get as far as the sugar maples, but thought I heard the telephone ringing, and possibly I did, but if so, the party had hung up by the time I got back to the house. It occurred to me that the caller might have been Wilbur, with some cock-and-bull yarn about where he had been for the past year, and as it might have been a mildly amusing story I stuck pretty close to the house for the next few weeks in case he should call again. On another occasion, when the cries had kept me awake for the better part of the previous night I started walking toward the lot but it began to look like rain and I had no umbrella with me and wasn't wearing overshoes or a raincoat, and also the hollering had stopped. I cite these instances only to show that I have been deeply concerned with Duykenfoos' welfare and by no means negligent or uncaring. On the other hand I'm not about to go traipsing all over hell's half acre every time some cretinous neighbor calls me in the middle of the night to say he thinks he heard someone yelling for help, when it's much more likely to have been the wind or someone's cat.)

At any rate the little twerp is back, having survived on a diet of raw frogs and salamanders, apparently, and whatever else had fallen into the well, in which the water had been only knee-deep because of the drought, and although he's scrawnier than usual I've no doubt he'll soon be back in full health, and none the worse for wear although his lower limbs may be permanently blue. I have restored him to full apprentice status, except that for the next eighteen months I shall dock half his pay each week until he has paid for damage to the boards through which he fell (which may not have been brand-new boards, I'll grant you, but they certainly weren't all *that* rotten, either) and to the masonry of the well's walls, which he had dislodged in several places in trying to claw his way to the top. (The kid has never been distinguished for upward mobility, and this is another case in point.)

And so I have once again taken this cruddy little ingrate under my wings, so to speak, and will, on occasion, permit him to try to develop his pitifully minimal writing skills at my expense. But—as I've already warned the kid—this time, no more Mister Nice Guy.

HOW TO BUY A HAT

At the most recent meeting of the Highlands Chapter of the Madison Avenue Rod, Gun, Bloody Mary & Labrador Retriever Benevolent Association, held in the lounge of the Seafield Lodge Hotel at Grantown On Spey, Scotland, and chaired by Mr. Arthur Oglesby, the following business was transacted:

Mr. Noel London of Kent said that speaking of towns on rivers he had one time been shooting snipe and duck in the west of Ireland and when heavy rains persisted he had gone into a haberdashery in Carrick-on-Shannon in order to buy a fore-and-aft shooting hat to prevent rain from running down the back of his neck, and had finally selected a hat and given it to the proprietor to wrap. The next morning when he put on the hat he found it to be considerably smaller than the one he had selected, and went around to the shop where he had bought it.

"You gave me the wrong hat yesterday," he told the merchant, who smiled smugly and said, "On the contrary, sir, I gave you the *right* hat. You had selected a lady's hat— see, there's the 'L' on the inner band of the very hat you selected—and I gave you a man's hat—see the 'M' on that little white tab."

"Hmm," said Mr. London. "Tell me, do you have any hats with an 'S' on the sweatband?"

"I do indeed," said the shopkeeper.

"What does the 'S' stand for?" asked London.

"I've never been able to figure that out," said the haberdasher, "but they seem quite small, and perhaps it stands for 'schoolboy.' "

"That must be it," said Mr. London, and told the shopkeeper he would like to take the hat marked 'L,' as he was subject to mild attacks of transvestism. The shopkeeper said he understood there was a lot of it going around, and graciously switched hats.

There being no further business at hand, the meeting was, on motion duly made and seconded, adjourned. On returning to the United States I left almost immediately for San Antonio, where the 8th bi-annual meeting of Game Conservation International (a.k.a. Gamecoin) was being held, at which I was scheduled to deliver a talk on fishing, and in fact did so, incurring only scattered boos and cat-calls. While there I bumped into a number of old friends, and heard a number of even older stories, including a plethora of Polish jokes which have recently been recycled as Texas Aggie jokes, such as the one about the Aggie who learned while at A&M that he wasn't actually a citizen of the United States as he had always assumed himself to be, as his parents had been Canadians living in the U.S. When a friend suggested he go down to the Federal courthouse and apply immediately for citizenship, he did so, and was referred to a Federal judge.

"Not to worry," said the judge. "You were born here, and have always lived here, and there shouldn't be any problem. Come in on Thursday at 10, when I'll be on the bench, and answer a few questions—purely a formality." When the Aggie showed up in the courtroom on Thursday, the judge said, "Son, I'm obliged by law to ask you a few questions, even if they sound a bit foolish. For example, do you advocate the overthrow of the United States government by force or violence?" The Aggie thought a minute, then said, "Force."

WOLF STORY

I stopped in at the Cock and Bull, our local tavern, the other evening and ran into Larry Ralston, who said he had just come back from a moose hunting trip to northern Quebec. He said he had harvested a respectably antlered moose, and that he had also seen and heard a number of wolves during his eight-day hunt. "It reminded me of that story you wrote in 'Exit Laughing' a long time ago," he said. "You know, about the moose hunter chased by wolves."

When I said I didn't recall any such story, which I didn't, he said, "Of course you do! You said you ran into a guy at a bar one time and got to talking about wolves." "I meet a lot of guys in bars, Larry," I said, "and we usually talk about something. Taxes, football, woodcock, fishing, whatever. I don't recall talking about wolves, but I may have."

"For Pete's sake!" Larry said. "You met this character and got talking, and he said he used to be a trapper and had spent a winter one time with a bunch of Cree Indians— the hardest winter they'd had there in fifty years. Maybe a hundred. Everybody in the village was starving. So this old coot went out hunting, on snowshoes, and one morning he killed a big bull moose 'way back in the bush, about 10 miles from the village. Then he snowshoed back to the village to get some help to bring it in. And one of the Crees got a horse and a sledge and went back with him to butcher the moose and haul it back to the village. Remember?"

"It rings a faint bell," I said, "but even before becoming senile I was always forgetful. What happened then?"

"Well," said Larry, "they got out there and found the moose and quartered it and loaded it onto the sledge and started back. Only shortly after they started, they looked back and saw a pack of twenty-eight big timber wolves following them. The wolves were starving, too, and they'd got the scent of that moose blood and were closing in rapidly on the sledge. So the old trapper, who was driving, told the Indian to toss one quarter of the moose off the sledge, and sure enough the wolves stopped and pitched into that nice fresh meat.''

"It's not much of a story," I said. "I can see why I forgot it."

"That's just the beginning!" Larry said. "Those wolves went through that hunk of moose in about two minutes flat, bones and all, and took off after the sledge again! And when they got uncomfortably close, the trapper made the Cree toss·off another quarter. And the same thing happened—the wolves stopped and wolfed down the meat and took up the chase again. Same thing with the other two quarters—the starving wolves paused just long enough to gobble them down, and kept on coming. So the trapper told the Indian to take the ax they'd used to butcher the frozen moose and stand in the rear of the sledge and try to fight off the pack when it got close enough. So the Cree started toward the back of the sledge, but slipped on the frozen moose blood and fell off, and when the trapper looked back to see what was going on there wasn't enough left of the Cree to matter.''

"It's starting to come back to me," I said. "What happened next?"

"Well, let's see," Larry said. "Oh, yes. The trapper kept on going, but when the wolves finished the Indian and started after him again and it was obvious they'd soon be on top of him, he stopped the sledge, shot the horse and took off toward a wooded hillside on snowshoes, with his .30/30 rifle and a handful of ammo. Of course it took the still ravenous wolves several minutes to polish off the horse, but as soon as they did they took off after the trapper. He was still a mile from the woods where he could climb a tree when the pack caught up with him, and he shot one of the brutes. The others ate the dead wolf and then came after him again.''

"Holy smokes!" I said. "That's pretty exciting!"

"Just wait!" Larry said. "When he shot the second wolf, the pack stopped again, and ate it. Same for the third wolf. And the fourth. And the fifth. But it wasn't long until he was down to the last two wolves. So he turned and shot one of them, and the other stopped to eat his dead companion. By this time the trapper had nearly got to the foot of a tree, but didn't have the strength, after all that running, to climb it. And then the last wolf took up the chase again.''

"Hoo boy!" I said. "Pretty exciting! And then what?"

"And when he reached for a cartridge to shoot the approaching wolf," Larry said, "he discovered he was out of ammunition!"

"The poor guy," I said. "Well, he gave it a good try."

"Then," said Larry, "when the last wolf was about 10 feet away and crouching to leap at his throat, it dropped dead. Of indigestion. And so would you, if you had a bull moose, a Cree Indian, a horse, and twenty-seven wolves on your stomach.''

"Hey!" I said. "That's some story. I think I sort of recollect it now."

"But what I never understood," Larry said, "was why the trapper, when he ran out of bullets, didn't just fling a handful of yoorse in that last wolf's face.''

"What's yoorse?" I said, and Larry said, "Why, thanks—I'll have a bourbon on the rocks.''

TEST YOURSELF AGAIN

It's apparent that with the population still growing apace, this country must sooner or later adopt some of the stringent measures used throughout Europe to limit the number of people pursuing these basic outdoor sports, and shunt them off onto tennis courts, carnivals, bowling alleys, massage parlors, bars, adult movies, Sunday school picnics, rock concerts, golf courses, orgies, piano recitals, opium dens, Tupperware parties, tea dances, amateur theatricals, saturnalias, hoe-downs, hootenannies, charity balls, pinball arcades, or any place that might be considered a substitute for overcrowded bass lakes or duck marshes.

In most European countries, in order to qualify for a hunting license, the would-be sportsman is obliged to undergo a series of oral, written, and physical tests, which cover, among other subjects, the ballistics of rifle and shotgun ammunition, the safe handling of firearms, the various breeds of gun dogs and their common diseases and their treatment, the traditions of hunting and other field sports and their importance as part of the applicant's cultural heritage, the identification of gamebirds and mammals, the common predators of gamebirds and their control, the legal seasons and the penalties for poaching, and so forth. Only after completing these examinations satisfactorily is the candidate able to purchase a firearm, join his local hunting or fishing club, and begin going afield.

It seems to me that sooner or later we in the United States shall be obliged to adopt a similar requirement, and I personally hope it will be sooner. In anticipation of that time, I wish to propose a simple test for those applying for a hunting license, with only those achieving a B-plus or better being licensed. Here are the questions:

I. (This is a three-part question; this is Part 1).

Seated in a duck blind with your old hunting buddy, you simultaneously notice a pair of mallard drakes coming into your rig and (b) a large cottonmouth moccasin that has just crawled onto the bench next to your partner and is coiled to strike. You realize that

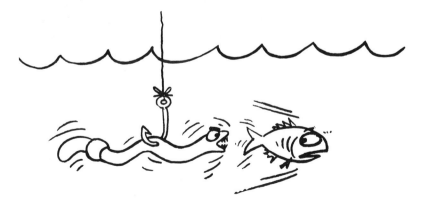

if you call your partner's attention to the snake, he will probably jump up and cause the mallards to flare off. On the other hand, if you or he shoot, the snake is likely to bite him. What do you do?

Part 2: Assuming you opted to keep quiet until you'd had a shot at the mallards, and that the snake had then bit your buddy and caused his instant death by venom or heart failure or both, would you (a) pick up the decoys, load your partner into the boat, and head back for the dock or (b) stay in the blind until you had your legal limit?

Part 3: If you elected to stay in the blind, would you (a) shoot only your own limit or (b) yours and your partner's?

II. While walking down the street in a strange city you hear an old lady crying, and when you peer inside her front door out of curiosity, she stops blubbering long enough to explain that her husband has died and left her penniless, with only a couple of worthless old shotguns as his entire estate. She shows you the guns, a Holland & Holland Royal matched pair with hand-detachable sidelocks in a fitted brassbound oak-and-leather case with a canvas cover, in mint condition. Between piteous sobs she says she intends giving the guns to the Salvation Army, but suggests you might be kind-hearted enough to buy them from her. When you ascertain that it's not a scam and that the guns have apparently never been fired, do you offer her $5/$7.50/$10/(check one)?

These are fairly easy problems, of course, but really difficult tests could be devised when necessary.

SECRETS OF SALESMANSHIP

I've always been a fairly easy-going guy, but a long time ago I did a considerable amount of fishing and shooting with a man who drove himself, and a hard bargain, and a late-model Upwardlymobile. He was a lot older than I was, and knew a lot of things I didn't know, and some I still don't know. He then owned a good stretch of a famous New Brunswick salmon river, which was how I had come to know him, and he belonged to a famous trout club in Pennsylvania, but I think he liked the idea of fishing more than he liked fishing. What he mostly liked doing was making money, and he made a lot of it before he died, in a lot of ways.

He had come off a small, run-down dairy farm in Ohio when his father died and had sold magazine subscriptions and then cheap encyclopedias door-to-door in small towns, learning about people and how to persuade them to buy whatever he happened to be peddling. Before I met him he got out of selling and into a lot of other money-making operations, some them fairly big time, and one day I asked him which one of them he liked best. This is what he told me, and I don't know how much of it is, or was, true. But it made a pretty good story, and I'll try to tell it:

"One of my first good jobs," he said, as we were sitting beside the Devil's Elbow pool on the Sevogle River, "was selling electric generators to farmers, long before there was such a thing as rural electrification. The generators were made by an Ohio company, and the product was good, but selling it to a bunch of suspicious, conservative, Midwestern farmers wasn't easy. But it could be done, and this is how I did it.

"I'd spend the morning," he said, "driving a Model-T Ford around the countryside, sort of casing the joint, and I'd pick out a fairly prosperous-looking farmhouse, and perhaps one next to it as a sort of back-up prospect. Toward evening, I'd hitch up a team of horses to my wagon, and head for the farmhouse. In the back of the wagon there was a generator powered by a two-cylinder gasoline engine, and about 150 feet of wire hooked up to a bare light bulb in a lamp stand.

"I knew about what time most farm families ate supper," he said, "and I timed it so I'd be turning into their driveway just about the time they had finished. Mostly, they'd eat at the big kitchen table, with a kerosene lantern on the table or hanging over it. I'd drive up to the house, knock on the door and ask if I could give them a free demonstration of a wonderful new invention, the electric light, and explain how easy it would be for them to enjoy this modern convenience.

"Well, usually the farmer said yes, or if he said no his wife might say, 'Oh, please, Hiram,' or the kids would plead with him, because some of them had never seen an electric light—only fair-sized towns had electricity. If he said no, and meant it, I'd head for the back-up prospect and hope he wouldn't have gone to bed by the time I got there. Mostly, though, it was a grudging yes, and so I'd drive around to the kitchen door, start the generator, run the wires into the kitchen and put the unlit light bulb on the table, beside the kerosene lantern. Sometimes, though, they'd have a Coleman pressurized lantern that gave a lot more light than the ordinary kerosene job, and that was tough competition.

"When I had the family around the table, I'd open my salesman case and take out a Bible. It was a good, leather-bound Bible, and I'd invite the farmer to read something from it, because these were usually Bible readers even if they never read anything else. I'd open it to a page in Deuteronomy, and say, "Why don't you start at the first verse on the right-hand page and read aloud, and the farmer would do just that. Oh, sometimes he'd have his wife read because she got more practice reading recipes, or the oldest child to show how smart he was at book-learning, but mostly the farmer himself would do the reading, by the light of the lantern.

"Then, just as he got to the last line on the page, and was turning it, I'd say, 'Now let me show you what *my* light does, and I'd turn off the lantern and switch on the electric bulb just as he was turning the page—I got to be pretty good at having the bulb come on just as the lantern flickered out—And when the farmer had adjusted his eyes to the new kind of light, he'd invariably say, 'Well, land sakes alive! That sure *is* some difference! My goodness, I can read a heap easier by this here electric light, I declare I can!'

"He could, too," my friend said. "Partly because the bulb shed quite a good light, but mostly because the page he had turned to was printed in type two sizes larger than the preceding page. Even for a prosperous farmer, that generator cost a pretty penny, but I sold and installed a slew of them in the course of two years—enough to buy me a half-interest in a hardware store in Cincinnati. Maybe my conscience should have bothered me, but I figured I was on the side of the angels, fighting the forces of darkness literally and figuratively. Let's throw a few more patterns at those salmon, then get back to the cabin for a sun-downer.''

I should have asked him whether that Bible was his own invention or the manufacturer's, but never did. And it always seemed to me it would have been more appropriate to have had the farmer read some pages from the Book of Mark.

WOULD A CAMEL WALK A MILE FOR YOU?

At a wildlife-conservation meeting a few weeks ago I ran into Dr. Wendell Swank, Professor of Wildlife Management at Texas A&M, whose houseguest I had been in Nairobi in 1967 and 1971 and with whom I had shot my first dove when (before going to Kenya to direct a game-cropping project for the United Nations FAO) he was Director of the Arizona Game and Fish Department. We sat down and talked about old times, and about some of the people Wendell had worked with in East Africa, but mostly we talked about Denis Zaphiro, an Englishman who has since become a citizen of Kenya but was then Senior Game Warden of the Northern Frontier District and had instituted a camel-mounted antipoaching patrol of tough Turkana tribesmen able to live, thrive, and fight under desert conditions. Denis was, and is, a delightful companion and storyteller (cf. Mary Hemingway's story in the old *Life* magazine about Ernest's last African safari, which Denis organized and led), and so when he invited me to go along on a ten-day patrol through the Mathews Range country south of what was then called Lake Rudolf, I leapt like a scared impala.

It was a marvelous trip, through country crawling with rhino and elephant, and I learned to ride a camel and even to enjoy it. At one remote waterhole, Denis conducted hearings on game-law violations, including a fifteen-year-old Rendille youth who, while herding cattle, had speared a young rhino to death under circumstances which, according to the local gamescout, hadn't called for such drastic action. "He'll be sent down to Nairobi," Denis said, "where he'll see six-story buildings, paved roads and other wonderful sights, eat better food than he ever has before, and when he comes back after ten days in the brig he'll be a hero and lord it over the other youngsters."

Later, Denis told me that in colonial times District Commissioners held court frequently, and were sometimes rather arbitrary in their judgments, which could not be appealed. In one instance, he said, a young and newly appointed District Commissioner paid a courtesy call on a much older and somewhat eccentric neighboring D.C., who invited him to go bird shooting one morning and lent him a shotgun.

When they returned with an ample bag of guinea fowl and sand grouse, and had had a pink gin or two and a pleasant lunch, the older commissioner announced that he would now hold court. When the staff of clerks and aides had been assembled, the visiting D.C. asked who was to be tried. "You are, old chap," said the older D.C., cheerfully.

"On what charge?" asked his astonished guest.

"Oh, it's nothing very serious, dear boy," his host said. "But specifically, you are charged with discharging a firearm without having in your possession a proper certificate, as required by Section 16-A of the Firearms Act. We shall now hear witnesses."

The older D.C. then got down from behind the bench, got into the witness box and testified that he had witnessed the defendant commit the offense as charged. He then returned to the bench, asked the defendant how he pleaded, and when the young D.C. pled guilty as charged, sentenced him to a fine of a hundred shillings (about $15). When the young D.C. had paid the fine to the court clerk, the older official declared the court adjourned.

The visiting D.C. then announced that he was reconvening the court, and, when his host protested that he was out of his district, reminded him of the emergency rules under which a D.C. could make use of the facilities of another district when, in his opinion, an emergency situation existed—as he thereupon declared it did. He then called the court to order, instructed the Sergeant-at-Arms to conduct the old D.C. to the prisoner's box, and declared the prisoner was forthwith charged with having lent a gun to an unauthorized person, in clear contravention of Section 17-B of the Firearms Act.

When he had left the bench and testified to having personally witnessed the offense, he resumed his seat on the bench and asked the prisoner how he pleaded. When the older D.C. grumpily pleaded guilty, the visiting commissioner said, "It is well known that in some circumstances offenses against the Firearms Act are rather lightly regarded. But in view of this court there are few violations more serious in their nature than the irresponsible handling of lethal weapons.

"And as there is apparently an alarming and almost epidemic tendency to flout and disregard this Act, as evidenced by the appearance before this court of *two self-confessed offenders within the past hour*, I am determined to make an example in this case, and do hereby sentence the defendant to pay a fine of 1,000 shillings."

Denis said the old D.C. grumbled considerably while paying his fine, but that the two of them then went off to have a gin-and-quinine and play some billiards, and were the best of friends thereafter.

ALL ABOUT GROUNDHOGS

I was happy to learn that Nick Lyons Books/Winchester Press has just published a nifty paperback edition of Roderick Haig-Brown's *A River Never Sleeps*, one of the classic angling books of this century, and I urge you to buy or steal a copy if you don't already own one. I was privileged to know Haig-Brown slightly, and admired him as a man as much as I admired him as a writer. I think it's in a *A Fisherman's Spring* that he tells of the time I took him to see the Beaverkill, about which he had heard so much, and in which he dutifully wet a line. But he didn't go into much detail, and so I shall do so.

Roderick was in New York to talk with publishers, and when I suggested that although it was early April and the weather was cold and nasty he should stay with me and drive up to the Beaverkill with me next day, he agreed. I threw some waders and tackle, enough for both of us, into the station wagon, and next morning off we went, arriving at the Antrim Lodge in Roscoe in plenty of time for lunch. I had a young, frisky, well-behaved Labrador retriever named Wullie with me, as he traveled well and Evelyn, my wife, was visiting her parents.

At the Antrim Lodge bar we bumped into my friend Bill N., a retired oil company executive who has one of the best angling libraries in these parts and is delightful company. Bill joined us for lunch, then invited us to come with him to visit a famous old club of which he's a member on the upper river and fling a few flies in the Home Pool, and we were happy to accept, as Roderick had heard of the club. I explained to Bill that we'd follow him in my wagon, as I had a Lab with me, but Bill insisted that he had his "fishing car" outside and that we all go with him. When I saw the almost brand-new maroon Lincoln he was leading us to, I again said, "Bill, you and Rod go in that, and Wullie and I will see you at the clubhouse." And again Bill, who's used to taking charge, insisted that we pile into the Lincoln. "This car's for fishing and shooting," he growled, "and Wullie's as welcome as anyone. Stop arguing, get your gear, and get in."

I sat Wullie on the back-seat floor and told him to stay there, which he did. At the clubhouse I let him out and while we were getting into our waders and setting up rods he explored the premises a bit, seeming fascinated by a pile of snow that the plow had left by the side of the road and romping in what was left of it.

The river was high and discolored, far too cold for good fishing, but we went through the motions for half an hour while a drizzle of sleet ran down our necks, and I think Rod took one shivering 10-inch brown. Then I looked up to check on Wullie and saw him rolling ecstatically in something he had unearthed, or unsnowed. (Ordinarily I'd have left him in the station wagon, but didn't want to use that beautiful sedan as a kennel.) I got out of the river and hurried to see what he had discovered. It was the well-rotted carcass of a groundhog that had been ripening under the pile for months, and the stench of it was godawful.

I called Wullie off, had him sit and stay, then found a cake of strong laundry soap and some old toweling in the clubhouse, and took him down to the river. I think both Roderick and Bill were glad to have an excuse to stop fishing and so, still wearing waders, I dragged Wullie into the Home Pool, lathered him up, and rinsed him off, perhaps seven or eight times. I've heard that this business of a dog's rolling in anything with a strong and usually unpleasant odor is an instinctive (or instinktive) effort to disguise or obliterate their own scent and thus protect themselves from predators, or perhaps in the case of predators it's to prevent their prey from getting a warning whiff of them while they're hunting. Could be.

When I had spent the better part of an hour lathering and rinsing Wullie thoroughly, holding him completely under water at times, both of us were cold and tired but the stench was considerably reduced. Or perhaps I had simply gotten used to it. (I remember when I was in college there was a pulp-and-paper factory thirty miles down the valley, and when the wind was from that direction half the student body suffered from nausea, but the several thousand people who lived near the mill never noticed it.)

Wullie, however, still stank noticeably, and when we had had a libation or two I asked Bill if he would take Roderick back to the Antrim Lodge so Rod could drive my station wagon back to the clubhouse and pick up Wullie and me. Bill was annoyed. "Dammit," he said, "I brought you up here and I'll take you back," and when I argued that that was no way to treat a new Lincoln, and to at any rate put the dog in the ventilated luggage compartment, Bill said that was no way to treat a Labrador retriever either. "Put some newspapers on the floor," Bill said. "It's just a short ride."

Actually it was about a twelve-mile trip, mostly on dirt roads, and took about half an hour, during which we were obliged to keep all windows wide open to avoid asphyxiation, and altogether it was hardly the way to introduce a revered fishing writer to a revered fishing river. But we all survived, and thanks largely to Bill it was a most enjoyable day. And three weeks and several baths later Wullie hardly smelled at all.

Rod had to go back to Campbell River next day, and about a week later I ran into Tom Yost at Abercombie & Fitch's tackle department, who said he had just come from the Beaverkill where he'd bumped into Bill N., who had told him of having met Haig-Brown the week before. "Tell me," I said, "did that brand-new maroon Lincoln smell peculiar?"

Tom looked puzzled. "It didn't smell at all," he said. "But it's not a brand-new maroon Lincoln. It's a brand-new *green* Lincoln."

ALL ABOUT FREE-LANCE WRITING

Ralf Coykendall Sr. was the best raconteur and most delightful gunning companion I've ever known, and it was a joy and a privilege to have been his friend. I met him at the Men's Bar at the Biltmore one Wednesday—Ralf's favorite day there, as the Chef's Special was always Beef Wellington—and when we had disposed of our bourbon-and-bitters, I told him that after thirty-odd years in various advertising agencies and some magazine writing on the side I had resigned my agency job and would henceforth try to make a living as a full-time free-lance writer.

Ralf, who frequently spoke in pertinent and sometimes impertinent parables, thought a minute and then said, "Ed, I used to live in a little Vermont town that was never very prosperous, but took pride in the fact that it took care of its own, and that no resident had ever been on government welfare. There was, however, a pleasant but somewhat addled chap who, in other, blunter towns might have been called the village half-wit. His name was Harold, and he lived in a small room over the feed-and-grain store.

"In most towns, Harold would have been on some kind of welfare, or stuck away in a funny farm, but in my town we didn't do that. Instead, the merchants in town took turns hiring Harold to do chores and odd jobs. This was a lot more charitable than it sounds, because Harold, despite his pleasant ways and his wish to be helpful, was disaster-prone. Harold left the spigot running on kerosene tanks. If something was precious and breakable, Harold dropped it. If a message was important, Harold forgot it. If something was combustible, Harold set it down on a red-hot stove, or knocked out his still-lit corn-cob pipe in it.

"Finally, the town ran out of merchants willing to put up with Harold, and one day at a village trustees' meeting someone said, 'Look, friends, we gotta do something about Harold. Last week he set fire to the drugstore twice and delivered the wrong prescriptions three times. Let's try to solve this problem now.'

"So they kicked it around for a while, until somebody said, 'Hey, I have an idea! That old World War I cannon has sat out there in the town square rusting away since the American Legion stuck it there in 1920. It's an eyesore, but nobody wants to haul it away and get the Legionnaires all het up. How about we hire Harold to keep that old cannon gussied up? Fifteen dollars a week is what us merchants have been paying him, and if each of us chipped in a dollar a week, we could set up a fund to pay him that much.'

"Everybody thought that was a fine idea, and when they called Harold in and said they had a mighty important job for him, and told him what it was and asked him if he thought he could handle it, Harold beamed with pride and allowed he reckoned he could. And by George, he did! Before the month was out, Harold had that cannon so dazzling shiny you couldn't bear to look at it in sunlight. And he kept it that way, too, for about three years. Everybody was happy, or so it seemed.

"Then one evening Harold showed up at the monthly meeting of the town trustees, and said he wanted to resign. This caused a lot of agitation among the trustees, who had visions of having to hire Harold again, and everybody wanted to know why he was resigning. 'Harold,' the chairman said, 'if it's more money you want, I'm sure we could give you a modest raise in salary. Because you've done a real fine job, and we're all proud of you. We're even proud of the cannon, now that you've taken such good care of it and made it so shiny and all. Tell us what the trouble is, and we'll try to make it right.'

" 'Oh, it ain't the money,' Harold said. 'Fact is, that $15 a week was more'n I needed to get by, and I saved about $5 or $6 every week and put it into the First National Bank. They give me a pass book and everything, and last month it come to nearly $900. So yesterday, by golly, I hitchhiked over to Burlington and *bought my own cannon.*' "

ALL ABOUT DAPPING

There seems to be a possibility I'll be fishing in Ireland when this appears, and I hope it works out that way. I haven't visited that splendid island for nearly twenty years, and recall its trout and snipe and woodcock and whisky with much pleasure, and its people with affection and respect. For example, I remember Arthur Knight, a real-estate man in Dublin who helped me arrange some driven-pheasant shooting in County Meath and some woodcock shooting in Galway and in whose office I sat one day swapping stories and passing the time of day (a rainy one, not surprisingly). "You collect stories," Arthur said, "and I have a friend in Kinvarra, about a dozen miles south of Galway City on Galway Bay, who's one of the greatest story tellers in Ireland. If you can spare a couple of days I could put you in touch with him, and I'm sure you'd get enough wild tales to see you through the next ten years of 'Exit Laughing'."

"I'm ready right now," I said, and when Arthur reached into a desk drawer and pulled out a skinny little telephone directory no more than a ¼-inch thick, and quickly found his friend's number, I asked how he happened to have a Kinvarra telephone directory in his desk. He laughed and said, "Ed, this is the directory for all of Ireland!" It was the first time I had realized how lacking that country then was in some material ways, and how little it seemed to matter.

At any rate Arthur called his friend Sean, a salesman of heating equipment, and arranged for me to meet him next day at noon. I drove to Kinvarra next morning, met Sean at the local pub, and spent the next two days and most of the nights listening to Sean, a cheerful, extroverted, highly articulate man, tell one story after another—stories so howlingly funny that Sean could scarcely keep from roaring with laughter every minute or two. I'm sure I would have roared too, if I had understood more than one word out of five that he was saying, but Sean had been raised on one of the western islands and spoke Gaelic long before he learned English, so that his English was spoken with the same sing-song inflection as if it had been Gaelic, and after the first few hours of trying to make him stop and repeat and repeat until I could figure out what he was saying, I gave up and didn't even bother to try translating. I just laughed when he laughed, whether we were golfing at the Kinvarra links or fishing for salmon and sea trout in the local spate river, and I heard enough stories to last me several lifetimes, and not a one I could understand and use.

I remember another time when snipe shooting near Athlone I met an Irish writer and teacher named Tim Cronin, who was famous for telling stories and told me about a local fishing guide named "Dummy" O'Callahan, so nicknamed because he usually talked a blue streak from morning to night, who was hired to ghillie for an American sportsman named Elmer Quigley, who wanted to fish for trout on a nearby lake by dapping live mayflies, the way they do in those parts.

The trouble was the American, hearing someone refer to his ghillie as "Dummy," got the idea that O'Callahan was a deaf-mute, and began ordering him around using hand-signals, pointing at the tackle and making motions for casting and rowing, until "Dummy" got the notion that Quigley was deaf and dumb, and tried to communicate with motions and gesticulations like the American's, with neither of them saying a word. They got along pretty well, too, except that Quigley kept striking too fast when a trout would rise to his dapped fly, pulling the hook out of the fish's mouth and missing it, and when "Dummy" tried to explain with sign-language that he shouldn't strike so soon it only convinced the American he was striking too slowly, which made matters worse.

"Dummy" even tried dropping the oars and waving his arms about with exaggerated slowness, so that Quigley thought O'Callahan was making fun of him and got kind of miffed, which didn't help. And this went on for several hours, with neither of them saying a word. Finally they were running out of live mayflies and hadn't caught a single trout despite numerous rises, and "Dummy" put the last three natural flies on the hook and rowed to the middle of the loch where he'd seen a big trout, maybe 5 pounds, rising, and when the monster rose slowly and inhaled the flies, and Quigley gave a great yank on the line and took the hook right out of the trout's mouth, "Dummy" couldn't stand it any longer. "Holy saints above!" he shouted, "I've had all of this I can take!", and jumped overboard and swam ashore, leaving Quigley to pick up the oars and row back to the dock.

Now "Quigley" wasn't a name you'd soon forget, Tim Cronin said, and it wasn't until several months later that one of the local folks came back from a visit to America and reported that while riding up New York's Fifth Avenue in a bus he had seen a freshly painted sign on an office building, and what it said was

THE ELMER QUIGLEY INSTITUTE
SPEECH RESTORED!

MORE ABOUT AXOLOTLS

Now that Wilbur Duykenfoos has defected to *Partisan Review* or *The National Enquirer* or wherever it was he went to—more on this next month—I've had to rely increasingly on the mail for assistance in keeping this department ticking along, and fortunately readers have been more reliable than the Duykenfoos kid ever was. Just this morning there came a nice note from David McCord, a Bostonian and erstwhile contributor of delightfully light verse to *The New Yorker*, the original *Vanity Fair*, and other publications. Mr. McCord wrote:

"Your good piece in the February *Field & Stream* delights me, particularly because of discovering the existence of, and origin of, the Axolotl Society. Long ago . . . I wrote a verse about the axolotl. Can't remember where it first appeared, but I put it into my own *Bay Window Ballads* (Scribner's, 1935; copyright by me). Perhaps you would like to print it in your column. That would please me.

"I grew up by the great Rogue River in Oregon, so I've been a fly fisherman (mostly dry now) since I was twelve. It makes me sad to think of the early days' fishing for big steelhead with a 4-ounce rod. Sincerely, David McCord."

I'm overjoyed to reprint the verse here, partly because I've been accused of inventing the axolotl out of the whole cloth, so that I welcome moral support, and partly because it will serve to add some much-needed luster to the department, which has not had a good classing-up since the original anti-poverty contest which involved translating the motto of the Madison Avenue Rod, Gun, Bloody Mary & Labrador Retriever Benevolent Association ("Keep Your Powder, Your Trout Flies, and Your Martinis Dry") into Latin—a competition that attracted large numbers of defrocked priests, seminarians, classical-language teachers, pharmacists, and language-droppers, and was won by a distinguished professor and theologian, then at Yale, Dr. Jan Pelikan, who has since gone on to even dizzier heights of intellectualism. Here it is:

THE AXOLOTL

"The axolotl
Looks a littl
Like the oxelotl.
Itl

"Drink a greatl
More than whatl
Fill the fatl
Whiskey bottl.

"The food it eatsl
Be no morsl;
Only meatsl
Drive its dorsl.

"Such an awfl
Fish to kettl!"
"You said a mawfl,
Pop'epetl!"

I have written to the Supreme Lizard of the Society proposing Mr. McCord for an Honorary Life Membership, but hasten to urge readers, if any, of this column to recognize that this is an exceptional event and to refrain from sending sonnets, triolets, couplets, cantos, rondelets, or any other verse forms to this department unless they are accompanied by one well-tied Silver Wilkinson or Thunder & Lightning on a No. 6 black-enameled double hook for each stanza and a self-addressed stamped return envelope. Do not affix the stamp too tightly.

HOW TO MAKE A MARTINI

One of several questions to which I don't know the answer is why most of the books on fishing, and especially those of some real or attempted literary merit, are devoted to the salmonids—trout and Atlantic salmon especially, and char, with an occasional nod to Pacific salmon and grayling—whereas authors of angling books are, as a rule, inclined to ignore squawfish, bullheads, suckers, carp, walleyed pike, fallfish, sheepsheads, shad, gars, and such. But it's a fact of angling literature: writers simply don't get dewy-eyed and choked up about grindles, or longeared sunfish, or chain pickerel.

Schubert never wrote a quintet and called it *Die Red-Horse Sucker*. Alfred Tennyson never, in reference to a brook, called attention to "here and there a shovelhead catfish, and here and there a big old hawg bass." No way. But I have shelves crammed with books whose authors grow positively giddy over brown and brook trout, rhapsodic over rainbows, starry-eyed over steelhead, and positively maudlin over Atlantic salmon and sea trout. Oh, it's true that non-salmonid species are sometimes the subject of passable verse, but usually the lines are less than laudatory, as witness this English bard's reaction to a suggestion that American catfish be introduced to British water, three-quarters of a century ago.

NO CATFISH PLEASE!

Oh, do not bring the catfish here!
The catfish is a name to fear.
Oh, spare each stream and spring:
The Kennet swift, the Wandle clear,
The lake, the loch, the broad, the mere,
From that detested thing!

The catfish is a hideous beast,
A bottom-feeder that doth feast
Upon unholy bait.
He's no addition to your meal,
He's rather richer than the eel
And ranker than the skate.

His face is broad, and flat, and glum;
He's like some monstrous miller's thumb;
He's bearded like the pard.
Beholding him the grayling flee,
And trout take refuge in the sea;
The gudgeons go on guard!

He grows into a startling size;
The British matron 'twould surprise,
And raise her burning blush,
To see white catfish, large as man,
Through waters dark and Stygian
Come with an ugly rush!

They say the catfish climbs the trees
And robs the roost, and, down the breeze,
Prolongs his caterwaul.
Ah, leave him to his western flood,
Where Mississippi churns the mud;
Don't bring him here at all!

(I lifted that from *Game Fishes of the World* by Charles Frederick Holder, published in 1913; he cribbed it from an even earlier issue of *Punch* but didn't give the author's name. And I prefer not to identify the guy who wrote:

To catch a one-pound trout than a hundred-pound tuna
I would suna.)

I thought of this predilection for certain subjects the other day when it occurred to me that there are scores of jokes about martinis, and none whatsoever, as far as I'm aware, about Pink Ladys or Harvey Wallbangers. Possibly it's because people are opinionated about martinis but have no strong views on Bloody Marys or Horse's Necks. I was fishing Upper Saranac Lake in the Adirondacks one evening, years ago, with David Kirkbride, and when I told him how I had nearly got myself flung into the pokey in Three Forks,

Montana, in 1955 on account of ordering a dry martini, Dave said, "Hell, everybody knows how to make a martini." We had passed a spiffy new diner that boasted a bar near Paul Smith's that morning, and I bet him a dollar they wouldn't know how to make a proper dry martini; it was a good excuse to knock off fishing, which was slow, and head for the diner.

Arriving there we ordered a brace of dry martinis, and I watched glumly as the bartender, only slightly consternated by the order, made the proper choice of French vermouth rather than Italian, and although he poured it with a too-lavish hand for my taste, his ratio of vermouth to gin, roughly one to four or five, was in the solid conservative stance extolled by Bernard De Voto and other traditionalists, and although I might have claimed a foul at the absence of the optional olive I reached for my wallet to pay my bet as the bartender set our properly chilled potions before us.

Then, before I could extract a dollar bill, the bartender said, "Oops—nearly forgot!" and popped a maraschino cherry into each of our drinks. David handed me a dollar and we paid for our martinis and left. So far as I can recall, it was the last time I won a bet on something important.

HOW TO CATCH SNOOK

On my way down to San Antonio last December to attend the annual meeting of the Winchester Irregulars, I picked up the inflight magazine of American Airlines and on page 21 read an interesting but presumptuous piece by Isaac Asimov on deoxyribonucleic acid, or DNA, the incredible molecule whose structure controls the physical characteristics of all living things. In the opening paragraph I found this statement: "Since every living thing is at least slightly different from every other living thing, and in some cases very different (you may be slightly different in appearance from your father but you are very different in appearance from an oak tree), this must come about because the DNA molecule is different in structure in different living things."

Hoo boy! This Asimov, without ever having laid eyes on me, says I look very different from an oak tree! Well the fact is, buster, I look amazingly *like* an oak tree. On several occasions I have been attacked by woodsmen with double-bitted axes. Twice, I have been inadvertently sprayed for tent caterpillars. I have had several severe attacks of oak gall. Young lovers keep trying to carve their initials into me. Birds often try to build nests on me, and Boy Scouts frequently look at my lower portion to see where the moss grows, and find north. When I suffer from hives, it's because bees have mistaken me for a bee tree. So much for science writers.

Annoyed, I switched to reading a fairly recent Travis McGee novel by my favorite murder-mystery writer, John D. MacDonald, and was reminded by a McGee reference to sailfishing that John lived in Sarasota during the 1950s and was a devout snook fisherman when not at his typewriter. He wrote to me one time during that decade to tell me that his wife routinely asked, ''What did you catch?'' when he came back from the inlet, and that he was almost always obliged to say, ''One snook,'' or ''Two snook,'' or ''Five snook,'' and kept hoping that some other make of fish would ingest his lure, as he felt sure his wife was getting awfully bored hearing the same old reply day after day.

Then recently, he wrote, he was fishing a feathered leadhead jig with a light spinning rod and when the monofilament snarled on the reel the jig sank and caught fast on the bottom. He said he pulled cautiously on the 6-pound line and finally managed to beach a barnacle-covered piece of pottery which appeared to be a chamber pot. A few minutes after he had unhooked the crockery and resumed fishing, he made a long, high cast and a low-flying pelican flew into the monofilament, which wrapped around its wing and brought it plunging into the water. It took him 10 minutes to play the bird into the beach and get it calmed down sufficiently to untangle the line and release it. While he was so engaged, a pod of commercial fishermen came by and one of them said to John, ''Watch this.'' He took the pelican's beak in his hand and walked it up and down the beach for about 2 minutes, holding the beak pointed skyward. When another of the group said, ''He's about done,'' the bird was turned loose. Instead of flying away, John wrote, the pelican put the point of his beak into the sand and stood staring at the ground for about 5 minutes. When one of the fishermen walked over and booted it gently in the fuselage, it looked up with a hey-where-am-I look of amazement, then flew off.

While this was going on an elderly onlooker came over and asked John what he was fishing for. When John said snook, the oldtimer said, ''You'll never get no big snook

on that little-bitty outfit. There's some real big snook in here, but you'd never hold 'em on line that light.'' John tried to explain that with a spinning reel (at that time still fairly newfangled) it would be awfully difficult for even a 30-pound snook to break off if properly handled, and when the geezer scoffed, John bet him a quarter he couldn't break the 6-pound line. ''Take that jig,'' John said, ''and make like you're a big snook. You've got 5 minutes to break off, any way except running out all the line.'' The oldtimer agreed, and for 5 minutes ran up and down the beach yanking and hauling on the line while John played him carefully. When the time was up the guy paid him the two bits and John went back to his apartment. When he walked in the door his wife said, ''What did you catch?'', and John was happy to be able to answer, ''An old man, a pelican, and a chamber pot.'' He said it was one of the best days he ever had, and that he was tempted to enter all three catches in the local fishing-rodeo under the unusual-species category, but had neglected to weigh and measure them.

On arriving at Stan Studer's ranch on the South Fork of the Frio I enthusiastically fell in with evil companions including not only the Studers *pere et fils* but wildlife painter Guy Coheleach, rancher Herb Toombs, publisher and pistoleer Steve Ferber, sporting-art collector George Coe, big-game hunter Jim Midcap, defrocked tennis pro Jimmy Moses, Gamecoin founder Harry Tennison, and sundry other Irregulars, and not long thereafter somehow found myself tramping with several accomplices across a stubble field stiff with bobwhite quail, just behind a nifty brace of well-trained Brittanys and just ahead of a safari truck carrying an eight-piece mariachi band which struck up ''The Yellow Rose of Texas'' (I think it was) each time the dogs went on point, which was frequently. I missed one going-away bobwhite, but ascribed it to the E string of the bass fiddle being slightly flat.

The annual meeting was dull. As chairman of the Genealogical Committee, I proposed doing an analysis of Steve Ferber's ancestry, to be titled ''Ferber's Forebears'' (or, if pursued in sufficient depth, ''Ferber's Fur-Bearing Forebears''), but a motion by pecan magnate Bob Leonard to disband the Committee was seconded and passed before I could rise to a point of order.

BOOK REVIEW

Although written many years ago, *Lady Chatterley's Lover* has just been reissued by Grove Press, and this fictional account of the day-to-day life of an English gamekeeper is still of considerable interest to outdoorminded readers, as it contains many passages on pheasant raising, the apprehending of poachers, ways of controlling vermin, and other chores and duties of the professional gamekeeper. Unfortunately one is obliged to wade through many pages of extraneous material in order to discover and savor these sidelights on the management of a Midland shooting estate, and in this reviewer's opinion this book can not take the place of J. R. Miller's *Practical Gamekeeping*.*

* I was a paragraph short one time, and looking around my study for inspiration I saw a copy of *Lady Chatterley's Lover* that had been sent to me by somebody at Grove Press, and so I wrote this "review." It was reprinted in *Reader's Digest, The Wall Street Journal, Time, The London Times Literary Supplement, The New York Times,* and a number of other publications, and was quoted by a Supreme Court Justice, Admiral Rickover (who thought it was serious but was told otherwise in a *Washington Post* column), twice on the BBC Third Program, and was otherwise bandied about for several months. What I liked most was the seven letters from *Field & Stream* readers asking where they could find a copy of J. R. Miller's *Practical Gamekeeping*.

ALPHABETICAL LISTING OF
"EXIT LAUGHING" COLUMNS